# COMPENSATING CHILD ABUSE IN ENGLAND AND WALES

Providing a detailed analysis of the legal principles in England and Wales, this book looks at governing compensation claims for the lasting trauma caused by child abuse. It discusses the merits and demerits of different forms of action as mechanisms for imposing liability for abuse, how compensable psychiatric damage can be proved and how the law deals with complex issues of duty of care, causation and extending limitation periods in the context of abuse cases. Whilst a substantial portion of the book deals with civil claims by the abused for the psychological harm caused by the abuse, coverage also extends to litigation by other parties involved directly or indirectly in abuse allegations. Also included is a significant comparative element, drawing upon jurisdictions such as Canada, Australia and New Zealand, as a means of speculating how our own legal system might develop.

PAULA CASE is a Lecturer in Law at the University of Liverpool, where her teaching focuses on torts and medical law. She has published papers on the subjects of claims by those falsely accused of abuse, regulation of the medical profession, medical negligence, claims for psychiatric damage, and environmental law and enforcement.

# COMPENSATING CHILD ABUSE IN ENGLAND AND WALES

PAULA CASE

CAMBRIDGE
UNIVERSITY PRESS

CAMBRIDGE UNIVERSITY PRESS
Cambridge, New York, Melbourne, Madrid, Cape Town, Singapore, São Paulo

Cambridge University Press
The Edinburgh Building, Cambridge CB2 8RU, UK

Published in the United States of America by Cambridge University Press, New York

www.cambridge.org
Information on this title: www.cambridge.org/9780521864022

© Paula Case 2007

This publication is in copyright. Subject to statutory exception
and to the provisions of relevant collective licensing agreements,
no reproduction of any part may take place without
the written permission of Cambridge University Press.

First published 2007

Printed in the United Kingdom at the University Press, Cambridge

*A catalogue record for this publication is available from the British Library*

ISBN 978-0-521-86402-2 hardback

Cambridge University Press has no responsibility for
the persistence or accuracy of URLs for external or
third-party internet websites referred to in this publication,
and does not guarantee that any content on such
websites is, or will remain, accurate or appropriate.

# CONTENTS

*Table of Cases*      *page* ix

*Table of Statutes and Statutory Instruments*      xxii

1   Law, Psychiatry, Society and Child Abuse      1
    Introduction      1
    Evolving constructions of child abuse      1
    Categorisations of abuse      3
        1. Physical abuse      5
        2. Childhood sexual abuse      12
        3. Emotional abuse      14
        4. Neglect      14
    The individual and abuse – abuse as a pathogen      16
        1. Psychiatric injury and dysfunction caused by sexual abuse      16
        2. Other types of abuse and psychological injury      19
        3. The law and psychiatry interface: psychological morbidity and disincentives to litigation      20
    Society and abuse      24
        1. Prevalence of abuse in childhood      24
        2. The context of abuse      25
        3. The law and society interface: the impact of media reporting and public inquiries – from hyperbole to understatement      27
        4. The onslaught of regulatory reforms      31
    Tort litigation and abuse      34
        1. Proliferation of claims pertaining to abuse      35
        2. Functions of tort litigation      36
        3. Trivialising, pejorative and demeaning language and the courts      47
        4. A comparative dimension      49
    Conclusion      50

2  Classifying Abuse as a Civil Wrong    52
   Introduction    52
   The current state of civil litigation relating to abuse    52
   Forms of civil action by the abused    54
   The perpetrator as defendant    54
       1. Trespass to the person (assault/battery)    54
       2. An action under the principle of *Wilkinson v. Downton*    61
       3. Breach of fiduciary duty    66
       4. Claims by bystander family members    69
   The non-perpetrator as defendant    71
       1. Litigation under the Human Rights Act 1998    72
       2. Breach of statutory duty    75
       3. The tort of negligence    76
       4. Breach of fiduciary duty    104
       5. Non-delegable duties    105
       6. The tort of misfeasance    107
       7. Vicarious liability and childhood abuse    108
   Insurance coverage    126
       1. Construction of the policy    126
       2. The insured perpetrator    128
       3. The insured non-perpetrator    129
   Alternative routes to compensation: criminal injuries compensation    131
       1. Awards for non-parasitic mental injury    134
       2. Awards for parasitic mental injury    135
       3. 'Directly attributable to'    135
       4. Direct attribution and bystander claims    135
       5. 'A crime of violence'    138
       6. Abuse claims    139
   Conclusion    141

3  Litigation Against the Accuser    144
   Introduction    144
   Claims against social services/local authorities    145
       1. The tort of negligence    145
       2. An action for breach of statutory duty    155
       3. Claims brought under the Human Rights Act 1998    157
       4. Misfeasance in public office    162
       5. Witness immunity    163
   Claims against the medical profession    164
       1. Confidentiality obligations    164
       2. The tort of negligence    168

3. Claims brought under the Human Rights
     Act 1998    178
  4. Disciplinary proceedings    178
Negligence claims against social services/local authorities
and medical practitioners in other jurisdictions    180
  1. Liability in Australia    180
  2. The Canadian position    182
  3. New Zealand    183
General claims against the accusers    184
  1. Actions in defamation    185
  2. Malicious prosecution    192
  3. Intentional infliction of psychiatric harm    194
Conclusion    195

4 Damage, Causation and Quantum    199
  Introduction    199
  Burden of proof    200
    1. English law and repressed memories    201
    2. Admissibility of recovered memory evidence in the US    206
  Damage    208
    1. Physical damage    208
    2. Psychiatric damage    209
    3. Damages for 'pure' psychiatric harm in tort    210
    4. The recognised psychiatric disorder requirement    216
    5. The role of expert evidence    218
    6. Classifications of mental illness    218
    7. Mental illness and credibility    225
  Causation and remoteness    225
    1. Proving 'causation in fact'    225
    2. Relaxation of the 'material contribution' test    227
    3. Future application of *Fairchild*    228
    4. Causation in law    229
    5. Remoteness of damage    231
    6. The thin skull (and crumbling skull) rules    233
    7. Breach of fiduciary duty    234
  Quantum    235
    1. Apportionment and the workings of the 'material
       contribution' test: divisible or non-divisible injury?    235
    2. Supervening traumatic events or incidents    238
    3. General and special damages    239
    4. Aggravating and exemplary damages    240
  Conclusion    242

5 Limitation Periods    244
  The limitation framework    244
    1. Limitation of actions and procedure    246
    2. Limitation Act 1980: a two-tier system    247
  Application of the Limitation Act to civil actions against perpetrators of abuse: *Stubbings v. Webb*    248
    1. Finding fault with *Stubbings v. Webb*    249
    2. Extending time for battery claims    252
    3. Application of *Stubbings* elsewhere in the UK    255
    4. Utilising alternative forms of action to circumvent *Stubbings v. Webb*    255
  Application of limitation periods to civil actions against non-perpetrator defendants    258
    1. Vicarious liability    258
    2. Non-battery claims    259
  Other issues    280
    1. Claims under the Limitation Act 1939    280
    2. Declaratory remedy    281
    3. Law Commission proposals for reform    282
  Conclusion    284

Conclusion    285

*Bibliography*    289

*Index*    299

# TABLE OF CASES

**A**

A v. Children's Aid Society 1996 ACWS (3d) 435
A v. UK (1999) 27 EHRR 611
A (A Child) v. The Ministry of Defence, Guys and St Thomas' Hospital NHS Trust [2003] EWHC 849; [2003] PIQR 33
A and Another v. Essex County Council [2004] 1 FCR 660; [2003] EWCA Civ 1848; [2003] PIQR 21; [2002] EWHC 2707
A v. Archbishop of Birmingham [2005] EWHC 1361; 2005 WL 1534633
A v. Bottrill [2002] UKPC 44; [2003] 1 AC 449
A B and Others v. Leeds Teaching Hospital NHS Trust [2005] 2 WLR 358; [2004] EWHC 644
Ablett v. Devon County Council (2000) (Court of Appeal, unreported)
A(C) v. Critchley (1998) 166 DLR (4$^{th}$) 475
Ackroyd v. MerseyCare NHS Trust [2003] EWCA Civ 663
Adam v. Ward [1917] AC 309
Alcock v. Chief Constable of South Yorkshire [1992] 1 AC 310
Adams v. Bracknell Forest Borough Council [2005] 1 AC 76; [2004] UKHL 29; [2003] EWCA Civ 706; [2003] ELR 409
A v. Hoare [2006] EWCA Civ 395; [2006] 1 WLR 2320
Aldersea and Others v. Public Transport Corporation; Chandler v. Public Transport Corporation (2001) 3 VR 473; [2001] VSC 169
Ali v. Courtaulds Textiles Ltd [1999] Lloyds Rep Med 301
Allen v. British Rail Engineering [2001] EWCA Civ 242; [2001] ICR 942
Althaus v. Cohen 756 A 2d 1166 (2000)
Amalgamated Television Services Pty Ltd v. Marsden [2002] NSWCA 419
AMP v. RTA and Others [2001] NSWCA 186
Anderton v. Clwyd CC (Disclosure of Records) [1999] ELR 1; [1998] ELR 533
Annetts and Anor v. Australian Stations Pty Ltd (2002) 191 ALR 449
Anns v. Merton LBC [1978] AC 728
Archer v. Brown [1984] 2 All ER 267
Arishenkoff v. British Colombia (2004) CCLT (3d) 163
Arnold v. Central Electricity Generating Board [1988] AC 228
Athey v. Leonati [1996] 3 SCR 458

Attorney General v. Guardian Newspapers (No 2) [1990] 1 AC 109; [1988] 3
    All ER 545
A(TWN) v. Clarke [2004] 3 WWR 11

**B**

B v. Attorney General (No 1 for 2003) [2003] UKPC 61; [2003] 4 All ER 833
Bagley v. North Hertfordshire Health Authority (1986) NLJ 1014
Baker v. Willoughby [1970] AC 467
Barber v. Somerset County Council [2004] UKHL 13; [2004] 1 WLR 1089
Barker v. Corus (UK) plc [2006] UKHL 20; [2006] 3 All ER 785
Barnett v. Chelsea and Kensington Hospital Management Committee [1969]
    1 QB 428.
Barrett v. Enfield LBC [2001] 2 AC 550; [1999] UKHL 25; [1998] QB 367
Battista v. Cooper (1976) 14 SASR 225
Bazley v. Curry (1997) 30 BCLR (3d) 1
BC v. Flintshire CC (formerly Clwyd CC) [2001] 2 FLR 33
B(D) v. Children's Aid Society of Durham (1996) 30 CCLT (2d) 310
B(E) v. Order of the Oblates of Mary Immaculate in the Province of British
    Columbia [2005] 3 SCR 45; [2003] 7 WWR 421
B (JP) v. Jacob (1998) 166 DLR 4$^{th}$ 125 NBCA
B (KL) v. British Colombia [2003] 11 WWR 203; [2001] 197 DLR (4$^{th}$) 431
B(M) v. British Colombia [2001] 5 WWR 6; (2001) 87 BCLR (3d) 12 CA
Beresford v. Royal Insurance Company Limited [1938] AC 586
Bernard v. Attorney General of Jamaica [2005] IRLR 398; [2004] UKPC 47
Bhandari v. Advocates Committee [1956] 3 All ER 742
Billings v. Read [1944] 2 All ER 415
Blackwater v. Plint [2004] 3 WWR 217; (2001) 93 BCLR (3d) 228
Bluebird Cabs v. Guardian Insurance (1999) 173 DLR (4$^{th}$) 318
Bolam v. Friern General Hospital Management Committee [1957] 2 All ER 118
Bolitho v. City and Hackney Health Authority [1997] 4 All ER 771
Bonnington Castings v. Wardlaw [1956] AC 613
Bradford-Smart v. West Sussex CC [2002] EWCA Civ 7; [2002] 1 FCR 425
Brandon v. Osborne Garrett and Co Ltd [1924] 1 KB 548; [1924] All ER Rep 703
Breen v. Williams (1996) 186 CLR 71
British Midland Tool Ltd v. Midland International Tooling Ltd and Others
    [2003] EWHC 466 (Ch)
Brown v. University of Alberta Hospital (1997) DLR (4$^{th}$) 63
Butler v. Southam [2001] NSCA 121

**C**

C v. C (1994) 114 DLR (4$^{th}$) 151
C v. Cairns [2003] Lloyds Med Rep 90
C v. D and another [2006] EWHC 166; 2006 WL 503014
C v. Flintshire CC [2001] EWCA Civ 302

C v. Middlesbrough Council [2004] EWCA Civ 1746; [2004] All ER (D) 339 (Dec)
Calascione v. Dixon (1993) 19 BMLR 97
Calveley v. Chief Constable of Merseyside [1989] AC 1228
Campbell and Cosans v. UK [1982] ECHR 1
Canadian Pacific Railway v. Lockhart [1942] AC 591
Caparo Industries Plc v. Dickman [1990] 1 All ER 568
Carmarthenshire CC v. Lewis [1955] AC 549
Carmichael v. National Power Plc [1999] 4 All ER 897
Carter v. Corporation of the Sisters of Mercy of the Diocese of Rockhampton [2001] QCA 335
Cartledge v. E Jopling and Sons Ltd [1963] AC 758
Caryl S v. Child and Adolescent Treatment Serv Inc 161 Misc 2d 563 (1994) affd 238 AD 2d 953 (Ct App 1997; 661 NYS 2d 168 (Ct App 1997)
Cassidy v. Minister of Health [1951] 2 KB 343
Cave v. Robinson Jarvis and Rolf [2002] UKHL 18
Chapman v. Hearse (1961) 106 CLR 112
Chatterton v. Gerson [1981] QB 432
Chester v. Afshar [2004] UKHL 41; [2005] 1 AC 134
Churchill Insurance v. Charlton [2001] EWCA Civ 112; [2002] QB 578
Cia de Seguros Imperio v. Heath (REBX) Ltd [1999] 1 All ER (Comm) 750
Clunis v. Camden and Islington Health Authority [1998] QB 989
C(LG) v. C(VM) (1996) 25 BCLR ($3^{rd}$) 107; [1996] BCJ no 1585
CLT v. Connon (2000) 77 SASR 449
Collins v. Hertfordshire County Council [1947] KB 598
Collins v. Tesco Stores Ltd [2003] EWCA Civ 1308
Collins v. Wilcock [1984] 3 All ER 374; 1984 1 WLR 1172 (ref in text chp 2 p 4.)
Commonwealth v. Introvigne (1982) 150 CLR 258
Commonwealth of Australia v. Nelson [2001] NSWCA 443
Connelly v. New Hampshire Insurance Co Ltd 1997 SLT 1341
Continental Insurance Company v. Dalton Cartage Company Ltd et al (1982) 131 DLR (3d) 559
Cornelius v. De Taranto [2002] EMLR 6; [2001] EMLR 12
Costello-Roberts v. UK (1993) 19 EHRR 112
Council for Healthcare Regulatory Excellence v. General Dental Council [2005] EWHC 87; *The Times*, 8 February 2005
Council for the Regulation of Health Care Professionals v. General Medical Council and Another [2005] EWHC 579 (Admin); [2005] All ER (D) 269 (Apr)
C(P) v. C(RJ) [1994] 114 DLR ($4^{th}$) 151
Crawford v. Board of Governors of Charing Cross Hospital *The Times*, 8 December 1953
Credit Lyonnais Bank v. Export Credits Guarantee Department [1999] 1 All ER 929 (HL)
Cutler v. Wandsworth Stadium [1949] AC 398

## D

D v. Bury Metropolitan Borough Council; H v. Bury Metropolitan Borough Council [2006] EWCA Civ 1; [2006] 1 FCR 148
Darker v. Chief Constable for the West Midlands Police [2000] 4 All ER 193
Davies v. City and Hackney Health Authority [1989] 2 Med LR 366
Daubert v. Merrell Dow 113 Sct 2786
Dobbie v. Medway Health Authority [1994] 4 All ER 450
Doe v. McKay 700 NE 2d 1018 (Ill 1998)
Donachie v. Chief Constable of the Greater Manchester Police [2004] EWCA Civ 405; (2004) SJLB 509
Donovan v. Gwentoys Ltd [1990] AC 472
Dooley v. Cammell Laird and Co Ltd [1951] 1 Lloyd's Rep 271
Doughty v. Turner Manufacturing Co Ltd [1964] 1 QB 518
D(P) v. Allen (2004) 132 ACWS (3d) 1098
DP v. UK [2003] 1 FLR 50
Driscoll Vaney v. Parkside Health Authority (1995) Med LR 345
Dubai Aluminium Co Ltd v. Salaam and Others [2003] 1 All ER 97; [2002] UKHL 48
Dulieu v. White and Sons [1901] 2 KB 669

## E

E v. K [1995] 2 NZLR 239
E v. UK (2003) 36 EHHR 31
Elguzouli-Daf v. Commissioner of Police of the Metropolis; McBrearty v. Ministry of Defence [1995] QB 335

## F

F v. Wirral Borough Council [1991] 2 All ER 648
Fairchild v. Glenhaven Funeral Services [2002] UKHL 22; [2002] 3 All ER 305
Fairlie v. Perth and Kinross Healthcare NHS Trust [2004] ScotCS 174
Farrell v. Avon Health Authority [2001] Lloyd's Rep Med 458
Fenton v. Thorley [1903] AC 443
Ferguson v. John Dawson and Partners (Contractors) Ltd [1976] 1 WLR 1213
Foley v. UK (2003) 36 EHRR 15
Forbes v. Wandsworth Health Authority [1997] QB 402
Frame v. Smith (1987) 42 DLR (4$^{th}$) 81
Frost v. Chief Constable of South Yorkshire; Duncan v. British Coal Corp; White v. Chief Constable of South Yorkshire [1999] 2 AC 455
Frye v. US 293 F193 (DC Civ 1923)
Furniss v. Fitchett [1958] NZLR 396

## G

GA v. British Colombia (1989) 61 DLR (4$^{th}$) 136
Garamella v. NY Medical College and Dr Ingram [1999] Lloyd's Rep Med 343
GBR v. Hollett (1996) 139 DLR (4$^{th}$) 260

G(ED) v. Hammer [2003] 11 WWR 244; [2001] 5 WWR 70
Glass v. UK [2004] 1 FCR 553
Gleaner Co Ltd v. Abrahams [2004] 1 AC 628; [2003] UKPC 55
Goldsworthy v. Brickell [1987] Ch 378
Gorris v. Scott (1874) 9 LR Exch 125
Goshen v. Lavin (1974) 46 DLR (3d) 137
G(R) v. Christison [1997] 1 WWR 641
Gray v. Barr [1971] 2 QB 554
Gray v. Reeves [1992] 89 DLR (4$^{th}$) 315; (1992) 64 BCLR (2d) 275 (SC)
Green v. Argyll Bute Council (OH) (2002) GWD 9
Green v. Matheson [1989] 3 NZLR 564
Gregory v. Portsmouth County Council [2000] 1 All ER 560

## H

H v. H [1997] 2 NZLR 700
H v. Isle of Wight [2001] WL 825780
H v. Norfolk CC [1998] QB 367; [1997] 1 FLR 384
H v. R [1996] NZLR 299
Halford v. Brookes [1992] PIQR P175
Hartley v. Birmingham City District Council [1992] 1 WLR 968
Hatton v. Sutherland [2003] EWCA Civ 76; [2002] 2 All ER 1
Hawley v. Luminar Leisure Ltd [2006] EWCA Civ 18; (2006) 150 SJLB
Heil v. Rankin [2000] 2 WLR 1173
Henderson v. Henderson (1843) 3 Hare 100
HF v. Canada (Attorney General) [2002] BCJ No 436
Hill v. Chief Constable for West Yorkshire [1990] 1 All ER 1046
Hill v. Rose [1990] IR 129
Hillman v. Black (1996) 67 SASR 490
Hinz v. Berry [1970] 2 QB 40
H (M) v. Bederman (1995) 27 CCLT (2d) 152
Hodges v. Northampton CC [2005] PIQR P7; [2004] EWCA Civ 52
Hodgkinson v. Simms [1994] 3 SCR 377
Hollis v. Vabin Pty Ltd [2001] 207 CLR 21
Holtby v. Brigham and Crane (Hull) Ltd [2000] 3 All ER 421
Home Office v. Dorset Yacht [1970] 2 All ER 294
Hopkins v. Secretary of Queensland [2004] QDC 021
Horne, Cherie Jayne v. Wilson, Graeme James Gregory (No 2) [1998] TASCC 44
Horrocks v. Lowe [1975] AC 135
Hospital Products v. US Surgical Corporation [2001] OCA 335; (1984) 156 CLR 41
Howell v. Young (1826) 5 B & C 259, 2 C & P 238
H(RL) v. H(M) 1998 ACWS (3d) 831
H(SG) v. Gorsline [2004] 23 CCLT (3D) 65; [2001] 6 WWR 132 (Alta QB)
Hudson v. Ridge Manufacturing [1957] 2 All ER 229

Hughes v. Lord Advocate [1963] AC 837
Hungerford v. Jones 722 A 2d 478 (NH 1998); 143 NH 203
Hunter v. Canary Wharf [1997] 2 All ER 246

## I
Ingram v. Chase Riverland and Robert Snyder (1995)
In the Dale Case [1992] PIQR P373

## J
Jacobi v. Griffiths [2003] 11WWR 244
Jane Doe v. Metropolitan Toronto (Municipality) Commissioners of Police (1998) 160 DLR (4$^{th}$) 697
JAH v. Wadle Associates 589 NW 2d 256 (1999)
JD v. East Berkshire Community NHS Trust [2005] UKHL 23; [2005] 2 WLR 993; [2003] Lloyd's Rep Med 9 (Chester CC)
JD, MAK & RKV v. East Berkshire Community NHS Trust [2003] EWCA Civ 1151; [2003] 2 FCR 1
J v. J et al (1993) 102 DLR (4$^{th}$) 177
Jobling v. Associated Dairies [1982] AC 794
John Doe v. Bennett [2004] SCC 17
John Doe v. O'Dell 2003 125 ACWSJ (3d) 928
Johnson v. Johnson 701 F.Supp 1363 (ND 111 1988)
Johnson v. Rogers Memorial Hospital Inc (2000) WI App 166
Jones v. Jones 242 NJ Super 195 (1990)

## K
K v. Gilmartin's Executrix 2004 SLT 1014; 2002 SLT 801
Kaiser v. Milliman 747 P 2d 1130 (Wash App 1988)
Kamloops City v. Nielson [1984] 2 SCR 2
Kelly v. Bastible [1997] 8 Med LR 15
Kerby v. Redbridge Health Authority [1994] PIQR Q1
Kershaw v. Whelan (No. 2) *The Times*, 10 February 1997
Khorasandjian v. Bush [1993] QB 727
Kirkby v. Leather [1965] QB 367
Knox v. Gye (1872) LR 5 HL 656
Knuppfer v. London Express Newspapers [1944] AC 116
KR and others v. Royal and Sun Alliance plc [2006] EWHC 48; 2006 WL 421839
KR and Others v. Bryn Alyn Community (Holdings) Ltd (In Liquidation), Royal & Sun Alliance Plc [2003] EWCA Civ 85; [2003] 1 FCR 385; 2001 WL 753345
Kuddus v. Chief Constable of Leicester Constabulary [2001] UKHL 29; [2001] 3 All ER 193
KW v. Pornbacher (1997) 32 BCLR (3d) 360 SC

## L

L (A Minor) and P v. Reading Borough Council [2001] PIQR 29
LAC Minerals Ltd v. International Corona Resources Ltd [1989] 2 SCR 574
Leame v. Bray (1803) 3 East 593 (102 ER 724)
Lepore v. New South Wales (2001) NSWLR 420
Letang v. Cooper [1965] 1 QB 232
Lewis v. Daily Telegraph [1964] AC 234
L (H) v. Canada (Attorney General) [2003] 5 WWR 421
Lillie and Reed v. Newcastle City Council [2002] EWHC 1600
Lister v. Hesley Hall Ltd [2002] 1 AC 215; [2001] UKHL 22
Livingstone v. Rawyards Coal Company (1980) 5 App Cas 25
Long v. Hepworth [1968] 1 WLR 1299
Lonhro v. Shell Petroleum Company [1982] AC 173
Louie v. Lastman (2001) 199 DLR (4$^{th}$) 741 (Ont Superior Ct of Justice)
Loutchansky v. Times Newspapers [2002] QB 783; [2001] EWCA Civ 1805
Lucas v. AVRO [1994] CLY 1444
Lucy v. Mariehamns Rederi [1971] 2 Lloyd's Rep 314

## M

M v. M (1988) 166 CLR 69
McDonald v. Mombourquette (1996) 152 NSR (2d) 109
McDonnell v. Congregation of Christian Brothers Trustees [2003] UKHL 63; [2003] 3 WLR 1627
McDonnell v. Congregation of Christian Brothers Trustees [2001] EWCA Civ 2095; [2002] CP Rep 31
McGhee v. NCB [1982] 3 All ER 1008
McInerney v. McDonald [1992] 2 SCR 138
McKerr v. UK (2002) 35 EHRR 23
McLoughlin v. Jones [2002] 2 WLR 1279; [2001] EWCA Civ 1743
McLoughlin v. O'Brian [1983] 1 AC 410
McManus v. Beckham [2002] EWCA Civ 939; [2002] 1 WLR 2982
Maguire v. Makaronis (1997) 188 CLR 449
Majrowski v. Guy's and St Thomas's NHS Trust [2006] UKHL 34; [2006] 4 All ER 395; [2005] QB 848; [2005] EWCA Civ 251
Mak and Rak v. Dewsbury NHS Trust and Kirklees Metropolitan Council [2003] Lloyd's Rep Med 13
M (A Minor) v. Newham LBC [1995] 2 AC 663
Mark v. Associated Newspapers [2002] EMLR 38
Market Investigations v. Minister of Social Security [1969] 2 QB 173
Marsden v. Amalgamated Television Services Pty [2002] NSWCA 419
Martin v. Watson [1995] 3 All ER 559
Mary D v. John D 264 Cal Rptr 633 (1989)
Mary M v. Los Angeles 54 Cal 3d 202 (1991)
Mattis v. Pollock [2003] 1 IRLR 603

Meadow v General Medical Council [2006] EWHC 146; [2006] 2 All ER 329
M(FS) v. Clarke [1999] 11 WWR 301 (BCSC)
Midland Insurance Company v. Smith (1881) 6 QBD 561
Mitchell v. Homfray (1881) 8 QBD 587 (CA)
M(K) v. M(H) [1992] 3 SCR 6
MK v. Dewsbury Healthcare NHS Trust [2003] Lloyd's Rep Med 13
M(M) v. F(R) [1999] 2 WWR 446
Montgomery v. Murphy (1982) 136 DLR 3d 525
Montoya v. Bebensee 761 P2d 285 (Colo Ct App 1988)
Moriarty v. Garden Sanctuary Church of God 511 SE 2d 699 (Ct App 1999); 334 SC 150 (Ct App 1999)
Morris v. Martin [1996] 1 QB 716
Mount Isa Mines Ltd v. Pusey [1971] ALR 253; (1970) 125 CLR 383
Myers v. Peel (County) Board of Education (1981) 123 DLR (3d) 1 SCC

## N

Nash v. Eli Lilly and Company [1993] 1 WLR 782
Nelson v. Rye [1996] 2 All ER 186
Nelson v. Washington Parish 805 F 2d 1236 ($5^{th}$ Cir 1986)
Nettleship v. Weston [1971] 2 QB 691
Newall v. Therm-A-Stor Ltd 17 January 1990 CA
Nicholson v. Westmorland County Council (1962) *The Times*, 25 October
Non-Marine Underwriters, Lloyds of London v. Scalera (2000) 50 CCLT(2d) 1
Norberg v. Weinrib (1992) 92 DLR ($4^{th}$) 449
North Essex Health Authority v. Spargo [1997] 8 Med LR 125
North Yorkshire County Council v. SA [2003] EWCA CiV 839; [2003] 2 FLR 849
Novak v. Bond (1998) DLR ($4^{th}$) 577

## O

O'Dowd v. Secretary of State for Northern Ireland [1982] 9 NIJB
Ontario Ltd v. Sagaz Industries Canada Inc [2001] 2 SCR 983
Ormiston v. Great Western Rly Co [1917] 1 KB 598

## P

Page v. Smith [1996] AC 155
Palmer v. Durnford Ford [1992] 2 All ER 122
Palmer v. Tees HA [2000] PIQR P1; [1999] Lloyd's Rep Med 351
Paramasivam v. Flynn (1998) 90 FCR 489
Parkinson v. St James and Seacroft University Hospital NHS Trust [2002] QB 266; [2001] EWCA Civ 530
Parmiter v. Coupland (1840) 6 M + W 105
P, C and S v. UK [2002] 3 FCR 1
Pereira v. Keleman [1995] 1 FLR 428
Perre v. Apand Pty Ltd (1999) 198 CLR 180

PH v. Chief Constable of H [2003] EWCA Civ 102
Phelps v. Hillingdon LBC [2001] 2 AC 619
Pirelli General Cable Works Ltd v. Oscar Faber and Partners [1983] 2 AC 1
Poland v. Parr and Sons [1927] 1 KB 236
Powell v. Boladz [1998] Lloyd's Rep Med 116; (1998) 39 BMLR 116 CA
Pratley v. Surrey County Council [2003] EWCA Civ 1067; [2003] IRLR 794
Primeaux v. US 102 F 3d 1458 (1996)
Prince v. Attorney General [1996] 3 NZLR 733
PS v. Germany (2003) 36 EHRR 61
PT v. Richard Hall Community Mental Health Care Centre 364 NJ Super 561, 837
    A 2d 436 (2002)
Purnell v. Roche [1927] 2 Ch 142
Pursell v. Horn (1838) 8 AD and E 602

**Q**
Quinn v. Leatham [1901] AC 495

**R**
R (on the application of Williamson) v. Secretary of State for Education and
    Employment [2005] UKHL 15; [2005] 2 WLR 590
R v. Brown [1994] 1 AC 212
R v. Browning (1994) CA; [1995] Crim LR 227
R v. Burstow (Anthony Christopher) [1997] 1 Cr App R 144
R v. Cannings [2004] EWCA Crim 1; [2004] 1 WLR 2607
R v. Clark [2003] EWCA Crim 1020
R (August) v. Criminal Injuries Compensation Appeals Panel [2001] QB 774
R v. Criminal Injuries Compensation Board ex parte Clowes [1977] 1 WLR 1353
R v. Criminal Injuries Compensation Board ex p Kent and Milne [1998] 1 WLR 1458
R v. Criminal Injuries Compensation Board ex p Warner; R v. Criminal Injuries
    Compensation Board ex p Webb [1987] QB 74
R v. Croydon Health Authority [1998] PIQR Q26
R v. Dawson (Brian); R v. Nolan (Stephen Thomas); R v. Walmsley (Ian) (1985)
    81 Cr App R 150
R v. Department of Health ex parte Source Informatics [2000] 1 All ER 786
R v. Flattery (1877) 2 QBD 410
R v. Harrow LBC ex parte D [1990] 1 FLR 79
R v. Hopley (1860) 2 F + F 202
R v. Ireland (Robert Matthew); R v. Burstow (Anthony Christopher) [1998] AC
    147; [1997] QB 114
R v. Mayes [1995] CLY 930
R v. Moloney [1985] AC 905
R v. Nedrick [1986] 1 WLR 1025
R v. Secretary of State for the Home Department ex parte Fire Brigades Union
    and Others [1995] 2 WLR 464

R v. St George (1840) 9 Car + P 483
R v. Tabassum [2000] Lloyd's Rep Med 404
R v. Williams [1923] 1 KB 340
R (on the application of KB) v. MHRT and SoS for Health [2004] QB 936; [2003] EWHC 193
Racz v. Home Office [1994] 2 AC 45
Rahman v. Arearose Ltd [2001] QB 351
Rahmetulla v. Vanfed Credit Union (1984) 29 CCLT 78 (BCSC)
Ramirez v. Armstrong 673 P 2d 822 (1983)
Ramona v. Isabella (No C61898 (Cal Sup Cr May 13, 1994)
Rawlinson v. Purnell Jenkison and Roscoe [1999] 1 NZLR 479
Ready Mixed Concrete v. Ministry of Pensions and National Insurance [1968] 2 QB 497
R(L) v. British Colombia 1998 ACWSJ (3d) 550
Re B (A minor) (Rejection of expert evidence) [1996] 3 FLR 272
Re C (HIV) [1999] 2 FLR 1004
Re Christian Brothers of Ireland in Canada 2004 128 ACWSJ (3d) 116
Reeves v. Commissioner of Police for the Metropolis [1999] 3 WLR 363
Re H [1991] FCR 736
Re H (Minors) Sexual Abuse: Standard of Proof [1996] AC 563
Re MB (C section) [1997] 2 FLR 426
Re Pauling's Settlement [1962] 1 WLR 86
Re Polemis and Furness, Withy and Co [1921] 3 KB 560
Re R (A minor) (Blood transfusion) [1993] 2 FLR 757
Revill v. Newbery [1996] 2 WLR 239
Reynolds v. The Health First Medical Group [2000] Lloyd's Rep Med 240
Rhodes v. Bates (1866) 1 Ch App 252
Rhodes v. Canadian National Rly (1990) 75 DLR $4^{th}$ 248
RK and MK v. Oldham NHS Trust and Dr B [2003] Lloyd's Rep Med 1 (QBD)
Robinson v. St Helens MBC [2003] PIQR 9; [2002] EWCA Civ 1099
Ronex Properties Ltd v. John Laing Construction Ltd [1983] QB 398
Rookes v. Barnard [1964] AC 1129
Ross v. Garabedian 742 NE 2d 1046 (Mass 2001)
Rowe v. Kingston upon Hull City Council [2003] EWCA Civ 1281; [2003] ELR 771

## S

S v. Attorney General [2003] 3 NZLR 450
S v. G [1995] 3 NZLR 681
S v. Gloucestershire CC; L v. Tower Hamlets LBC [2001] Fam 313
S v. Walsall MBC [1995] 3 All ER 294
Samuels v. Southern Baptist Hospital 594 So 2d 571 (1992)
Savile v. Roberts (1698) 1 Ld Raym 374
Sawyer v. Midelfort 595 NW 2d 423 (Wis 1999)

Scott v. Shepherd (1773) 2 BI R 892
Secretary of State for Transport, Local Government and the Regions v. Snowdon [2002] EWHC 2394; [2003] RTR 15
Seymour v. Williams [1995] PIQR 470
Shahzade v. Gregory 923 F Sup at 289 (D Mass 1996)
Sheldon v. RM Outhwaite (Underwriting Agencies) Ltd [1995] 2 All ER 562
Sidaway v. Board of Governors of the Bethlem Royal Hospital [1985] AC 871; [1984] QB 493
Silcott v. Comr of Police for the Metropolis (1996) 8 Admin L R 633
Sim v. Stretch [1936] 2 All ER 1237
Smith v. Advanced Electrics P/L [2002] QSC 211
Smith v. Clay (1767) 3 Brown CC 639
Smith New Court Securities Ltd v. Scrimgeour Vickers (Asset Management) Ltd [1997] AC 254
Sparham v. Callaghan [2000] 1 QB 75
Speight v. Gosnay (1891) 60 LJ QB 231
Spring v. Guardian Assurance [1995] 2 AC 296; [1994] 3 All ER 129
ST v. North Yorkshire County Council [1999] 1 IRLR 98
Stanton v. Callaghan [2000] 1QB 75
Starks v. RSM Security (2004) NSWCA 351
State v. Hungerford 697 A 2d 916 (NH 1997)
State of New South Wales v. Seedsman [2000] NSWCA 119
Stovin v. Wise [1996] 3 All ER 801
Stubbings and Others v. UK (1996) 23 EHRR 213
Stubbings v. Webb [1993] AC 498; [1992] QB 197; [1991] 3 All ER 949
Sullivan v. Moody (2001) 28 Fam LR 104
Surtees v. Kingston Upon Thames RBC [1991] 2 FLR 559
Swales v. Glendinning 2004 128 ACWSJ (3d) 853
Swindle v. Harrison [1997] 4 All ER 705

**T**

T (A Minor) v. Surrey County Council [1994] 4 All ER 577
T v. Boys and Girls Welfare Services [2004] EWCA Civ 1747; [2004] All ER (D) 361 (Dec)
T v. H [1995] 3 NZLR 37
Tarasoff v. Regents of University of California (1976) 551 P 2d 334 131 Cal R 14
Target Holdings Ltd v. Redfern [1996] 1 AC 421
Taylor v. Director of the Serious Fraud Office [1999] 2 AC 177
Taylor v. McGillivray (1993) 110 DLR ($4^{th}$) 64
Teece v. Honeybourne (1974) 54 DLR (3d) 549
Theaker v. Richardson [1962] 1 WLR 151
Thompson v. Smith Ship Repairers Ltd [1984] 1 QB 405
Three Rivers DC v. Governor and Company of the Bank of England [2000] 2 WLR 1220

T(L) v. T(RW) (1997) 36 BCLR (3d) 165
TP and KM v. UK (2002) 34 EHRR 42
Transco Plc v. Stockport Metropolitan Borough Council [2004] 2 AC 1; [2003] UKHL 61
Trear v. Sills 69 Cal App 4$^{th}$ 1341 (Cal Ct App 1999)
Tremain v. Pike [1969] 3 All ER 1303
Trim Joint District School Board of Management v. Kelly [1914] AC 667
Trotman v. North Yorkshire County Council [1998] ELR 625
Tucker v. News Media Ownership [1986] NZLR 716
Tuman v. Genesis Associates 894 F Supp 183 (1995)
Tyson v. Tyson 727 P2d 226 (Wash 1986)

V

Vasey v. Surrey Free Inns [1996] PIQR 373
Venema v. Netherlands [2003] 1 FCR 153
Venning v. Chin (1974) 10 SASR 299
Victoria General Hospital v. General Accident Assurance Co of Canada [1995] 8 WWR 106
Victorian Railway Commissioners v. Coultas (1888) LR 13 App Cas 222; (1816) 1 Stark 493
Vorvis v. Insurance Corp. of British Colombia (1989) 58 DLR (4$^{th}$) 193
VP v. AG and William Starr (1999) SKQB 180
Vukelic v. The Mayor and Burgesses of the London and Hammersmith and Fulham [2003] EWHC 188

W

W v. Attorney General [1999] 2 NZLR 709
W v. Edgell [1990] 1 All ER 835
W v. Essex CC [2001] 2 AC 592
W v. Home Office [2002] 3 WLR 405
W v. Meah [1986] 1 All ER 935
W v. Westminster City Council [2005] EWHC 102; [2005] 4 All ER 96 (Note *The Wagon Mound* [1961] AC 388)
Wainwright v. Home Office [2003] UKHL 53; [2002] 3 WLR 405
Walker v. Northumberland County Council [1995] 1 All ER 737
Watkins v. Birmingham County Council *The Times*, 1 August 1975
Watkins v Secretary of State for the Home Department [2006] UKHL 17; [2006] 2 WLR 807
Watson v. Haines (1987) Aust Tort Reps 80–94
White v. JF Stone [1939] 2 KB 827
White v. Jones [1995] 2 AC 207
Whitfield v. Calhoun (1999) 242 AR 201
Widenmaier v. Jarvis [1981] 9 ACSW (2d) 364
Wilkinson v. Downton [1897] 2 QB 57

Williams v. Milotin (1957) 97 CLR 465
Williams v. The Minister, Aboriginal Land Rights Act 1983 and Anor [1999] NSWSC 843
Wilsher v. Essex Area Health Authority [1988] AC 1074; [1986] 3 All ER 801
Wilson v Governors of Sacred Heart Roman Catholic School [1998] ELR 637
Wilson v. Pringle [1987] QB 237
Wilsons & Clyde Co. v English [1938] AC 57
Wodrow v. Commonwealth (1993) 45 FCR 52
Wong v. Parkside Health NHS Trust (2002) 99(2) LSG 28; [2001] EWCA Civ 1721
Wood v. Hills [2003] EWCA Civ 1537
Wood v. Kennedy (1998) 165 DLR (4$^{th}$) 542
Wood v. State of New South Wales [2004] NSWCA 122
Woodhead v. Elbourne [2000] QSC 42
Wright v. John Bagnall and Sons Ltd [1900] 1 QB 240

# X
X (Minors) v. Bedfordshire CC [1995] 2 AC 633
X v. Chief Constable of West Midlands [2004] EWCA Civ 1068
X (HA) v. Y [1988] 2 All ER 648

# Y
Y(AD) v. Y(MY) [1994] 5 WWR 623
Yewens v. Noakes (1880) 6 QB 530
Youssoupoff v. Metro-Goldymn Mayer (1934) 50 TLR 581
Y(S) v. C(FG) [1997] 1 WWR 229

# Z
Z v. United Kingdom (2002) 34 EHRR 97
Zamstein v. Marvasti 692 A 2d 781 (Conn 1997)

# TABLE OF STATUTES AND STATUTORY INSTRUMENTS

European Convention of Human Rights 1950
Human Rights Act 1998
Care Standards Act 2000, s.23, s.72, s.73, s.79A, B, F, U
Convention on the Rights of the Child
Children Act 1989, ss.17, 26(3), 31, 47
Children Act 2004, s.1, 3–4, 58
Children and Young Persons Act 1933, s.1
Children and Young Persons Act 1969, s.29
Civil Evidence Act 1968, s.11
Civil Liability (Contribution) Act 1978
Congenital Disabilities (Civil Liability) Act 1976, s.1
Criminal Injuries Compensation Act 1995
Criminal Justice Act 1988, s.39
Day Care and Child Minding (National Standards) (England) 2001 (SI 2001/1828)
Day Care and Child Minding (National Standards) (England) Regulations 2003 (SI 2003/1996)
Education (No 2) Act 1986, s.548
Education Act 1996, s.47
Education Reform Act 1988, s.218
Fatal Accidents Act 1976
General Medical Council Preliminary Proceedings Committee and Professional Conduct Committee (Procedure) Rules 1988 (SI 1988 No. 2255)
Health and Social Care (Community Health and Standards) Act 2003, s.76, s.77, s.79, s.80
Human Rights Act 1998, s.7
Injury Prevention, Rehabilitation, and Compensation Act 2001
Limitation Act 1939
Limitation Act 1954
Limitation Act 1963
Limitation Act 1980, s.2, s.11, s.11(4)(a), s.11(4)(b), s.14, s.14(2), s.14(3), s.28, s.32(1)(b), s.32(2), s.33, s.33(3)(d), s.36(1), s.38(1), s.38(3)
Limitation (Northern Ireland) Order 1989 (SI 1989/1339) (NI II).
Local Authority Services Act 1970, s.7

Local Authority Social Services (Complaints Procedure) Order 1990 (SI 1990 No. 2244)
Medical Act 1983, s.36(1), s.36A, s.37
Medical (Professional Performance) Act 1995
National Health Service (Regulation of Health Care Professionals) Act 2002, s.29
Partnership Act 1890, s.10
Prescription and Limitation (Scotland) Act 1973, s.17, s.19A
Protection from Harassment Act 1997, ss.1, 3
Protection of Children Act 1999, ss.5, 7
Offences Against the Person Act 1861, ss.18, 20, 34, 47
Rehabilitation of Offenders Act 1974
School Standards and Framework Act 1998, s.131
Sex Offenders Act 1997
Sexual Offences Act 1956, ss.7(2)(c), 12, 13, 45
Sexual Offences Act 1997
Sexual Offences Act 2003, s.16, s.18
Sexual Offences (Amendment) Act 2000

# 1

# Law, Psychiatry, Society and Child Abuse

## Introduction

As will become apparent, the identification of child abuse is a multi-disciplinary affair, drawing upon the combined but not necessarily compatible wisdom of medicine, law and sociology. This book seeks to provide an account of the journey of child abuse through the evolution of these different perspectives culminating in the legal, clinical and sociological discourse which prevails today. It is hoped that this discussion will serve as a useful backdrop and prelude to examination of the legal issues which have arisen in the context of abuse claims, and that it will assist in explaining judicial attitudes to abuse claims and some of the peculiar difficulties which abuse claimants face.

## Evolving constructions of child abuse

The concept of child abuse has been described as 'more like pornography than whooping cough':[1] in other words, it is a socially constructed phenomenon which reflects the operative values and opinions of a particular culture at a given point in time rather than an objectively defined occurrence. A striking example of this fact is the story of the Pitcairn Islanders recently convicted of having sex with adolescent girls from the age of 12.[2] The case for the defence (although ultimately unsuccessful) was built upon the revelation that the practice of sex with adolescent girls on the islands had become the cultural norm and was an accepted ritual in Pitcairn Islands' society.

Real shifts in the portrayal of child abuse are also evident when a longitudinal assessment is made of such abuse in the UK. Generally

---

[1] C. Wattam, 'The Social Construction of Child Abuse for Practical Policy Purposes' (1996) CFLQ 189, relying on N. Parton, *The Politics of Child Abuse* (Macmillan, 1985).
[2] And on the cultural defence, see A. Trenwith, 'The Empire Strikes Back: Human Rights and the Pitcairn Proceedings' (2003) 7(2) *Journal of South Pacific Law* 1.

speaking, the socially constructed concept of child abuse has undergone a process of redefinition from being depicted largely as a medical concern to being defined as a problem requiring a multidisciplinary focus. In the 1960s child abuse was defined by the medical or disease model of abuse, a fact which was attributable in no small part to the seminal research into physical abuse by Kempe et al. which ascribed many cases of childhood skeletal lesions/fractures to parental abuse.[3] The label applied to this discovery (the 'battered child syndrome') was a deliberate ploy to attract the attention and support of the medical profession to the issue and to alert them to the danger of misdiagnosing physical injuries as accidental or unexplained without considering the possibility of trauma being inflicted by the parent.[4] By the 1980s child abuse was being portrayed less as a private family matter requiring an emphasis on medical diagnosis and therapeutic intervention, and increasingly as a social phenomenon requiring bureaucratic solutions. The many public inquiries which have been conducted into exposed incidents of child abuse have progressively imposed the social phenomenon construction by focusing on social and economic depravation within the family, outlining the role and functions of the various welfare agencies involved and producing a set of legislative and policy recommendations for the future – a pattern which, although originally noted in 1985,[5] remains evident in inquiries published 20 years later.

From medicalised and sociological conceptualisations of the problem of abuse we have now moved to an era in which concerted efforts are made to adopt a multidisciplinary approach to the problem of child abuse; a methodology which draws upon medical, social and legal expertise.[6] This has been the result of concerns regarding both over-reliance on single methodologies or paradigms for the purposes of identifying child abuse (*false positives*)[7] and incidents where a lack of coordination between public bodies has been blamed for missed signs

---

[3] R. S. Kempe, H. Kempe et al., 'The Battered Child Syndrome.' (1962) 181 JAMA 17.
[4] See also the follow up in Britain under the banner the 'battered baby syndrome' by D. L. Griffiths and F. J. Moynihan in 'Multiple Epiphyseal Injuries in Babies (Battered Baby Syndrome)' (1963) 11 BMJ 1558.
[5] Parton, *The Politics of Child Abuse*.
[6] This is the essence of Department of Health, *Working Together to Safeguard Children* (Home Office, Department for Education and Employment, 1999), the government's guidance to doctors and social workers issued under s. 7 of the Local Authority Services Act 1970.
[7] As appears to have occurred in the Cleveland story, see below.

and missed opportunities to prevent abuse (*false negatives*).[8] The rationale of the multidisciplinary approach is that it serves as a network of checks and balances which are designed to optimise the number of accurately identified cases of child abuse. Whilst the net of accountability for identifying and dealing with child abuse has been cast wider than ever before, this multidisciplinarity has had some unexpected legal consequences. Interestingly, the complexity introduced by the multidisciplinary approach was relied upon by the House of Lords as a ground for denying liability on the part of social services towards children who were not rescued from abuse, as it would be too difficult to define the lines of accountability.[9] One other consequence of multidisciplinarity is allegedly that once a child is labelled as a cause for concern, or the child's parents are labelled as abusers, these classifications become more thoroughly entrenched because they are often legitimated by both medical and police authority.[10]

## Categorisations of abuse

The common law's mechanisms of compensation in England and Wales do not recognise a concept of child abuse as such, only forms of tort actions such as battery, negligence or misfeasance.[11] There are, however, legal instruments which do recognise abuse as a concept and which, to a lesser or greater degree, have influenced the evolution of claims for compensation:

- Article 3 of the European Convention of Human Rights ('ECHR') (as incorporated into UK law via the Human Rights Act 1998), recognises the right to freedom from inhuman and degrading treatment. This provision has been explicitly associated with cases of child abuse and neglect.[12]

---

[8] For example, the death of Victoria Climbié in 2000.
[9] *X (Minors) v. Bedfordshire CC* [1995] 2 AC 633 (see Chapter 2).
[10] H. D'Cruz, 'The Social Construction of Child Maltreatment – the Role of Medical Practitioners' (2004) 4 *Journal of Social Work* 99.
[11] The criminal law has long recognised an offence of child cruelty which is broadly compatible with abuse and would include all four types of abuse discussed in this book. Section 1 of the Children and Young Persons Act 1933 makes it an offence for anyone with custody, charge or care of a child to 'wilfully assault, ill-treat, neglect, abandon or expose the child in a manner likely to cause unnecessary suffering or injury to health'.
[12] *Z v. UK* (2002) 34 EHRR 97; *TP & KM v. UK* (2002) 34 EHRR 42.

- The Convention on the Rights of the Child which echoes the above prohibition in Article 37 states that 'No child shall be subjected to torture or other cruel, inhuman or degrading treatment'. The Convention provides further in Article 19 that:

> State parties shall take all appropriate legislative, administrative, social and educational measures to protect children from physical or mental violation, injury or abuse, neglect or negligent treatment, maltreatment or exploitation including sexual abuse, while in the care of parent(s), legal guardians or other persons who have the care of the child.

This last provision illustrates that child abuse is a generic term used to refer to a multitude of acts or omissions which society defines as wrongs against the child.

Although the law of torts does not define child abuse, the civil procedures designed to protect children from abuse employ four categories of child abuse which will be adopted for the purposes of this book: physical abuse, sexual abuse, emotional abuse and neglect. The definitions reproduced here are largely taken from *Working Together to Safeguard Children*, a document published by the Department of Health in 1999 which has become the working manual for professionals dealing with child abuse. Entries on the Child Protection Registers by category of abuse for the year ending 31 March 2005 were as follows:[13]

- Physical abuse – 15%.
- Sexual abuse – 9%.
- Emotional abuse – 20%.
- Neglect – 44%.
- Mixed (i.e. more than one of the above categories) – 12%.

Despite the fact that sexual abuse represents the category of abuse with the smallest number of annual registrations, it is this category with which the majority of claims for compensation have been concerned and which the courts have devoted most time to. The reasons for this apparent disparity will be explored below.

---

[13] *Referrals, Assessments and Children and Young People on Child Protection Registers: Year Ending 31 March 2004* (TSO, 2006) (accessible via the Department for Education and Skills website: www.dfes.gov.uk).

## 1. Physical abuse

Physical abuse may involve hitting, shaking, throwing, poisoning, burning or scalding, drowning, suffocating, *or otherwise causing physical harm to a child*. Physical harm may also be caused when a parent or carer feigns the symptoms of, or deliberately causes ill health to a child whom they are looking after. This situation is commonly described using terms such as factitious illness by proxy or Munchausen syndrome by proxy.[14]

As the definition suggests, there are many forms of physical abuse and the term is used here to include corporal punishment by parents, teachers and others with the care of children, playground bullying and the fabrication or induction of illness in a child.

### Corporal punishment

Although neither tort law nor criminal law defines physical abuse, the legal position outlined below suggests that any force used to punish a child which leaves a mark is now to be regarded as physical abuse. Thus, the 'physical harm' threshold implied in the *Working Together* definition is applied so as to require medically diagnosed harm or at least visible evidence of force which is more than transient. A higher threshold is applied in schools and childcare facilities where smacking (whether harmful or not) is outlawed. Ironically, the moves towards banishing corporal punishment were originally articulated in the guise of protecting parental rights. In *Campbell and Cosans v. UK*,[15] corporal punishment in grant-aided schools against the wishes of the parent was held by the European Court of Human Rights ('ECtHR') to be a violation of the *parents'* rights under Article 9 of the ECHR (the right to freedom to manifest beliefs, namely the belief that children ought not to be the subject of disciplinary force). The ban on corporal punishment introduced in 1986 after *Campbell and Cosans* extended only to state schools.[16] Then in 1998 the ban was extended to fee paying schools,[17] and has thereafter been applied to childminders and day care providers.[18] It should be noted that these absolute prohibitions on corporal punishment go further than is strictly necessary for the protection of the child from inhuman and

---

[14] *Working Together*, at 2.4 (emphasis added).    [15] [1982] ECHR 1.
[16] S. 47 of the Education (No. 2) Act 1986, followed by s. 548 of the Education Act 1996.
[17] S. 131 of the School Standards and Framework Act 1998.
[18] Imposed by the Day Care and Child Minding (National Standards) (England) Regulations 2003, SI 2003/1996, para. 5.

degrading treatment under the ECHR. In *Costello-Roberts v. UK*,[19] punishment of a 7-year-old by three smacks on the buttocks through clothing and causing no visible injury was found by a narrow majority not to attain the minimum level of severity to amount to a violation of Article 3. This judgment suggests that corporal punishment in itself does not violate the ECHR, but rather that compliance with the ECHR requires explicit controls on the severity of the punishment so as to preclude harm which is more than transient or trivial.

In *R (on the application of Williamson) v. Secretary of State for Education and Employment*[20] the claimants (parents and teachers from four independent schools) unsuccessfully challenged the ban on corporal punishment in all schools[21] as a violation of parents' Article 9 rights to manifest their religious beliefs. Such rights were based on the allegedly widely held Christian tenet that moderate use of physical punishment was an essential form of discipline if children were to be deterred from unacceptable or ungodly behaviour.[22] The House of Lords ruled that the outright ban on corporal punishment in schools did interfere materially with the parents' rights under Article 9, but decided that such interference was justified as necessary in a democratic society. This was on the grounds that interference with the parents' rights was necessary for the protection of the rights and freedoms of others; children were vulnerable citizens and the ban was necessary to protect them from distress and the other harmful effects of physical violence.[23] Baroness Hale of Richmond remarked: 'if a child has a right to be brought up without institutional violence, as he does, that right should be respected whether or not his parents and teachers believe otherwise.'[24]

The issue of corporal punishment by parents was raised in *A v. UK*, where the ECtHR ruled that the defence of reasonable chastisement as then expressed did not give sufficient protection to the child from inhuman and degrading treatment prohibited under Article 3.[25] This inadequacy had led a jury to acquit a man of assault causing actual bodily harm, despite the fact that use of the garden cane on his 9-year-old 'stepson to be' had caused several bruises on his legs. The court

---

[19] (1993) 19 EHRR 112.   [20] [2005] UKHL 15; [2005] 2 WLR 590.
[21] S. 548 Education Act 1996 as amended in 1998.
[22] Based in part on passages from the Bible including Proverbs 13:24: 'He who spares the rod hates his son, but he who loves him is diligent to discipline him.'
[23] [2005] UKHL 15; [2005] 2 WLR 590, *per* Lord Nicholls at [49].
[24] [2005] UKHL 15; [2005] 2 WLR 590 at [86].   [25] (1999) 27 EHRR 611.

found that hitting a nine-year-old child with a garden cane on more than one occasion, and with enough force to leave bruises, was sufficient to reach the level of severity prohibited by Article 3. Therefore, the availability of the reasonable chastisement defence[26] in this case was a violation of the state's obligation to protect vulnerable children from treatment contrary to the ECHR. Section 58 of the Children Act 2004 now removes the defence of reasonable chastisement, from offences of wounding and causing grievous bodily harm,[27] assault causing actual bodily harm[28] and cruelty to children.[29] As actual bodily harm includes superficial injuries such as bruising, scratching or reddening of the skin which persists for hours or days[30] and also psychiatric injury,[31] the effect of this provision is to ban smacking where it leaves a mark on the child that is more than transient or trifling. The defence of reasonable chastisement remains available to parents for minor forms of common assault[32] on their children.

Thus, there exists a real (but not always easy to apply) demarcation between the absolute prohibition on corporal punishment as applied to schools and childcare facilities and the ban on 'harmful' corporal punishment applied to parents and guardians. During the passage of the Children Bill, the Joint Committee on Human Rights[33] expressed concerns that whilst s. 58 probably fulfilled the UK's obligations under Article 3 as expressed in *A v. UK*, the retention of a diluted reasonable chastisement defence for common assault violated other international commitments (for example, the Committee for the Rights of the Child's

---

[26] Dating from 1860 – see *R v. Hopley* (1860) 2 F & F 202, where Cockburn CJ ruled that a parent, or a person who has the parental authority 'may for the purpose of correcting what is evil in the child, inflict moderate and reasonable corporal punishment'.
[27] S. 18 or 20 of the Offences Against the Person Act 1861.
[28] S. 47 of the Offences Against the Person Act 1861.
[29] S. 1 of the Children and Young Persons Act 1933.
[30] Current Crown Prosecution Service ('CPS') charging standards would still allow the charge of common assault against a parent who hit their child causing reddening of the skin (*Offences Against The Person, Incorporating Charging Standard*, accessible via the CPS website (www.cps.gov.uk), although this is to be revised so as to require reddening of the skin which persists for more than hours or days. CPS charging standards are not binding on the courts but are used to guide police and prosecutors and represent the interpretation of the ingredients appropriate to an offence.
[31] *R v. Chan-Fook* [1994] 1 WLR 689 (to qualify the psychiatric harm must be something more than a strong emotion, e.g. extreme fear or panic).
[32] An offence under s. 39 of the Criminal Justice Act 1988.
[33] *Joint Committee on Human Rights – 19th Report: Children Bill* (2003–4) HL 161/HC 537 at 135.

interpretation of Article 19 of the Convention on the Rights of the Child (see above)). There remains pressure to outlaw any corporal punishment applied to children, with references made to the example set by Sweden, where smacking was outlawed in 1979. The supporters of a complete ban argue that retaining the defence of reasonable punishment, albeit in a reduced form, conveys the message to parents that smacking is acceptable and discriminates against the child, given that adults would have the protection of a common assault charge in cases of minor hitting, whereas a child's claim to this effect would be subject to the defence of reasonable chastisement.

Given that the concept of reasonable chastisement outside schools has diminished so as to allow only *de minimis* corporal punishment, it is perhaps no coincidence that entries on the child protection registers under the heading of physical abuse have dropped dramatically from 1995 (8,700 entries) to 31 March 2004 (4,100 entries).[34]

### Abuse by fabrication or induction of illness

The popularised term 'Munchausen's Syndrome by Proxy' ('MSBP') was first coined by paediatrician Professor Sir Roy Meadow, whose evidence has since been rejected in several high-profile cot death cases.[35] The discrediting of Professor Meadow, along with the fact that the MSBP label focuses attention on the perpetrator of the harm rather than the child, explains why many professional bodies involved in child protection are now using the term FII (fabricated or induced illness (by proxy)).[36]

There are two main ways in which FII occurs:[37]

- **fabrication** of signs and symptoms. This may include fabrication of past medical history, falsification of hospital charts and records, specimens of bodily fluids or letters and documents;

---

[34] *Referrals, Assessments and Children and Young People on Child Protection Registers*, at table 3C.

[35] R. Meadow, 'Munchausen Syndrome by Proxy: The Hinterland of Child Abuse' (1977) *Lancet* 343. Munchausen's Syndrome itself was named by Richard Asher in 'Munchausen Syndrome' (1951) 1 *Lancet* 339.

[36] Psychiatrists focusing on the perpetrator's mental state would be more likely to refer to 'factitious disorder by proxy' as it is known in the *Diagnostic Statistical Manual Fourth Edition, Text Revision* (American Psychiatric Association, 2000): 'the deliberate production or feigning or physical or psychological signs or symptoms in another person who is under the individual's care.' (at 781).

[37] *Safeguarding Children in Whom Illness is Fabricated or Induced* (Department of Health, 2002).

- **induction** of illness (e.g. by poisoning, starvation, forced vomiting, suffocation).

The perpetrator of this type of abuse is usually identified as the parent (more often the mother than the father) or carer, or even healthcare worker.[38] The result for the child can include physical harm inflicted to induce illness in the child or even death,[39] unnecessary clinical investigations or treatment ('medical abuse') and psychiatric disturbance resulting from the dysfunctional nature of the child's relationship with the perpetrator.

Despite widespread media attention, FII is thought to be very rare, with a national survey suggesting there were only around 50 new cases each year in the UK.[40] Given the level of deception implicit in FII, the fact that almost any disorder can be mimicked (giving rise to a wide range of FII scenarios) and that children may adopt their parents' perception of illness and comply with the presentation of bogus symptoms,[41] it is notoriously difficult to distinguish the parent who is fabricating or inducing illness from the over-anxious parent. Clinicians and social workers are instructed to look out for unexplained and persistent illness in the child and hypervigilance in the carer who is eager for clinical intervention despite the lack of medical indication. Signs of FII are largely behavioural or relate to conflicts in clinical evidence (e.g. therapy for the supposed illness is inexplicably ineffective or the symptoms are unexplained or are followed by negative diagnostic results). Of course, these indicators have to be viewed against the backdrop of the knowledge-base of medicine which is constantly subject to review and realignment, meaning that

---

[38] Interestingly, in Munchausen's Syndrome the perpetrator of the fraud is usually identified as male (F. Raitt and S. Zeedyk, 'Mothers on Trial: Discourses of Cot Death and Munchausen's Syndrome by Proxy' (2004) 12 *Feminist Legal Studies* 257 at 259), whereas in MSBP the perpetrator is usually female. This distinction illustrates the arbitrariness with which the labels of Munchausen's Syndrome and Munchausen's Syndrome by Proxy have been applied to very different 'disorders'.

[39] E.g. the conviction of Petrina Stocker for manslaughter of her 9-year-old son by administering salt into his hospital drip: 'Mother found guilty in case of fabricated illness' (2005) BMJ 330.

[40] R. McClure, P. Davis, R. Meadow and J. Sibert, 'Epidemiology of Munchausen Syndrome by Proxy, Non-accidental Poisoning, and Non-accidental Suffocation' (1996) *Archives of Disease in Childhood* 57.

[41] Royal College of Paediatrics and Child Health, *Working Party Report: Fabricated or Induced Illness by Carers* (London, RCPCH, 2002).

inconsistencies in medical data should not necessarily be assumed to constitute evidence of foul play.

Litigation associated with FII in England and Wales has tended to take the form of parents claiming compensation for having been wrongly accused of deliberately injuring or falsifying injury in their child, as to which see later in Chapter 3.[42]

## Bullying at school

Bullying is defined as 'the use of strength or power to frighten or hurt weaker people'.[43] The suggestion that the victim of bullying is weak is not uncontroversial and, in the context of psychiatric damage claims, this definition might be taken as suggesting that the claimant does not possess ordinary phlegm, a fact which might have an impact on liability. A preferable definition might therefore be: 'deliberately hurtful behaviour repeated over a period of time in circumstances where it is difficult for those being bullied to defend themselves.'[44]

Whilst bullying can occur in any interpersonal context, it is particularly associated with the playground. A Department for Education and Employment Circular identifies three types of bullying; *physical* (kicking, hitting and theft), *verbal* (e.g. name-calling or racist remarks) and *indirect* (spreading rumours, excluding from social groups).[45] The effects of bullying are similarly diverse. Bullying is increasingly being associated with psychological harm, and may result in a detrimental impact on the victim's schooling and subsequently their earning capacity, and, in extreme cases, can be blamed for suicide.[46]

So how is bullying to be identified? First, the term 'bullying' suggests ongoing behaviour and not single events. Secondly, although bullying is

---

[42] *JD v. East Berkshire Community NHS Trust* [2005] UKHL 25; [2005] 2 WLR 993 and *P, C & S v. UK* [2002] 3 FCR 1. See also *Venema v. Netherlands* [2003] 1 FCR 153.
[43] *Oxford English Dictionary* (www.oed.com).
[44] *Protecting Children from Abuse: The Role of the Education Service* (Department for Education and Employment Circular 10/95).
[45] *Protecting Children from Abuse*. The proposition that bullying can be non-physical was also supported by Wright J in *H v. Isle of Wight* (2001) WL 825780 (see below).
[46] It has been estimated that there are around 16 suicides by minors in the UK each year which are the direct result of bullying: N. Marr and T. Field, *Bullycide: Death at Playtime* (Success Unlimited, 2000).

discussed here under the heading of physical abuse for the sake of convenience, as the circular mentioned above clarifies, bullying does not necessitate physical contact:[47]

> It can take the form of name calling, insulting and deliberately wounding remarks, or social ostracism, which can be just as hurtful and perhaps in a more penetrating and permanent way than physical violence.

Further, the occurrence of bullying in law is to be objectively determined:[48]

> The criterion of what does or does not amount to bullying in any given circumstances is not to be judged solely by the subjective perception of the victim himself ... but involves an objective assessment of the observed behaviour, taken in conjunction with any apparent vulnerability in the target of the behaviour complained of.

Thus, the legal test of what might be identified as bullying is objective in nature, and whilst the vulnerability of the victim forms part of the equation, that vulnerability must be 'apparent', therefore maintaining the objectivity of the test. Non-statutory guidance from the Department for Education and Employment in 2000 identified factors which made certain individuals more vulnerable to bullying, which might be used to support arguments that this individual was foreseeably at risk. The factors included: the possession of expensive items (e.g. a state-of-the art mobile phone), ethnic minority, shyness and idiosyncracies such as speech impediments.[49] The comment was also made that whilst boys tended to indulge in physical forms of abuse, girls were more likely to use verbal or indirect means which would be more difficult to detect.

Of course, in a claim for compensation arising out of bullying there are often two potential defendants: the perpetrator (unlikely in the case of a child bully) and the school or employers of the bully. Claims for psychiatric harm occasioned by bullying in the school years are likely to be targeted at local education authorities (LEAs) on the basis of either vicarious liability for the negligence of teaching staff, or even,

---

[47] Per Wright J in *H v. Isle of Wight* (2001) WL 825780.   [48] *Ibid*.
[49] *Bullying: Don't Suffer in Silence – An Anti-Bullying Pack for Schools* (Circular 64/2000).

potentially, direct liability.[50] LEAs cannot, however, be vicariously liable for the torts of their bullying pupils.[51]

## 2. Childhood sexual abuse

> Sexual abuse involves forcing or enticing a child or young person to take part in sexual activities, whether or not the child is aware of what is happening. The activities may involve physical contact, including penetrative (e.g. rape or buggery) or non-penetrative acts. They may include non-contact activities, such as involving children in looking at, or in the production of, pornographic material or watching sexual activities, or encouraging children to behave in sexually inappropriate ways.[52]

The *Working Together* definition of sexual abuse is typical in extending far beyond sexual intercourse to include paedophilia, exhibitionism, sexual sadism, child pornography and child prostitution.[53] Notably, registrations on the Child Protection Register under the heading of sexual abuse have declined to less than half their number in 1995 (from 5,600 to 2,700 as of 31 March 2005[54]). It is difficult to gauge exactly what these statistics indicate; they may be indicative of the multidisciplinary approach producing less false positive identifications of abuse, or they may be the result of defensive practice by child protection professionals prompted by increased litigation on the part of the victims of false allegations.

Discourse on the subject of childhood sexual abuse tends to be founded upon an assumption that this form of deviance is unique and therefore merits special treatment from policy-makers, legislatures and the courts. This uniqueness is predicated on a subset of assumptions, including:

- that recall of sexual abuse is often, or even typically, repressed by the victim and is only recovered many years later, therefore meriting special legal considerations in terms of limitation periods;[55]

---

[50] Lord Slynn in *Phelps v Hillingdon LBC* [2001] 2 AC 619 at 658 did not accept that education authorities owed no duty of care. The two other detailed judgments, of Lord Clyde and Lord Nicholls, stated that the issue did not have to be decided for the purposes of this appeal.
[51] *Watkins v. Birmingham City Council* (1975) *The Times*, 1 August.
[52] *Working Together*, at 2.6.
[53] R.S. Kempe and H. Kempe, *The Common Secret: Sexual Abuse of Children and Adolescents* (W. H. Freeman, 1984).
[54] *Referrals, Assessments and Children and Young People on Child Protection Registers*, at table 3C.
[55] E. Wilson, 'Suing for Lost Childhood: Child Sexual Abuse, the Delayed Discovery Rule and the Problem of Finding Justice for Adult Survivors of Child Abuse' (2003) 12 *UCLA Law Review* 145.

- that sexual abuse is more morally reprehensible than any other form of abuse and is comparable with murder in terms of the levels of social approbation it attracts;[56]
- that sexual abuse is more likely to cause long-term psychological, life-altering damage than any other form of abuse;[57] and
- that sexual abuse has no acceptable level of expression – its prohibition is absolute (zero tolerance) unlike physical abuse in the home, which is currently defined in English law by its degree in order to exclude the concept of reasonable chastisement.[58]

Most of these assertions of uniqueness can be readily rebutted, for example, it is inexplicable why trauma arising out of sexual incidents should produce the phenomenon of recovered memories when other forms of trauma do not,[59] and whilst sexual abuse is quite probably regarded as more heinous than other forms of child abuse, as we have seen, this would not be the case in all ages or in all societies. Nevertheless, it seems that in Canada and the US at least, acceptance of the rhetoric of 'uniqueness' has resulted in sexual abuse claims being given preferential legal treatment in the application of limitation and causation principles, to the detriment of claimants affected by other kinds of abuse (physical abuse, emotional abuse and neglect).[60] It is certainly the case that the majority of the case law in England and Wales and other jurisdictions on compensating abuse, criminal prosecutions for child abuse offences,[61] research efforts into the psychological consequences of abuse, and consequently much of this book, is taken up with exploring the specific issues which sexual abuse during childhood raises.

---

[56] *Ibid.* [57] *Ibid.*
[58] S. Ashenden, *Governing Child Sexual Abuse: Negotiating the Boundaries of Public and Private, Law and Science* (Routledge, 2004) at 9. It is seemingly this reason which motivated Butler Sloss LJ to distinguish between physical and sexual abuse in *Trotman v. North Yorkshire CC* [1998] ELR 625, concluding that whilst vicarious liability could exist for physical assaults, it could never apply to sexual assaults which were inevitably a negation of the teacher's duty. Now overturned by *Lister v. Hesley Hall Ltd* [2002] 1 AC 215.
[59] S. Brandon et al., 'Reported Recovered Memories of Child Sexual Abuse' (1998) 172 *British Journal of Psychology* 296.
[60] For an example of preferential treatment in Canada, see *Arishenkoff v. British Colombia* (2004) CCLT (3d) 163, where s. 3(4)(K) of the Limitation Act, which provides unlimited time for sexual abuse claims to be brought, is discussed and its application to other forms of abuse is ruled out. As to the US position, see Wilson, 'Suing for Lost Childhood'.
[61] L. Hoyano, G. Davies, R. Morgan and L. Maitland, *The Admissibility and Sufficiency of Evidence in Cases of Child Abuse* (Home Office Occasional Paper 100, 1999) at vii.

### 3. Emotional abuse

> Emotional abuse is the persistent emotional ill-treatment of a child such as to cause severe and persistent adverse effects on the child's emotional development. It may involve conveying to children that they are worthless or unloved, inadequate, or valued only insofar as they meet the needs of another person. It may feature age or developmentally inappropriate expectations being imposed on children. It may involve causing children frequently to feel frightened or in danger, or the exploitation or corruption of children. Some level of emotional abuse is involved in all types of ill treatment of a child, though it may occur alone.[62]

As the *Working Together* definition suggests, emotional abuse embraces both acts and omissions[63] and is often accompanied by another form of abuse. Consequently, emotional abuse is generally registered under other headings,[64] and for this reason the incidence of emotional abuse of children is widely regarded as underreported. This under-reporting is also due to the fact that this form of abuse rarely climaxes in an 'incident' and leaves no physical scar or mark;[65] in other words, as with neglect and FII, emotional abuse is descriptive of a dysfunctional relationship rather than an event.[66] The difficulty of proving a causal relationship between emotional abuse and impairment of a child's health or social development results in delay in registration for emotional abuse alone. Clearly, the existing definition of this category of abuse is not well suited to current child protection procedures with their emphasis on immediacy of harm or imminent peril.[67]

### 4. Neglect

> Neglect is the persistent failure to meet a child's basic physical and/or psychological needs, likely to result in the serious impairment of the child's health or development. It may involve a parent or carer failing

---

[62] *Working Together*, at 2.5.
[63] J. Garbarino, E. Guttmann, and J. Seeley, *The Psychologically Battered Child* (Jossey-Bass, 1986).
[64] D. Iwaniec, 'An Overview of Emotional Maltreatment and Failure to Thrive' (1997) *Child Abuse Review* 370.
[65] J. Garbarino, 'The Elusive "Crime" of Emotional Abuse' (1978) 2 *Child Abuse and Neglect* 89 at 90.
[66] D. Glaser and V. Prior, 'Is the Term Child Protection Applicable to Emotional Abuse?' (1997) 6 *Child Abuse Review* 315.
[67] *Ibid*.

to provide adequate food, shelter and clothing, failing to protect a child from physical harm or danger, or the failure to ensure access to appropriate medical care or treatment. It may also include neglect of, or unresponsiveness to, a child's basic emotional needs.[68]

Two of the most well-known English cases where compensation was claimed for child abuse can most accurately be described as falling under the heading of 'neglect' (*X v. Bedfordshire CC*[69] and *Barrett v. Enfield LBC*[70]). In both of these cases the defendant local authorities were alleged to have failed in their duties to protect children from abuse and neglect either in their home (*X v. Bedfordshire*) or once they had been taken into care (*Barrett*). As, ultimately, the system designed to protect these children from abuse was being accused of neglect, these cases have been described as examples of 'iatrogenic neglect'.[71]

In *Barrett* the claimant had been taken into care by the local authority aged ten months and remained in care until the age of 17 years. His complaint was that during that time, inadequate steps had been taken to arrange for his adoption, provide psychiatric treatment or to monitor his foster care. Suits for parental neglect are complicated by a rule that a child ought not to be able to sue his parents for their lack of reasonable care exercised in his upbringing.[72] This rule does not, however, apply where the defendant is a local authority with the care of the claimant and has access to trained staff to consult on matters relating to the child's circumstances;[73] therefore *Barrett*'s claim survived a striking out application.

In addition to iatrogenic neglect cases such as *X* and *Barrett*, the courts have recently been exposed to a barrage of what might be termed 'educational neglect' cases, where the claimant alleges that their schooling was deficient in failing to recognise and/or cater for their special educational needs and consequently they have suffered psychiatric and pecuniary disadvantages. Very little is said in this book on educational neglect cases, as they are far from what most would regard as cases of child abuse.[74]

---

[68] *Working Together*, at 2.7.   [69] [1995] 2 AC 633.   [70] [2001] 2 AC 550.
[71] C. Lyon, *Child Abuse* (Jordan Publishing, 2003) at 91.
[72] Lord Woolf MR in *H v. Norfolk* [1998] QB 367 at 377; *Barrett v. Enfield LBC* [1998] QB 367, *per* Lord Woolf MR at 378.
[73] [2001] 2 AC 550.
[74] For further detail on these claims see M. A. Jones and P. Case, *Claims for Psychiatric Damage* (Tottel Publishing, 2007).

## The individual and abuse – abuse as a pathogen

The aforementioned dominance of sexual abuse in the profile of child abuse claims brought in England and Wales is largely due to the fact that recollections of this type of wrong are more likely to be articulated using a discourse of 'incidents' and 'events' rather than abusive environments and relationships. Incidents and events are far better suited to the torts lexicon of wrongs, trespasses and damage and are therefore far easier to conceptualise as tort claims. The 'success' of sexual abuse claims in dominating the legal stage is, however, also attributable to links identified by psychiatry between this form of abuse and psychological dysfunction, links which have been persistently reinforced by the ongoing publication of more and more research on the topic.

### 1. Psychiatric injury and dysfunction caused by sexual abuse

Sexual contact with children has undergone a dramatic process of redefinition, with society changing its stance from the early 1900s when such contact was seen as morally damaging, with implications for the corruption of the child, shifting to the contemporary focus on such contact as being psychologically damaging.[75] Many regard the received wisdom concerning sexual abuse and its psychological effects as owing its origins to Sigmund Freud's seduction theory, published in the 1890s, which asserted that the repression of traumatic sexual experiences in childhood was the trigger for the later emergence of 'hysteria' in women.[76] The insinuation of sexual exploitation in the respectable homes of Victorian society proved unpalatable, particularly given that Freud was essentially asserting that *all* hysteria was rooted in repressed sexual abuse during childhood, thereby suggesting that sexual misconduct with children was widespread. These unpopular suggestions resulted in the medical community ridiculing and ostracising Freud,[77]

---

[75] C. Smart, 'A History of Ambivalence and Conflict in the Discursive Construction of the "Child Victim" of Sexual Abuse' (1999) 8(3) *Social and Legal Studies* 391 at 399.
[76] Note that Freud suggested only a correlation between the repression of sexual abuse and psychopathological outcomes. He did not make the more general link which is made between sexual abuse, whether repressed or not, and psychiatric illness: M. McCullough, 'Freud's Seduction Theory and its Rehabilitation: A Saga of One Mistake After Another' (2001) 5 *Review of General Psychology* 3.
[77] D. Gleaves and E. Hernandez, 'Recent Reformulations of Freud's Development and Abandonment of his Seduction Theory' (1999) 2 *History of Psychology* 324.

and condemning his seduction theory as 'scientific fairy tale'.[78] The negative feedback directed at Freud appears to have prompted him to retract his theory of repression in favour of an alternative theory which portrayed such abuse as the product of the patient's fantasy (the Oedipus theory).[79] This alternative explanation served to disguise the link between abuse and psychological harm, a move which has been described as a betrayal of both Freud's patients and sexual abuse victims generally.[80]

It was not until much later that the real turning point in the recognition of abuse-related trauma occurred. The turning point was seemingly prompted by the coincidence of research into the devastating post-traumatic effects of the Vietnam War and emerging feminist perspectives, which encouraged a focus on exploitation in the home and between the sexes. Today, sexual abuse appears in the *Diagnostic Statistical Manual of Disorders* (DSM IV) as a trigger for one of the most frequently utilised psychiatric diagnoses in the English legal system – post-traumatic stress disorder (PTSD).[81] The formal recognition of sexual abuse as causative of psychiatric disorder in DSM IV signals a fairly conclusive acceptance by the profession of psychiatry of the phenomenon of psychiatric harm occasioned by abuse. That is not to say that this acceptance is without its critics. Whilst there is a broad consensus that the psychological impact of repeated acts of sexual abuse can be devastating, it would not be quite true to state that this view is unanimously held. Research by Rind et al.[82] published in 1998 suggested that the subjects of abuse were almost as likely as control groups to be

---

[78] McCullough, 'Freud's Seduction Theory'.
[79] J. M. Masson, *The Assault on Truth: Freud's Suppression of the Seduction Theory* (1984) and L. B. Richardson, 'Missing Pieces of Memory: A Rejection of the "Type" Classifications and a Demand for a More Subjective Approach' (1999) 11 *St Thomas Law Rev* 515. The term 'dissociation' originates from the work of one of Freud's contemporaries, Pierre Janet, in P. Janet, *L'Automisme Psychologique* (Felix Alcan, 1889).
[80] McCullough, 'Freud's Seduction Theory'. Although see Wilson, 'Suing for Lost Childhood', who argues that Freud's Oedipus theory still maintained the link between childhood sexuality and psychopathology and without this model the link between sexual abuse and psychological harm would never have been accepted as readily in the 1980s.
[81] At 309.81. The current definition of PTSD as applied in DSM IV states that PTSD can be prompted by directly experienced violent personal assault (including sexual assault).
[82] B. Rind, P. Tromovitch and R. Bauserman 'A Meta-Analytic Examination of Assumed Properties of Child Sexual Abuse Using College Samples' (1998) 124(1) *Psychological Bulletin* 22.

well-adjusted individuals. This research sparked national controversy in the US, with the *American Psychological Association*, which had published the paper, being forced publicly to condemn the research and apologise for not having considered the policy implications of what it had published.[83] The Rind research is, however, very much in the minority, and literature tends to reinforce the belief that sexual abuse has a potentially far-reaching and debilitating psychological impact. Finkelhor and Brown outline what they refer to as the 'traumagenic dynamics' of sexual abuse, including:[84]

1. an impact on the child's sexual development;
2. the experience of betrayal by a trusted individual (e.g. a parent, teacher or priest);
3. powerlessness, which may be reinforced by threats of violence or coercion; and
4. stigmatisation leading to feelings of shame and an assumption of responsibility for the abuse by the victim.

The synergistic effect of these dynamics inflicts a particularly deep psychological scar on the abused. Similarly, Alpert et al. point to the unique stressors associated with child abuse, such as the fact that the incidents involve an immature dependent child and that the trauma will likely be repeated rather than confined to a single incident.[85]

Sexual abuse during childhood is associated with vulnerability to psychological disorder in general, but with no condition in particular.[86] The particular form of dysfunction through which the psychological scar inflicted by abuse manifests itself can include: post-traumatic stress disorder,[87] borderline personality disorder, anxiety, depression, suicidal

---

[83] R. J. McNally, 'Progress and Controversy in the Study of Posttraumatic Stress Disorder' (2003) 54 *Annual Review of Psychology* 229.
[84] D. Finkelhor and A. Browne, 'The Traumatic Impact of Child Sexual Abuse: A Conceptualisation' (1985) 55 *American Journal of Orthopsychiatry* 541.
[85] J. Alpert, L. S. Brown and C. A. Courtois, 'First Report of the American Psychological Association Working Group on Investigation of Memories of Childhood Abuse: Symptomatic Clients and Memories of Childhood Abuse – What the Trauma and Child Sexual Abuse Literature Tells Us' (1998) 4 *Psychology Public Policy and Law* 941.
[86] S. Brandon et al., 'Reported Recovered Memories of Child Sexual Abuse' at 299.
[87] K. L. Nabors, 'The Statute of Limitations: A Procedural Stumbling Block in Civil Incestuous Abuse Suits' (1990) 14 *Law and Psychology Review* 153 at 158. Note also D. H. Schetky (1990) (in 1998 Working Party document refs), where the author concludes that almost 50% of abuse survivors display symptoms of PTSD.

tendencies,[88] phobias, low self-esteem,[89] somatic disorders affecting the immune, central nervous, endocrine and reproductive systems, sexual dysfunction, confusion about sexual orientation, dysfunction in interpersonal relationships and anti-social behaviour.[90] These mental health problems have also been associated with an increased likelihood that individuals affected will lead lives involving prostitution, violent crime (including becoming the perpetrator of sexual abuse[91]), drug abuse and imprisonment.[92] These adverse outcomes for the victim's health and behaviour raise complex medico-legal issues, not only as to how causation and quantum are to be decided, but also as to how these symptoms can affect the claimant's decision/willingness to litigate, causing delay in the launching of proceedings and raising the issue of how limitation provisions can fairly be applied.

## 2. Other types of abuse and psychological injury

Whilst literature on the association between sexual abuse during childhood and psychological problems abounds, identifying studies on the mental health consequences of other types of abuse is far more taxing. There is little evidence that psychological harm flows from mild smacking as opposed to child-beating, and research even suggests that the benefits of mild parental smacking between the ages of 2 and 6 years outweigh the disbenefits.[93] There is as yet little in the way of litigation by

---

[88] C. Bagley, *Child Sexual Abuse and Mental Health in Adolescents and Adults* (Avebury, 1995) observed that 23% of abused interviewees in his South London study experienced suicidal thoughts in the last year as compared with 3% of the control group (at 4).

[89] Sexual abuse is a risk factor in the development of many psychiatric disorders: *Memories of Childhood Abuse* (1994) American Medical Association, Council on Scientific Affairs.

[90] Alpert, Brown and Courtois, 'First Report'. See also now *Working Together to Safeguard Children: A Guide to Inter Agency Working to Safeguard and Promote the Welfare of Children* (Department of Health, 1999) at para 2.13.

[91] 'Abused Boy of 12 who Raped His Teacher is Jailed for Life.' *The Times*, 12 March, 2005. See also the story of the paedophile attempting to sue the Catholic Church, claiming the priest who abused him caused him to become an offender himself: 'Paedophile to Sue Catholic Church over Alleged Abuse.' *The Times*, 19 August 2005.

[92] C. Bagley, *Child Sexual Abuse and Mental Health in Adolescents and Adults* (Avebury, 1995) at 4 and W. Kisch, 'From the Couch to the Bench: How Should the Legal System Respond to Recovered Memories of Childhood Sexual Abuse?' (1996) 5 *American University Journal of Gender and the Law* 207.

[93] R. Larzelere, 'A Review of the Outcomes of Parental Use of Nonabusive or Customary Physical Punishment' (1996) 98 *Pediatrics* 824.

adults who were physically abused during childhood claiming compensation for the psychiatric harm such abuse has caused them. Yet it has been argued that there is equal reason for delay in bringing a claim based on physical abuse given the fact that in relatively recent times there was widespread social acceptance of corporal punishment, and also that the uncertainty of the line between 'discipline' and 'abuse' has meant that the injury would often be 'hidden in plain view'.[94] The long-term psychiatric effects of fabricated or induced illness on the child are unknown, although it is suspected that it may result in children developing distorted perceptions of themselves and of their health, and possibly affect their future parenting skills.[95] Children who have been subjected to emotional abuse show multiple indicators of impairment, including educational and developmental under-achievement and low self-esteem,[96] and although emotional abuse is hardly ever considered fatal, this form of abuse is capable of triggering suicide attempts and other forms of self-harm.[97]

Much of the available research tends to assume that the psychological fallout of sexual abuse is more serious than that produced by physical or emotional abuse, neglect or separation from the mother.[98] There is, however, research which suggests that sexual abuse is often wrongly identified as the sole trigger of the psychological injury whereas, in truth, the psychological effects of abuse have more to do with the dysfunctional environment in which such abuse generally occurs.[99]

### 3. The law and psychiatry interface: psychological morbidity and disincentives to litigation

The precise psychological sequelae of abuse are of importance to determinations of liability and compensation insofar as the courts need to identify the 'damage' to be compensated and whether a causal nexus can be demonstrated between the abuse and the harm. Another legal

---

[94] Wilson, 'Suing for Lost Childhood'.
[95] Royal College of Paediatrics and Child Health, Working Party Report, *Fabricated or Induced Illness by Carers* (RCPCH, 2002).
[96] D. Glaser and V. Prior, 'Is the Term "Child Protection" Applicable to Emotional Abuse?' (1997) 6 *Child Abuse Review* 315.
[97] C. Doyle, 'Emotional Abuse of Children: Issues for Intervention' (1997) 6 *Child Abuse Review* 331.
[98] Bagley, *Child Sexual Abuse and Mental Health in Adolescents and Adults* at 21.
[99] Wilson, 'Suing for Lost Childhood'.

dimension of the psychological effects of abuse concerns the impact these effects are reputed to have on the claimants' willingness to approach the courts. Such claimants are perhaps more likely than most to be less assertive in claiming their right to compensation. Should the law accommodate this reticence when it comes to applying the rules of limitation where it can be shown that such reserve is a result of the defendant's wrong?

### Repressed memory/dissociative amnesia

Quite independently of the pathological symptoms and other functional disturbances mentioned above, child abuse, particularly sexual abuse, is frequently alleged to result in repressed memories, 'the process of burying memories of painful or traumatic experiences'.[100] This repression of traumatic memories is a well-documented self-defence mechanism which is now represented in DSM IV as 'disassociative amnesia'.[101] The phenomenon of repressed memory is regarded as affecting only a minority of abuse victims,[102] but for those it does affect, it represents grave obstacles to the pursuit of compensation. Repression can cause delay on the part of the claimant in bringing the abuse to the court's attention and can cause further difficulties in terms of whether the court can be convinced that the memories are reliable evidence of the occurrence of the abuse. These obstacles arise, in part, out of the dissonance between the goals of the legal system and the discipline of psychiatry. The retrieval of repressed memories is viewed by psychiatry as a therapeutic tool upon which a treatment programme can be built, and the veracity of those memories is not the therapist's primary concern. The law's emphasis is, however, on whether repressed memory is a mechanism through which the truth can reliably be ascertained in order that any litigation will be conducted fairly between the parties. Thus, the goals of

---

[100] L. Holdsworth, 'Is it Repressed Memory with Delayed Recall or is it False Memory Syndrome?' (1998) 22 *Law and Psychology Review* 103 at 105.

[101] 4th edn, at 300.12. Although see H. G. Pope et al., 'Attitudes Towards DSM IV Dissociative Disorders Diagnoses Among Board-Certified American Psychiatrists' (1999) 156 *American Journal of Psychiatry* 321, where research showed only approximately one-third of psychiatrists in the US thought dissociative disorders should be included without question in the DSM. Amnesia also features as a possible symptom of PTSD.

[102] Alpert, Brown and Courtois 'First Report'. Cf. S. Feldman-Summers and K. Pope, 'The Experience of "Forgetting" Childhood Abuse: A National Survey of Psychologists' (1994) 62 *Journal of Consulting and Clinical Psychology* 636–9, who put the figure of 'forgetting' at around 40% of victims and who also linked the likelihood of repression with the severity of abuse.

law and psychiatry are at odds, despite the fact that the existence of the claim for psychiatric damage arising out of abuse assumes a great degree of cooperation and compatibility between the two disciplines.

Apparently, despite the inclusion of dissociative amnesia in the profession's diagnostic criteria, the world of psychiatry is still divided on the existence of repressed memory,[103] and indeed there is even disagreement as to whether the profession has reached a position of consensus or not.[104] One of the most frequently cited studies on repression is the study by Williams, which asked women who had been treated in hospital for injuries arising out of sexual assault, whether they had ever been abused. The study concluded that 38% of these women failed to disclose the abuse, and yet they were willing to disclose other equally intimate details of later incidents (suggesting that the reason for non-disclosure was memory related rather than any unwillingness to disclose on their part).[105] This research has, however, been the subject of caustic criticism on the grounds that many of those who did not disclose the abuse were under 4 years of age at the time the abuse came to the attention of the authorities.[106] It is widely understood that abuse which occurs when the child is 4 years old or under will be difficult for the adult to recall verbally due to the limited development of linguistic skills of young infants.[107] Given these circumstances, it is quite feasible that, at least in some of the cases studied by Williams, the forgetting was due to ordinary childhood amnesia rather than trauma induced memory impairment.

Earlier research by Briere suggests that 42–59% of individuals who report childhood sexual abuse can identify a period in their lives when they had no recollection of their abuse.[108] With respect, it seems self-contradictory to suggest that a subject can recall having forgotten something. It is possible that much of what is described as repressed/recovered memories refers to something in the subject's past which they have not thought about for a long period of time rather than that mechanisms

---

[103] For a renowned attack on the principle of repression, see Loftus and Ketcham, *The Myth of Repressed Memory*.

[104] See the discussion of *State v. Hungerford* 697 A 2d 916 (NH 1997) and *Shahzade v. Gregory* 923 F Sup at 289 below.

[105] Williams, 'Recall of Childhood Trauma'. See Reagan, 'Scientific Consensus on Memory Repression and Recovery' for an analysis of this research.

[106] McNally, 'Progress and Controversy'.

[107] C. Gore-Felton et al., 'Psychologists' Beliefs and Clinical Characteristics Judging the Veracity of Childhood Sexual Abuse Memories' (2000) 31 *Professional Psychology Research and Practice* 372.

[108] J. Briere, *Child Abuse Trauma: Theory and Treatment of Lasting Effects* (Sage, 1992).

of their subconscious have actively blocked it out. In fact, in the case law of England and Wales there is little reference to repression or recovered memories, a state of affairs which is in all probability a result of the damning conclusions of the Brandon Report.[109] This report, which is widely regarded as the Royal College of Psychiatrists' guide to the profession on the issue of repressed memory, is highly sceptical of the theory of repression and recovery of traumatic memory and has seemingly stopped dead in the water any attempt to persuade the judiciary that recollections of abuse can be forgotten for many years and retrieved at a later date.[110]

Our jurisprudence does, however, accept that the claimant's psychological response to the abuse may be delayed or may take many years to manifest itself and that the abuse may distort perceptions of the victim or might reasonably produce an overwhelming urge to avoid any activity which involves reliving the abuse (such as litigation).

## Distorted perceptions

Aside from the possibility of recovered memories, the circumstances of the abuse can cause a distorted perception of the incidents of abuse which inhibits claimants in the pursuit of legal remedies until therapy adjusts those perceptions. These distorted perceptions can manifest themselves in a belief that the claimant is in fact responsible for the abuse and that the abuser is therefore not a 'wrongdoer'. Placing the victim under an 'illusion of responsibility' is a frequent ploy used by the abuser to maintain the conspiracy of silence surrounding the abuse.[111] Alternatively, where the perpetrator is a family member, the decision not to reveal or report the abuse either inside or outside the family may have been procured by undue influence or duress with the use of explicit or implicit threats. These threats may take the form of the abuser suggesting that disclosure will inflict crisis and possibly breakdown of the family unit,[112] will harm individuals in the family unit by causing the abuser to take vengeance or will cause psychological trauma to an already fragile relative.[113]

---

[109] S. Brandon et al., 'Reported Recovered Memories of Child Sexual Abuse'.
[110] See Chapter 4.
[111] J. Lamm, 'Easing Access to the Courts for Incest Victims' (1991) 100 *Yale Law Journal* 2189 at 2192.
[112] K. L. Nabors, 'The Statute of Limitations: A Procedural Stumbling Block in Civil Incestuous Abuse Suits' (1990) 14 *Law and Psychology Review* 153 at 156.
[113] Recognised in *Gray v. Reeves* [1992] 89 DLR (4th) 315 at 330, per Hall J.

## Avoidance behaviours

Even claimants who have always had full recollection of their experiences may be expected to exhibit a reluctance to engage in any activity which requires them to re-live or discuss their abuse or encounter their abuser. This general avoidance behaviour may be the reason for a claimant not considering bringing a civil action sooner, whereas the progress of time may make litigation a less threatening prospect.

The potential for repression of memories and the distorted perceptions of abuse and avoidance behaviour discussed above raise a number of distinct legal issues:

1. Should abuse be categorised as a 'trespass' or a 'breach of duty' for the purposes of limitation of actions? (The latter would secure access to a more flexible limitation period so that account could be taken of the psychological factors which might have caused the claimant to procrastinate.) *(Form of action – see Chapter 2)*;
2. In jurisdictions where the theory of repression and recovery of memories of abuse is accepted as credible, should memory based testimonies procured by therapeutic intervention be admissible in civil cases? *(Admissibility – see Chapter 4)*;
3. In these jurisdictions what have the courts' views been on the reliability of recovered memories of abuse? *(Reliability – see Chapter 4)*;
4. Should limitation statutes be 'tolled' (i.e. suspended) to allow the claim of an abuse victim who has experienced repressed memory, a distorted perception of the abuse or avoidance behaviour to be brought beyond the usual limitation period? If so, on what grounds? *(Limitation periods – see Chapter 5)*.

## Society and abuse

### 1. Prevalence of abuse in childhood

Research from the US suggests that around 20% of women and 5–10% of men have experienced sexual abuse.[114] A survey undertaken by the National Society for the Prevention of Cruelty to Children (NSPCC) among 2,869 adults aged 18–24 years old, revealed the disturbing findings that 1% of those surveyed reported being sexually abused by a

---

[114] Alpert, Brown and Courtois, 'First Report'.

parent and 3% reported sexual abuse by another relative.[115] Another study claimed to reveal that 21% of young women attending further education colleges in Britain had experienced sexual abuse involving physical contact before the age of 18, as compared with 7% of the same male population.[116] It should be noted, however, that statistics proclaiming to reveal the prevalence of abuse tell us nothing about the likely proportion of responses which are genuine.[117] The actual figure may be either under-estimated (many abuse victims may be too traumatised or fearful to reveal or report their experiences) or over-estimated (false reports may be a product of other psychological problems, the desire for financial gain or vindictive motives).

## 2. The context of abuse

### Abuse in the home

Concerns regarding the physical and sexual abuse of children began with a focus on abuse in the family home. Although sexual activity with children in the family home has been stigmatised and criminalised for many years, it was not until the Punishment of Incest Act 1908 that sexual abuse within families became a matter for state jurisdiction rather than a matter of ecclesiastical law. Even then, the purpose of this Act was not purely to protect children but was also designed to prevent the birth of 'feeble-minded' offspring due to interbreeding.

It has been noted that even in the 1960s the prevailing policy in England and Wales dictated that where incest was discovered offenders were to be prosecuted only in the worst, most persistent cases.[118] The evacuation of children during the Second World War also left its mark on childcare policy, with research revealing the deleterious effects of children being separated from their families. Consequently, up until 1975 one of the legacies of wartime evacuation was a widely held belief that, notwithstanding the fact that the child was the victim of abuse in the home, it was far better to keep the family together than to take the child into care. This conviction that a family ought not to be divided

---

[115] P. Cawsom et al., *Child Maltreatment in the UK: A Study of the Prevalence of Child Abuse and Neglect* (National Society for the Prevention of Cruelty to Children, 2000).

[116] L. Kelly, L. Regan and S. Burton, *An Exploratory Study of the Prevalence of Sexual Abuse in a Sample of 16–21 Year Olds* (University of North London, 1991).

[117] E. Greer, 'Tales of Sexual Panic in the Legal Academy: The Assault on Reverse Incest Suits' (1998) 48 *Case Western Reserve* 513.

[118] Bagley, *Child Sexual Abuse and Mental Health in Adolescents and Adults*.

is illustrated by the defendant's conduct in the case of *C v. Cairns*.[119] A general practitioner became aware that one of his patients had been sexually abused by her stepfather. In line with common practice in 1975, he kept this information confidential, allegedly in the belief that resolving the problem was best left to the child's mother. Whilst it is not doubted that such inaction would at one time have been regarded as good practice, it would likely result in findings of negligence and professional misconduct today. Another stark contrast between contemporary attitudes towards incest and those of 30 years ago is evidenced by the fact that a book published as recently as the late 1970s advocated incest within certain boundaries.[120]

## Abuse in child care institutions

It was not until the early 1990s that concerns were raised regarding the abuse of children in residential care.[121] This was because residential care was often regarded as a last resort and as a remedial or punitive option, therefore abuse was not readily associated with these institutions as society did not expect residential homes to be congenial environments.[122] *Lost in Care* (the 'Waterhouse Report')[123] highlighted not only the prevalence of physical and sexual abuse and neglect in local authority homes, privately run children's homes and foster homes, but also the gross system failures which had allowed the abuse to continue undetected. These failures ranged from regular omissions to make proper checks and obtain references for persons recruited to work in the child care sector, to inadequate monitoring and inspection of these institutions by local authorities. The report found that complaints systems for residents and staff were largely non-existent until the late 1980s and that, in any case, complaints by children in these institutions were largely discouraged. This 'cult of silence' was only broken when

---

[119] [2003] Lloyd's Med Rep 90.
[120] 'Non-coercive Father-daughter Incest Can in Fact Produce Competent and Notably Erotic Young Women. Childhood is the Best Time to Learn' in A. Yates, *Sex Without Shame* (William Morrow, 1978), cited in E. Olafson, D. Corwin and R. Summit, 'Modern History of Child Sexual Abuse Awareness: Cycles of Discovery and Suppression' (1993) 17 *Child Abuse and Neglect* 7.
[121] B. Corby, A. Doig and V. Roberts, *Public Inquiries into Abuse of Children in Residential Care* (Jessica Kingsley Publishers, 2001) at 38.
[122] *Ibid.*
[123] *Lost in Care: Report of the Tribunal of Inquiry into the Abuse of Children in Care in the Former County Council Areas of Gwynnedd and Clwyd Since 1974* (2000) (HC 201).

pressure mounted from staff employed by the local councils and media coverage resulted in the Tribunal of Inquiry being set up in 1996.[124]

3. *The law and society interface: the impact of media reporting and public inquiries – from hyperbole to understatement*

Societal awareness of abuse is likely to have an enormous influence on the receptiveness of the courts towards claims seeking compensation for abuse. Low-level awareness can be of importance in explaining why a claimant has taken so long to approach the courts, whereas high-level awareness can increase judicial scepticism towards arguments that the claimant did not appreciate until many years after the abuse that they might have a claim. A number of factors have been identified as significant in tuning society's ear more acutely to child abuse generally as a problem to be addressed:

- the trend towards smaller family units affording parents more time and energy to focus on the welfare and potential of each individual child;[125]
- the 'invention' of battered child syndrome in the United States by Kempe et al. in the late 1950s;[126]
- the public inquiry into the death of Maria Colwell in 1973 at the hands of her violent stepfather;
- the launch of ChildLine in 1986, a 24-hour telephone counselling service for children with an emphasis on child sexual abuse; and
- the Waterhouse Report revealing widespread abuse in all its forms in children's homes and foster homes in Wales.

In light of the above, arguments regarding the unforeseeability of the general risks of sexual abuse will soon lose their currency. For example, it might be argued that ignorance of the risk of child abuse in the family home could not be reasonably sustained beyond the late 1980s when the publication of the Cleveland Inquiry brought the issue to the public's notice in such a dramatic fashion (see below).[127] Indeed, in the

---

[124] The North Wales Child Abuse Tribunal of Inquiry, the report of which became the Waterhouse Report (*Lost in Care*).
[125] Corby, Doig and Roberts, *Public Inquiries into Abuse of Children in Residential Care*.
[126] Kempe and Kempe et al., 'The Battered Child Syndrome'.
[127] The Cleveland Inquiry (1987) is identified as the turning point by both Bingham LJ in *Stubbings v. Webb* [1992] QB 197 (CA) at 208 and Lyon, *Child Abuse* at 2.102. See also Corby, who regards sexual abuse as largely hidden in Britain until the late 1980s (Corby, Doig and Roberts, *Public Inquiries into Abuse of Children in Residential Care* at 76).

previously mentioned case of *C v. Cairns*, the High Court determined that whilst the decision of a GP not to disclose sexual abuse of a child patient in the mid-1970s was not negligent when judged against the prevailing knowledge of abuse at the time; such non-disclosure today would give rise to an 'irresistible' conclusion of negligence.[128]

In civil claims for compensation arising out of the different forms of child abuse, the extent to which the occurrence of that abuse has been recognised and the degree to which its prevention has been explicitly on the public agenda are of crucial importance to the extent to which the law will waive the usual time limits in bringing an action. Bingham LJ made explicit reference to this fact in the Court of Appeal judgment in *Stubbings v. Webb*:[129] '... during the period in question [late 1970s] there was not that general awareness among the public of the psychological effects of child abuse which certain well-publicised events since then have caused.' The level of society's awareness is also pivotal to issues such as the willingness of claimants to seek compensation and arguments about the foreseeability of such harm for the purposes of liability in negligence.

The 'moral panic' concerning childhood abuse which crescendoed in the mid to late 1980s in Britain[130] has allegedly produced outcomes which are seriously prejudicial to the contemporary victims of abuse, including an aftermath of decline in preventive activity and prosecutions for incest.[131] The incident which is most associated with prompting the downturn in concern for the abuse victim came in the shape of the Cleveland scandal which erupted in 1987. Two local paediatricians, Geoff Wyatt and Marietta Higgs, diagnosed an unprecedented number of children in the Cleveland area as having been sexually abused. Over 120 children were taken from 57 family homes using place of safety orders,[132] often without warning and without being allowed to say goodbye or retrieve their toys and other belongings. Concerns were raised when foster homes and residential home places were filled and a

---

[128] *C v. Cairns* [2003] Lloyd's Rep Med 90.

[129] [1991] 3 All ER 949 at 955.

[130] J. Kitzinger, *Framing Abuse: Media Influence and Public Understanding of Sexual Violence Against Children* (Pluto Press, 2004), observing that reporting of sexual abuse in *The Times* increased by 300% from 1985 to 1987.

[131] K. Soothill and B. Francis, 'Moral Panics and the Aftermath: A Study of Incest' (2002) 24 JSWFL 1, using Home Office statistics to demonstrate that incest prosecutions have fallen to lower than those in the 1970s, when incest was not regarded as a significant problem at 15. See also R. Persaud, 'Keeping Mum Over Child Abuse' (2005) 330 BMJ 152.

[132] Under the now superseded s. 28 of the Children and Young Persons Act 1969.

special hospital ward was established to accommodate the overspill of removed children. The Orkney scandal of 1991[133] featured a similar story of children being removed peremptorily from their parents and was followed by media coverage which provoked echoes of Cleveland and reinforced the sentiments of public outrage at authoritarian officials destroying family homes.

The Cleveland and Orkney scandals became symbols of malpractice by child protection professionals, particularly social workers.[134] They also marked a shift in the public's sympathies from the 'child as victim' to the 'family unit as victim', the latter being characterised by media portrayals of loving parents needing protection from over-zealous social workers who saw child abuse lurking around every corner.[135] The inquiry into the Cleveland affair did not reach clear conclusions on whether the children had been abused by their parents but focused instead on the poor quality of care provided by the authorities,[136] reporting many criticisms of the working practices of the child protection workers involved in the case,[137] and portraying the children as 'double victims' of abuse.[138] The inquiry published 12 rules to be followed in conducting interviews with children suspected of being the victims of abuse (e.g. that interviews should be approached with an open mind, should comprise open-ended questions and should be undertaken by persons of experience and trained with an aptitude for talking to children).

Media coverage of the Cleveland/Orkney affairs was as enthusiastic as coverage of the horrors of the prevalence of child abuse itself,[139] a popular allegation being that the child protection agenda was out of control resulting in unfounded allegations which were comparable to

---

[133] Nine children were removed from four families due to suspicions of ritualistic abuse by parents in collusion with other members of the community, including the local minister.
[134] Kitzinger, *Framing Abuse* at 64.
[135] Soothill and Francis, 'Moral Panics and the Aftermath: A Study of Incest' at 13.
[136] Corby, Doig and Roberts, *Public Inquiries into Abuse of Children in Residential Care* at 43.
[137] *Report of the Inquiry into Child Abuse in Cleveland 1987* (1988) Cm 412.
[138] These children were possibly victims of abuse in their own homes, and had subsequently been subjected to further bureaucratic abuse in the form of intrusive medical examinations and inappropriate interviewing techniques: C. Lyon, 'Legal Developments following the Cleveland Report in England – A Consideration of Some Aspects of the Children's Bill' (1989) *Journal of Social Welfare Law* 200.
[139] Kitzinger, *Framing Abuse* at 55; J. Myers, 'New Era of Skepticism Regarding Children's Credibility' (1995) 1 *Psychology Public Policy and Law* 387.

the Salem witch trials of 1692. The hyperbole of this comparison overlooked the fact that, whilst none of the Salem accused was a witch, it was unlikely that all of the allegations of child abuse were false.[140] Just as Freud's professional peers forced him to recant his seduction theory, it has been argued that societal awareness of sexual abuse as a pathogen has again been repressed. The backlash against over-zealous child protection has served society's instinct to avoid contemplating such a distasteful possibility as the widespread sexual abuse of children.[141]

The years following the backlash have seen a fairly steady trend of decline in the number of entries on the child protection registers from 1995 (approximately 35,000 entries) through to 2005 (approximately 25,900 entries).[142] As noted above, however, it is impossible to tell whether the figures for 2005 are closer to being representative of true cases of abuse or whether they are an underestimation of the problem due to the litigation-fuelled defensive practice of social workers and other professionals. What is of particular note for the purposes of this book is the fact that the English courts' exposure to civil litigation concerning sexual abuse, including the House of Lords' judgment in *Stubbings v. Webb*,[143] which has had a devastating effect on civil litigation in this area, did not occur until the aforementioned backlash had caused an entrenched scepticism in the UK towards claims of childhood sexual abuse.

The Cleveland and Orkney scandals offer proof, if proof were needed, that the pendulum of societal awareness of child abuse is profoundly influenced by media attention and public inquiries, both of which have the potential to give rise to distorted constructions of the problem of abuse and to misinform policy designed to deal with it. Child protection work is beleaguered by the recent torrent of public inquiries,[144] each of which has been followed by government responses, recommendations

---

[140] Myers, 'New Era of Skepticism'.
[141] Olafson, Corwin and Summit, 'Modern History of Child Sexual abuse Awareness'.
[142] *Referrals, Assessments and Children and Young People on Child Protection Registers: Year Ending 31st March 2005* (Stationery Office, 2006) (accessible via the Department for Education and Skills website: www.dfes.gov.uk).
[143] [1993] AC 498.
[144] Corby, Doig and Roberts, *Public Inquiries into Abuse of Children in Residential Care* reports that there have been 79 such inquiries between 1973 and 2000 (at 7). See also *Report of the Inquiry into the Removal of Children from Orkney in February 1991* (The Clyde Report) (1992) (HC 195); *The Victoria Climbié Inquiry: Report of an Inquiry by Lord Laming* (the Laming Report) (Stationery Office, 2003); *An Independent Inquiry Arising from the Soham Murders* (the Bichard Inquiry) (2004).

and professional guidance. In the context of institutional care, it has been argued that the weight of inquiries has resulted in residential care once more being regarded as a last resort rather than a positive option, the effect being that some children are left in abusive environments rather than being offered a place in an institution. Local authorities have been reluctant to expand their child care facilities and have relied instead on placement with foster homes or private institutions. Many such homes are given the care of children they are ill-equipped to deal with and private homes have traditionally been less well regulated than their local authority counterparts.[145]

### 4. The onslaught of regulatory reforms

Since the publication of the Waterhouse Report, childcare provision has been subject to an ongoing assault of new regulatory bodies and inspectorates (some of which have already been abolished and replaced),[146] extended regulatory powers and new requirements of registration, suitability and compliance for all care providers. The inspection function for residential care homes, children's homes and fostering agencies was removed from local authorities[147] and now rests with the Commission for Social Care Inspection ('the Commission'),[148] an independent inspectorate for all social care services in England (but not Wales)). The Commission is empowered to review or investigate the provision by local authorities in England of social services.[149] Its general function is described as being to encourage improvement in the provision of social services,[150] and in exercising this function it is to be concerned in particular with, *inter alia*, the availability, accessibility, management, economy and efficiency of these services and of the need to safeguard and promote the rights and welfare of children.[151] The Commission is under a duty to keep the Secretary of State informed about social

---

[145] Corby, Doig and Roberts, *Public Inquiries into Abuse of Children in Residential Care* at 182.
[146] For example, the National Care Standards Commission, created by the Care Standards Act 2000, replaced in its childcare regulatory functions by the Commission for Social Care Inspection.
[147] Care Standards Act 2000.
[148] Health and Social Care (Community Health and Standards) Act 2003, as of 1 April 2004.
[149] Ss. 79–80 of the Health and Social Care (Community Health and Standards) Act 2003.
[150] S. 76 of the Health and Social Care (Community Health and Standards) Act 2003.
[151] S. 76(2).

services provision and it is permitted to give advice to the Secretary of State on matters connected with this subject as it sees fit.[152] In particular, the Commission may advise the Secretary of State of any changes to national minimum standards[153] that, if made, could secure an improvement in the performance by local authorities in England of their adoption and fostering functions.

In each local authority area the Commission registers the private and voluntary care services that are required to meet national standards, inspects, assesses and reviews all care services, inspects boarding schools, residential special schools and further education colleges with residential students aged under 18, publishes inspection reports, deals with complaints about care service providers. It now also reviews complaints about local authority social services departments.[154]

The regulation of childminding and day care provision for young children was similarly removed from local authority control and placed under a new arm of Ofsted[155] and national standards have been devised for this field of child care[156] (note that these arrangements are subject to further change under the Child Care Act 2006 provisions). Childminders are defined as those who look after one or more children under the age of 8 on domestic premises for reward (excluding parents, those with parental responsibility for the child, relatives of the child or foster parents of the child).[157] Childminders must register with Ofsted (registration being contingent on the suitability of the childminder(s) and the suitability of all persons employed or living on the premises being suitable for contact with children, the premises being suitable for their purpose and the provision complying with Ofsted regulations[158]) and be inspected regularly. Providing childminding services without being registered and having been served with an enforcement notice from Ofsted to this effect is an offence.[159] An offence is also committed by the provision of day

---

[152] S. 77.
[153] Issued by the Secretary of State under s. 23 of the Care Standards Act 2000.
[154] *Learning from Complaints: Consultation on the Changes to the Social Services Complaints Procedures for Adults* (Department of Health, 2004).
[155] S. 79B of the Care Standards Act 2000.
[156] See Day Care and Child Minding (National Standards) (England) Regulations 2001, SI 2001/1828 and the Day Care and Child Minding (National Standards) (England) Regulations 2003, SI 2003/1996, set out in *Childminding: Guidance to the National Standards* (Ofsted, 2001) and *Childminding: Guidance to the National Standards – Revisions to Certain Criteria* (Ofsted, 2004).
[157] S. 79A.   [158] S. 79B.   [159] S. 79D(4).

care services without registration, although no prior service of an enforcement notice is required. Nursery education settings which are on their local authority's directory to provide free places for 3–4-year-olds must also be inspected regularly by Ofsted. Powers of inspection are extensive and include a right of entry at a reasonable hour to premises where the inspector has a reasonable belief that a child is being looked after, powers to interview, seize evidence and a right to inspect computer records at the premises.[160] A new programme of 'early years' inspections started in April 2005. Providers have been warned that Ofsted will give little or no notice that they intend to carry out an inspection and will inspect all provision at least once every three years and more often in some circumstances.

To these regulatory initiatives can be added the recently established Children's Commissioner, created to act as a voice for children and young people in England with the general function of 'promoting awareness of the views and interests of children'. This remit has been criticised as being a much diluted version of the role given to the Commissioner for Children in Wales, which includes reviewing and monitoring arrangements with a view to their effectiveness in safeguarding and promoting the rights and welfare of children.[161] The Children's Commissioner harks back to proposals made by the Waterhouse Report.[162] The Commissioner is permitted to hold inquiries, on direction by the Secretary of State or on his own initiative, into cases of individual children with wider policy relevance in England, provided the inquiry would not duplicate the work of another body.[163]

This regulatory onslaught makes for an incredibly complex matrix of responsibilities. In terms of seeking compensation for abuse, the standards issued by these regulatory bodies and frameworks provide a benchmark which can be utilised to fix the relevant standard of care in negligence actions, although not retrospectively. It also increases, at least superficially, the range of potential defendants in abuse claims, although as has been seen already in the context of the multidisciplinary approach to child protection, complexity can have the converse effect by diluting the accountability of each individual player.

---

[160] S. 79U(4).  [161] S. 73 of the Care Standards Act 2000.
[162] S. 1 of the Children Act 2004, with a remit of England only. For Wales see the earlier creation of Children's Commissioner for Wales under s. 72 of the Care Standards Act 2000. There are also separate Commissioners for Scotland and Northern Ireland.
[163] Ss. 3–4 of the Children Act 2004.

## Tort litigation and abuse

Whilst the world of psychiatry has for many years associated child abuse and exploitation with psychological dysfunction, it is only relatively recently that the legal community has recognised child abuse, particularly sexual abuse, as a foreseeable reality which produces long-lasting harm and which must therefore be subject to specific preventative controls and compensatory mechanisms. The judiciary were initially resistant to the notion that abuse inflicted legally recognised harm on the victim; rather children were not yet recognised as the beneficiaries of legal rights and therefore meriting protection. Once they had been the subject of inappropriate sexual contact they became moral lepers, a source of contagion which might corrupt other children around them.[164] This can be contrasted with the last decade in which Parliament has enacted a number of statutes which have extended and redefined sexual offences, with particular reference to child victims,[165] including the offences of abusing a position of trust in relation to a child by engaging in sexual activity with a child, sexual activity in the presence of a child or causing a child to watch a sexual act.[166]

A central theme of this book will be that any litigation-based system of compensating the victims of abuse requires that law and medicine join forces to identify the wrong, the damage suffered, its cause and the impact of abuse on legal issues such as the delay in bringing litigation. This contrived medico-legal union is frequently an uneasy one, particularly in the context of litigation by the abused, as the disciplines of law and medicine are founded upon different sets of goals and assumptions. Another example of dissonance arises from the fact that developmental strands of psychology and psychoanalytical theory often look to critical incidents during childhood to explain adulthood neuroses. Yet, this longitudinal search for the causes of mental trauma, and the idea that stored experiences can cause behavioural mutations in later life, do not sit well with the law's traditional search for a 'cause' accompanied by an immediate 'effect'.

It is not only delay in litigating which has made the compensation of abuse such an intricate field of litigation. As indicated above, the

---

[164] Smart, 'A History of Ambivalence and Conflict' at 403.
[165] Sexual Offences Act 1997; Sexual Offences (Amendment) Act 2000; Sexual Offences Act 2003.
[166] Ss. 16, 18 and 18 respectively of the Sexual Offences Act 2003.

psychological response to abuse can result in symptoms which are many and varied. However, accepting that an association exists between sexual wrongs and psychological dysfunction is a long way from convincing a court that the wrongdoer caused the dysfunction in a particular case. Issues of causation and contribution are particularly intractable given that abuse victims are often subject to traumatic experiences both preceding the abuse (e.g. by family problems resulting in the child being taken into an institutional setting where the abuse occurs) and after the abuse (e.g. where behavioural change caused by abuse steers the claimant into a life of crime or drug-taking which brings its own problems).

This book will map the application of legal principles to the complexity of abuse-related injury, and chronicle the law's struggle to adapt traditional concepts of 'duty', 'damage', 'causation' and 'limitation' to a wrong which is often characterised by the delayed onset of intangible psychological injuries or which produces defence mechanisms in its victims causing delay in the launch of legal proceedings (e.g. by way of distorted perceptions of the abuse or avoidance strategies).

## 1. Proliferation of claims pertaining to abuse

The chapters which follow will provide a detailed analysis of the legal principles in England and Wales and the underlying values governing, *inter alia*, compensation claims for the lasting trauma suffered by adult survivors of child abuse and claims brought by those wrongly accused of abuse. This analysis will necessarily include:

- discussion of the merits and demerits of different forms of action as mechanisms for imposing liability for abuse (e.g. liability in negligence, trespass to the person, breach of fiduciary duty, misfeasance in public office, vicarious liability and non-delegable duties);
- an analysis of how compensable psychiatric damage can be proved;
- exploration of how the law deals with complex issues of duty of care and causation; and
- detailed scrutiny of how limitation periods may be extended in the context of abuse cases.

Whilst a substantial portion of the book will deal with civil claims by the abused for the psychological sequelae of abuse, the book's coverage also extends to litigation by other parties involved directly or indirectly in abuse allegations. For example, the issue of whether a person wrongly accused of child abuse can sue the authorities/professionals responsible for (falsely) reporting that they are responsible for abuse, raises distinct legal issues.[167] Other litigation possibilities include workers dealing with abuse victims or perpetrators, who seek compensation from their employers for exposing them to distressing experiences without adequate training or support,[168] or claims by bystanders (e.g. family members) to the abuse who are traumatised by witnessing the effects of the abuse.

### 2. Functions of tort litigation

The functions of tort are explored in brief here with particular reference to abuse claims so as to presage discussion as to the effectiveness of the torts regime in compensating abuse in the following chapters. Whilst a functional analysis of torts can give rise to a host of different purported functions, for the purposes of this text the common and 'elegantly simplistic'[169] assumption that the main functions of tort are 'compensation' and 'standard setting' is adopted. To these dual functions can be added the third and fourth dimensions of 'accountability' and the 'therapeutic function'.

#### Compensation

Academics are in general agreement that the primary goal of torts is the compensation of injury.[170] The level of damages awarded in civil claims is designed to put the claimant in the position they were in before the tort was committed, insofar as money is able to do so.[171] The assessment of damage and lost opportunities in abuse cases, as with many personal injury cases is necessarily fictional. How can a monetary value be placed

---

[167] Although disciplinary proceedings provide a mechanism of accountability in such cases (as *per* the recent case of Professor Southall's appearance before the General Medical Council), the courts are reluctant to impose any civil liability, preferring to protect the independence of the professional: *B v. Attorney General (No. 1 of 2003)* [2003] UKPC 61; [2003] 4 All ER 833; *JD, MAK and RK v. East Berkshire Community NHS Trust* [2005] UKHL 23; [2005] 2 WLR 993; *Sullivan v. Moody* (2001) 28 Fam LR 104.

[168] *State of New South Wales v. Seedsman* [2000] NSWCA 119; *Wood v. State of New South Wales* [2004] NSWCA 122.

[169] Brennan, 'An Empirical Analysis of Accidents and Accident Law'.

[170] P. Cane, *Atiyah's Accidents Compensation and the Law* (Weidenfeld and Nicolson, 1990) at 498; *Royal Commission on Civil Liability and Compensation for Personal Injury* (1978) Cmnd 7054 at para 49 and T. G. Ison, *The Forensic Lottery* (Staples Press, 1967) at 3.

[171] *Livingstone v. Rawyards Coal Co.* (1980) 5 Ap Cas 25.

on the suffering associated with abuse (e.g. the diminished self-esteem and detrimental impact on social relationships or future parenting). Moreover, given the impact of abuse on a young person's development, how is it possible to calculate the effect of abuse by comparing the damaged adult with the prosperous confident adult that might have been if the claimant's childhood had not been blighted by an abusive relationship? The intractable problems of placing an economic value on the harms caused by abuse mean that criticisms of quantum are difficult to rebut. What is clear, however, is that from the claimant's perspective tort is superior to other routes of redress insofar as the total damages award is concerned. The level of damages for sexual assault is likely to be between two and three times that available in a criminal injuries case.[172] It might be questioned how the function of compensation can be of any value at all to the victim of abuse, but it should be remembered that a compensation award does more than provide financial recompense for the economic disadvantages which abuse and psychiatric injury have inflicted, it also performs a subset of functions; damages have symbolic force as, *inter alia*, an expression of the wrong done to the claimant and a vindication of the claimant's character.

Aside from the question of how the level of compensation is to be fixed, the compensation function of tort raises the issue of who must pay: what are the principles of defendant selection applied by the torts regime? Whilst historically the torts system focused on identifying the cause of the claimant's loss as a means of determining liability to pay compensation, the rise of freedom of action led the courts to insist on 'no liability without fault'.[173] The central importance now attached to the *defendant's responsibility* rather than the *claimant's need* for compensation in determining tortious liability (and particularly in the context of the tort of negligence) demonstrates a primary concern with 'corrective justice'. The Aristotelian concept of corrective justice rests on a notion of righting wrongs, or of the defendant's responsibility for the

---

[172] C. Keenan, 'A Plea Against Tort Liability for Child Protection Agencies in England and Wales' (2003) 42 *Washburn Law Journal* 235 at 250.
[173] J. Fleming, *The Law of Torts* (9th edn, LBC Information Services, 1998) at 10. Abel attributes such a shift to mass migration and urbanisation as strangers have a lesser incentive to exercise due care towards each other: R. Abel, 'A Critique of Torts' (1990) 37 *UCLA Law Review* 785. The tension between fault and no-fault liability in tort continues to be played out in the context of nuisance and *Rylands v. Fletcher* (1868) LR HL 330, with liability creeping ever closer to 'fault based' forms. See M. A. Jones, *Textbook on Tort* (7th edn, Blackstone Press, 2000) at 7.1.8 and 8.1.9.

claimant's plight. This notion is bilateral, in the sense that decisions as to liability are made by reference to both parties of the action, to the exclusion of the impact of liability or the lack thereof on broader society.[174] In order that the integrity of corrective justice is assured, account must be taken of the defendant's interests in a fair decision-making process, hence the complex rules of limitation explored in Chapter 5, which attempt to protect defendants from stale, unprovable and false claims. The bilateral concern for justice between the parties is, however, far from sufficient to explain the intricacies of tort liability and is only one component in a much broader picture. Consider, for example, the case of negligence actions against local authorities or social workers where the substance of the complaint is that an identified perpetrator deliberately inflicted harm in the form of sexual abuse upon the claimant and that the defendants failed to rescue the claimant from the abuse.[175] A purely 'corrective' approach would surely require the perpetrator to be the source of compensation, and yet the recent success of iatrogenic neglect cases demonstrates that corrective justice represents only one dimension of torts litigation in this area.

A system of compensation which is concerned to effect a fair distribution of goods throughout society reflects the concept of 'distributive justice'.[176] Even in the tort of negligence, where an expression of the defendant's culpability in the form of a breach of the common law duty of care appears to be of central importance, considerations of distributive justice permeate judicial reasoning in the guise of considering the justice, fairness and reasonableness of imposing a duty of care. For example, the answer to the question of whether the wrongly accused can sue the doctors/social workers who unreasonably persisted in their allegations of abuse is intertwined with the perceived burdens on child protection work and the implications that a duty to the accused would have for the protection of the abused. These cases, discussed in Chapter 3, demonstrate that the duty assessment in such cases goes far beyond a consideration of corrective justice between the instant parties.

---

[174] J. Stapleton, *Disease and the Compensation Debate* (OUP, 1986). See also J. L. Coleman, 'Tort Law and the Demands of Corrective Justice' (1992) 67 *Indiana Law Journal* 349.
[175] E.g. *X (Minors) v. Bedfordshire CC* [1995] 2 AC 633.
[176] A. Grubb, *The Law of Tort* (Butterworths, 2002). It has been argued that corrective justice and distributive justice are independent and even incompatible principles: J. Wright, 'Right, Justice and Tort Law' in D. G. Owen (ed.), *Philosophical Foundations of Tort Law* (OUP, 1995) at 171.

The broad coverage of liability insurance appears to have driven a slight shift in tort liability towards distributive justice as opposed to corrective justice considerations. Where tort has the effect of imposing liability on insured defendants, academics have pointed to the beneficial effects of loss spreading. The claimant's loss is diffused into the cost of increased insurance premiums, and possibly passed onto consumers. But, given the courts' reluctance to avert to insurance as a relevant factor in fixing liability, such loss diffusion cannot be regarded as a formal policy objective of torts.[177] The distinct and more specific effect of risk allocation[178] can, however, be regarded as part of the philosophy of torts. Here liability attaches to those individuals/organisations who are best placed to manage such risks and prevent the reoccurrence of such injury in the future (and who, as a result, are often incidentally also insured). For example, the principle of vicarious liability, in regarding the defendant employer as the best cost absorber and generally imposing liability on employers in the absence of personal fault, can be regarded as a further example of distributive justice at work. Further, the fact that there is a clearly identifiable trend of increasing the vicarious liabilities of the employer, particularly notable in cases of physical violence and sexual wrongs by employees,[179] suggests that the courts are happy to increase the redistributive capacity of torts.

Many tort judgments display elements of both corrective and distributive justice. Even in cases of 'no-fault' vicarious liability where it might be assumed that corrective justice has little role to play, the House of Lords' recent step of bringing some instances of sexual abuse under the mantle of an employer's vicarious liabilities makes reference to corrective justice ideals by importing a moral dimension into its decision, saying that it is 'just, fair and reasonable' that, on the facts, the employer ought to be liable for the abuse perpetrated by its employee.[180] And with regard to negligence actions, Mullender attaches significance to the ordering of considerations within the 'tripartite' duty of care test. The primacy of corrective justice is, he argues, demonstrated by the reasonable foreseeability of harm being accorded lexical priority amongst the three limbs of the modern test for duty of

---

[177] Although see now *Transco plc v. Stockport MBC* [2003] UKHL 61; [2004] 2 AC 1, where their Lordships refer to liability according to who is the cheapest insurer.
[178] Stapleton, *Disease and the Compensation Debate*, at 121.
[179] See Chapter 1.
[180] *Lister v. Hesley Hall Ltd* [2002] 1 AC 215.

care: foreseeability, proximity and justice, fairness and reasonableness.[181] In the bigger picture of tort liability, where distributive justice is afforded priority it is the exception rather than the general rule.

### Setting standards and incident prevention

The philosophy of risk allocation described above is instrumental in enabling tort to function as a mechanism of deterrence or accident prevention. Whilst the common law of torts only rarely makes direct reference to deterrence or accident prevention as an objective, it is easy to agree with the preference some academics have expressed for accident prevention over compensation as a goal.[182] Welfare is maximised if adverse incidents do not happen at all, rather than if they happen but are compensated. Deterrence is a far simpler matter in the context of intentional torts such as battery than for non-intentional torts such as negligence. Moreover, deterrence is even less readily associated with a lack of care which involves inadvertence (i.e. if the defendant has not even addressed his mind to the risk in question, no conscious decision is ever made between 'liability attracting conduct' and 'liability avoiding conduct'). Talk of deterrence in such situations is largely defunct (although deterrence may operate in cases where potential defendants put in place a system to reduce the risk of inadvertence itself).

Negligence as a tort acts as a general deterrent in the sense that what constitutes a lack of reasonable care will only be decided by the courts after the incident has occurred.[183] In cases of a recurring risk in the provision of child protection services, a clear precedent to the effect that given conduct is a breach of the local authority's duty of care provides a mechanism of specific deterrence for future practice. It is quite possible that the torts regime works as a more effective deterrent at this institutional level, as large organisations such as NHS trusts and local authorities are in a better position to improve risk management and the prevention of future accidents than individuals are.[184] There is cause, however, for doubting the deterrence value of pro-claimant rulings in this field given the fact that the claim is often brought many years after

---

[181] R. Mullender, 'Corrective Justice, Distributive Justice and the Law of Negligence' (2001) 17 *Professional Negligence* 35 at 37.
[182] Ison, *The Forensic Lottery* at 80.
[183] Cane, *Atiyah's Accidents Compensation* at 493.
[184] G. Schwartz, 'Reality in the Economic Analysis of Tort: Does Tort Law Really Deter?' (1994) 42 *UCLA Law Review* 377 at 378. On the other hand, see J. Allsop and L. Mulcahy, *Regulating Medical Work* (Open University Press, 1996) at Chapter 8.

the abuse coupled with the additional years taken for the courts to process the claim. This 'double time-lag' means that, for example, by the time the ECHR in *Z v. UK*[185] decided that the state had failed in its positive duty to protect children from peril in the home, child protection practice had changed beyond recognition. Just as the prevalence of professional, employer and motorist insurance has influenced torts' pursuit of compensation, its impact has also been felt in terms of the capacity of tort as a mechanism of accident prevention. The existence of a relevant insurance policy, for the most part, severs the connection between liability and the defendant's purse.[186] Nevertheless, it should not be assumed that insurance cannot provide a substitute set of incentives for defendants to act in a precautionary manner. If insurance is 'experience rated' – the higher the rate of adverse incidents arising out of the defendant's conduct, the higher the premium – and if policies carry upper and lower limits on cover, liability can penetrate the shield of insurance. Therefore, whilst insurance insulates the defendant from the excesses of liability, it should be capable of mimicking the effects of liability for the purposes of incident prevention. If the cost of liability is absorbed by insurance, it might be supposed that individuals responsible for the failure in child protection will be subject to professional costs in the form of disciplinary action. There is, however, no formal connection between the judicial system and the disciplinary system. The court has no power to launch an investigation into the circumstances giving rise to the failure, and the social worker or medical practitioner concerned (even if personally at fault) will not necessarily be subject to any disciplinary action.

The further shortcomings of tort liability as a mechanism of deterrence include the fact that the measure of damages is calculated by the court's best guess as to what is necessary to compensate the claimant and therefore is not necessarily proportionate to the gravity of the wrong or the defendant's culpability. Additionally, the threat of liability can induce quite the opposite of incident-preventing behaviour with potential defendants failing to take remedial/preventive steps out of fear that their conduct will be interpreted as an admission of fault.[187] Whilst data from litigation might be regarded as a potentially rich source of learning from failure,[188] such a small number of cases reach the courts, that the

---

[185] *Z v. UK* (2002) 34 EHRR 97.
[186] Cane, *Atiyah's Accidents Compensation* at 490.
[187] Ison, *The Forensic Lottery* at 85.
[188] *An Organisation with a Memory* (Department of Health, 2000) at 4.33.

information derived from these cases is only the tip of the iceberg. Perversely, the more serious the case in terms of the severity of the error, the more likely the case is to be settled. In this sense, court cases are an unreliable indicator of lessons to be learned for child protection. The randomness of cases selected for a hearing before the courts means that tort judgments cannot be regarded as a reliable learning tool for the sectors involved in child protection work. Potential defendants can only speculate as to the content of their obligation of care and the risk of incurring liability by pursuing or departing from current practice. It is here that the deterrence capacity of tort has been doubted, given the prevailing uncertainty as to the exact content of the duty of care.[189] The guidance value of judgments delivered in court cases is very often superseded by the passage of time. For example, the complaint in the case of *Barrett v. Enfield LBC*[190] that the claimant had been placed in five different residential care homes during his childhood loses resonance given the shift away from institutional care prompted by the *Lost in Care* report.[191]

It should also be remembered that torts litigation is claimant-dependent. For the torts regime to be activated, a claimant must step forward and undertake the burden of protracted litigation. In this sense, the regulatory power of tort is randomised as the courts only have the opportunity to rule on randomly raised questions determined by the pool of litigants resolute enough to go all the way. The focus in torts is therefore on what might be isolated cases of abuse. The nature of claimant-focused negligence litigation deprives the court of the opportunity to examine the system of care operated by the defendant and its impact on persons beyond the instant claimant.[192] Even when the courts express disapproval of child protection practice, there is no reliable medium for communicating such disapproval to the professions at large. Having said this, litigation can often generate publicity and external public pressure to reform practice. The problem lies in the unpredictability with which such publicity mechanisms operate. It is worth noting, in particular, that the publicity generated by a case which concludes with a finding of no liability can equal that in a finding of liability, thus, as distinct from the function of compensation, litigation, whether successful or not, can have a significant deterrent effect.

---

[189] Grubb, *The Law of Tort* at 28.
[190] [2001] 2 AC 550.   [191] Keenan, 'A Plea Against Tort Liability' at 253.
[192] Keenan, 'A Plea Against Tort Liability' at 252.

### The public forum function – accountability and arbitration

Suggestions that tort exists to 'pass moral judgment' on the defendant's acts can be subsumed under the heading of accountability.[193] The notion of the public forum function of torts litigation is traceable back to an article by Linden, cited with approval by many academics, including Atiyah.[194] The public forum proposition involves the portrayal of negligence litigation as operating in an 'ombudsmanlike' fashion, investigating the cause of the relevant incident and scrutinising the defendant's conduct.[195] Once again, it is easy to see that the claimant's belief in the forum function of litigation does not necessarily require a finding of liability. Issues can be publicly aired and examined in a formal setting without an order of damages being made against the defendant. In this sense, the media attention triggered by a high profile court case may achieve more in terms of satisfying the claimant's needs than the legal process itself.

In the context of abuse claims, the arbitration/accountability function is confounded by the peculiar difficulties of verifying the claimant's allegations. Practitioners and academics are divided on whether the legal system is capable of differentiating effectively between genuine and fabricated claims of abuse with the help of mental health experts.[196] This is the dynamic at the core of this area of law which lurks behind the prevailing reluctance to throw open the doors of litigation. First, there is the fact that many allegations surface several years after the abuse occurred, therefore an assessment of the reliability and truthfulness of the claimant's account is crucial. The law's search for reliable and accurate evidence of past events for the purpose of fixing liability is, however, frustrated in abuse claims, both by the therapeutic process and the protracted nature of litigation. Both involve examination and re-examination of the claimant's version of events, yet it is axiomatic that repeated 'retelling' of the circumstances of the abuse can reshape the claimant's memory. This creates acute problems when the claimant is the only witness available to the court, which is often the case due to the secrecy which often surrounds abuse. Finally, the adversarial process

---

[193] Abel, 'A Critique of Torts'.
[194] A. M. Linden, 'Tort as Ombudsman' (1973) 51 *Canada Bar Review* 155.
[195] G. Stephenson, *Torts Sourcebook* (Cavendish, 2002) at 8–9.
[196] Cf. for example, C. G. Bowman and E. Mertz, 'A Dangerous Direction: Legal Intervention in Sexual Abuse Survivor Therapy' 109 *Harvard Law Review* 549 and E. Greer, 'Tales of Sexual Panic in the Legal Academy: The Assault on Reverse Incest Suits' (1998) 48 *Case Western Reserve* 513.

of tort litigation can obscure the fact finding process as the inquiry is led by the advocates of the parties and focuses on the issues they have selected as crucial to their client's case.[197]

Independent professional corroboration of the claimant's allegations is not always possible either. For example, the harm inflicted by sexual abuse is not tangible and the deception of carers who induce illness in children means that this form of abuse, as with sexual abuse, is not instantly verifiable by the usual medical means. These difficulties are responsible for the continuing controversy over the legitimacy of criteria and forms of evidence used to determine intervention in a suspected case of child abuse.[198] Where such uncertainty exists, it is often argued that the judicial process is not an efficient mechanism for the arbitration of competing scientific theories. This has been a particular feature which has lent force to the backlash against claims of abuse. For example, the Cleveland Report noted that magistrates' courts (where the place of safety order ('PSO') hearings were heard) could not handle either the volume of cases, or the complexities of scientific evidence put before them regarding the reliability of the reflex anal dilatation test.[199]

Whilst it might have been thought that expert evidence could ameliorate the shortcomings of the courts in identifying genuine claims of abuse, the Cleveland scandal marked the beginning of an era of distrust of professional judgement in the particular context of protecting children, both at the level of social work practice and the ability of medical science to perform the forensic function of identifying when abuse had occurred.[200] These patterns of distrust have been revived, *inter alia*, by the expert witness controversy surrounding the overturned murder convictions of Angela Cannings[201] and Sally Clarke.[202] Both Cannings and Clarke had been convicted of murdering their young children, both convictions being in part based on the assistance of expert evidence from Professor Roy Meadow. Statistical estimations of the incidence of

---

[197] Keenan, 'A Plea Against Tort Liability' at 252.
[198] Ashenden, *Governing Child Sexual Abuse* at 9.
[199] Lyon, 'Legal Developments following the Cleveland Report in England'.
[200] The use of the reflex anal dilatation test by the two paediatricians at the heart of the Cleveland affair was particularly controversial resulting in the publication of guidelines in the Cleveland Report which were recently updated in the form of *Guidance on Paediatric Forensic Examinations in Relation to Possible Child Sexual Abuse* (2004), issued jointly by the Royal College of Paediatric and Child Health and the Association of Forensic Physicians.
[201] *R v. Cannings* [2004] EWCA Crim 1; [2004] 1 WLR 2607.
[202] *R v. Clark* [2003] EWCA Crim 1020.

Sudden Infant Death Syndrome on which the prosecution's evidence was based have since been discredited and cases in which this evidence was used have been reviewed. Meanwhile, Professor Southall, an internationally renowned paediatrician whose evidence has been crucial in many child protection cases, has been found guilty of serious professional misconduct by the GMC. His peremptory allegations to the police that the husband of Sally Clark had murdered two of his children were made after watching a television documentary in which Mr Clark was interviewed. Professor Southall remained steadfast in his expression of these views despite the emergence of evidence which highlighted the flaws in his hypothesis. That the evidence could so blight the lives of one family has shaken the public's confidence in the expert witness system and has paved the way for attempts to sue professionals who instigate abuse allegations.

## The therapeutic function of tort litigation

It is commonly assumed that legal action serves not only to provide compensation to the abuse claimant which may help cover the medical expenses arising out of the abuse, but that it also serves a therapeutic function by directly facilitating recovery. There are a number of books encouraging readers who have experienced abuse to bring civil actions as a step in their recovery which provide testimony to this assumption.[203] This connection between litigation and therapy is made with particular reference to tort actions, as opposed to criminal prosecution or submitting a claim to a compensation scheme, on the grounds that civil action places the abused in a position of equal or greater power than the abuser who takes the defensive role,[204] whereas with a criminal prosecution, the abused individual is portrayed as a passive 'victim' or 'witness' and has little control over the confrontation. The lesser burden of proof in civil litigation (proof of the claimant's case on the balance of probabilities) has also been identified as facilitating the therapeutic value of tort litigation given that, in some circumstances, it allows the claimant to succeed on the basis of their own uncorroborated evidence.[205] There is some evidence in judgments relating to civil abuse claims that the

---

[203] E. Bass and L. Davies, *The Courage to Heal* (HarperCollins, 1988) being perhaps the best known of these.
[204] Nabors, 'The Statute of Limitations' at 159.
[205] B. Feldthusen, 'The Civil Action for Sexual Battery: Therapeutic Jurisprudence?' in D. Wexler and B. Winick *Law in a Therapeutic Key: Developments in Therapeutic Jurisprudence* (Carolina Academic Press, 1996) at 855.

judiciary assume that the process of litigation is in fact non-therapeutic and likely to aggravate the claimant's symptoms, but that once the litigation is resolved there may be therapeutic gains.[206]

It should be remembered, however, that the cost of litigation will put the therapeutic gains of court action beyond the reach of most abuse claimants[207] and that even where the outcome is favourable to the claimant, the process may be anti-therapeutic. Empirical research on the therapeutic and anti-therapeutic effects of civil litigation for the abused has found that the protracted nature of torts litigation was anti-therapeutic in depriving the abused of control over the liability determining process.[208] Some research subjects commented on being 'assaulted' again by the legal system which denied them the opportunity to tell the court anything beyond the facts surrounding the abuse and allowed bureaucrats to wrest control from claimants. Also, in cases where the defendant chose not to appear in court, or not to defend the claim at all, some claimants felt denied the opportunity to have a public airing of their story. This experience is likely reinforced by the fact that the court process is often dominated by the evidence of experts rather than that of the parties themselves. Furthermore, the fact that some forms of action often require something very specific in terms of proof of damage or a relationship with the accused may mean that lawyers distort the truth of the abused's experiences to fit the legal forms required for a successful suit, thereby again neutralising the therapeutic value of the tort action.

Where litigation ends in settlement, much of the potential therapeutic value of bringing a claim may be lost. Equally, a loss in litigation can be anti-therapeutic,[209] and a finding for the defendant can leave the claimant feeling humiliated or rejected.[210] Greer agrees, pointing out that in recovered memory cases, the memories may well be false, in which case, the 'abuse victim' is likely to suffer psychological damage and, even if the

---

[206] E.g. in *KR* at first instance, Connell J stated of one claimant that her 'distress has been if anything amplified by her subsequent involvement in this litigation' (*KR and others v. Bryn Alyn Community (Holdings) Ltd (in liquidation), Royal and Sun Alliance plc* (2001) WL 753345 (QBD) at [84]) and in *A B and others v. Leeds Teaching Hospital NHS Trust* [2004] EWHC 644; [2005] 2 WLR 358.

[207] Feldthusen, 'The Civil Action for Sexual Battery' at 873.

[208] N. Des Rosiers, B. Feldthusen and O Hankivsky, 'Legal Compensation for Sexual Violence' (1998) 4 *Psychology, Public Policy and Law* 433.

[209] *Limitation of Civil Actions – A Discussion Paper (Preliminary Paper 39)* (Law Commission, New Zealand, 2000) at 50.

[210] Des Rosiers, Feldthusen and Hankivsky, 'Legal Compensation for Sexual Violence'.

memories are true, there is a significant possibility that the litigation will be unsuccessful.[211] The adversarial process of litigation can also discourage defendants from making apologies or accepting responsibility, thereby obstructing much of the therapeutic value of resolution.[212] Some support for this argument can be gleaned from the fact that prior to the Waterhouse Inquiry, Clwyd County Council had commissioned its own reports into allegations of child abuse in residential care but had not made the findings public due to its fears of invalidating its insurance by being seen to admit liability. Other authors have commented on the potential of retaliatory litigation by the accused to silence the voice of the abused, thereby undermining therapeutic attempts to regain self-confidence and self-reliance.[213] To this point can be added the possibility that the perpetrator may involve the non-intervening parent in the litigation by claiming that they should share liability because of their failure to prevent the abuse, thus causing a destruction of other family ties.[214]

### 3. Trivialising, pejorative and demeaning language and the courts

Central to the potential therapeutic function of torts litigation is the role of the judicial process in providing public legitimation of the claimant's complaint. The power of the terminology used to describe the parties and incidents which are the subject of the court hearing confers legitimacy on one version of events at the expense of competing explanations of the same events. The abused may be portrayed by lawyers or judges as worthy claimants setting a positive example to those in a like position or in a demeaning fashion which aggravates the existing hurt caused by abuse. Linguistic studies of judgments in this field have tended to focus on the transcripts of criminal trials, but nevertheless give rise to some interesting insights into the characterisations of the parties to abuse litigation, and lay bare the assumptions upon which judicial determinations are based. Legal narratives define the sources of valid knowledge and, in the context of abuse claims, it has been asserted that women and children are frequently

---

[211] Greer, 'Tales of Sexual Panic in the Legal Academy'.
[212] Keenan, 'A Plea Against Tort Liability' at 251.
[213] C. G. Brown and E. Mertz, 'A Dangerous Direction: Legal Intervention in Sexual Abuse Survivor Therapy' 109 *Harvard Law Review* 549.
[214] E. Grace and S. Vella, 'Vesting Mothers With Power They Do Not Have: The Non-Offending Parent in Civil Sexual Abuse Cases' (1994) 7 *Canadian Journal of Women and the Law* 184 at 195.

portrayed as fabricators of sexual offences, but that the judicial rhetoric of neutrality disguises this pro-defendant bias.[215]

It is also well documented, for example, that early judicial responses to claims by the victims of abuse tended to characterise them as delusional or hysterical,[216] sick and broken,[217] or as deviant or unreliable witnesses.[218] The fact that large damages awards are generally framed in terms of compensatory damages rather than punitive damages has been identified as tending to reinforce the portrayal of the claimant as sick and broken.[219] Current restrictions on punitive damages (e.g., the fact that they are generally unavailable where the abuser has already been convicted and served a sentence) mean that the role for punitive damages is limited (see Chapter 4).

Today there are signs that these characterisations of the abuse claimant are being replaced by more enlightened portrayals. Studies of sentencing decisions in Canadian criminal abuse trials have charted a shift from a traditional approach, which tended to trivialise the harm caused by abuse by dwelling on the absence of tangible harm resulting from abuse, to a lexicon of physical harm as a metaphor for the lasting psychological effects of abuse (with frequent use of terms such as 'scarring' and 'carnage').[220] Another linguistic strategy which Canadian judges now use to counteract the traditional view of abuse as 'harmless' is to analogise sexual offences with theft by referring to victims being 'robbed' of their innocence or of their childhood. These developments have led to suggestions that the psychological harm flowing from abuse is now taken for granted by the judiciary, indicating a growing judicial awareness of the typical impact of sexual abuse.

It is one of the aims of this book to assess the portrayal of the abuse victim in contemporary judicial accounts of abuse claims. Particularly telling in this regard is the prominence of limitation arguments in abuse litigation and its potential to throw the spotlight on the claimant's

---

[215] C. Taylor, *Court Licensed Abuse: Patriarchal Lore and the Legal Response to Intrafamilial Abuse of Children* (Peter Lang, 2004).
[216] E. Mertz and K. Lonsway, 'The Power of Denial: Individual and Cultural Constructions of Child Sexual Abuse' (1998) 92 *Northwestern University Law Review* 1415.
[217] Des Rosiers, Feldthusen and Hankivsky, 'Legal Compensation for Sexual Violence'.
[218] C. Smart, 'A History of Ambivalence'.
[219] Des Rosiers, Feldthusen and Hankivsky, 'Legal Compensation for Sexual Violence'.
[220] C. Macmartin, 'Judicial Constructions of the Seriousness of Child Sexual Abuse' (2004) 36 *Canadian Journal of Behavioural Science* 66, following on the work of K. E. Renner, C. Alksnis and L. Park, 'The standard of social justice as a research process' (1997) *Canadian Psychology* 38.

behaviour and the reasonableness of their delay in approaching the courts and thereby diminish focus on the defendant's wrong (see Chapter 5).

## 4. A comparative dimension

Given the paucity of authority in England and Wales on many of the issues which are pertinent to abuse claims, this book indulges in some comparative discussion, examining the experience of the jurisdictions of Canada, Australia, New Zealand on selected issues. Whilst it is not intended that this book will provide a systematic account of how each issue has been dealt with in Canada, Australia and New Zealand, it is hoped that the comparative flavour of the discussion will facilitate critical reflection on the current rules in England and Wales and will throw light on the options available for the development of tort claims in this jurisdiction. The value of this comparative dimension may also be of value to readers from other jurisdictions seeking information on how English law has dealt with this emergent area of law. As far as decisions in England and Wales are concerned, the impact of the Human Rights Act 1998 has been considerable, and it is likely that this will lessen the persuasive weight of English judgments for Commonwealth jurisdictions which are not bound by ECHR requirements.

Private law in both Australia and Canada, although possessing distinct features which are not readily transplantable to other jurisdictions,[221] are both based on the English common law system. Both jurisdictions are traditionally more liberal than the English common law in providing remedies in tort and have a much more progressive approach to the recovery of damages for psychological injury. The Canadian legal system, in particular, has been the pioneer in developing solutions to the difficulties faced by the abuse victim seeking civil damages. The result is a body of law which clearly recognises the uniqueness of the problems faced by the abuse victim as claimant and which fashions remedies to accommodate these idiosyncracies. The rules regulating limitation of actions, vicarious liability and breach of fiduciary duty in cases of abuse have been given far more consideration in Canada than in the courts of England and Wales, where

---

[221] E.g. the Canadian Charter of Rights and Freedoms was embedded in the Canadian Constitution in 1982, meaning that the courts can declare legislation to be invalid as incompatible with the Charter. Australia has recently seen wide-ranging reform of its torts regime following the *Review of the Law of Negligence Report* (2002) ('Ipp Review') designed to address the issue of increasing premiums for, and reduced availability of, public liability insurance.

the stranglehold of inflexible limitation rules has stymied the development of abuse jurisprudence.

Where appropriate, case law from New Zealand is also referred to for its persuasive value and progressive approach to claims for abuse, although it must be noted that its direct applicability is limited due to the influence of the Accident Compensation Scheme, which ousts many of the common law remedies for personal injury. Where the claimant suffers 'personal injury by accident' this statutory no-fault regime provides compensation to the person injured and a civil action for the same injury is generally barred. Despite the fact that sexual abuse is not normally regarded as fitting the definition of an 'accident', the scheme was extended to cover mental trauma caused by sexual offences,[222] whereas mental trauma which is not associated with a physical injury would usually fall outside the scheme. Amongst others, sexual abuse claims have been associated with an upsurge of claims made to the scheme and the source of fraudulent claims giving rise to calls for tighter controls.[223] The common law bar on damages for claims covered by the scheme used not to apply to abuse which occurred prior to 1975 (the beginning of the accident compensation scheme). Now, the Injury Prevention, Rehabilitation, and Compensation Act 2001 provides that the date the injury occurred is deemed to be the date upon which the claimant first received treatment for their mental injury.[224] The result of this provision is that, since 2001, the majority of sexual abuse litigation is dealt with under the scheme, thereby limiting the value of this jurisdiction as a source of influence on the common law.

Reference is also made in this book on occasion to cases from Scotland and the US (particularly in the context of recovered memories and claims brought by those wrongly accused of abuse which have been rife in the US), although with less frequency.

## Conclusion

In this book's survey of the intricacies and obstacles which the parties and legal representatives face in abuse claims, it is claims pertaining to sexual abuse which will, for the most part, monopolise the discussion.

---

[222] S. 40 of the Accident Insurance Act 1998 (now repealed).
[223] J. Miller, 'Compensation for Mental Trauma Injuries in New Zealand' (1998) Australasian Journal of Disaster and Trauma Studies.
[224] S. 36(1).

This is owing to the weight of research which confirms the psychological ramifications of this form of abuse and the fact that it is more likely to be articulated in a language which is compatible with traditional tort claims. Having said that, there are a number of features of society's awakening to sexual abuse which present real difficulties for abuse claims. The move to a multidisciplinary approach to protecting children blurs the lines of accountability, making it difficult to identify defendants in civil litigation, at least where the claim is one of 'iatrogenic neglect' by a non-perpetrator defendant. The increased complexity of regulation of child care arrangements triggered by the *Lost in Care* report has only added to this fragmentation of responsibility and, whilst it may superficially appear that the range of potential defendants in iatrogenic neglect cases has increased, it may be far more difficult to identify a single body or agency as responsible for failures in an individual case. In addition to the difficulties posed by the layered regulatory framework of child protection, there are a number of factors which potentially set the scene for abuse claims to be met with judicial scepticism. The Cleveland and Orkney scandals and the hyperbole which characterised media coverage of these stories immediately preceded the House of Lords' first experience of an abuse claim (*Stubbings v. Webb*), a fact which may have had a negative bearing on abuse claims heard at that time. Furthermore, for these claims to succeed the courts must be prepared to invest significant faith in the profession of psychiatry and its evidence regarding the damage inflicted by abuse. The legal issues which face an abuse claimant and the tenor of the courts' judgments in these cases are the subjects of Chapter 2.

# 2

# Classifying Abuse as a Civil Wrong

The hidden horrors of physical violence, sexual abuse and emotional damage to children in schools and in care are now beginning to surface in personal injury claims brought by victims years after the event . . . The harm suffered can have catastrophic consequences and if a life has been blighted by that degrading conduct a remedy in damages, ought, in justice, to be available if the balance of fairness between the parties can accommodate it.[1]

## Introduction

This chapter explores civil litigation by adult claimants alleging that they were abused during their childhood years and examines the different forms of action which might be used to launch such proceedings. The particular difficulties in establishing each cause of action will be addressed and, where the courts of England and Wales have yet to hammer out these issues, case law from other jurisdictions is referred to as a means of providing tentative suggestions as to how English law might develop. Generic issues of proof of damage, causation, remoteness and limitation are dealt with in later chapters.

## The current state of civil litigation relating to abuse

The number of civil claims for the harm caused by child abuse appears to be rising steadily and promises to continue to do so. This is not necessarily part of any compensation culture (which in any case has been rejected as fictional[2]) but is the result of the fact that the prevalence of child abuse and the association between sexual abuse and long-lasting

---

[1] *Per* Ward LJ, in *McDonnell v. Congregation of Christian Brothers Trustees* [2001] EWCA Civ 2095; [2002] C P Rep 31.
[2] *Compensation Culture* (House of Commons Constitutional Affairs Committee 3rd report session 2005–06) HC 754, concluding that the UK is not moving towards a compensation culture.

psychological trauma are now widely accepted. The courts are therefore far more receptive to the essence of abuse claims, even if discharging the burden of proof remains extremely onerous. The threat of abuse claims has reached such proportions in some sectors that institutions have used bankruptcy as a shield against further civil claims.[3] There have also been suggestions that the area is proving so lucrative to the legal profession that the investigation of abuse allegations is being hampered by false accusations prompted by solicitors advertising their services in connection with group civil litigation.[4]

Concerns surrounding the escalation of litigiousness in this area are bound to be translated by the courts into either explicit or implicit limitations on recovery in the name of public policy. Fears that abuse claims are spiralling out of control are likely to spur the courts on to divert claimants away from the civil justice system, to protect institutional defendants from liability for wrongs which they could not realistically prevent, to combat the spectre of defensive practice and to prevent distortion of the criminal justice system, for example, by instructing claimants to seek damages through the criminal injuries compensation scheme instead. It should be noted, however, that the amount of compensation awarded via the criminal injuries compensation route tends to be much lower than in a successful civil claim. In 2001 a total of 48 institutional abuse claims were resolved by the Criminal Injuries Compensation Authority, resulting in an average payment of £6,400. Civil claims, when successful, can result in damages of over £600,000.[5] The difference in award levels is thought to explain why less than 20% of complainants in criminal cases seek criminal injuries compensation.[6] Aside from the lower levels of compensation, and perhaps

---

[3] See S. Goldberg, 'Boston Archdiocese Threatens Bankruptcy' *Guardian*, 3 December (2002) and *Re Christian Brothers of Ireland in Canada* [2004] 128 ACWS (3d) 116 (winding up by reason of insolvency due to civil claims relating to abuse). In England and Wales the Catholic Office for the Protection of Children and Vulnerable Adults recorded in its annual report for 2004 that it had referred 100 complaints of abuse in a church setting to statutory authorities as compared with 62 in 2003: *Annual Report 2004* (Catholic Office for the Protection of Children and Vulnerable Adults, 2005) available at www.copca.org.uk.

[4] *The Conduct of Investigations into Past Cases of Abuse in Children's Homes – Fourth Report of the Home Affairs Committee* (2002), Select Committee on Home Affairs (2001–2), HC 836.

[5] An award of £635,000 was made by the High Court against the Archbishop of Birmingham and trustees of the Birmingham Archdiocese of the Roman Catholic Church, to A, who suffered schizophrenia and PTSD after being abused by a priest for 11 years: 'Record Damages for Sex Abuse by Catholic Priest', *The Times*, 1 July 2005.

[6] *The Conduct of Investigations into Past Cases of Abuse in Children's Homes*.

more important to the claimant, the criminal injuries compensation scheme offers nothing by way of deterring those responsible for the abuse.

## Forms of civil action by the abused

### The perpetrator as defendant

Where a claimant is contemplating litigation for its therapeutic capacity it could readily be assumed that a cause of action against the alleged perpetrator (as opposed to non-perpetrator defendants such as the abuser's employer) would be preferred. Yet litigation against non-perpetrator defendants is probably more common, a fact which is due to the greater likelihood that insurance will be in place, the possibility that a non-perpetrator defendant may have survived the death of the perpetrator and, last but not least, the fact that limitation rules are far more likely to bar an action against the perpetrator for intentional wrongs than actions against non-perpetrator defendants for a lack of care.

An action against the perpetrator of abuse may take the form of an action in trespass to the person, intentional interference with the person or (possibly) an action for breach of fiduciary duty. Civil claims in this area now have the added ammunition of rulings from the European Court of Human Rights that child abuse can constitute 'inhuman and degrading treatment' under Article 3 of the ECHR.[7]

### *Defining the cause of action*

The particular cause of action by which the abuse is litigated is crucial in determining how limitation provisions are applied,[8] the defences available and the applicability of insurance indemnities, and can therefore determine the success or otherwise of the claim.

### *1. Trespass to the person (assault/battery)*

Traditionally, sexual abuse and physical abuse have been actioned as a battery,[9] a form of action which requires an intentional touching without lawful authority.[10] For the purposes of civil battery, a broad

---

[7] *Z v. UK* [2001] 2 FLR 612; *E v. UK* (2003) 36 EHHR 31; *DP v. UK* [2003] 1 FLR 50.
[8] Although this is less of an issue under Australian law, as to which see later.
[9] *W v. Meah* [1986] 1 All ER 935; *Stubbings v. Webb* [1993] AC 498 (HL).
[10] *Collins v. Wilcock* [1984] 1 WLR 1172.

meaning of 'intentional' is applied, requiring only that the conduct which constituted the tort (i.e. in battery the touching) was intended as opposed to the harm.[11] Although in *C v. D and another*[12] counsel appeared to concede that removing clothing from a claimant did not constitute the touching required for a battery, it is submitted that if there was such a concession it was made in error. Battery does not require skin-to-skin contact.[13] Furthermore, the purpose of the law of trespass is to protect citizens from violations of bodily integrity and it would be incongruous to adopt a construction of civil battery which prohibits an unwanted kiss but permits unwanted undressing.

Whilst consent usually operates as lawful authority in battery claims, it is unlikely that consent could ever operate as a defence in a case of childhood physical or sexual abuse, given the minority of the victim and the frequent association of sexual abuse with manipulation and deception on the part of the adult. There is even the possibility that such a defence would be ruled out on the grounds of public policy.[14] As to the consent of an adult victim, no action in battery lies where the claimant consented,[15] unless that consent was procured by fraud, misrepresentation or duress.[16] Where that consent is procured by means of deception as to the nature of the sexual contact, it is possible that consent is negated and a battery action will lie. This is most likely to occur in a medical context, for example, where a doctor seeks to persuade his patient that sexual contact was in fact therapeutic.[17]

Neeb and Harper forcefully argue that the complexities of sexual abuse cannot be adequately defined in a charge of assault or battery,[18] citing as support the seminal Canadian case of *M(K) v. M(H)*, where La Forest J remarked that '[a]ssault and battery could only serve as a crude legal description' of incest or abuse.[19] Certainly in most other instances of battery, the harm, if any, manifests itself immediately after the unauthorised touching. Yet, in cases of sexual abuse, the lasting damage may not manifest itself until years later. Nonetheless, however 'crude'

---

[11] *Wilson v. Pringle* [1987] QB 237.   [12] [2006] EWHC 166; 2006 WL 503014.
[13] *Pursell v. Horn* (1838) 8 AD & E 602.
[14] Following the approach of the House of Lords in *R v. Brown* [1994] 1 AC 212.
[15] *D(P) v. Allen* (2004) 132 ACWS (3d) 1098.
[16] *Chatterton v. Gerson* [1981] QB 432.
[17] See *R v. Flattery* (1877) 2 QBD 410; *R v. Williams* [1923] 1 KB 340 and, more recently, *R v. Tabassum* [2000] Lloyd's Rep Med 404.
[18] J. W. W. Neeb and S. J. Harper, *Civil Action for Sexual Abuse* (Canada, Butterworths, 1994) at 104.
[19] *M(K) v. M(H)* [1992] 3 SCR 6.

battery is as a descriptor of sexual abuse, the essence of the battery action presents distinct advantages to the abuse victim in that no damage is required to be proven (thus, where damages are sought for the psychological sequelae of abuse, no recognised psychiatric disorder needs to be demonstrated) and the intentional nature of the act means that the harm for which compensation is sought need not be foreseeable.

The difficulties posed by the battery action relate not as much to the fundamental requirements of the action, but to the statutory limitation periods imposed on these claims. These difficulties stem from the unsatisfactory resolution in *Letang v. Cooper* of the issue of whether an intentional act, such as sexual assault or battery, can be regarded as a 'breach of duty'.[20] The case concerned a dispute regarding the application of limitation provisions, the crucial distinction being between actions for personal injury caused by a 'breach of duty' (which is subject to a flexible three-year limitation period) and other actions (the latter being subject to an inflexible six-year limitation period).[21] Lord Denning, dissenting from the majority, stated that intentional acts should be actioned as trespasses and that such were not embraced by the phrase 'breach of duty' in the statute. However, if he was wrong on this, he postulated that the law of torts rested on the general assumption of a duty not to unlawfully injure fellow citizens.[22] The majority in *Letang* preferred to say that a negligent trespass was actionable but that damage would have to be proved.

According to the majority reasoning in *Letang* and the alternative reasoning of Lord Denning, sexual assault could feasibly be categorised as a 'breach of duty' – the duty to not to unlawfully injure our fellow citizens – therefore, it appeared that abuse did not necessarily need to be characterised as an intentional act of battery.[23] Later case law has, however, approved Lord Denning's dissent in *Letang v. Cooper* and the

---

[20] [1965] 1 QB 232.
[21] Sections 2 and 11 of the Limitation Act 1980 discussed later.
[22] [1965] 1 QB 232 at 241.
[23] This liberal interpretation of 'breach of duty' is not without later support. In *Long v. Hepworth* [1968] 1 WLR 1299 (a High Court decision), Cooke J accepted the broader definition of breach of duty as embracing intentional acts of trespass. (He reached this decision relying on *Letang* and the earlier case of *Billings v. Read* [1944] 2 All ER 415. This case was not referred to in the *Stubbings* judgment.) He also stated, however, that he would have reached the same decision without the earlier authority of *Letang*, because the draftsman was concerned to avoid the mischief of delay in litigation. The distinction between unintentional and intentional injuries had no relevance for the purposes of such a policy objective (at 246).

proposition that intentional/unintentional acts are mutually exclusive for the purposes of civil suits and that intentional acts must be actioned under trespass has become firmly entrenched in English law.[24] Further, when the issue of categorisation of sexual abuse arose for consideration in the House of Lords case of *Stubbings v. Webb*[25] (discussed in more detail in Chapter 5), Lord Griffiths expressly rejected the liberal construction of 'breach of duty', saying: 'If I invite a lady to my house, one would naturally think of a duty to take care that the house is safe, but would one really be thinking of a duty not to rape her?'[26] This is tantamount to saying that the very idea of sexual assault is so extreme and abhorrent that it is taken for granted that it should not occur and it would be far from the minds of decent people – therefore, to articulate the law in terms of a duty not to rape another is unnecessary. The flaws in this argument are not difficult to spot. The fact that a wrong is abhorrent does not mean that it cannot be the subject of a duty not to do it. What use would a law be if it imposed a duty to be nice to one's neighbour but not a duty to abstain from inflicting serious injury? Furthermore, Lord Griffiths' denial that sexual assault could constitute a breach of duty was made notwithstanding earlier English authority which clearly recognises the potential for a trespass action and an action on the case arising out of the same facts, a fact which had prompted criticism of Lord Denning's dissenting judgment in *Letang* as 'judicial legislation'.[27] Notably, the rigid distinction between intentional and unintentional wrongs maintained by the English courts is not endorsed elsewhere. In Australia it is clear that intentional acts can be actioned as trespass or negligence,[28] and there is specific authority to suggest that sexual assault can be actioned as negligence.[29] In Canada the mutually

---

[24] *Wilson v. Pringle* [1987] QB 237. [25] [1993] AC 498 (HL).
[26] At 508. Cf. Lord Hoffmann in *Wainwright v. Home Office* [2003] UKHL 53; [2002] 3 WLR 405 at [41], where he commented that in cases of psychiatric injury there was no point in arguing about whether the injury is intentional if negligence will do just as well, and the House of Lords decision in *Reeves v. Commissioner of Police for the Metropolis* [1999] 3 WLR 363, where, in the context of the defence of contributory negligence, 'negligence' included deliberate and intentional self-harm. See also *Horne, Cherie Jayne v. Wilson, Graeme James Gregory (No. 2)* [1998] TASCC 44, where sexual assault was treated as a breach of the defendant's duty not to expose the claimant to the risk of harm (conceded by defence counsel).
[27] Per Bray CJ in *Venning v. Chin* (1974) 10 SASR 299, the earlier English authority being *Leame v. Bray* (1803) 3 East 593 (102 ER 724).
[28] *Williams v. Milotin* (1957) 97 CLR 465, followed in *Venning v. Chin* (1974) 10 SASR 299.
[29] *Lepore v. New South Wales* (2001) NSWLR 420 (McHugh J at 455).

exclusive approach also appears to have been rejected[30] and in New Zealand the courts have left open the issue of whether a claim can be brought in negligence when the allegations were of intentional acts constituting battery.[31]

The consequence of *Stubbings v. Webb* is that, generally, sexual abuse is to be actioned against the perpetrator as an intentional act; a battery.[32] In consequence, any psychiatric harm manifesting itself years after the abuse occurred goes only to quantification of damages and not completion of the tort, as an action in trespass, which requires no proof of damage, causes time to run from when the wrong is committed.[33] If abuse were to be regarded as actionable in negligence, or under the principle in *Wilkinson v. Downton*,[34] both of which require damage as an essential ingredient of liability, it could be argued that the tort was not complete until the manifestation of psychiatric harm, thus the claim would not crystallise and the limitation period would not start to run until that time. Thus, the claimant will usually only have six years from the occurrence of the abuse or reaching the age of majority in which to bring the claim, no matter how much later the damage manifested itself or was discovered. The implications of this ruling for abuse claimants can not have been missed by their Lordships. As indicated above, it is perhaps no coincidence that this case was heard not long after the Cleveland and Orkney scandals had raised serious questions regarding whether false allegations of abuse had become the latest pandemic.[35]

Aside from the difficulties which *Stubbings* creates for historical claims against the perpetrator of abuse, it also produces an unconscionable distinction between the perpetrator as defendant and the non-perpetrator as defendant who is accused of having failed to prevent the abuse. For example, when the non-offending parent is sued for their failure to procure the removal of their spouse from the family home, thereby 'permitting' the abuse to continue, the action will typically be in negligence not battery. Consequently, more liberal limitation provisions

---

[30] *Goshen v. Lavin* (1974) 46 DLR (3d) 137; *Teece v. Honeybourne* (1974) 54 DLR (3d) 549 and, in the context of abuse, *McDonald v. Mombourquette* (1996) 152 NSR (2d) 109 (CA) and, more recently, *B(M) v. British Colombia* [2001] 5 WWR 6 and *John Doe v. O'Dell* 2003 125 ACWSJ (3d) 928.

[31] *S v. Attorney General* [2003] 3 NZLR 450 (at [46] and [120]).

[32] Confirmed in *A v. Hoare* [2006] EWCA Civ 395; 2006 WL 901084.

[33] *Howell v. Young* (1826) 5 B&C 529.    [34] [1897] 2 QB 57.

[35] See Chapter 1 at pp. 27–31.

will apply, and hence the perpetrator will often prove to be a less accessible defendant than the non-perpetrator defendant.[36]

At the time of writing, it is forecast that the ruling in *Stubbings* as it affects limitation rules will be amended either by a House of Lords' decision reviewing the damaging effects of *Stubbings* or by Parliament implementing the Law Commission's recommendations of 2001.[37] Much more is said about the implications of *Stubbings v. Webb* for issues of limitation in Chapter 5.

## The human rights challenges

The ruling in *Stubbings v. Webb*[38] that abuse was to be actioned as a trespass with less favourable limitation provisions was challenged in the European Court of Human Rights as a violation of the claimant's right of access to a court under Article 6(1) of the ECHR and the right under Article 14 to equal treatment.[39] Both challenges were unsuccessful, the court taking the view that access to a court had not been impaired given that claimants had six years from the age of majority to bring a claim and that the alternative of prosecution, with the possibility of attaching a compensation order, was subject to no time limits. The right of access to a court was not an absolute right but gave rise to exceptions, including the pursuit of legitimate aims. Limitation periods advanced the legitimate aims of protecting defendants from stale claims, unreliable evidence and ensuring legal certainty and finality.[40] The Court's reasoning in respect of Article 6 neglects the fact that a prosecution for child abuse is particularly difficult, given that often the only witness to the abuse is the victim themselves. The chance of proving abuse 'beyond a reasonable doubt' in the absence of corroborating evidence is exceedingly slim and, as Mullis argues, compensation is by no means automatic even if prosecution is successful.[41] The Court noted, however, that limitation periods in Member States may need to be amended to incorporate special provisions for child abuse in light of developing awareness of the problems caused by child abuse.

---

[36] *Seymour v. Williams* [1995] PIQR 470, discussed later in Chapter 5.
[37] *Limitation of Actions*, Report No 270 (Law Commission, 2001).
[38] [1993] AC 498.
[39] *Stubbings and others v. UK* (1996) 23 EHRR 213. The three other claimants had repressed all memory of the abuse and also fell outside the six-year period.
[40] Judges Foighel and MacDonald dissenting.
[41] A. Mullis, 'The Abuse Continues? *Stubbings and Others v. UK* in the ECHR' (1997) 9 *Children and Family Law Quarterly* 291 at 297.

The crux of the claimant's alternative argument under Article 14 was that the application of a rigid time limit to claims brought against intentional harms was unreasonable and disproportionate when compared with actions against unintentional harms where discretion to extend the time limit exists. The court found that any difference in treatment between the victims of intentional and unintentional injuries was reasonable and objectively justified and did not violate the ECHR. Generally, victims of negligence suffered less obvious injuries and therefore more time should be afforded for the realisation that a wrong had been committed and compensation needed.[42] This conclusion fails to recognise the fact that in cases of sexual abuse, this usual order of events is precisely reversed.

The essence of the challenge in *Stubbings v. UK* was revived in *A v. Hoare*[43] with the assertion that the passage of time and the enactment of the Human Rights Act 1998 breathed new life into Article 6 arguments. The claimants argued that s. 3 of the 1998 Act required the courts to read legislation in a way that was compatible with Convention rights and taking this together with the suggestion in *Stubbings v. UK* that developing awareness may merit a review of the issue of limitation meant that continuing to follow *Stubbings v. Webb* constituted a violation of Article 6. This argument was rejected on the grounds that the Human Rights Act only came into force in October 2000 and was not intended to have retrospective effect. The defendant's reliance on limitation arguments involved the exercise of a right which accrued as soon as time expired six years after the abuse occurred and in the present appeals that was long before the year 2000. Thus s. 3 was of no assistance, as it could not be used to extinguish rights which were extant before the Act came into force.

### Other post-*Stubbings* developments

Although *Stubbings* was a House of Lords judgment which is yet to be overruled, it has not been the final word on the form of action to be used by an abuse claimant. In *KR and others v. Bryn Alyn Community (Holdings) Ltd (In Liquidation), Royal & Sun Alliance plc* (the *Bryn Alyn* litigation),[44] there was an *obiter* suggestion that *Stubbings* did not decide that deliberate assault could not ever be regarded as a breach of

---

[42] A challenge under s. 15 of the Canadian Charter of Rights and Freedoms (equal treatment) was similarly regarded as doomed to failure in *Gray v. Reeves* [1992] 89 DLR (4th) 315 at 354.
[43] [2006] EWCA Civ 395; [2006] 1 WLR 2320.
[44] [2003] EWCA Civ 85; [2003] 1 FCR 385.

duty. The question in any given case was whether the particular facts gave rise to an action for 'breach of duty' for the purposes of limitation provisions, *whether or not those facts might also be regarded as another action such as trespass to the person.* This conclusion was supported with authorities which recognised the overlap of various causes of action with the tort of negligence.[45] This *obiter* statement appeared to leave open the possibility that future cases could deal with deliberate assault as a 'breach of duty'. Further, in *McDonnell v. Congregation of Christian Brothers Trustees*,[46] Lord Bingham regarded the suggestion that sexual abuse might be actioned against the perpetrator as a breach of duty, thereby triggering the flexible three-year limitation period as 'arguable'.[47] However, in *A v. Hoare* the Court of Appeal rejected suggestions that *Stubbings* could be distinguished where the acts of abuse could be described concurrently as breach of a non-delegable duty.

In 2001 the Law Commission recommended a general overhaul of limitation, one of the consequences of which would be to undo the effect of *Stubbings* without changing the rule that a claim against the perpetrator should be in trespass. (See Chapter 5 for further detail on the Law Commission's report.)

## 2. An action under the principle of Wilkinson v. Downton

The case of *Wilkinson v. Downton*, albeit a humble English High Court decision, provided the foundations of an independent cause of action in torts for wrongfully caused physical or psychiatric harm which also seems well suited to many abuse claims.[48] The rule has been applied to different effect in different jurisdictions, yet in its country of origin a number of unresolved questions persist so that the precise scope of the rule remains elusive. The defendant in *Wilkinson* falsely told the claimant that her husband, who had been to the races, had broken both his legs and had requested that his wife should come to collect him. The claimant, believing the story to be true, incurred the unnecessary expense of rail fares in her effort to collect her husband and suffered a

---

[45] An example not cited in the *Bryn Alyn* case is to be found in *Spring v. Guardian Assurance* [1994] 3 All ER 129 (HL), which recognised the possibility of contemporaneous actions in defamation and negligence on the same facts.
[46] [2003] UKHL 63; [2003] 3 WLR 1627.   [47] At [26].
[48] Although see the words of Clarke MR in *A v. Hoare* [2006] EWCA Civ 395; [2006] 1 WLR 2320 at [136] preferring that abuse claims proceed without recourse to 'this obscure tort, whose jurisprudential basis remains unclear'.

violent shock to her nervous system, for which she sued the defendant in damages. Wright J rejected the claimant's argument based on liability for damage caused by fraud, apparently because it was not clear that the defendant intended the statement to be acted upon. Admitting that the present case was without precedent, he found the defendant liable on the alternative ground that liability existed for wilful acts calculated to cause physical harm to the claimant which in fact caused physical harm where there was no justification for the act. Thus it seems that there does not need to be proof of a 'wrong' but rather conduct without justification.[49] The judge also rejected the defendant's argument that the damage was too remote, as cases which suggested mental harm might be too remote[50] were concerned with liability in negligence and not wilful wrongs. There seems to be no reason why emotional or sexual abuse could not be actioned under the principle in *Wilkinson v. Downton*,[51] particularly given the fact that the damages sought are often focused upon the psychiatric scars of abuse.

## 'Calculated to cause harm'

Within the requirement of conduct 'calculated to cause harm' there are at least two further issues. First, how is the defendant's calculation of causing harm to be assessed – is intention required or will recklessness suffice? Secondly, where the harm complained of is psychiatric harm, does the action require that the defendant calculated to cause a recognised mental illness or will the calculation of distress or upset be enough to establish liability?

## Will recklessness suffice?

Trindade has argued that the courts have indulged in the use of a fiction to impute to the defendant an intention to cause physical or psychiatric harm, giving as an example the fact that in *Wilkinson* itself, Wright J was prepared to infer such an intention, a fact which seems inconsistent with the judge's reference to the statement as a practical joke.[52] The same fiction-based reasoning appears in the Canadian case of

---

[49] See C. Witting, 'Tort Liability for Intended Mental Distress' (1998) 21(1) *University of New South Wales Law Journal* 55 for further discussion of the extent to which this is a requirement of liability.
[50] *Victorian Rlys v. Coultas* (1816) 1 Stark 493.   [51] [1897] 2 QB 57.
[52] F. A. Trindade, 'Intentional Infliction of Purely Mental Distress.' (1986) 6(2) *Oxford Journal of Legal Studies* 219 at 221.

*Bielitski v. Obadiak*.[53] The claimant alleged that she had suffered shock after hearing a rumour initiated by the defendant that her son had hanged himself from a telegraph pole. The defendant was found liable on the basis of the rule in *Wilkinson v. Downton*, notwithstanding that the statement was not made directly to the claimant.[54] As to whether the statement was 'calculated to cause harm', the court showed considerable favouritism to the claimant by assuming that the harm was inflicted deliberately – for what other reason would the defendant have said such a thing but to cause harm (given that any reasonable man would know that the claimant would be caused physical pain and mental anguish on hearing the rumour)? The imputation of intention under the rule in *Wilkinson* is little different from the extended meaning of intention in criminal law which encompasses both anticipated and desired consequences and those which are virtually certain to follow from the defendant's acts.[55]

A more thorough discussion of this issue was conducted in *Wainwright v. Home Office*,[56] following allegations that prison officers had strip-searched visitors to the prison in breach of prison rules, and in a manner which caused them humiliation and distress. The second claimant, who had cerebral palsy, allegedly suffered PTSD following the incident. The Court of Appeal accepted that physical or recognised psychiatric harm had to be proved,[57] but considered that even the second claimant's case must fail as there was no evidence of intention or recklessness on the part of the prison officers as to the infliction of such harm.[58] The House of Lords refused to disturb this ruling, saying that the necessary intention had not been established.

There would be distinct advantages in pursuing an abuse claim under the mantle of *Wilkinson v. Downton*. For example, time does not start to run for limitation purposes until the tort is completed by damage. This may therefore provide the abuse claimant with a means of extending the limitation period for a few years. Difficult evidentiary questions would, however, be raised as to how long it takes for the mental illness to crystallise following the abuse. Further, it is unclear whether a claim

---

[53] (1922) 65 DLR 627.
[54] The chain of communication involved at least five persons (other than the claimant).
[55] *R v. Nedrick* [1986] 1 WLR 1025; *R v. Moloney* [1985] AC 905.
[56] [2003] UKHL 53; [2002] 3 WLR 405.  [57] [2003] UKHL; [2002] 3 WLR 405 at [41].
[58] Buxton LJ noted that a strong case could have been made under the Protection from Harassment Act 1997, although establishing a 'course of conduct' may have been difficult.

under *Wilkinson v. Downton* might be regarded as an action for 'breach of duty' and therefore provide access to the flexible three-year limitation period referred to above.[59]

The potential advantages of framing an action as an intentional interference with the person have yet to be utilised. Given the observations made above regarding the fiction employed to impute to the defendant an intention to cause harm, it seems likely that the courts would be convinced of such an intention in the case of serious physical, emotional or sexual abuse. As subjective recklessness regarding the infliction of psychiatric harm suffices for conduct 'calculated to cause harm', abuse from the 1970s onwards would surely demonstrate such recklessness with little difficulty; indeed, acts of repeated sexual abuse would probably be regarded as an instance of true intention to cause harm. Whilst the Canadian courts are reluctant to allow this form of action to be used between family members,[60] it seems that English courts would be unlikely to express any such reservation.[61] Despite the lack of apparent obstacles, there is as yet no English authority endorsing the use of the intentional interference action against an abuser,[62] although the case of *Wainwright v. Home Office* discussed above could be used as authority for its use in connection with unwanted touching.

## The type of harm[63]

As to the type of harm to be suffered for the rule to be applicable, it should be remembered that in *Wilkinson v. Downton* itself, Wright J referred to 'physical injury'. The original judgment therefore provides no direct guidance on whether in cases of mental harm, a recognised psychiatric disorder is required or whether mental distress falling short of such illness will suffice. The House of Lords has, however, since confirmed that in cases of imputed intention, such as *Wilkinson v. Downton*, the need for a recognised psychiatric disorder or other

---

[59] W. V. H. Rogers, 'Tort Law and Child Abuse: An Interim View from England.' (1994) 3 *Tort Law Journal* 17 seems to suggest that the six-year limit would apply to these actions also.

[60] *Louie v. Lastman* (2001) 199 DLR (4th) 741, following Wilson J (dissenting) in *Frame v. Smith* (1987) 42 DLR (4th) 81.

[61] No objection was raised in *Stubbings v. Webb* [1993] AC 498 (HL) to the fact that the claimant was suing her stepfather for sexual assault.

[62] Although the argument was raised in *W v. Essex CC* [1998] PIQR 346, its application to the facts was dismissed without reasons by the Court of Appeal.

[63] See also Chapter 4 on this.

physical harm stands.[64] The seeds of a possible exception to this rule were sown by an *obiter* statement from Lord Hoffmann in *Hunter v. Canary Wharf*, where he stated:

> I see no reason why a tort of intention should be subject to the rule which excludes compensation for mere distress, inconvenience or discomfort in actions based on negligence. The policy considerations are quite different.[65]

If the usual rules relating to remoteness and limitation are adjusted when the harm is intentionally caused in the strict sense (as opposed to imputed intention), it is conceivable that the threshold of damage might be altered in the claimant's favour also. In *Wainwright v. Home Office*,[66] Lord Hoffmann was faced with what he had said in *Hunter* and elaborated by saying that distress may be actionable where the 'defendant acted in a way which he knew was unjustifiable and intended to cause harm or at least acted without caring whether he caused harm or not'. Nevertheless, he was mindful that Parliament had chosen to restrict the tort of harassment to a 'course of conduct', and therefore the common law was bound to be reluctant to encroach on Parliament's territory by fashioning rules which would enable distress damages to be recoverable in incidents of single intentional acts.

As Lord Hoffmann reserved his opinion on whether in cases of true intention damages for distress were payable, it remains open whether in an extreme case of intentionally caused harm such as sexual abuse, damages for distress might be available.[67] In any case, the claimant in such an action would also have open to them the argument that psychiatric harm was a result of an invasion of physical integrity comparable to physical injury, and therefore consequential damages for distress are payable as part of the pain and suffering award.[68]

---

[64] *Wainwright v. Home Office* [2003] UKHL 53; [2003] 3 WLR 1137. Confirmed in *C v. D and another* [2006] EWHC 166; 2006 WL 503014.

[65] [1997] AC 655 at 706. There are certainly statements in many cases to the effect that the usual bounds of liability have no application where harm was intended: see the statements in *Battista v. Cooper* (1976) 14 SASR 225 and *M(K) v. M(H)* [1992] 3 SCR 6.

[66] [2003] UKHL 53; [2002] 3 WLR 405.

[67] In *C v. D* [2006] EWHC 166 at [94], Field J appears to assume that liability under *Wilkinson v. Downton* can never yield damages for distress falling short of a recognised disorder, although leaving open the possibility that Lord Hoffmann intended to create a new category of liability for mere distress.

[68] *Parkinson v. St James and Seacroft University Hospital NHS Trust* [2002] QB 266, per Hale LJ likening an invasion of physical integrity to a physical injury.

## 3. Breach of fiduciary duty

The breach of fiduciary duty action hails not from tort but from equity. In some jurisdictions (although probably not England and Wales) this action can be used either against a perpetrator or against the defendant who has knowledge of the abuse but fails to act to protect the child.

A breach of fiduciary action, if available, would likely outclass actions in battery or intentional interference with the person in terms of the benefits offered to claimants. There are authorities which suggest that the measure of damages can be more generous to the claimant, a more pro-claimant view may be taken of the appropriate limitation period, the rules of causation are less strictly applied than in common law actions and the defence of contributory negligence is less likely to apply. To determine the application of the breach of fiduciary duty action to abuse litigation in English law, it is necessary to identify which relationships are fiduciary in nature. Attempts to define the essential element of fiduciary relationships include references to 'inequality' and 'dependence',[69] emphasis on the 'control of opportunism',[70] and a minimum requirement of 'dependency or vulnerability'.[71] In *Norberg v. Weinrib*, the necessary conditions were regarded as being an imbalance of power, potential for interference with a legal interest or vital and substantial practical interest and an undertaking to exclusively look after the interests of the beneficiary of the relationship.[72] These characteristics of inequality, dependence and undertakings would seem particularly suited to the 'usual suspects' in cases of sexual abuse: the parent, the child minder, the priest, the teacher and the doctor. Indeed, Flannigan refers to the doctor/patient and parent/child types of fiduciary relationship as based on 'deferential trust' and as denoting an even greater degree of vulnerability than the traditional trustee/beneficiary relationship.[73]

---

[69] 'The hallmark of the fiduciary relation is that the relative legal positions are such that one party is *at the mercy* of the other's discretion'. E. Weinrib, 'The Fiduciary Obligation' (1975) 25 *University of Toronto Law Journal* 1 at 7 (emphasis added).
[70] R. Flannigan, 'Fiduciary Regulation of Sexual Exploitation' (2000) 79 *Canada Bar Review* 301 at 304.
[71] *LAC Minerals Ltd v. International Corona Resources Ltd* [1989] 2 SCR 574.
[72] *Norberg v. Weinrib* (1992) 92 DLR (4th) 449, *per* Sopinka J at 501.
[73] R. Flannigan, 'The Fiduciary Obligation' (1989) 9 *Oxford Journal of Legal Studies* 285. Not all sexual contact with a fiduciary gives rise to a breach of duty – it is rather that the fiduciary must somehow have exploited their access to fiduciary assets, for example, the sexual capacity of the fiduciary (Flannigan, 'Fiduciary Regulation of Sexual Exploitation' at 308).

Nowhere is the vulnerability and dependence associated with fiduciary relationships more pronounced than in the parent/child relationship.[74] Yet, whilst English law recognises that parents have a legal duty to act in their children's best interests,[75] recognition of fiduciary obligations is restricted to the child's economic interests and the operation of undue influence on the child. This is because fiduciary obligations in English law have generally only been recognised in the context of the protection of economic interests, rather than physical integrity. Consequently, the House of Lords' judgment in *Sidaway v. Governors of Bethlem Royal Hospital*[76] rejected the proposition that the doctor/patient relationship should be defined as a fiduciary one,[77] despite its currency in other jurisdictions.[78] Lord Scarman regarded the doctor/patient relationship as being 'a very special one – the patient putting his health and his life in the doctor's hands',[79] but not a fiduciary one. His reasoning was that fiduciary duties existed to provide redress where a right recognised in law would otherwise have no protection. In the context of doctor/patient communications, the right was adequately protected by the tort of negligence.[80] That is not to say that the answer would have been the

---

[74] New Zealand similarly recognises fiduciary obligations as arising out of the parent: child relationship: *Broeke v. White* (unreported, 12 March 1992), Williams J (Whangerei HC) cited in Neeb and Harper, *Civil Action for Sexual Abuse*, at 224. See also *B (KL) v. British Colombia* [2001] 197 DLR (4th) 431, where it appears to be accepted that the relationship between foster parent and child might be fiduciary. The relationship between the Crown, who had negligently supervised foster homes, and the children was not a fiduciary one as there was no relevant conflict of duty and self-interest.

[75] *Re C (HIV)* [1999] 2 FLR 1004; *Re R (A Minor) (Blood Transfusion)* [1993] 2 FLR 757.

[76] [1985] AC 871.

[77] Most other Commonwealth jurisdictions do portray doctor–patient relations as fiduciary: e.g. *Taylor v. McGillivray* 110 DLR (4th) 64, which illustrates that a consenting sexual relationship between physician and patient gives rise to an actionable breach of fiduciary duty in Canadian law. The refusal to recognise such in English law seems to have a lot to do with the common law's determination that patients are not entitled to all available information regarding their medical treatment, rather that such a right is subject to therapeutic privilege – a concept which would be at odds with the fiduciary relationship.

[78] E.g. *Taylor v. McGillivray* (1993) 110 DLR (4th) 64 (Canada) and *Norberg v. Weinrib* (1992) 92 DLR (4th) 449 at 499, where McLachlin J stated that fiduciary obligations were capable of protecting 'not only narrow legal and economic interests, but can also service to defend fundamental human and personal interests'. See also *Breen v. Williams* (1996) 138 ALR 259, which suggests that the doctor owes fiduciary obligations to the patient, although not giving rise to a right of equitable compensation for personal injury.

[79] [1985] AC 871 at 884.

[80] There are, however, authorities that are consistent with the doctor–patient relationship as fiduciary: *Rhodes v. Bate* (1866) 1 Ch App 252; *Mitchell v. Homfray* (1881) 8 QBD 587 (CA). See also P. Bartlett, 'Doctors as Fiduciaries: Equitable Regulation of the Doctor–Patient Relationship' (1997) 5 *Medical Law Review* 193 at 196.

same had the case for redress been presented as one of serious physical or sexual abuse, for here it can be argued that protection is inadequate due to the non-extendable limitation period applied to battery actions.[81] Moreover, surely the protection of physical integrity has lexical priority over economic interests;[82] therefore, there ought to be no objection in principle to extending the protective powers of the fiduciary duty to physical integrity.

Canada is by far the leading light in terms of extending fiduciary obligations to the protection of physical integrity. Recognised relationships trigger a rebuttable presumption that they give rise to fiduciary obligations.[83] Thus, in *M(K) v. M(H)*[84] the Canadian Supreme Court confirmed that an action for psychiatric damage triggered by sexual abuse arose not only in assault and battery, but also for breach of fiduciary obligation. Given that the child was at the mercy of the parent and that the 'non-economic interests, of an incest victim were particularly susceptible to protection from the law of equity, parent-child abuse could be regarded as a breach of fiduciary obligations.[85]

Canadian law not only embraces the preservation of physical integrity as a fiduciary obligation, but also adopts an expansive construction of non-parental relationships giving rise to fiduciary duties. The duty has also been found to exist between a member of the clergy and his parishioners,[86] and the Crown and children under its

---

[81] Cf. also the case of *Goldsworthy v. Brickell* [1987] Ch 378, where Nourse LJ explored the kind of trust required for a presumption of undue influence to arise, a concept which is often associated with fiduciary relationships, and concluding that the doctor/patient relationship was one such instance of presumed influence.

[82] *Parkinson v. St James and Seacroft University Hospital NHS Trust* [2002] QB 266, per Hale LJ.

[83] *LAC Minerals Ltd v. International Corona Resources Ltd* [1989] 2 SCR 574.

[84] [1992] 3 SCR 6.

[85] *J v. J et al* (1993) 102 DLR (4th) 177 – parents, 'whether biological or otherwise' (e.g. the common law spouse of the natural parent if treated as a parent), stood in a fiduciary relationship to their child. The issue of abuse as breach of fiduciary duty has yet to be definitively stated in Australian case law, although the weight of authority would seem to be against the parent/child relationship giving rise to fiduciary obligations: *Woodhead v. Elbourne* [2000] QSC 42; *Paramasivam v. Flynn* (1998) 90 FCR 489 and in *Hospital Products v. US Surgical Corporation* [2001] QCA 335, where the established categories of fiduciary relationship in Australian law were listed, parent and child do not appear. Cf. the dissenting judgment of Atkinson J in *Carter v. Corporation of the Sisters of Mercy of the Diocese of Rockhampton*, where he treated the categorisation of abuse in an orphanage setting as breach of fiduciary duty as 'not fanciful' (1984) 156 CLR 41. See also *Prince v. Attorney General* [1996] 3 NZLR 733.

[86] *KW v. Pornbacher* (1997) 32 BCLR (3d) 360 SC; *D(P) v. Allen* (2004) 132 ACWS (3d) 1098.

guardianship.[87] The limits of the fiduciary duty concept as a cause of action for abuse victims are well illustrated in the New Zealand case of *H v. R*.[88] The alleged abuse in *H v. R* was perpetrated by a party unrelated to the claimant, who had no prior relationship with the victim other than the fact that he had a holiday home close to his victim's family's holiday home. Harman J distinguished this abuser from an abusing parent or doctor, saying of more 'intermittent relationships':

> There are obvious problems with the establishment of a fiduciary duty. An otherwise admirable end cannot be met by utilising an important concept and one which has a distinct moral and functional presence in our law, by watering down the basic concept of a fiduciary.[89]

Despite the difficulties experienced in Canada with regard to defining the boundaries of this cause of action, the mechanism of fiduciary duty could provide the key to improved legal remedies for the victims of sexual abuse in English law where a relationship of dependence could be established. The concept of fiduciary duty is recognised in English law, and it seems at least arguable that the concept of fiduciary duty could similarly be adapted to afford protection of the psychological victims of childhood abuse from particular perpetrators. The closest our courts have come to this is the ruling in *Lister v. Hesley Hall Ltd*,[90] which uses the concept of bailment to develop a principle of non-delegable responsibility for children in the defendant's care.

### 4. *Claims by bystander family members*

The courts of England and Wales have yet to fully explore the issue of whether a bystander parent/sibling, or perhaps even a professional carer of the immediate victim, would have a claim against the abuser or (occasionally) against a third party for failing to prevent the abuse for the psychiatric harm they suffer by reason of their helplessness and a feeling of responsibility they suffer as a result of the abuse. A bystander[91] claim against the perpetrator would likely be in negligence as although the act is intentional, it is not a trespass against the claimant, but is only

---

[87] *A(C) v. Critchley* (1998) 166 DLR (4th) 475; *B (KL) v. British Colombia* (conceded at [38]).
[88] [1996] NZLR 299.  [89] [1996] NZLR 299, *per* Harman J at 307.
[90] [2001] UKHL 22; [2002] 1 AC 215. Discussed later.
[91] Admittedly, the term 'bystander' would possibly be resisted as it does not adequately encapsulate the relationship between, say, a child being abused by his stepfather and the victim's mother.

negligent as to the mental harm that might be caused to a relative or carer of the immediate victim. It is unusual, but not entirely without precedent, for a defendant to owe a duty of care to the close relative of their immediate victim.[92] Particular difficulties arise out of the fact that the damage for which compensation is being claimed is psychiatric and the claim would therefore be subject to all the restrictive conditions attached to such claims. First, the suffering of the relative must equate to a recognised psychiatric disorder.[93] Second, if these claims were to be brought in negligence, such claimants would have difficulty demonstrating where they sit on the primary/secondary victim dichotomy which governs psychiatric damage claims. On the one hand, their position would not sit easily with the primary victim definition which has traditionally required physical endangerment of the claimant by the defendant and involvement in a sudden traumatic event.[94] Alternatively, they may be categorised as secondary victims, not being in physical danger themselves,[95] but suffering trauma due to the endangerment of a loved one. If classed as secondary victims, they would face the difficulty of proving the direct perception of a 'sudden shocking event' as required by *Alcock v. Chief Constable of South Yorkshire*.[96] It is not difficult to imagine that, in some contexts of childhood abuse, a sudden shocking event would be present where, for example, the claimant stumbled upon an incident of abuse. However, in many cases there will be a gradual realisation that the abuse is occurring, the gradualness of which might be reinforced by denial that such an atrocity could be happening in their own family. Would the courts insist upon the fulfilment of the *Alcock* criteria in such a case? In *W v. Essex*, their Lordships accepted as arguable, a claim for psychiatric damage by foster parents based on their discovery that their

---

[92] Largely in the context of 'secondary victims' suffering psychiatric damage. See also *R(L) v. British Colombia* 1998 ACWSJ (3d) 550 (class action by parents of abused children arguing that defendants owed them a duty of care was not plainly and obviously bound to fail). See to the opposite effect: *Powell v. Boladz* [1998] Lloyd's Rep Med 116; (1998) 39 BMLR 116 CA and *A B and others v. Leeds Teaching Hospital NHS Trust* [2004] EWHC 644; [2005] 2 WLR 358 (no duty of care to the relatives of a patient).
[93] *Hinz v. Berry* [1970] 2 QB 40; *Alcock v. Chief Constable of South Yorkshire* [1992] 1 AC 310 and see further, Chapter 4.
[94] *Page v. Smith* [1996] AC 155; *White v. Chief Constable of South Yorkshire* [1999] 2 AC 455. Although the sudden traumatic event criterion appears now to be in doubt: *Donachie v. Chief Constable of the Greater Manchester Police* [2004] EWCA Civ 405; (2004) 148 SJLB.
[95] Unless, as is often the case, the abusing parent abuses their spouse as well as their children.
[96] [1992] 1 AC 310.

children had been sexually abused by a foster child they had innocently brought into their home.[97] The fact that their psychiatric injury stemmed from their feeling of responsibility for the abuse did not prevent them qualifying as primary victims and the fact that their discovery of the abuse was not immediately after the sexual incident occurred did not prevent them from being secondary victims. As the issue of duty of care was not finally determined, however, the *W* case is of limited assistance. Further litigation in bystander cases would give the courts the opportunity to reconsider the authority of *Dooley v Cammell Laird & Co Ltd*.[98] This case was interpreted in later cases as an instance of a claimant entitled to a remedy as a primary victim by virtue of their reasonable feeling of responsibility for the peril of another.[99] Although this reasoning has subsequently been abandoned by the House of Lords in *White*,[100] a claim by the parent or sibling bystander could convince the court that the 'responsibility' category of primary victim should be revived.

Additional guidance in bystander cases is available in the form of *State of New South Wales v. Seedsman*,[101] the claim of a young, untrained police officer working in a child abuse unit and exposed to horrific cases of child abuse. Although the Australian courts are not bound by the *Alcock* criteria, the court did have to decide (analogously) whether this claim for post-traumatic stress disorder was recoverable despite the fact that the diagnostic criterion of physical endangerment of self or a loved one[102] was missing (see Chapter 4). Nevertheless, the court readily concluded that, given the advisory status of the diagnostic criteria and the exceptional nature of child abuse, the plaintiff's psychiatric harm was readily foreseeable.[103]

## The non-perpetrator as defendant

There are a number of reasons why a non-perpetrator may be identified as a defendant in abuse litigation: lack of knowledge as to the

---

[97] [2001] 2 AC 592.    [98] [1951] 1 Lloyd's Rep 271.
[99] *Alcock v. Chief Constable of South Yorkshire* [1992] 1 AC 310.
[100] *White v. Chief Constable of South Yorkshire* [1999] 2 AC 455.
[101] [2000] NSWCA 119.
[102] *Diagnostic Statistical Manual Fourth Edition, Text Revision* (American Psychiatric Association, 2000) at 309.81.
[103] This case, based as it was on the employment relationship, would be unlikely to have succeeded in English law, see *Barber v. Somerset County Council* [2004] UKHL 13; [2004] 1 WLR 1089.

perpetrator's whereabouts; the perpetrator is deceased or unable to satisfy a claim; or a belief that the non-perpetrator should be brought to account for their failures. It is here in particular that the law has the potential to perform a standard setting or deterrence function.

There are really two types of non-perpetrator:

1. those who have responsibility for the perpetrator and are effectively being sued for having failed to exert proper influence, supervision or control to prevent the abuse taking place (the employer of the perpetrator as defendant is typically in this category); and
2. those defendants who have responsibilities associated with the care or protection of the claimant (the so-called 'iatrogenic neglect' cases[104]).

The following sections deal with the potential liabilities of the employer, schools, health care professionals, social workers, local authorities, police force, correctional services and hospitals as non-perpetrators whom the law might fix with responsibility for the incidence of abuse. Much more detail is provided on claims against the employer of the perpetrator as this covers a host of different scenarios and also raises questions of vicarious liability.

## 1. Litigation under the Human Rights Act 1998

The Human Rights Act 1998 has had a significant impact on litigation in this area by both changing the shape of the tort of negligence as it applies to public authority defendants that have allegedly failed to prevent abuse occurring (s. 2 of the Act requires the courts to take into account ECtHR jurisprudence when determining questions arising in connection with human rights) and in extending the range of remedies available (s. 7 of the Act provides a right of action against public authorities that have acted incompatibly with a Convention right). The term 'public authority' includes not only defendants such as local authorities, but also domestic courts which have perhaps acted incompatibly with Convention rights by not providing adequate redress for an identified violation. This new cause of action is only available to 'victims' of the incompatible conduct, only where the specified incompatibility occurred after 2 October 2000 and the s. 7 right of action must be exercised within a year of the action complained of.[105] Having said

---

[104] C. Lyon, *Child Abuse* (Jordan Publishing, 2003) at 91.   [105] S. 7(5)(a).

that, the court has the discretion to extend time where it is adjudged fair to do so in all the circumstances.[106]

In the context of the s. 7 right of action, Article 3 (paired with Article 13) of the ECHR has emerged as a useful avenue of redress to child abuse claimants. Decisions from the European Court of Human Rights have repeatedly confirmed that long-term physical and sexual abuse constitutes a violation of the right to be free from inhuman and degrading treatment under Article 3.[107] Further, this Article imposes a positive obligation on the state to protect children from abuse amounting to inhuman and degrading treatment and, provided the failure of the public authority had a realistic prospect of altering the outcome or mitigating the harm, the state's liability is engaged.[108] The state's positive obligation to protect children from abuse is not breached unless there was actual or constructive knowledge that the claimant was being abused. Thus, in *E v. UK* the local authority's failure to act on their suspicions that a convicted sex offender was living with E's family in breach of a probation order (the sex offences having been committed against members of E's family) constituted a violation of Article 3, as the local authority had constructive knowledge that the abuse was continuing.[109] This is to be distinguished from the case of *DP v. UK*,[110] where the local authority was found not to have violated Article 3, as it was not proved that the authority knew that abuse was occurring in the family home (particularly as the claimants' mother had actively hidden the abuse). Long-term physical and emotional abuse or neglect of children can also constitute 'inhuman and degrading treatment' under Article 3.[111]

The role of Article 13 is to guarantee the availability of a remedy at national level for violation of the other Convention rights.[112] In the context of violations of Articles 2 and 3 (the most important fundamental human rights) the 'remedy' must constitute a mechanism for establishing the liability of public authorities in addition to providing compensation for the non-pecuniary loss flowing from the violation. Article 13 requires that the remedy must be effective, both legally and practically.[113] In this regard it has been found that in cases of serious abuse:

---

[106] S. 7(5)(b).   [107] *Z v. UK* [2001] 2 FLR 612; *E v. UK* (2003) 36 EHHR 31.
[108] *E v. UK* (2003) 36 EHHR 31 at H8.   [109] *E v. UK* (2003) 36 EHHR 31.
[110] [2003] 1 FLR 50.   [111] *Z v. UK* [2001] 2 FLR 612.
[112] This Article was not explicitly incorporated into domestic law under the Human Rights Act, as the government took the view that the remedies under the Act itself implemented the right to a remedy.
[113] *E v. UK* (2003) 36 EHHR 31 at H11.

- Judicial review does not provide an adequate remedy – presumably because the tight time limits mean that review is not in practice available to an abuse victim who is a child at the time of the abuse.[114]
- The criminal injuries compensation scheme does not provide an adequate remedy as, whilst providing compensation, it does not make awards for pecuniary losses, nor does it provide a mechanism for determining the liability of either the perpetrator or the public authority.[115]
- A complaint to the ombudsman regarding the social services' inaction does not constitute an effective remedy under Article 13 as the ombudsman only has the power to make recommendations and does not make a binding determination.[116]
- A civil action may, however, provide an effective remedy.[117] Therefore, provided an action in negligence or under s. 7 of the Human Rights Act is available in law and in practice, the right to a remedy is *prima facie* fulfilled.

As to the last of these, the right of action under the Human Rights Act only exists where the conduct complained of post-dates 2 October 2000, therefore other remedies ought to be available to satisfy the requirements of Article 13 before this time. Recent adjustments to the duty of care analysis for the purposes of the tort of negligence indicate that such an action would be available.[118]

A violation of Article 13 may be established notwithstanding a claimant's failure to show breach of any of the named rights in the ECHR. Provided the claimant brings forward allegations that named rights were violated and that those allegations are sufficiently well founded to require examination on the merits, Article 13 requires that a remedy is in principle available.[119]

Article 41 of the ECHR provides that, where a violation has been found, the decision of the court shall afford 'just satisfaction'. Some cases brought in the European Court of Human Rights seeking damages for injured feelings fail because the finding of a violation is sufficient of itself to provide just satisfaction to the applicant.[120] Damages awarded

---

[114] *E v. UK* (2003) 36 EHHR 31.  [115] (2003) 36 EHHR 31 at H14.
[116] (2003) 36 EHHR 31 at H14.
[117] (2003) 36 EHHR 31 and *McKerr v. UK* (2002) 35 EHRR 23.
[118] *JD v. East Berkshire Community NHS Trust* [2005] UKHL 23; [2005] 2 WLR 993.
[119] *DP v. UK* [2003] 1 FLR 50.   [120] *Goodwin v. UK* (2002) 35 EHRR 18.

under the Human Rights Act 1998 are to be comparable in amount to those which would have been awarded in tort.[121]

Delay in the context of legal proceedings has also given rise to damages for distress under the guise of a violation of Article 6(1) – the right to a fair trial. In *Foley v. UK*,[122] the Court of Human Rights awarded such damages for the distress caused by delays of over 14 years in appeals, only some of which were attributable to state authorities. The court did not require objective proof of such distress but considered that: '... emotional distress cannot always be the object of concrete proof. This does not prevent the court from making an award if it considers that it is reasonable to assume that the applicant has suffered injury requiring financial compensation.'

## 2. Breach of statutory duty

An action for breach of statutory duty against local authorities for failing to rescue the claimant from an abusive environment could dispense with the need to prove negligence and would therefore constitute an attractive alternative to the negligence action. This form of action arises where breach of a statutory obligation causes damage and the courts can be convinced that the statute in question was intended by Parliament to provide a civil remedy for its infraction.[123] Where the statute itself is silent on the availability of civil remedies, the courts engage in speculation as to parliamentary intention applying a series of restrictive presumptions established by case law to determine the issue. To take an example, it might be thought that the Children Act 1989 gives rise to a civil action where breach of the duty on local authorities to make enquiries where there is reasonable cause to suspect that a child is suffering or likely to suffer significant harm can be established.[124] The decision as to whether the threshold of actual or potential significant harm is satisfied and decisions regarding what to do thereafter are not, however, subject to a breach of statutory duty action. Applying the principle that the claimant must be a member of a specific group which the statute in question was designed to protect, Lord Browne-Wilkinson in *X* found that the Children Act was designed to protect not just children but the social welfare of the community (a striking revelation given the title of the Act). His Lordships also considered that the work

---

[121] *R (on the application of KB) v. MHRT and Secretary of State for Health* [2003] EWHC 193; [2004] QB 936.
[122] (2003) 36 EHRR 15.  [123] *Cutler v. Wandsworth Stadium* [1949] AC 398.  [124] S. 47.

necessitated such difficult sensitive decisions regarding the balance between protecting the child from harm and protecting the family unit from disruption that 'exceptionally clear statutory language' would have been required before the duty bearer could be regarded as potentially liable in damages for breach. Given that the breach of statutory duty action can effectively impose strict liability on the defendant it is submitted that the negligence action is a far more appropriate mechanism for compensating abuse as it is capable of importing a significant margin of error in liability for work which is characterised by 'tough calls'.

## 3. The tort of negligence

As is clear from the discussion of *Stubbings v. Webb* above,[125] English courts have resisted attempts to categorise the perpetration of sexual abuse as negligence. It is nevertheless possible to pursue a case in negligence against non-perpetrators whose failure to act to prevent the abuse can be regarded as a breach of their duty of care, or whose positive act of negligence provided the abuser with the opportunity to abuse. Such defendants have ranged from non-intervening parents and social services to the perpetrator's employer. Bringing a claim in negligence requires proof that a duty of care was owed by the defendant to the claimant in respect of the type of harm suffered, that the duty was breached and that the breach caused the damage. As the harm for which the claimant seeks compensation will very often be psychiatric harm, it is necessary to be aware of the special rules relating to the duty not to cause psychiatric harm. The courts tend to categorise claimants seeking compensation for pure psychiatric harm as either 'primary victims' (persons personally endangered by the defendant's negligence)[126] or 'secondary victims' (bystanders observing the endangerment of a loved one)[127] for the purposes of identifying when the duty of care arises. Although the courts have not yet applied this terminology to the sexual abuse claimant, that is not to say that they will not do so at a later date.[128] The sexual abuse claimant will either be regarded as falling outside the primary/secondary dichotomy altogether, or will be classed as a primary victim by virtue of the fact that they are analogous to

[125] [1993] AC 498 (HL).   [126] *Page v. Smith* [1996] AC 155.
[127] *Alcock v. Chief Constable of South Yorkshire* [1992] 1 AC 310.
[128] The primary/secondary victim distinction has been applied in analogous contexts where C alleged that D was negligent in failing to prevent the perpetration of harm by a third party: *Palmer v. Tees HA* [2000] PIQR P1.

primary victims,[129] or that in abuse scenarios there is no-one else who might qualify as the primary victim.[130]

Bringing an action in negligence rather than in trespass would provide the claimant with a potentially more generous limitation period. Not only would the claimant have access to the flexibility of statutory delayed discovery provisions,[131] they would also have the opportunity to argue that, aside from delayed discovery of the injury, the tort was not complete until damage was suffered, and that the damage did not immediately follow the abuse.

## Duty of care and the range of defendants

For the law to impose a duty of care on the defendant, it must be reasonably foreseeable that a failure to take care could result in harm to the claimant, there must be a relationship of proximity between the claimant and defendant and it must be just, fair and reasonable to impose a duty of care.[132] Where the defendant is a public authority, counsel for the defence routinely seek to have the claim struck out as disclosing no reasonable cause of action because the danger of impeding public bodies' work by opening the floodgates of litigation renders it unjust or unfair to impose a duty of care. Consequently, the 'justice, fairness and reasonableness' segment of the duty of care analysis has dominated the court's determinations in this area.

## Employer liability in negligence for child abuse

The employment relationship has special status in the tort of negligence. This special status means that the employer of the abuser may be liable in damages for abuse committed by an employee under one of the following mechanisms:

- the principles of direct liability for negligence in the hiring, failure to supervise or failure to dismiss the errant employee;
- breach of the employer's non-delegable duties of care (dealt with in section 5 below); or
- vicarious liability for torts committed by employees within the course of their employment (dealt with in section 7 below).

---

[129] Per Butler-Sloss LJ in *McLoughlin v. Jones* [2001] EWCA Civ 1743; [2002] 2 WLR 1279 and *Parkinson v. St James and Seacroft University Hospital NHS Trust* [2002] QB 266, per Hale LJ.
[130] *W v. Essex CC* [2001] 2 AC 592; *Farrell v. Avon Health Authority* [2001] Lloyd's Rep Med 458.
[131] Under s. 11(4)(a) and (b) of the Limitation Act 1980.
[132] *Caparo Industries plc v. Dickman* [1990] 1 All ER 568.

An employer may be found liable in negligence for failing to heed warning signs that their employees were abusing their position in order to exploit children in their care. Such liability is now recognised as a real risk endemic to foster homes, child care services, borstals and boarding schools, but the fact that the true scale of institutional sexual abuse has only recently been exposed has meant that the law attributing responsibility for such abuse on employers is at an early stage in its development. Claimants suing on events which occurred 20 or 30 years ago face the difficulty of showing that, at the relevant time, child abuse was a foreseeable risk.

In the main, therefore, abuse claims in negligence against employers only succeed where it can be shown that the risk posed to the children was brought specifically to the defendant's attention and ignored.[133] This can be illustrated by reference to two Canadian cases; *H(SG) v. Gorsline*[134] and *GBR v. Hollett*.[135] In *Gorsline* the Canadian court found the School Board not negligent, as in 1979 'the prospect of sexual misconduct by a teacher with a student was not in anyone's contemplation', sexual abuse was simply not a foreseeable risk. This can be compared with *Hollett* where the employer's failure to promptly dismiss their school counsellor at a residential school for juvenile girls was found to be negligent. Reports had been received that the counsellor was dealing in drugs, helping girls to escape from the school and that there had been some instances of physical abuse. As to the foreseeability of damage, the defendants argued that it was not foreseeable that in three months from these adverse reports, their employee would help the claimant to run away to live with him and subject her to physical and sexual abuse. It was held that it was not necessary to foresee that these specific events might transpire, but rather that it was foreseeable that allowing the employee to remain in employment might result in physical abuse to the claimant.

Another instance of negligent failure to act upon a warning can be found in *Garamella v. New York Medical College and Dr Ingram*,[136] where the US District Court imposed liability upon the defendant analyst (and vicarious liability upon his employers) for the harm

---

[133] See *John Doe v. Bennett* [2004] SCC 17 – defendants found directly liable in negligence due to the fact that, when the Bishop had been informed of the abuse, no action was taken and no system existed for dealing with such matters.
[134] [2001] 6 WWR 132 (Alta QB); approved on appeal at [2004] 23 CCLT (3D) 65.
[135] (1996) 139 DLR (4th) 260.   [136] [1999] Lloyd's Rep Med 343.

inflicted by a psychiatrist's sexual abuse of his child patient. Garamella's paedophilic tendencies had come to light during psychoanalysis with the defendant that he was required to undergo as part of his training. The analyst failed to advise anyone of the unsuitability of Garamella as a psychoanalyst or the risks of him dealing with children. Dr Ingram argued that his professional duty of confidence was binding upon him unless an imminent threat to an individual was identified. The court rejected such an argument identifying two factors of particular importance. First, this was not an ordinary psychiatrist/patient relationship but one where the defendant exercised a great degree of control over the perpetrator of harm due to his role in progressing the career of trainee psychiatrists. Secondly, the means by which Garamella could be stopped from inflicting harm on child patients were easily accessed by simply blocking his progress to a career involving children. Certainly, English courts might decide that in a case such as this, whilst a breach of confidence may not be unlawful, no actionable duty to disclose would be found due to an absence of proximity.[137]

### Vetting mechanisms and the standard of care

In negligence litigation the conduct of workers involved in child protection, whether in a child care institution or in the capacity of clinicians or social workers deciding on a care plan for a particular child, is to be judged by the *Bolam* test.[138] Thus, the standard required is that of the ordinary skilled individual working in that particular field and the worker is not negligent if their action or inaction is supported by a responsible body of professional opinion (and that course of conduct is capable of withstanding logical analysis).[139]

When considering the common law standard of care, particularly as it applies to employers and voluntary organisations, note must be taken of the vetting mechanisms now available to check whether individuals have been convicted of relevant criminal offences in the past. Indeed, the existence of these vetting mechanisms, accompanied by the criminal sanctions for their non-observance, may tempt a court to find that employers involved in the provision of childcare services owe a non-delegable

---

[137] As per *Hill v. Chief Constable for West Yorkshire* [1990] 1 All ER 1046 and *Palmer v. Tees Health Authority* [1999] Lloyd's Rep Med 351.
[138] *KR v. Bryn Alyn Community (Holdings) Ltd (In Liquidation)* (2001) WL 753345 at [81].
[139] *Bolam v. Friern General Hospital Management Committee* [1957] 2 All ER 118, as applied in the light of *Bolitho v. City and Hackney Health Authority* [1997] 4 All ER 771.

duty to ensure that their employees are not disqualified from working with children.

There are currently three ways in which an individual can be disqualified from working with children. First, they may appear on the Protection of Children Act 1999 list (the 'POCA list') of persons considered to be unsuitable to work with children.[140] Secondly, such persons might appear on the Department of Education and Skills' list of teachers who are disqualified from working with children under the Protection of Children Act 1999.[141] Childcare organisations are under a duty to check both lists before employing someone in a 'child care position' and must not offer employment to anyone who appears on either list.[142] Finally, the criminal courts can make an order disqualifying a person from 'working with children' if they have been convicted of a relevant offence.[143] Here, the criminal law relies upon the disqualified person to behave responsibly as to employment decisions. Disqualified persons commit an offence if they knowingly apply for, offer or accept work with children.[144] Employers will be guilty of an offence if they knowingly offer employment to someone disqualified by any of the three mechanisms set out above, or if they fail to remove such an individual from employment involving 'working with children'.[145] 'Working with

---

[140] This list, often referred to as the '99 List', is maintained by the Secretary of State under s. 1 of the Protection of Children Act 1999 and encompasses the non-statutory Department of Health Consultancy Index.

[141] Amending s. 218 of the Education Reform Act 1988.

[142] S. 7 of the Protection of Children Act 1999. If the employee comes through an agency, it is sufficient if the child care organisation is satisfied that the agency has in the last 12 months checked the list and that they have received written confirmation that the person does not appear on either list. S. 12 defines 'child care positions' as those concerned with the provision of accommodation, social services or health care services to children which enables regular contact with children.

[143] Ss. 26–30 of the Criminal Justice and Court Services Act 2000. Relevant offences are listed under Schedule 4 to the Act include cruelty, indecent conduct or sexual intercourse with a child and possession of child pornography.

[144] S. 35(1). It is also the prospective employee's duty to disclose information in an enhanced criminal record certificate if that information might be relevant to the post applied for, unless there is good reason for not doing so: s. 115 of the Police Act 1997; *X v. Chief Constable for West Midlands Police* [2004] EWCA Civ 1068; (2004) 101 (35) LSG 34.

[145] S. 35(2) and (3). Note that if the employment of a barred person is not done knowingly, no criminal provision is breached, but performing checks on new recruits will undoubtedly be part of the employer's common law duty of care to clients and the duty to employees to provide a safe working environment: *Wilsons & Clyde Co. v. English* [1938] AC 57.

children' is defined broadly as encompassing paid or unpaid work in 'regulated positions' which includes specified posts in local government and children's charities[146] and those positions where the 'normal duties' include work:

- in day care premises;[147]
- involving caring for, training, supervising or being in sole charge of children;[148]
- involving unsupervised contact with children;[149]
- which includes caring for children under the age of sixteen in the course of the children's employment;[150]
- in institutions exclusively or mainly for the detention, reception, treatment, care or education of children;[151] or
- supervising or managing an individual in his work in a regulated position.[152]

The reference to 'normal duties' excludes positions involving one-off contact with a child. Therefore, if a mother rings for a taxi to pick up her child, the taxi firm is not breaking the law in sending a disqualified person.[153] The employer's duty to vet those employees working in regulated positions constitutes an exception to the Rehabilitation of Offenders Act 1974, which would normally require that spent convictions not be used to discriminate against prospective employees. The employer is entitled to take into account both spent and unspent convictions when filling child care positions.

The three lists of disqualified employees outlined above are to be distinguished from the sexual offences register which identifies persons convicted of relevant offences (including pornography) convicted in the Crown Court.[154] Persons on the register must comply with requirements to notify the police of their home address periodically[155] and it is the duty of the police to check the accuracy of the information on the register at least annually. The potential liability of the police in this regard is discussed below at p. 101. Employing someone whose name appears on the Sexual Offences Register in a job where the worker may

---

[146] S. 36(6). [147] S. 36(1)(a). [148] S. 36(1)(c). [149] S. 36(1)(d). [150] S. 36(1)(e).
[151] S. 36(2). [152] S. 36(1)(h). [153] Lyon, *Child Abuse* at 9.271.
[154] Sexual Offences Act 1997. The register does not, however, include persons found to have abused children in the course of Children Act proceedings (these persons are listed on the lists maintained by government departments), nor does it detail persons convicted of sexual offences before 1997.
[155] Sexual Offences Act 2003, s. 85.

come into contact with children is not necessarily negligent. For example, it seems that registration on the Sex Offences Register does not automatically make someone unfit to be a bus driver.[156]

The Criminal Records Bureau, established in 2002, administers what are now known as 'disclosure checks' to identify whether the subject of the inquiry has any criminal convictions. Employers offering employment involving more than *de minimis* contact with children will undoubtedly be negligent if they fail to obtain a criminal records bureau disclosure for job applicants. The Criminal Records Bureau has access to the national police database containing records of criminal convictions, cautions and reprimands, but also to the disqualification lists mentioned above. Applications to screen an individual's criminal record must be made direct to the Criminal Records Bureau or via a registered body and must be made for the appropriate type of disclosure:

- 'basic', for general recruitment purposes (disclosure extends to all offences which are not 'spent' under the Rehabilitation of Offenders Act 1974);
- 'standard', for posts which involve regular contact with children (disclosure includes spent and unspent convictions and entry on the above named lists prohibiting work with children); and
- 'enhanced' for posts involving regularly caring for or being in sole charge of children (extends beyond convictions to information from local police records which might be regarded as relevant).

Guidance has been issued to assist employers to determine whether any disclosed convictions are relevant or not.[157]

These arrangements are due to be reformed later this year once the Safeguarding Vulnerable Groups Bill is passed. The Bill seeks to implement the recommendations of the Bichard Inquiry,[158] following the Soham murders, which identified a number of shortcomings in existing procedures for vetting and barring those believed to present a risk to children from employment involving contact with children. Under the Bill the existing List 99 and the POCA list would be consolidated into a composite list of persons barred from working with children. Of particular significance is the duty under cl. 11 of the Bill requiring 'regulated

---

[156] *Secretary of State for Transport, Local Government and the Regions v. Snowdon* [2002] EWHC 2394; [2003] RTR 15
[157] *Employing People with Convictions* (Criminal Records Bureau, 2001).
[158] *The Bichard Inquiry Report.* HC 653 (TSO, 2004).

activity providers'[159] to make 'appropriate checks' before permitting anyone to engage in a regulated activity. Thus, an employer who has not knowingly employed a barred person will not be safe from prosecution if they failed to check the list of barred individuals.

Under existing arrangements, it is likely that failure to check or to heed an applicant's criminal record will result in liability in negligence if a recruit with a relevant record abuses any of the children which the perpetrator accessed via his or her employment. Moreover, a positive assurance to, for example, a parent that an individual is not a risk to children when they have relevant convictions can give rise to liability of the *Hedley Byrne* variety if a child comes to harm as a result.[160] Thus, it is possible that the Criminal Records Bureau or registered body may be liable for negligence in the preparation or passing on of disclosures.

Of course, the employer's duty extends beyond the vetting process to the oversight of staff once they are employed and being alert to the possibility that their workers may be a source of harm or danger to others in the course of their work.[161] The little case law that there is on this subject suggests that the courts are sympathetic to employers' ignorance in this regard and require little in the way of proactive steps to investigate unusual behaviour towards children. In *C v. Middlesborough BC*[162] the Court of Appeal chose to emphasise the fact that paedophiles employ deviant and manipulative techniques designed to avoid discovery and deflect criticism, thus pointing to the difficulty of identifying a potential abuser in the employer's workforce. In the context of sexual abuse committed by a teacher in the early 1980s, the court was told that there had been warning signs, such as the fact that pupils frequently visited the teacher's rooms and the teacher in question gave cigarettes and presents to the victim and visited his home (referred to as a classic technique used by the paedophile to ingratiate himself with the child's family). Despite these warning signs, the employer was not negligent in failing to investigate matters further as to impose liability on these facts would involve the application of wisdom gleaned from

---

[159] Regulated activity with children is defined in Schedule 3 to the Bill and includes teaching, training, instruction, supervision, treatment or therapy of children.
[160] *T (A Minor) v. Surrey CC* [1994] 4 All ER 577; *W v. Essex CC* [1998] PIQR 346 (CA), argument not dealt with on appeal to the House of Lords.
[161] *Hudson v. Ridge Manufacturing* [1957] 2 All ER 229, although in the context of harm to another employee.
[162] [2004] EWCA Civ 1746; [2004] All ER (D) 339 (Dec).

hindsight.[163] Notwithstanding this reluctance to fix the standard of care with reference to hindsight, enough is now known about the vulnerability of children to the predations of determined offenders that certain checks and safeguards can be expected to be put into place. English courts have not spoken on this issue as yet, but they might be invited to adopt the approach of a judge in the High Court of Australia in *New South Wales v. Lepore*, who asserted that any residential school or facility which allowed its workers personal contact with children without supervision or accompaniment by another adult should be held liable in negligence if abuse occurred.[164]

## Cases of iatrogenic abuse or neglect

Claims asserting that the abuse or neglect was caused by the intervention or lack thereof by a defendant whose professional responsibility was to safeguard the claimant from abuse might be termed 'iatrogenic abuse cases'.

**Local authorities**  Under the Children Act 1989, local authorities are under a statutory duty to safeguard and promote the welfare of children within their area who are in need.[165] Children are 'in need' if they are unlikely to achieve or maintain a reasonable standard of physical or mental health or physical, emotional, intellectual or social development.[166] A child who is being abused or neglected clearly qualifies as being 'in need'. The extent to which local authorities owe an enforceable private law duty of care to children being abused in their home or to the children it places into care is an issue which has produced a web of conflicting case law and has attracted considerable academic scrutiny. The overall approach of the courts can be identified as a three point analysis as follows:

- The starting point is that the courts must not impose a duty of care which conflicts with or undermines a pre-existing statutory duty.[167]

---

[163] Cf *Swales v. Glendinning* 2004 128 ACWSJ (3d) 853 where the court found the defendant diocese liable in negligence for sexual abuse from 1969–74 by one of its priests on the grounds that it was common knowledge that young boys visited this particular priest in his private rooms on a regular basis. Such activities should have prompted further inquiries and interviewing of the children.
[164] (2003) ALR 412 *per* Gaudron J at [125].
[165] S. 17. This is to be viewed within the context of the modern broader duty to 'improve the wellbeing' of children in the local authority's area as set out in s. 10(4) of the Children Act 2004.
[166] S. 17(10).
[167] *Stovin v. Wise* [1996] 3 All ER 801 at 810, *per* Lord Nicholls and followed in *X (Minors) v. Bedfordshire CC* [1995] 2 AC 633 by Lord Browne-Wilkinson.

There is, however, no conflict where the defendant's conduct was so unreasonable as to fall outside the permissible limits of the exercise of statutory powers.[168]
- Secondly, a distinction is to be drawn between the conduct of policy matters which are non-justiciable and operational matters to which a duty of care may be applied.[169] The former include decision-making which necessitates considerations of social policy, allocation of public resources and 'the balance between pursuing desirable social aims as against the risk to the public inherent in so doing'.[170]
- Finally, if the negligence relates to operational rather than policy matters, the usual tripartite test is to be applied to determine whether a duty of care is owed, but the application of the test will be 'profoundly influenced by the statutory framework within which the acts complained of were done'.[171]

The House of Lords' judgment in *X v. Bedfordshire CC*, although now apparently qualified by the ECtHR and marginalised by later cases, has left an indelible mark on this area of law. In *X*, their Lordships considered, *inter alia*, the complaints of five claimants alleging negligence against the local authorities for not rescuing them from long-term physical and emotional abuse and neglect in their parental home.[172] The defendants had been on notice that the claimants were malnourished, regularly stole food from bins at school and that their cleanliness and hygiene were seriously neglected, but the defendants had failed to take action to remove them from the family home. Their Lordships dealt first of all with the issue of whether the performance of statutory responsibilities for the care of individual children was justiciable. The policy/operational distinction described above came into play – if the claim related to an exercise of statutory discretion (policy), no common law action was available unless the defendant's action fell outside the ambit of the discretion. Where the complaint related to implementation of a previously agreed policy (operations), the usual foreseeability, proximity and justice, fairness and reasonableness test applied with

---

[168] *X (Minors) v. Bedfordshire CC* [1995] 2 AC 633.
[169] *Per* Lord Wilberforce in *Anns v. Merton LBC* [1978] AC 728 at 754. See the criticisms of this distinction in *Barrett v. Enfield LBC* [2001] 2 AC 550, *per* Lord Slynn at 571 and R. A. Buckley, 'Negligence in the Public Sphere – Is Clarity Possible?' (2000) 51 *Northern Ireland Law Quarterly* 25.
[170] *X (Minors) v. Bedfordshire CC* [1995] 2 AC 633.
[171] *Ibid.* [172] *Ibid.*

particular regard to the statutory framework within which the defendant operated. In the given case, although it was reasonably foreseeable that damage would result if the defendants carried out their statutory duties negligently and there was sufficient proximity between the children and the local authority, special considerations meant that the actions should be struck out on the grounds that it would not be just, fair and reasonable to impose a duty of care on the local authorities regarding their failure to take the claimants into care. This was because, according to Lord Browne-Wilkinson:

- a common law duty would cut across the existing statutory regime for protecting children – the existing regime of child protection was interdisciplinary, requiring the cooperation of many agencies and it would be impossible to disentangle the responsibilities of one agency from another;
- child protection responsibilities involved difficult and delicate tasks and it would not be desirable for the threat of litigation to discourage social workers from executing their duties in this sensitive work;
- the threat of liability could cause social workers to act defensively and with excessive caution to the detriment of children at risk;
- moreover, Parliament had provided a raft of remedies in the legislation (including complaints to the local authorities ombudsman and criminal injuries compensation) and the common law should not add to them.[173]

The assumptions made by Lord Browne-Wilkinson regarding the negative impact of liability in tort (in particular the risk of defensive practice and the difficulties of performing such sensitive tasks in a climate of potential litigation) are typical of the English courts' confident reliance on assumptions without reference to any supporting empirical evidence.[174] Furthermore, it is difficult to identify the distinguishing factors which led the House of Lords to dwell on the negative impact of liability in *X* when in another case of the same year against local authority defendants (*Phelps v. Hillingdon LBC*[175]) their Lordships' emphasis was very much on the positive impact of potential liability

---

[173] [1995] 2 AC 663 at 749–751.
[174] J. Hartshorne et al., '*Caparo* Under Fire: a Study into the Effects upon the Fire Service of Liability in Negligence' (2000) 21 *Modern Law Review* 502.
[175] [2001] 2 AC 619. Cf. what is said in *Barrett v. Enfield LBC* [2001] 2 AC 550 on the effectiveness of alternative remedies.

on service standards, mirroring the sentiments of Lord Browne-Wilkinson in X.

The effect of the ruling in X was to create a rebuttable presumption that no duty of care extended from local authorities to children in the exercise of their statutory child protection powers. There is an element of absurdity in the conclusion reached in X given that the statute in question accords the interests of the child paramount importance, yet the beneficiaries of that guiding principle are denied any civil remedy for the careless performance of those duties. It is hardly surprising that ten years later, the X v. Bedfordshire case now stands marooned after a three stage assault which began with a number of authorities confining its effect by distinguishing the particular facts of X:

*Stage 1 – sidelining* X v. Bedfordshire

**Children already removed from the family home** – The House of Lords in *Barrett v. Enfield LBC* refused to follow X where the complaint arose in relation to the poor management of a child's welfare once separated from his parents. The claimant alleged that he had been damaged by a badly coordinated programme of care, in which he had been moved between homes nine times with no consideration being given to the possibility of being returned to his mother or the alternative of adoption. Their Lordships construed X as applying only in cases of a failure to take a child into care to remove the child from an abusive or neglectful environment, although the logic of distinguishing between children who are in care and children still living at home is far from self-evident.[176] Their Lordships also took the view that the courts should only strike out claims where they could be certain that it would not be just, fair and reasonable to impose a duty of care.

**Educational neglect cases** – Then in *Phelps v. Hillingdon LBC*,[177] the House of Lords considered claims brought against a local education authority for failing to identify the special educational needs of the claimants during their school years. As indicated above, their Lordships found that the policy factors identified by Lord Browne-Wilkinson in X had less application to 'educational' cases than 'abuse'

---

[176] [2001] 2 AC 550, *per* Lord Slynn at 568. See also May LJ in *S v. Gloucestershire CC; L v. Tower Hamlets LBC* [2000] 2 FCR 345 at 375 where the ruling in X was confined to its particular facts.
[177] [2001] 2 AC 619.

cases and refused to strike out claims on the grounds that no duty of care was owed. The wisdom of the presumption against a duty of care was implicitly questioned by Lord Slynn's comment that whilst in some cases liability would interfere with the performance of a local authority defendant's duties, it was for the defendant authority to establish that, it was not to be presumed. Fears of a rash of gold-digging claims causing defensive practice were misplaced. 'Denial of the existence of a cause of action is seldom, if ever, the appropriate response to fear of its abuse', rather claims would be controlled by the courts exercising their case management powers to weed out frivolous claims. Lord Clyde added that any fear of a flood of claims may be countered by the fact that the claimant must show that the defendant's standard of care fell below the *Bolam* standard, a 'deliberately and properly high standard' in recognition of the difficult nature of some decisions which the defendant makes and 'leaving room for differences of view on the propriety of one course of action over another'.

**Abuse by a 'child in need'** – The Court of Appeal in *W v. Essex CC* also refused to follow *X* where a complaint was brought by children harmed by the placement of a foster child in their home, without warning the claimants' parents that the foster child was known or suspected to have been the perpetrator of sexual abuse. A duty of care was arguable on these facts because the child claimants were not the subjects of the local authority's statutory duties.[178]

**Duty to prospective adoptive parents** – Finally, the House of Lords in *A & another v. Essex County Council*,[179] whilst approving the policy reasoning in *X*, found that adoption agencies owed a duty of care to prospective adopters where the conduct complained of constituted 'operational negligence' rather than the negligent exercise of discretion. Here the identified negligence was an administrative failure to pass on information regarding the extent of the adopted child's difficulties despite a decision to communicate that information.

---

[178] [1998] PIQR 346. Much also seemed to rest on the positive assurances made to the claimant's parents that the perpetrator was not an abuser. See also *H v. Norfolk CC* [1997] 1 FLR 384 (CA), distinguishing *X* as not applicable where the complaint related to placing or continuing the child in foster care as opposed to whether to put the child into care or not).

[179] [2003] EWCA Civ 1848; [2004] 1 FCR 660.

*Stage 2 – The ECHR challenge* The real death knell for *X v. Bedfordshire* came in the form of the ECHR challenge launched by some of the claimants from *X*, and the later judgment of the English courts in *JD v. East Berkshire Community NHS Trust* on the impact of the Human Rights Act. In *Z v. UK*, the ECtHR ruled that the state had a positive obligation to protect children from treatment contrary to Article 3, and that the parental neglect and abuse of the children in *X v. Bedfordshire* had been a violation of Article 3 of the ECHR.[180] The government conceded that, where a civil action for compensation was not available, the remedies provided by complaint to the local authorities ombudsman and the right to claim criminal injuries compensation fell short of what was required to provide a remedy in the circumstances of these cases (e.g. in *X*, criminal injuries compensation was minimal as much of the abuse did not conform to the eligibility criterion of a 'crime of violence'). The court consequently found a violation of Article 13.[181] The government argued that for the future, similar claimants could have a right of action under s. 7 of the Human Rights Act 1998 independently of the negligence suit.

*Stage 3 – Pre-emptive overruling* In light of the ruling in *Z v. UK*, the Court of Appeal in *JD v. East Berkshire Community NHS Trust*[182] determined that the House of Lords' stance that no duty of care could be owed to children with regard to decisions about their care arrangements could not survive enactment of the Human Rights Act 1998.[183] Given that child protection legislation established that the interests of the child were paramount,[184] recognising a common law duty of care towards the child was consistent with this duty and would not have an adverse effect on its exercise. Breach of such a duty of care would frequently amount to a breach of Article 3 of the Convention. For claims relating to conduct before 2 October 2000, no action under the Human Rights Act 1998 would be available, but the absence of an alternative remedy for victims before this date pointed in favour of the recognition

---

[180] See also *E v. UK* (2003) 36 EHHR 31.
[181] *Z v. United Kingdom* (2002) 34 EHRR 97; *TP and KM v. UK* (2002) 34 EHRR 42.
[182] [2003] EWCA Civ 1151; [2003] 2 FCR 1.
[183] [2003] EWCA Civ 1151; [2003] 2 FCR 1 *per* Lord Phillips MR at [83]. The decision of *X v. Bedfordshire* would, however, continue to have currency as regards claims brought by the parents of children thought to be at risk of abuse as the child's interests were potentially in conflict with the interests of the parents (at [86]).
[184] S. 1 of the Children Act 1989.

of a common law duty of care. Generally, a duty of care to the child would exist in relation to the investigation of abuse allegations and the initiation and pursuit of child care proceedings, although there may be cases where on the particular facts it would not be just, fair and reasonable to impose a duty of care.[185]

In the author's view it may now be tentatively stated that the presumption against a duty of care in *X* has been reversed. When *JD* was considered by the House of Lords, the duty of care owed to children in abuse investigations by the doctors who examined and assessed the children was conceded.[186] It is therefore unclear whether the pre-emptive overruling of *X* in the Court of Appeal has their Lordships' support, although Lord Nicholls stated that the law had 'moved on' since the decision in *X* and Lord Rodger acknowledged that local authorities may owe a common law duty to children in the exercise of their child protection duties.[187] This does not, however, speak clearly on the issue of whether such a duty of care arises on the facts of *X* where the complaint concerns a failure to take children into care or only other distinguishable situations (e.g. where the child suffers abuse once in care as *per Barrett*).

### Abuse in the foster home

The local authority is also responsible for arranging foster care where necessary.[188] Where abuse takes place in a foster home, the local authority may be sued for failure to adequately monitor the foster placement.[189] The court in *Surtees v. Kingston Upon Thames BC*[190] heard a complaint relating to a 2-year-old child suffering third-degree burns whilst in foster care. The court refused to find the local authority liable for negligent supervision of the foster home in the absence of deliberate wrongdoing by the parents.[191] It is not clear that this decision survives the rulings in *Z v. UK* and *JD v. East Berkshire*.

---

[185] At [84].   [186] [2005] UKHL 23; [2005] 2 WLR 993.
[187] [2005] UKHL 23; [2005] 2 WLR 993 at [82].
[188] Part IX of the Children Act 1989.
[189] In *B (KL) v. British Colombia* [2003] 11 WWR 203 the Supreme Court accepted that an action in negligence lay against the Crown for negligent supervision of foster care, but that on the facts it was out of time.
[190] [1991] 2 FLR 559.
[191] In any case, the court in *Surtees* relied upon *H v. Norfolk CC* [1997] 1 FLR 384 (action against local authority for negligent foster care struck out following *X v. Bedfordshire*), a case which has since been overruled in *S v. Gloucestershire CC* [2001] Fam 313.

**Social workers and health care professionals** The individual who has suffered abuse may bring a claim in negligence on the grounds that a doctor or social worker knew or suspected that the claimant was being abused but failed to alert the authorities. The individual social workers and psychologists involved in the *X* case referred to above were found not to be liable to the children because they had not assumed responsibility towards them. Their remit was to advise the local authority, not the claimants, and any duty of care was therefore owed to their employer. Even if this were not the case, their Lordships felt that the same reasons of justice and fairness as precluded a duty of care being owed by the local authority would also apply to the liability of the individual professionals. Of course, this now seems to be subject to adjustment following the developments discussed above and, in any case, the finding that the local authority employees assumed no responsibility to the claimants seems hard to reconcile with the finding in *Phelps* that individual professionals owed a duty of care to school pupils in the education cases.

The feasibility of a contemporary claim against health care professionals, at least where there is actual knowledge that abuse is occurring, is confirmed in *C v. Cairns*. The claimant, then 40 years old, brought an action in negligence against her general practitioner (GP), arguing that he had been aware that as a child in 1975 she was the victim of sexual abuse at the hands of her stepfather. By failing to alert the relevant authorities, her GP had exposed her to years of further abuse. The court found for the defendant, saying that, in 1975, responsible colleagues at that time would also have kept their knowledge of the abuse confidential and hoped for the best (although according to the court, a finding of negligence on such facts if occurring in 2002 would have been irresistible). It is perhaps not the case that all non-disclosures of suspected abuse would now be regarded as negligent. Currently, the General Medical Council advises that if a patient is believed to be the victim of physical, sexual or emotional abuse, disclosure must be made to the relevant authorities if it is in the patient's best interests. If it is decided not to be in the patient's best interests, the case must be discussed with an experienced colleague and the doctor must be prepared to justify a decision not to disclose.[192]

---

[192] *Protecting and Providing Information* (GMC, 2004), para 29.

Even if negligence had been proved, the case of *C v. Cairns* also presented difficult issues of causation, as to which see Chapter 4.

## Witness immunity

Where an individual is alleged to have failed to prevent the abuse occurring, defendants have raised arguments of witness immunity in an attempt to prevent the imposition of a duty of care. Both expert witnesses and non-expert witnesses have immunity from suit extending to the evidence they present in court and any work which can be regarded as preparatory to giving that evidence. The rationale for the immunity is twofold. First, in the interests of justice, witnesses ought to be able to give their evidence freely and without fear of consequent litigation and this freedom must not be undermined by challenges to the preparation of that evidence. Secondly, it is in the public interest that, subject to the appeals procedure, court rulings should be final and witness immunity prevents a multiplicity of actions designed to challenge a court's decision by surreptitious means.[193] In *Darker v. Chief Constable for the West Midlands Police*,[194] the House of Lords confirmed the distinction between 'carrying out investigations' and 'preparing evidence' to be given as a witness at a trial. Public policy did not justify extending the immunity to things said or done which could not be fairly said to be part of their participation in the judicial process.[195] This distinction is not always easy to apply, and the limits of the immunity are drawn by balancing the public interest in the administration of justice and the competing policy that a wrong should not be without a remedy.[196] Case law establishes that whereas the drafting of documents in anticipation of court proceedings attracts immunity,[197] the immunity does not apply to work done primarily to advise a client of their litigation prospects.[198]

In cases of alleged child abuse, the distinction between work which is preparatory to giving evidence in court and 'investigations' might be regarded as particularly difficult to apply given that most health care professionals and social workers know that once there has been a suggestion of child abuse, it is fairly likely that either care proceedings

---

[193] *Silcott v. Comr of Police for the Metropolis* (1996) 8 Admin L R 633.
[194] [2000] 4 All ER 193.
[195] *Ibid.*, per Lord Hope of Craighead at 197.   [196] *Ibid.*
[197] *Taylor v. Director of the Serious Fraud Office* [1999] 2 AC 177.
[198] *Palmer v. Durnford Ford* [1992] 2 All ER 122.

or criminal proceedings will follow. In *M v. Newham*, mother and child were separated due to a mistaken belief that the mother's boyfriend had been abusing the child. The Court of Appeal rejected arguments that the psychiatrist and social worker whose evidence had been pivotal in procuring the separation had the benefit of witness immunity, for whilst both parties might have anticipated that their words would be used in litigation, they did not in the event become involved in any litigation.[199] Doubt was cast on this ruling, however, on appeal to the House of Lords where Lord Browne-Wilkinson[200] stated, *obiter*, that the Court of Appeal had adopted too narrow a construction of witness immunity – the fact that the defendant was never ultimately involved in a trial would not prevent the application of the immunity.[201] Where a psychiatrist was instructed to examine a child for the purpose of discovering whether the child had been abused and by whom, the examination had such an immediate link with possible proceedings that the immunity applied.[202] The psychiatrist would have known that an affirmative report from her would likely be used to launch proceedings for the protection of the child and it was in the public interest that they should be able to speak freely. Aside from this apparent reversal, further confusion has been added by the Court of Appeal in *JD v. East Berkshire Community NHS Trust*.[203] Here, Lord Phillips suggested that the liberal approach to witness immunity expressed by Lord Browne-Wilkinson in the *Newham* appeal was to be tempered by what their Lordships had since said in the *Darker* case. Broad support for the narrower construction of witness immunity is also evident in *Meadow v. General Medical Council*, where Collins J states that, for a report to attract witness immunity, it 'must have been prepared with a view to its being used or in the knowledge that it will probably be used in evidence in court'.[204]

**Hospitals/NHS trusts** The therapeutic relationship involves an assumption of responsibility on the part of the doctor for the welfare of the patient, which can include protection of that patient from third parties who could foreseeably cause harm.[205] In the Canadian case of

---

[199] *Per* Thomas Bingham MR [1995] 2 AC 633 at 661.
[200] *X (Minors) v. Bedfordshire CC* [1995] 2 AC 633.
[201] *Stanton v. Callaghan* [2000] 1 QB 75.   [202] [1995] 2 AC 633 at 755.
[203] [2003] EWCA Civ 1151; [2003] 2 FCR 1.
[204] *Meadow v. General Medical Council* [2006] EWHC 146 at [10].
[205] Or sometimes when the patient is the perpetrator rather than the victim: *Tarasoff v. Regents of University of California* (1976) 551 P 2d 334 131 Cal R 14.

*H(M) v. Bederman*,[206] the defendant doctor was liable for failing to prevent the assault of a post-operative patient by a fellow patient sharing the same ward. The vulnerability of the claimant patient in terms of her lack of clothing and her inability to protect herself due to grogginess caused by the anaesthetic meant that the hospital owed a duty to protect her from predatory individuals, either by constant supervision or by a separation of male and female patients. There was also a suggestion that a fuller ward (safety in numbers) would have sufficed to have prevented the assault.

The duty to protect the patient may potentially be sufficiently extensive to encompass cases where the harm is inflicted in the victim's home. In *Brown v. University of Alberta Hospital*,[207] the court heard a claim for physical damage to a child and psychological damage to the mother caused by violent shaking of the child by its father. The hospital was liable in negligence for failing to identify the risk of physical abuse when the child had been presented to hospital with head injuries one week earlier.

**Schools and teachers** It seems self-evident that a school stands in a proximate relationship to its pupils by reason of the fact that children at school are the subject of a regime over which they have little control and given the quasi-parental obligations which schools owe towards children in their care.[208] The duty arising out of this proximity requires that reasonable care be taken as to the provision of education[209] and 'for the health and safety of the pupils in its charge'.[210] 'As with parents, the duty is high'.[211]

Whilst the duty upon schools and teachers to protect their pupils from predatory members of staff undoubtedly exists,[212] negligence litigation against schools has tended to focus on pupil-to-pupil bullying. A cluster of recent cases have paved the way for claims against schools for failing to protect pupils from the psychological, physical and financial consequences of bullying campaigns by fellow pupils or from other

---

[206] (1995) 27 CCLT (2d) 152.   [207] (1997) DLR (4th) 63.
[208] Sometimes referred to as *in loco parentis*, although see Hyams, *Law of Education* at 474, where it is argued that this concept has been displaced by ss. 2(9) and 3(5) of the Children Act 1989.
[209] *Gower v. London Borough of Bromley* [1999] ELR 356.
[210] *Van Oppen v. Clerk to the Bedford Charity Trustees* [1990] 1 WLR 235, *per* Balcombe LJ at 250.
[211] *Scott v. Lothian Regional Council* 1999 Rep LR 15.
[212] *A v. Hoare* [2006] EWCA Civ 395 at [83].

forms of abuse. Not only do these cases confirm the viability of claims for psychiatric harm inflicted through the medium of bullying *per se*, they also demonstrate the further growth of litigation for psychiatric harm in the sector of education.

The House of Lords' decision in the dyslexia claims in *Phelps v. Hillingdon LBC*[213] was instrumental in this area by confirming that teachers and schools could be in liable in negligence, not only to pupils with special needs, but to any of their pupils.[214] Furthermore, the Court of Appeal ruling in *Bradford-Smart v. West Sussex CC*,[215] establishes that the proximity that exists between school and pupil gives rise not only to obligations to avoid the direct infliction of harm, but the duty to take reasonable steps to safeguard children from the harmful conduct of their other charges.[216]

## Liability for bullying beyond school premises

If a school can in principle be liable for pupil-to-pupil bullying, what if the bullying should arise outside the school's gates or outside school hours? Should the school have any legal responsibility for the harm that flows from bullying and harassment off school premises? In *Bradford Smart v. West Sussex CC*,[217] the claimant allegedly suffered psychiatric injury due to bullying by pupils at the defendant's school. As much of the conduct complained of took place on the claimant's journey to and from school, the High Court took the view that justice, fairness and reasonableness required that the duty of care should not extend beyond the school gate: 'If the school chooses as a matter of judgment to be proactive *then that is a matter of discretion not obligation*.'[218] The Court of Appeal reversed these findings, saying that although 'the school cannot owe a general duty to its pupils, or anyone else, to police their activities once they have left its charge', nevertheless, there could be circumstances where a failure to exercise powers of discipline against pupils for violent conduct outside school premises could constitute a

---

[213] [2001] 2 AC 619; [2000] 3 WLR 776.
[214] [2001] 2 AC 619, *per* Lord Nicholls at 667. See also L. Berman and J. Rabinowicz, 'Bullying in School Claims'. [2001] JIPL 247. The content of the duty in relation to pupils with special needs is likely however to be higher. Cf. *Nwabudike v. Southwark LBC* [1997] ELR 35 and *J v. Lincolnshire CC* [2000] ELR 245.
[215] [2002] 1 FCR 425.
[216] *Bradford Smart v. West Sussex County Council* [2002] 1 FCR 425.
[217] *Ibid.*   [218] Emphasis added. *Per* Garland J [2001] ELR 138.

breach of the school's duty of care to the victim pupil.[219] Clearly, the duty extending beyond the school premises could be triggered by school trips, exchanges and school organised extra-curricular activities, but the court indicated that the duty could also potentially extend beyond school hours,[220] beyond the spatial boundaries of school buildings and beyond school-related activities.

The limits of the duty of care as it relates to bullying are not clearly defined. If the duty can extend beyond the perimeter of the school fence, the further question arises of whether schools could be liable for bullying perpetrated on a school bus provided by the school[221] or for failing to identify the fact that a child is being abused by non-pupils (e.g. siblings in the family home). A court wishing to limit the scope of the duty to curtail bullying, or its effects, would likely refer to the oft-repeated statement made by Balcombe LJ in *Van Oppen v. Clerk to the Bedford Charity Trustees*[222] that '... it would be neither just nor reasonable to impose upon the school a greater duty than that which rests on a parent'. Similarly, it might be argued that the school should not assume the responsibility of sole guardians and should expect that parents will also exercise reasonable care in the protection of their child.[223]

### Standard of care: the professional parent?

In a bullying claim, the claimant must first of all have been a reasonably foreseeable victim of bullying. For the foreseeability of harm to be satisfied, it is likely that the child or parents would need to have actively confided in the teachers, or at least that the claimant could show that a sudden decline in their academic performance or manner should have been observed by responsible members of the teaching profession.

---

[219] Per Judge LJ, relying on the authority of *R v. London Borough of Newham, ex parte X* [1995] ELR 303 at 306 which confirms that disciplinary powers can extend to violence outside school premises. Cf. the decision in *Good v. Inner London Education Authority* (1980) 10 Fam Law 213, where it was held that the standard of reasonable care does not require supervision from the classroom to the place where pupils were picked up by their parents at the end of the school day. See also *Wilson v. Governors of Sacred Heart Roman Catholic School* [1998] ELR 637, CA.

[220] See e.g. the Australian case of *Geyer v. Downs* (1977) 138 CLR 91 – duty extended to injuries on school grounds before teachers started work if pupils allowed on the premises.

[221] A. Ruff, *Education Law: Text, Cases and Materials* (Butterworths, 2002) at 271.

[222] [1990] 1 WLR 235, per Balcombe LJ at 261.

[223] As in the context of occupier's liability in *Phipps v. Rochester Corporation* [1955] 1 QB 450 at 473.

Witnessing a single incident of bullying may not suffice as violence is likely to be regarded as a normal part of school life.[224]

Just as the scope of the duty has been measured by what could be expected of a reasonable parent, so the standard applicable has traditionally been regarded as akin to that of a parent.[225] In *Nicholson v. Westmorland CC*,[226] the teacher's standard of care was articulated as 'the reasonable careful parent looking after a family as large as twenty'. This formulation may need revising in light of current class sizes. The difficulties of applying a standard of reasonable parenting to a school environment were noted in the Canadian case of *Myers v. Peel*:

> The standard of care to be exercised by school authorities in providing for the supervision and protection of students for who they are responsible is that of the careful or prudent parent ... It has, no doubt, become somewhat qualified in modern times because of the greater variety of activities conducted in schools, with probably larger groups of students using more complicated and more dangerous equipment than formerly ... It is not, however, a standard which can be applied in the same manner and to the same extent in every case. Its application will vary from case to case and will depend upon the number of students being supervised at any one time, [and] the nature of the exercise or activity in progress.[227]

It is perhaps because of the modern context of schooling, with its increased numbers and heightened risks, that formulation of the standard has shifted from one of the reasonable parent to that of the reasonable professional.[228] The standard of care to be exercised by schools in the protection of pupils appears to be that of the *Bolam* standard (i.e. that the defendant is not negligent if a 'responsible body of professional opinion' supported her conduct).[229] Of course, the modern construction of *Bolam* means that if the court regards the opinion expressed

---

[224] *H v. Isle of Wight* (2001) WL 825780.
[225] Per Lord Reid in *Carmarthenshire County Council v. Lewis* [1955] AC 549 at 566.
[226] (1962) *The Times*, 25 October.
[227] *Myers v. Peel (County) Board of Education* (1981) 123 DLR (3d) 1 SCC at 10. See also *Geyer v. Downs* (1977) 138 CLR 91 at 102, where the Australian court rejected the reasonable parent standard because it was unrealistic to apply it to the headmaster with 400 pupils or a master with a class of 30.
[228] See Lord Nicholls in *Phelps v. Hillingdon LBC* [2001] 2 AC 619 at 666.
[229] Per Auld LJ in *Gower v. London Borough of Bromley* [1999] ELR 356 at 359 and Lord Nicholls in *Phelps* [2001] 2 AC 619 at 667, where he speaks of teachers as 'professionals'. See also *Scott v. Lothian Regional Council* (1999) Rep LR 15, where the court said that liability required that the teacher concerned must have been guilty of 'such failure as no teacher of ordinary skill would be guilty of if acting with ordinary care'.

by the defendant's experts as 'not capable of withstanding logical analysis' then it may reject such evidence.[230]

As to the content of a school's legal obligation to safeguard against bullying, the Court of Appeal in *Bradford Smart*[231] stated that the problem of bullying was sufficiently well known for it to be reasonable to expect schools to have policies and practices to address the problem. Presumably, failure to implement a bullying policy would be influential in convincing a court that the school had not addressed the issue.[232] It is also likely that courts will in future be referred to the requirements of the School Standards Framework Act 1998, which obliges headteachers to implement measures to prevent bullying.[233] Such measures are to be published and disseminated to pupils, parents and employees of the school.[234] Beyond the implementation of a bullying policy, the Court of Appeal in *Bradford-Smart* did not express any practical steps to be taken to fulfil the requirement of reasonable care. It should be noted, however, that guidance to schools explicitly states that 'strong sanctions such as exclusion may be necessary in cases of severe and persistent bullying'.[235] Thus, it is possible that in some cases the standard of care required to protect the victim might require expulsion of the bully. Furniss also suggests that there should be resort to police involvement in serious cases as a last resort.[236]

The judgment in *Bradford Smart* does, however, expressly recognise that the duty to intervene to safeguard from bullying is problematic and will likely involve the courts providing a degree of latitude. It has to be recognised, for example, that the duty to minimise bullying may conflict with duties to other children (presumably in terms of supervisory manpower and resources). The duty will also be affected by the difficulties of deciding to intervene where parents or police had not done so, and the further risk of intervening and thereby making the victim's predicament worse or accelerating the miscreant's behaviour. From the foregoing it

---

[230] *Bolitho v. City and Hackney HA* [1997] 4 All ER 771.   [231] [2002] 1 FCR 425.
[232] This is despite the fact that a bullying report has concluded that bullying policies are ineffective: A. Katz, A. Buchanan and V. Bream, *Bullying in Britain: Testimonies from Teenagers* (Young Voice, 2001).
[233] S. 61(4)(b), which requires that measures be determined with a view to encouraging good behaviour and in particular preventing all forms of bullying. See also DfEE Circular 10/99 *Social Inclusion: Pupil Support*.
[234] S. 61(7).
[235] *Bullying: Don't Suffer in Silence – An Anti-Bullying Pack for Schools* (Circular 64/2000).
[236] C. Furniss, 'Bullying in Schools – It's Not a Crime Is It?' (2000) 12(1) *Education and the Law* 9.

would appear to be difficult to establish a breach of this newly recognised duty and that successful actions against schools for the psychiatric harm occasioned by bullying will be extremely rare. Add to these issues the fact that, like the victims of sexual abuse, the victim of bullying is often frightened into silence and is therefore unlikely to volunteer information leading to the discovery of the bullying or the identity of the bully. The secrecy which the victim often exhibits will generally exacerbate the difficulties of showing that it was reasonably foreseeable that this claimant would suffer recognised psychiatric harm.

In light of the above, it might easily have been predicted that the claim in *Bradford Smart* would fail (as it in fact did) for want of negligence. The claimant's teacher, in whom the claimant had confided, had closely monitored the victim by offering support and encouragement and allowing her to stay indoors during break time to avoid confrontation with the bullies. The court concluded that a reasonable body of professional opinion would have approved the teacher's actions. It is worthy of note that in the knowledge of a specific risk of bullying, the duty was regarded as having been fulfilled without any steps being taken to confront the bully or intervene directly. The court did not enquire as to whether other teachers or the head teacher had been notified about the bullying.

### Other non-perpetrators as defendants in negligence actions

**The police and correctional services** These parties may be named as defendants where the perpetrator of a physical or sexual assault ought to have been under the control or supervision of the relevant authorities. It is well established in English law that a defendant who negligently fails to keep a dangerous criminal confined can be liable for the damage caused by the criminal's escape, provided: the damage is foreseeable; there is sufficient proximity between the claimant suffering damage and the place from which the detainee escaped; and it is just, fair and reasonable to impose a duty of care on the defendant for the perpetrator's escape (a factor which may pose a particular obstacle in litigation against the police or correctional services). In *Home Office v. Dorset Yacht*, the Home Office was found to owe a duty of care to persons in the vicinity of a detainee's escape. In particular, its duty of care encompassed the damage caused to the claimant's yacht, as its location rendered it foreseeable that it would be used as a means of escape from the island on which the escapee had been detained.[237] Analogously, in

---

[237] [1970] AC 1004.

*S(J) v. Clement*,[238] the Canadian correctional services were found liable in negligence for failing to inform the police promptly of the escape of a convict with a history of taking out his frustrations by sexually assaulting women and who had been showing signs of agitation the night before the escape. The escapee, who had been missing for almost two hours before the police were notified, broke into the claimant's home and assaulted her. The court found that, had the police been notified sooner, a police presence in the area would likely have pre-empted the attack. As in *Home Office v. Dorset Yacht*,[239] the claimant's home was geographically proximate to the place of the convict's detention (two miles away).[240]

Where the perpetrator of the harm has not yet been brought into custody, the proximity requirement is more difficult to satisfy as the defendant cannot be regarded as having control over the offender and there is no place of escape from which to assess geographical proximity. The response of the House of Lords in *Hill v. Chief Constable for West Yorkshire* was to say that no proximity existed between the police and the victim of a serial killer on the loose, as the victim was not identifiable as especially at risk – she was just one of any number of women who might have become the murderer's next target. Nevertheless, proximity can be established where it can be demonstrated that the defendant ought to have realised that the claimant was especially at risk, perhaps because they have identified a pattern in the offender's attacks which indicate that the claimant is a likely victim. In *Jane Doe v. Metropolitan Toronto (Municipality) Commissioners of Police*,[241] the police were liable in negligence for a violent assault by the 'balcony rapist'. The defendants had failed to publicise the rapist's repeated attacks in the media or inform local residents that there was a predator in the area who used first floor balconies to access his victims. The court found that the police had used local women as bait, organising a covert police presence in the area where they thought he would strike next, but not warning the

---

[238] (1995) DLR (4th) 449.   [239] [1970] AC 1004.
[240] Cf. *Nelson v. Washington Parish* 805F. 2d 1236 (5th Cir. 1986) – no proximity between sheriff and claimant raped by escaped convict 13 days after escape and 750 miles away from place of detention. See also *K v. Secretary of Sate for the Home Department* [2002] EWCA Civ 775 – rape by illegal immigrant who had been released from prison after being convicted of serious sexual offences. C was unlikely to succeed in establishing liability on the part of the Home Office for releasing the offender from prison without immediately deporting him (*per* Smith J).
[241] (1998) 160 DLR (4th) 697.

public so that they could protect themselves.[242] This discernible pattern of offending means that *Jane Doe* is distinguishable from *Hill*, where no real pattern of attacks had emerged. Even if a pattern of offending had been identified in *Hill*, this may not in itself have been sufficient to convince the court that it was just, fair and reasonable to impose a duty of care. Their Lordships in *Hill* thought that, even if proximity were established, imposing a duty of care would be counter-productive in distracting manpower and resources from the police which could otherwise be utilised in protecting the public. Despite recent case law suggesting a more flexible application of the justice, fairness and reasonableness criterion to cases against public bodies (such as those mentioned above in the context of local authorities), it seems unlikely that the police will be held to owe a duty of care in respect of a criminal who has never been in custody. This is perhaps the real distinction between the finding of a duty of care in *Dorset Yacht* and the rejection of such a duty in *Hill*.

As mentioned above, the police are under a statutory duty to check the whereabouts of persons on the sex offender's register and it might be thought that a failure to do so may give rise to a cause of action if a registered sex offender were to move to a new address without notifying the police and committed sexual offences close to their new home.[243] Again, it is unlikely that a court would find sufficient proximity between the police and an individual who happened to fall prey to the offender in the vicinity of the offender's new address.

**Non-intervening parents or foster parents** There is nothing to prevent a claimant suing their parents, whether they are suing on an intentional wrong[244] or whether they are suing in negligence,[245] and arguments that it may not be just, fair and reasonable to do so do not seem to have featured in claims against parents. In *Seymour v. Williams*, the Court of Appeal allowed a claim in negligence to proceed against a mother who failed to prevent her husband's abuse of their daughter. This case illustrates what the court called the 'illogical and surprising' shape of the law after *Stubbings*, for the limitation provisions had halted the claimant's suit against her father in trespass, but the delayed

---

[242] The court found the reason for the police failing to warn the women at risk was fear of jeopardising their investigation and a mythical belief that women would become hysterical and falsify allegations.
[243] S. 1 of the Sex Offenders Act 1997, now Part II of the Sexual Offences Act 2003.
[244] *Stubbings v. Webb* [1993] AC 498 (HL); *Pereira v. Keleman* [1995] 1 FLR 428.
[245] *Young v. Rankin* 1934 SC 499 (negligent driving); *Seymour v. Williams* [1995] PIQR 470.

discovery provisions were available to save the claim in negligence against the non-perpetrator mother.[246] In *Pereira v. Keleman*,[247] the court had some sympathy with the non-offending mother who had married young, was entirely dominated by her husband and whose objections and protestations were unlikely to have had any effect. The court also accepted that she had been unable to bring herself to acknowledge the scale of the father's interference with his children. Notably this was not a case in which the mother's conduct was the subject of a civil action, therefore the court was not being invited to criticise her conduct.

The negligence action against non-intervening parents has been subject to more thorough analysis in the Canadian courts with mixed messages emanating from the case law as to the degree of protection to be afforded by the non-perpetrator parent. In *Y(AD) v. Y(MY)*, the claimant's father was found liable for 'knowingly preserving an abusive environment in which his son was ensnared' by failing to remove him from an abusive mother.[248] It is worthy of note that the non-intervening parent in *Y(AD)* had actual knowledge of the claimant's abuse, whereas the courts have been reluctant to make a finding of negligence on the grounds that the defendant was aware of certain facts which pointed to abuse in the family home, but did not make the connection. In *M(M) v. F(R)*,[249] for example, the claimant sued her foster mother in negligence and breach of fiduciary duty for failing to realise that her adult son had a sexual interest in children and had abused the claimant for nine years during the 1970s. It was argued that complaints by other parties regarding her son and the discovery of a vibrator in his room should have alerted her to the fact that something was wrong. The main issue in determining liability became whether the standard of care in such a case took account of the defendant's subjective characteristics, including her sexual naiveté and her unshakeable trust in her son. The majority of the court held that the question was whether a reasonable person, having the background and capacity for understanding of this defendant would have appreciated the risk. Although there is English authority to suggest that the objective standard of care is insisted upon despite the defendant's inexperience,[250] the court distinguished this authority as confined to Road Traffic Act cases where policy required a high standard be imposed so as to ensure that the injured party is compensated by the

---

[246] [1995] PIQR 470.   [247] [1995] 1 FLR 428.   [248] [1994] 5 WWR 623.
[249] [1999] 2 WWR 446.   [250] *Nettleship v. Weston* [1971] 2 QB 691.

defendant's insurance.[251] The lack of personal fault was an exception that did not apply in cases of defendants who were bystanders in the perpetration of criminal wrongs by a third party. A similarly subjective empathy is evidenced by the court's treatment of the bystander mother in *T(L) v. T(RW)*.[252] The claimant's mother had been aware of a single incident of inappropriate touching and, unaware that this was part of an ongoing state of affairs, she decided not to inform the police despite her friend's advice to do so. She did, however, believe (mistakenly) that her husband had no opportunity to continue the abuse, as the claimant's brothers had been instructed never to leave their sister alone with her father and her daughter had raised no more complaints. The court accepted that the defendant mother had not breached her duty to her daughter as she was 'of limited education and imagination' and felt powerless to stop any further abuse.

Again, it is doubtful whether such a result would obtain today in an English court. The responsibilities of a foster parent or natural parent may well be regarded as requiring a high standard of care, one which does not afford such reference to the naiveté of the bystander defendant. Moreover, it is unlikely that a contemporary court would accept alleged ignorance of the possibility of abuse, rather it would probably expect anyone with the care of children to be vigilant to such risks.

The subjective empathy displayed in the *M* and *T* cases is absent in the case of *J v. J et al.*,[253] where the non-offending spouse was found liable in negligence and breach of fiduciary duty and was made to pay both compensatory and punitive damages.[254] The court found that the defendant had come across her child and husband in the act of sexual intercourse on one occasion and that this, accompanied by other suggestive facts (including rough play and the presence of contraceptives under her daughter's bed), indicated actual knowledge that the incest was ongoing. Despite this knowledge, the victim's mother deflected the investigations of the Children's Aid Society and failed to report the father's conduct to the authorities. The finding of liability in this case has been criticised on the grounds that the standard of care expected of the mother failed to take into account the social, economic and political realities which combine to make

---

[251] At [22].   [252] (1997) 36 BCLR (3d) 165.   [253] (1993) 102 DLR (4th) 177.
[254] An award of exemplary damages in English courts is unlikely in a negligence case given the restrictions imposed by *Rookes v. Barnard* [1964] AC 1129.

many women married to abusive men powerless to change the fate of their family.[255] The court failed to inquire whether the defendant was psychologically robust enough to tackle her husband or what the financial and physical ramifications might be if she were to remove herself and her daughter from the family home.[256] Whilst there may be some merit in making such points to reaffirm the distinction in culpability between the perpetrator parent and the non-perpetrator parent, given that a zero-tolerance approach exists towards sexual abuse, it is no surprise that a finding of negligence should follow in a case where the non-perpetrator witnesses an act of intercourse but does nothing.

### 4. Breach of fiduciary duty

As *J v. J* indicates, the breach of fiduciary duty action has been applied also to the non-perpetrator defendant. If a breach of fiduciary duty action were to be available for non-economic harms (see above), this would also have implications for the non-intervening parent who failed to protect their child from abuse in the home. The finding of a breach of fiduciary duty by the bystander mother in *J v. J et al.*[257] was based upon the court's conclusion that she was at best guilty of 'wilful blindness' in failing to remove her child from the setting of the abuse and for deflecting the inquiry of the Children's Society when it was alerted to the possibility of abuse. The fiduciary duty owed by parents requires that they put the child's interests ahead of their own. Thus, a parent must choose destruction of the family unit over the risk that serious abuse will continue, as the risks of long-term psychological damage and perpetuation of the cycle of abuse are regarded as greater than the psychological injury caused by the breakdown of the family unit.[258]

The Canadian court in *M(FS) v. Clarke*[259] concluded that an action for breach of fiduciary duty existed between the abuse victim and the Anglican Church as employers of the abuser. The fiduciary duty arose because the victim 'absolutely trusted that he would be properly cared for', and the fact that the institution was an Anglican one 'lent a superior moral tone to the residence that created an additional level of

---

[255] Grace and Vella, 'Vesting Mothers With Power They Do Not Have'.
[256] Ibid., at 190.   [257] (1993) 102 DLR (4th) 177.
[258] *J v. J et al.* (1993) 102 DLR (4th) 177.   [259] [1999] 11 WWR 301 (BCSC).

assurance'.[260] Notably, the duty did not arise from the time the pupil victim enrolled at the defendant's school, but rather after the abuse was reported.[261] Similarly, the Alberta Court of Queens Bench has held that a fiduciary duty arose in relation to a school board, where the abuser was one of its teachers,[262] as there was a 'significant power imbalance between the student on the one hand and the combined forces of teachers, principals and administrators on the other, combined with the legislative authority of the School Board'.[263]

Once a relevant fiduciary duty is established there is the further issue of how breach of a fiduciary obligation is to be established. Whilst this is not likely to be an issue in cases against the perpetrator (breach would be assumed), establishing breach has proved far more problematic against non-perpetrator defendants. In *Clarke*, the finding of a fiduciary duty did not result in liability as there was no indication of negligence, and breach of fiduciary duty connoted at least offensive conduct.[264]

The Canadian authorities are at present unsettled on this point.[265] Although parents are expected to act in the best interests of their children, failure to do so does not of itself give rise to breach of a fiduciary duty. Some of the leading cases suggest that, in fact, something in the order of 'dishonesty', 'bad faith' or 'intentional disloyalty' is required,[266] whereas there are other judgments which indicate that a lack of bad faith or improper motive will not necessarily preclude a finding of breach of fiduciary duty.[267]

For details on the causation rules applicable to breach of fiduciary duty actions, see Chapter 4.

## 5. Non-delegable duties

A non-delegable duty of care involves strict liability upon the defendant – no personal fault is required. That is not to say that proof of injury itself

---

[260] At??  [261] Cf. *McDonald v. Mombourquette* (1996) 152 NSR (2d) 109.
[262] *H(SG) v. Gorsline* [2001] 6 WWR 132 (Alta QB). Cf. *J(A) v. D(W)* – social worker in breach of fiduciary duty for failing to protect a minor from abuse.
[263] [2001] 6 WWR 132 at [113]. Not disturbed on appeal *H(SG) v. Gorsline* [2004] 23 CCLT (3D) 65.
[264] [2001] 6 WWR 132 at [117].
[265] E. Grace and S. Vella, *Civil Liability for Sexual Abuse and Violence in Canada*. (Butterworths, 2000) at 67.
[266] *A(C) v. Critchley* (1998) 166 DLR (4th) 475.
[267] *B (KL) v. British Colombia* [2001] 197 DLR (4th) 431; *McInerney v. McDonald* [1992] 2 SCR 138.

establishes breach of the non-delegable duty. The defendant's responsibility is to ensure that reasonable care is exercised by those who are entrusted with the care of the matter concerned. An employment relationship does not have to be proved, therefore the duty can be implicated by the negligence of an independent contractor engaged by the defendant. Thus, although liability for a non-delegable duty requires fault on the part of someone, there is no need to prove an act within the course of employment and it is not necessary to point to exactly who failed to exercise reasonable care to establish breach of the defendant's non-delegable duty, merely that in the circumstances, a reasonable employer or school would have taken precautions against such harm.[268] Examples of non-delegable duties which might be relevant to a claim relating to sexual abuse include: school/pupil[269] and, tentatively, NHS trusts and patients.[270]

There are *obiter dicta* which suggest that the concept of non-delegable duty may apply even where the 'wrong' is a deliberate one;[271] therefore, the intentional assault of a child in the defendant's care by someone whom the defendant entrusted with the care of that child can amount to an actionable breach of the non-delegable duty. More attention has been afforded to the issue of whether the non-delegable duty can be breached by intentional wrongs in Australia than has been the case in England and Wales.[272] In Australia, school authorities owe a non-delegable duty to their pupils,[273] due to the immaturity and inexperience of their pupils and their need for protection. Such a duty includes taking reasonable care to provide suitable and safe premises and taking reasonable care to provide an adequate system to ensure that no child is exposed to unnecessary injury.[274] In *NSW v. Lepore* the High Court of Australia

---

[268] *Carmarthenshire CC v. Lewis* [1955] AC 549; *Watson v. Haines* (1987) Aust Tort Reps 80–094.

[269] *Lister v. Hesley Hall Ltd* [2002] 1 AC 215, per Lord Hobhouse and Lord Clyde; *Carmarthenshire CC v. Lewis* [1955] AC 549, referred to with approval in *A (A Child) v. Ministry of Defence, Guys and St Thomas' Hospital NHS Trust* [2003] EWHC 849; [2003] PIQR 33. Cf. *G(ED) v. Hammer* [2003] 11 WWR 244, the Schools Act did not place a non-delegable duty on the School Board for the safety of its pupils.

[270] *Cassidy v. Minister of Health* [1951] 2 KB 343.

[271] *Lister v. Hesley Hall Ltd* [2002] 1 AC 215, per Lord Hobhouse and *Morris v. Martin* [1966] 1 QB 716, per Denning LJ.

[272] See *New South Wales v. Lepore* (2003) ALR 412, where Gummow and Hayne JJ appear to say that non-delegable duties are breached only by negligence, but McHugh J regards intentional harms as also implicating non-delegable duties.

[273] *The Commonwealth v. Introvigne* (1982) 150 CLR 258.

[274] Per Murphy J in *The Commonwealth v. Introvigne* (1982) 150 CLR 258.

heard three cases relating to sexual abuse in school settings which were argued on the basis of the school authorities' non-delegable duty to safeguard children and additionally on the grounds of vicarious liability for the wrongs of their employees. The majority decided that the non-delegable duty analysis did not apply to cases involving intentional wrongs of third parties. To decide otherwise would be to encroach on the realms of vicarious liability which was far better suited to dealing with intentional wrongs.[275] The non-delegable duty of care related to the conduct of care, supervision and control of the children. To extend it any further would have no deterrent value and would interfere with the development of vicarious liability principles.[276] The appeal of these arguments is far from self-evident: why is deterrence important for the law relating to non-delegable duty, but not for vicarious liability? And why are the principles of vicarious liability to be developed at the expense of those relating to non-delegable duties? The answer seems to be, at least in part, the court's expressed wish to keep Australian law in line with that in England and Canada.

## 6. The tort of misfeasance

The tort of misfeasance in public office can be utilised where a public officer in the exercise of their official powers abuses those powers in bad faith. The claimant must have suffered some special damage over and above that suffered by other members of the public,[277] such special damage requiring proof of physical, psychiatric or economic harm.[278] It is not necessarily enough that the claimant's constitutional rights (e.g. to freedom from inhuman and degrading treatment under the Human Rights Act 1998) are affected by the alleged misfeasance. Lord Steyn in *Three Rivers DC v. Governors of Bank of England (No. 3)*[279] set out two forms of the tort of misfeasance:

1. The 'targeted malice' form – where the officer engages in misconduct which was intended to injure the claimant or a class of people of which the claimant was a member.
2. The 'subjective recklessness' form – where the officer carries out an act knowing that he has no power to do so *and* that the act will probably injure the claimant or a class of which the claimant is a

---

[275] McHugh J dissenting.   [276] Per Gummow and Hayne JJ.
[277] [2000] 3 All ER 1 (HL) per Lord Hobhouse at 45.
[278] *Watkins v Secretary of State for the Home Department* [2006] UKHL 17; [2006] 2 WLR 807.
[279] [2000] 3 All ER 1 (HL).

member. Lord Steyn was clear that for the second form of the misfeasance action only subjective recklessness would suffice. Thus the officer must have no honest belief in the lawfulness of the act and must be recklessly indifferent as to whether it will cause harm.

The tort fills the lacuna in the law due to the fact that no action in negligence arises for an act of maladministration[280] (although it should be clear from the above that the tort of misfeasance requires something beyond negligence in the line of bad faith or dishonesty) or can provide a useful remedy where a negligence claim may otherwise fail (e.g. due to a finding that no duty of care attaches to the exercise of discretion pertaining to policy matters). The tort can be committed by an individual public officer (for which the appropriate public body may be vicariously liable[281]) or by a public body.

### 7. Vicarious liability and childhood abuse

Vicarious liability is a principle by virtue of which the defendant is held liable in damages for the tort of another. This no-fault liability bears more than a passing resemblance to liability for breach of non-delegable duties, but unfortunately the law lacks clarity as to when vicarious liability is to be preferred over the non-delegable duty analysis and vice versa. The usual context in which vicarious liability is imposed is that of the employer being held vicariously liable for the tort of the employee. That is not to say that vicarious liability is confined to such relationships, although English law seems to be less willing to extend the application of vicarious liability than, say, Canada, which has extended vicarious liability principles to the relationship between the Roman Catholic Church and its priests.[282]

Establishing vicarious liability on the part an employer requires proof:

- that a tort was committed (e.g. trespass,[283] intentional interference with the person[284] or negligence,[285] but presumably not breach of a fiduciary duty as that does not qualify as a tort[286]);

---

[280] *Calveley v. Chief Constable of Merseyside Police* [1989] AC 1228.
[281] *Racz v. Home Office* [1994] 2 AC 45.
[282] *John Doe v. Bennett* [2004] SCC 17; *K. W. v. Pornbacher* (1997) 32 BCLR (3d) 360 SC.
[283] *Lister v. Hesley Hall Ltd* [2001] UKHL 22; [2002] 1 AC 215.
[284] *Janvier v. Sweeney* [1919] 2 KB 316 (award made against private detectives' employers).
[285] *Century Insurance v. Northern Ireland Road Transport Board* [1942] AC 509.
[286] *Credit Lyonnais Bank v. Export Credits Guarantee Department* [1999] 1 All ER 929 (HL).

- that the tort was committed by an employee of the defendant; and
- that it was committed within the course of employment.

### Establishing an employment relationship

In light of the above, the usual prerequisite to the operation of vicarious liability is that there is an employment relationship between the tortfeasor/wrongdoer and the defendant. There is currently no satisfactory universal test for establishing this, and what is worse, most of the tests proposed are derived from cases outside the law of torts, for example, employment law, social security law or the law of intellectual property. The statements or intentions of the parties themselves are a useful starting point in determining this issue, but will not be conclusive as the courts are alert to the possibility that employers have the upper hand in defining the relationship and will do so to suit themselves. Employers should not be able to sidestep their liabilities to their workers, or indeed to third parties, by describing their workers as independent contractors.[287] The defendant's 'control' over the work of the tortfeasor will be an essential element in an employment relationship, although the test of control has shifted from one of control of the manner in which the work is done[288] to one of control at a more abstract level, for example, control of the temporal or spatial features of the work task.[289] Mutuality of obligations must also be present, that is, the defendant must be obliged to provide work just as the worker is obliged to accept it.[290] In addition to the essential factors of control and mutuality, the court will generally apply what has become known as the 'entrepreneur test'. Here the courts make a qualitative decision as to whether the worker is an employee by assessing who takes the risks presented by the enterprise, and whether the worker has the opportunity to maximise their profit from the work task.[291]

---

[287] *Ferguson v. John Dawson & Partners (Contractors) Ltd* [1976] 1 WLR 1213; *Young & Woods Ltd v. West* [1980] IRLR 201 (CA).

[288] *Yewens v. Noakes* (1880) 6 QB 530.

[289] *Collins v. Hertfordshire CC* [1947] KB 598; *Walker v. Crystal Palace FC* [1910] 1 KB 87.

[290] *Carmichael v. National Power plc* [1999] 4 All ER 897; *Montgomery Johnson v. Underwood* (CA) [2001] IRLR 269. Although the inclusion of mutuality as a requirement and prerequisite to the imposition of vicarious liability has been criticised, see R. Kidner, 'Vicarious Liability: For Whom should the Employer be Liable?' [1995] 15 *Legal Studies* 47 at 47.

[291] *Market Investigations v. Minister of Social Security* [1969] 2 QB 173; *Ready Mixed Concrete v. Ministry of Pensions and National Insurance* [1968] 2 QB 497. See also *Ontario Ltd v. Sagaz Industries Canada Inc*, 2001 SCC 59.

It has recently been established that in an exceptional case dual vicarious liability might be imposed; that is, vicarious liability for a worker's torts may be shared by more than one employer.[292] For example, in the case of a nursery nurse who abuses children during a temporary placement, vicarious liability could potentially be imposed upon the nursery which employed her and the agency that supplied the nursery with the predatory worker. The sharing of liability in such cases is not to be determined solely by reference to the degree of control exercised by each employer but rather by whether it is 'just' in all the circumstances that both employers be vicariously liable.[293]

### Other relationships to which vicarious liability might apply

As mentioned above, relationships to which vicarious liability might apply have not been definitively determined, although few seem to exist in English law beyond the usual employment relationship. One exception to this is the fact that a statutory form of vicarious liability gives rise to liability of partnerships for the wrongs of partners where the wrongful act is in the 'ordinary course of the business of the firm'.[294] More important in the context of abuse claims is the rejection of the relationship between government and foster parents as one giving rise to vicarious liability on the grounds that the relationship is more akin to that of independent contractor than employer/employee.[295]

This can be contrasted with the position in New Zealand, where the Crown can be vicariously liable for the negligence of foster parents as the latter act in the capacity of a unique form of agents as opposed to independent contractors (there being no formal contract and neither party undertaking a business venture for profit).[296] Additionally, the ongoing duty the Crown owed to children in foster care meant that they could be regarded as principals in this arrangement (the relevant statute providing that the Crown could cancel foster care arrangements, foster parents were to abide by the Crown's manual of fostering practices and the Crown had the right to inspect the foster home at any time). Tipping

---

[292] *Viasystems (Tyneside) Ltd v. Thermal Transfer (Northern) Ltd* [2005] EWCA Civ 1151; [2006] 2 WLR 428, approved in *Hawley v. Luminar Leisure Ltd* [2006] EWCA Civ 18; (2006) 150 SJLB.
[293] *Hawley v. Luminar Leisure Ltd* [2006] EWCA Civ 18; (2006) 150 SJLB.
[294] Partnership Act 1890, s. 10.
[295] *S v. Walsall MBC* [1995] 3 All ER 294; *B (KL) v. British Colombia* [2003] 11 WWR 203.
[296] *S v. Attorney General* [2003] 3 NZLR 450.

J added that refusing to impose vicarious liability on the defendants for the acts of foster parents would produce an undesirable and potentially unjust anomaly between the remedies available to children in institutional care and those in foster care.[297]

In Australia[298] and Canada[299] the courts also recognise vicarious liability as broader in application than the traditional employment relationship. In Canada the courts ask whether the relationship between defendant and tortfeasor is sufficiently close to make the imposition of vicarious liability appropriate and look for something which can be described as akin to an employment relationship[300] or, alternatively, can it be said as a matter of policy and analogy that vicarious liability should be found to exist.[301] Under this expansive version of vicarious liability the secular arm of the church has been found vicariously liable for the conduct of its priests. In *John Doe v. Bennett*,[302] a Roman Catholic Priest had abused a number of young boys in his geographically remote parishes. The claimants brought actions against, *inter alia*, the perpetrator, two bishops under whose supervision the priest was employed, the Roman Catholic Church and the Roman Catholic Episcopal corporation. The Supreme Court found the Roman Catholic Episcopal Corporation to be vicariously liable, given the fact that the relationship between bishop and priest is akin to an employment relationship; the priest takes a vow of obedience to the bishop and the bishop exercises significant control over the priest including the power to remove and discipline.[303]

It is unlikely that the vicarious liability principle will be extended in English law to other relationships at the present time given that there is a general resistance in other areas to the imposition of strict liability in tort.

---

[297] At [114].
[298] *Hollis v. Vabu Pty Ltd* (2001) 207 CLR 21, which demonstrates that the test for contract of employment in Australia is open-ended and indicates that the answer to the question of for whom is the defendant vicariously liable may differ depending on the context in which it is asked.
[299] The categories of relationship which attract vicarious liability are 'neither exhaustively defined nor closed'. *671122 Ontario Ltd v. Sagaz Industries Canada Inc* [2001] 2 SCR 983 at [25].
[300] *B(KL) v. British Colombia* [2003] 11 WWR 203 at [197], *per* MacLachlin CJC.
[301] *S v. Attorney General* [2003] 3 NZLR 450 at [102]. [302] [2004] SCC 17.
[303] See also *KW v. Pornbacher* (1997) 32 BCLR (3d) 360 SC and *D(P) v. Allen* (2004) 132 ACWS (3d) 1098 (vicarious liability conceded by defendant Diocese). Cf. *McDonald v. Mombourquette* (1996) 152 NSR (2d) 109, where no vicarious liability was found because the priest acted contrary to his religious tenets (although this was decided prior to *Curry* and *Griffiths*).

## Sexual abuse and the course of employment

Whilst such acts of sexual deviance have nothing to do with the employer's business, it is clear that the particular vulnerability of children gives rise to a special danger of abuse. And although sexual misconduct of this kind might be regarded as 'extreme', in the sense of being abhorrent, it can sadly no longer be regarded as extreme and extraordinary to the extent of being unforeseeable in the context of organisations involved in the care of children.[304] Indeed, a recent report on child abuse in religious institutions has concluded that the church has encouraged sexual frustration and shame, thereby contributing to the creation of tendencies towards paedophilia amongst its brethren, and that, moreover, the culture of secrecy which demands forgiveness from the victim has in part perpetuated the molestation of children.[305] Given, therefore, that certain institutional activities can be said to give rise to a risk of abuse, the law may wish to establish some responsibility on employers for minimising the risk of and dealing with the consequences of abuse, but falling short of liability in negligence.

The concept of the 'course of employment' acts as a control device limiting the liability of employers and is therefore the perfect conduit for effecting shifts in liability to reflect judicial thinking on the moral responsibilities of the modern employer. Recent developments in English law suggest a widening of the course of employment, particularly in the context of acts of assault and battery occasioned by an errant employee.[306] The means of establishing whether deliberate or intentional wrongs fall within the course of employment appears to have shifted from an application of Salmond's test which states that 'an act is within the course of employment if it is either: a wrongful act authorised by the employer; or a wrongful and unauthorised mode of doing some act authorised by the employer'[307] (originally appearing in a student text of 1907) to a test which emphasises a different aspect of Salmond's classic statement on the course of employment, that is, whether the

---

[304] Hall has argued that these institutional settings act as a 'crucible' for rogue paedophiles (M. Hall, 'After Waterhouse: Vicarious Liability and the Tort of Institutional Abuse' (2000) 22(2) *Journal of Social Welfare and Family Law* 159).

[305] *Time for Action: Report of Sexual Abuse Issues* (Churches Together in Britain and Ireland, 2002).

[306] See D. Bennett, 'Employers' Vicarious Liability: Assaults at Work and Sexual Abuse Claims' [2002] *Journal of Personal Injury Law* 359.

[307] J. Salmond, *Salmond on Torts* (1st edn, 1907), approved in *Canadian Pacific Railway v. Lockhart* [1942] AC 591.

wrong bears a 'sufficiently close connection' with the wrongdoer's employment.[308] Although the connectedness test was apparently favoured over Salmond's test on the grounds of the vagueness of the latter, Lord Nicholls has commented that the test of 'connection' offers no guidance as to the type or degree of connection required and that such imprecision is inevitable given the range of circumstances in which vicarious liability applies.[309]

On the issue of whether child abuse could ever be regarded as 'within the course of employment', it must therefore be demonstrated that the connection between the abuse and the work task is so close that the abuse can 'fairly and properly' be regarded as done in the course of employment,[310] supported by reasoning from analogy with relevant cases. A sufficient 'connection' is not satisfied merely by showing that employment of the wrongdoer in this post provided the opportunity for the tort to be committed.[311] The English courts had provided no definitive answer to whether child abuse, particularly sexual abuse, could fall within the course of employment until 1999. Prior to this date, any attempt to predict the outcome of such a case would likely have been founded on analogy and extrapolation from cases dealing with whether physical violence by employees falls within the course of employment. Such analysis would likely have concluded that sexual assault would fall outside the 'course of employment', for in cases of assault and battery the English courts had previously held employers vicariously liable *only* where the act complained of could be regarded as protecting the employer's interests.[312] Whilst the courts have indicated that this notion of protecting the employer's interests could be applied liberally so as to extend beyond the *de facto* protection of the employer's property from risks of damage to exacting physical violence as a means of retribution for damage done to the property,[313] depraved acts of sexual exploitation

---

[308] *Lister v. Hesley Hall Ltd* [2001] UKHL 22; [2002] 1 AC 215, confirmed in *Dubai Aluminium Co Ltd v. Salaam and others* [2002] UKHL 48; [2003] 1 All ER 97 and *Bernard v. Attorney General of Jamaica* [2004] UKPC 47; [2005] IRLR 398 as the test for intentional torts.
[309] *Dubai Aluminium Co Ltd v. Salaam and others* [2002] UKHL 48; [2003] 1 All ER 97 at [25].
[310] *Ibid.*, at [23].
[311] *Lister v. Hesley Hall Ltd* [2001] UKHL 22; [2002] 1 AC 215, *per* Lord Steyn at 235. Note the impossibility of distinguishing between 'connection' and 'opportunity' was precisely the criticisms levied at the connectedness test in *New South Wales v. Lepore* (2003) ALR 412.
[312] *Poland v. Parr and Sons* [1927] 1 KB 236. See also *Deatons Pty Ltd v. Flew* [1949] 79 CLR 370.
[313] *Vasey v. Surrey Free Inns* [1996] PIQR 373 and *Mattis v. Pollock* [2003] IRLR 603.

could surely never be regarded as fulfilling some loyalty to an employer.[314]

*English law and the 'connectedness test':* Lister v. Hesley Hall   The sentiment of imposing a degree of legal responsibility on employers for minimising the risk of child abuse in institutions such as schools and care homes appears to be at the heart of the ruling in *Lister v. Hesley Hall Ltd*,[315] the second English case to deal with abuse and vicarious liability. The House of Lords in *Lister* heard allegations that the claimant had suffered psychiatric harm as a result of systematic sexual abuse at a school for maladjusted boys run by the defendant. The perpetrator of these assaults was employed as the warden of the school with responsibilities for discipline, supervision and day-to-day tasks such as putting the boys to bed and getting them up for school. Particular note was taken of the fact that the warden created the opportunities for abuse by implementing what appeared to be a very relaxed regime of discipline with the use of gifts and undeserved leniency. The House of Lords unanimously found the abuse to be within the course of employment, although their Lordships did not speak with one voice as to the route to this finding. There were broadly two *ratios*; the sufficient connection analysis and the non-delegable duty analysis.

*Ratio 1: 'sufficient connection'*   Lord Steyn and Lord Clyde took the view that the abuse in *Lister* was so closely connected to the 'nature of the employment' that it was 'just, fair and reasonable' to hold the employers liable. Lord Hobhouse thought that vicarious liability would also attach if the warden had not been the perpetrator but had discovered the fact of

---

[314] The blanket rejection of sexual assaults as constituting part of the course of employment for the purposes of vicarious liability was endorsed in the now overruled English case of *ST v. North Yorkshire County Council* [1999] IRLR 98. Applying Salmond's test, acts of sexual assault could not be regarded as an unauthorised mode of an authorised task, but were rather a negation of the duty of the council to look after the children for whom it was responsible. This restrictive approach is illustrated by the case of *NX v. Carbrini Medical Center* (2002) NY Int 15, where a hospital was held to be free of vicarious liability in respect of the sexual assault of one of its patients recovering from anaesthetic by one of its doctors. The reasons given were that the torts were committed for the doctor's own personal motives and did nothing to further the employer's business or interests. Cf. the contrasting US cases of: *Primeaux v. United States* 102 F 3d 1458 (1996); *Mary M v. Los Angeles* 54 Cal 3d 202 (1991); *Samuels v. Southern Baptist Hospital* 594 So 2d 571 (1992).
[315] [2001] UKHL 22; [2001] 2 All ER 769.

abuse by fellow employee and had negligently failed to report it. Again, sufficient connection between the tort and the employment would have existed. The defendants would not, however, have been vicariously liable for abuse by a groundsman whose duties had nothing to do with the tort. In addition to the language of 'sufficient connection', later judgments have extracted an alternative expression of the test from *Lister* as being that the 'employer ought to be liable for a tort which can fairly be regarded as a reasonably incidental risk to the type of business he carried on'.[316]

The introduction of the terminology of 'just, fair and reasonable' into vicarious liability is worthy of comment. Given that the usual home of this terminology is the duty of care, their Lordships could be regarded as having confused the streams of primary and secondary liability.[317] However, by transplanting this language from duty of care to rules on the 'course of employment', the Law Lords have introduced a theme of moral responsibility into vicarious liability principles, as the determination of what falls within the course of employment will more likely be influenced by the court's view as to whether the employer *ought* to be liable.

Ratio 2: *non-delegable duty* In an alternative *ratio*, Lord Diplock and Lord Hobhouse appeared to be particularly influenced by argument from the claimants' counsel that a finding against vicarious liability would create the impression that the law was granting greater protection to personal possessions than to children. This argument was based on the case of *Morris v. CW Martin*,[318] in which an employer was held liable for the theft of a client's mink stole by an employee who had been entrusted with cleaning the mink. In *Morris*, liability had been imposed on the grounds that the employers had a non-delegable duty of care to safeguard their client's property. Lord Diplock and Lord Hobhouse in *Lister* took the view that as the claimants were entrusted to the care of the defendant's home, the employer should be liable for harms occasioned to the children by those allocated with responsibility for their care.

---

[316] *Bernard v. Attorney General of Jamaica* [2004] UKPC 47; [2005] IRLR 398 and *Majrowski v. Guy's and St Thomas's NHS Trust* [2005] EWCA Civ 251; [2005] QB 848 (not disapproved in the House of Lords judgment: [2006] UKHL 34, [2006] 4 All ER 395).
[317] See also the similar reference to justice, fairness and reasonableness in the context of vicarious liability in *Phelps v. Hillingdon LBC* [2001] 2 AC 619, *per* Lord Slynn at 654.
[318] [1966] 1 QB 716.

Whichever *ratio* is adopted, the *Lister* judgments represent a significant broadening of the employer's legal responsibilities for sexual abuse, and possibly any form of deliberately inflicted child abuse. This sudden extension of employer liability prompted the House of Commons Home Affairs Committee to suggest that the law was encouraging unscrupulous individuals to make false allegations against employers and that *Lister* should be overturned by legislation, or, that failing a retraction of *Lister*, legal aid ought to be withdrawn from abuse claims.[319]

*Other jurisdictions and the connection test*   The connection test appears in the case law of Australia and owes much to Canadian authorities which predate *Lister*. It is worth examining these jurisdictions with a view to gleaning from the case law the factors which might be drawn upon when applying the sufficient connection test in future cases in the courts of England and Wales. These factors have so far included:

- whether the employment has anything to do with the care of or responsibility for children;[320]
- the time and place of the abuse (i.e. during work hours, on work premises or outside of these);[321]
- whether the employee or employer acted *in loco parentis* to the child;[322]
- the degree to which the job for which the perpetrator was employed provided the opportunity to commit the abuse;[323]
- whether chastisement, confrontation or intimacy (physical or psychological) with children was inherent to the work task;[324]
- the vulnerability of the child in relation to the employee's work role (e.g. age, disability);[325]
- the degree of isolation which the child experiences from their home/parents;
- whether the care offered by the defendant institution is residential or non-residential;[326]

---

[319] *The Conduct of Investigations into Past Cases of Abuse in Children's Homes.*
[320] *G(ED) v. Hammer* [2001] 5 WWR 80.   [321] *Jacobi v. Griffiths* [1999] 2 SCR 570.
[322] *Jacobi v. Griffiths* [1999] 2 SCR 570; *Bazley v. Curry* (1997) 30 BCLR (3d) 1.
[323] *Bazley v. Curry* (1997) 30 BCLR (3d) 1.
[324] *Bazley v. Curry* (1997) 30 BCLR (3d) 1; *John Doe v. Bennett* [2004] SCC 17; *VP v. Attorney General and William Starr* (1999) SKQB 180; *Lister v. Hesley Hall Ltd* [2002] 1 AC 215; *M(FS) v. Clarke* [1999] 11 WWR 301 (BCSC).
[325] *New South Wales v. Lepore* (2003) ALR 412.
[326] *H(SG) v. Gorsline* [2004] 23 CCLT (3D) 65. Cf. *K v. Gilmartin's Executrix* 2004 SLT 1014 and *L (H) v. Canada (Attorney General)* [2003] 5 WWR 421.

- ratio of adults to children in the defendant's workplace;[327]
- whether the employer's organisation is an ordinary business enterprise or a non-profit institution[328] (the latter may mean a stronger connection is insisted upon).

The context in which these factors have arisen is discussed in the sections below.

*Canadian law and the increased risk test:* Bazley v. Curry   The decision in *Lister* bears some parallels with the earlier judgment in *Bazley v. Curry*[329] from the Supreme Court of Canada.[330] The defendant in *Bazley* was a non-profit organisation which managed a residential care facility of last resort and acted as the parent of the children in its charge. As to whether the defendant should be liable for the conduct of their employee (a paedophile eventually convicted of 19 child abuse offences) the Supreme Court decided unanimously in favour of the claimant. McLachlin J designed a test for such cases incorporating, but not determined by, Salmond's test for the course of employment. First, the court should assess whether precedent unambiguously determined that the tort was within or outside the course of employment. Secondly, the court should decide whether liability *ought to be imposed* on the employer given the policy rationales underlying the law of vicarious liability. As there were no decisive precedents on the issue of sexual abuse, the outcome of this particular case depended upon the court's application of the second stage. McLachlin J took the view that the primary policy underlying vicarious liability was one of:

> ... providing a just and practical remedy to victims. Those who introduce the risk have a duty to those who may be harmed. This policy of effective compensation, though, must be fair in imposing liability on the employer. This fairness is present, given that the employer puts the risk into the community. The employer should therefore bear the loss.[331]

Thus, if the employer's business 'materially enhanced the risk' of the particular harm being inflicted by employees (in the sense of

---

[327] *New South Wales v. Lepore* (2003) ALR 412.   [328] *John Doe v. Bennett* [2004] SCC 17.
[329] (1997) 30 BCLR 3d 1.
[330] On vicarious liability in Canada as it relates to sexual abuse, see Grace and Vella, *Civil Liability for Sexual Abuse and Violence in Canada*, Chapter 3.
[331] (1997) 30 BCLR (3d) 1.

significantly contributing to it), vicarious liability ought to be imposed.[332] The old approach of disguising policy decisions with opaque discussion of the 'course of conduct' and 'scope of employment' was henceforth to be abandoned.

The 'increased risk' test involves approaching vicarious liability by assessing explicitly whether legal responsibility *ought* to rest with the defendants because of the causal link between the broad risks associated with the defendant's enterprise and the abuse. As to the assessment of the risk created by the employer's activities, a number of factors were to be weighed, including: the opportunity afforded to the employee to abuse their power; the extent to which the wrong related to confrontation or intimacy inherent in the employee's work; and the vulnerability of the potential victims in relation to the employee's role. This analysis led to a finding of vicarious liability on the facts given that the defendant's employees were encouraged to act as substitute parents for the children in their care, and were given duties including general supervision, and more intimate tasks such as bathing the children and tucking them in at night.

There is more than a superficial similarity between the approaches of *Lister* and *Bazley*: the test of connectedness in *Lister*, although probably influenced by the judgment of *Bazley v. Curry*, was in fact derived from the Salmond test. The Salmond test states that unauthorised acts can still fall within the course of employment 'provided they are *so connected* with acts which [the employer] has authorised' (emphasis added) that they be regarded as unauthorised modes of doing them. However, the test of close connection in *Lister* lacks explicit reference to the risk rationale enunciated in *Bazley* and has been criticised for failing to articulate deterrence-based objectives.[333]

*Australian law and the connectedness test:* NSW v. Lepore    In *New South Wales v. Lepore*[334] (the case concerning three joined appeals relating to sexual abuse in school environments discussed above), the High Court of Australia was asked to decide whether sexual assault of a pupil in the guise of the teacher's disciplinary powers could be within the course of

---

[332] (1997) 30 BCLR (3d) 1, *per* MacLachlin J at [57].
[333] C. Brennan, 'Third Party Liability for Child Abuse: Unanswered Questions.' (2003) 15 *Journal of Social Welfare and Family Law* 23 at 25.
[334] (2003) ALR 412. The *Lepore* case is in fact three joined appeals from *Lepore v. NSW; Samin v. State of Queensland* and *Rich v. State of Queensland*.

employment. The majority adopted versions of the connectedness test developed in *Lister*,[335] but the court was divided on whether sexual harms could ever be within the course of employment. A narrow majority thought that such conduct could potentially fall within the course of employment and ordered a retrial on the basis of vicarious liability. According to Gleeson CJ, the risk of sexual abuse was not to be regarded as *ordinarily* incidental to the conduct of most schools or as within the course of a teacher's employment.[336] There were, however, exceptions where the relationship between child and employee involved such power and intimacy that abuse could be regarded as sufficiently connected to the employee's duties for vicarious liability to operate. Relevant considerations used to distinguish a teacher being given the *opportunity* for abuse and a teacher's duties being *connected* with the abuse included:

- the age of the children;
- the number of adults responsible for the children;
- the tasks involved;
- the particular vulnerability on the part of the children; and
- the circumstances of the misconduct.

For example, abuse which could be said to result from excessive or inappropriate chastisement of children would be within the course of employment,[337] even if its inappropriateness stemmed from the employee's desire for sexual gratification. The context of chastisement provided sufficient connection between the abuse and the employment. This can be contrasted with the judgment of Kirby J, who found the potential 'connection' to be made out by the immature and vulnerable state of the pupils, meaning that all teaching enterprises carried an inherent risk of abuse.[338] Gummow and Hayne JJ dissented, finding that there was no vicarious liability unless the wrong was done in the pursuit of the employer's interests or was done with ostensible authority.[339] Gaudron J also adopted the 'ostensible authority'

---

[335] See also *Starks v. RSM Security* (2004) NSWCA 351, where the close connection test appears to have been used to find that a security guard who head-butted a patron of the hotel he was employed at was within the course of employment as the battery was closely and directly connected with acts authorised by his employer.
[336] (2003) ALR 412.   [337] (2003) ALR 412 at [78].   [338] (2003) ALR 412.
[339] Criticised by K. Adams, 'The High Court on Vicarious Liability' (2003) 16 *Australian Journal of Labour Law* 10 for allowing abhorrence of child abuse to drive the way in which the test for vicarious liability was applied (i.e. how could such heinous acts be described as within the course of employment?).

reasoning, but found that vicarious liability probably was established. Two of the joined cases were dismissed as the majority found no vicarious liability for the intentional wrongs of the teachers and the third was sent back to the lower courts for a new trial. The lack of agreement between the judges of the High Court of Australia as to either principle or outcome in *Lepore* does little to quell further speculative litigation, something which it is generally hoped that the higher courts will seek to prevent.

Although *Lepore* signifies a broad acceptance of the connectedness test as part of Australian law, the judgments also include some strident criticism of it. Callinan J rejected the connectedness test outright, implying that its application depended too heavily on how the court chose to define the work allocated to the employee.[340] Gummow and Hayne JJ were also critical of the connection test, preferring to say that vicarious liability would not apply on the facts because the predatory nature of the teacher's act was contrary to a core element of the employment contract. The teacher must have actual or ostensible authority to do the act complained of before the employer would be vicariously liable. They also rejected the increased risk test on the grounds that it obscured the distinction between primary and secondary liability.[341]

*The spectrum of risk*   In the case of both the connection test and the increased risk test, determinations of whether abuse is within or without the course of employment will be a question of fact in each case. It will depend upon where on the spectrum of risk the particular case lies, and as case law accumulates it may be possible to extract some general principles. The cases reviewed below are largely from the Canadian courts, as it is this jurisdiction which has addressed various points on the spectrum of risk in the most detail.

*Bazley* was followed by *Jacobi v. Griffiths*, another Supreme Court of Canada case, which culminated in a finding that the relevant acts of abuse fell outside the course of employment.[342] The errant employee in *Jacobi* was employed as a Program Director of a children's club which organised after-school activities. Although his role required him to develop a 'rapport' with the children at the club, the Supreme Court of Canada decided against vicarious liability. *Jacobi* was regarded as

---

[340] P. Vines, 'Schools' Responsibility for Teachers' Sexual Assault: Non-Delegable Duty and Vicarious Liability' [2003] *Melbourne University Law Review* 22.
[341] (2003) ALR 412 at [224].   [342] [1999] 2 SCR 570.

distinguishable from *Bazley* on the grounds that all the assaults (excepting one) took place outside working hours and away from the club. Further, the club did not act *in loco parentis* toward the children, and it was therefore not at the 'same end of the spectrum of risk' as the *Bazley* case.[343] In *John Doe v. Bennett*,[344] the Supreme Court likened the psychological intimacy which a parish priest shared with local children with the physical intimacy found in *Bazley*. This psychological intimacy encourages the victim's submission to the abuse and increases the opportunity for the perpetrator to abuse. It was also significant in *Bennett* that the parishes were geographically isolated and there were few other authority figures.

At the opposite end of the spectrum, in *M(FS) v. Clarke*,[345] the increased risk was such that the court stated that the employer could not possibly have given the employee a greater opportunity to abuse children, except perhaps by allowing the children to reside in the employee's accommodation.[346] The factors contributing to this conclusion were that the employee was a dormitory supervisor in a residential school with access to the dormitory at all hours and he was responsible for discipline and supervision of the children throughout the day excepting during class times. The children's vulnerability was further amplified by the fact that they could not leave the school, they were away from home in an isolated rural location and parents could be jailed for keeping their children at home. The dormitory supervisor was therefore the closest these children had to a parent. No interview had been held, no references were sought and no training had been given. One of the interesting facets of this case was the claim in negligence against the abuser's employers. The court asked whether there were considerations which ought to restrict, reduce or negative the duty of care.[347] It concluded that the size of an institution would not serve to limit the duty of care. The court instead focused on the magnitude of the risk created by placing children in residential schools in these circumstances.[348] This judgment illustrates well the convergence of vicarious liability and direct liability in these cases. Both the primary and vicarious liability aspects of

---

[343] Per Binnie J, although the suggestion that parental responsibility is necessary for vicarious liability was rejected in *VP v. Attorney General and William Starr* (1999) SKQB 180, discussed later.
[344] [2004] SCC 17.   [345] [1999] 11 WWR 301 (BCSC).   [346] At para 140.
[347] Applying Lord Wilberforce's two-stage test from *Anns v. Merton LBC* [1978] AC 728, now superseded in English law.
[348] Relying on *H(M) v. Bederman* (1995) 27 CCLT (2d) 152 (Ont Gen Div).

the judgment seemingly focus on the size of the risk of abuse, evidence that courts will often search for indications of fault when determining vicarious liability issues. Surely, however, a clear distinction is to be maintained in the sense that employers of those with close contact with children may recognise a risk and address that risk by chaperoning or supervision arrangements. Reasonable care should not constitute a defence to vicarious liability.

A case positioned between *Bazley* and *Jacobi* on the spectrum of risk is *VP v. Attorney General & William Starr*.[349] In this case, Hunter J, sitting in the Queen's Bench of Saskatchewan, attempted to further reconcile the judgments in *Bazley* and *Jacobi*, and in so doing offered a useful perspective on how issues of vicarious liability might be resolved. The claimant had been physically and sexually assaulted by an administrator at a residential school and sought compensation from his abuser and the Attorney General of Canada (as responsible for supervising daily operations at the school). Of vital importance in this case was the fact that the abuser's role included the non-administrative function of disciplining pupils at the school, and it was during the punishment of VP for running away from school, that the acts of abuse took place. The judgment of Hunter J confirmed that employment involving contact with children and thereby presenting the opportunity for abuse did not suffice for vicarious liability to be imposed on the abuser's employer.[350] He went on to say that the judgment in *Jacobi* did not require parental authority as a precondition of vicarious liability. It is rather that the enterprise creates the risk of abuse, and such risk may be introduced by 'job created power' over the potential victim. In *Jacobi* it was not only that the abuse generally took place off club premises that took the abuse outside the course of employment, but that the children returned home to their parents in the evening and were free to leave at any time. Vicarious liability therefore rested on the degree of *power wielded by the abuser over their victim by virtue of their employment role*. In *Starr*, the function of disciplining pupils was regarded as advancing the employer's aims and also created a relationship of power and vulnerability between abuser and victim. This quasi-parental power meant that the employer/master took the risk of a wrongful exercise of such a power. The dicta of Hunter J also made it clear that although a quasi-parental power had been found

---

[349] (1999) SKQB 180.
[350] Relying on *B (JP) v. Jacob* (1998) 166 DLR (4th) 125 NBCA and *Barrett v. The Ship 'Arcadia' et al.* (1977) 76 DLR (3d) 535 (BCSC) as support for this proposition.

to exist in this case, vicarious liability was not confined to such instances, citing a case of a police officer having sufficient 'job created power' over ordinary citizens for abuse to fall within vicarious liability principles.[351]

As mentioned above, the vicarious liability principles have been applied in Canada to the relationship between the state and the foster parents that it entrusts the care of children to. In *B(M) v. British Colombia*,[352] the court followed *Bazley* in finding that as the state had placed the claimant in the day-to-day care of the foster parents, materially increasing the risk of the harm suffered, they should be vicariously liable. A non-delegable duty to the same effect was also found and the court was unimpressed by arguments against liability grounded in public policy, such as that liability would deter authorities from offering child protection services. Where the perpetrator was employed as a baker in a residential school with no authority to discipline, direct or care for the children, vicarious liability would not be imposed on the employer.[353] To decide otherwise would be to make the employer the involuntary insurer of the risks of abuse.

### Vicarious liability for abuse in non-residential settings

Where does abuse in non-residential settings sit along the spectrum of risk?[354] This will depend upon the duration of contact anticipated by the employer between worker and children and the level of intimacy and dependence anticipated. For example, there is a great deal of difference in terms of intimacy and dependence between a supply mathematics teacher and his or her pupils and between a sports coach and the gifted children they are assigned to instruct. In *A v. Hoare*,[355] the Court of Appeal seemed satisfied that sexual abuse by a teacher with pastoral responsibilities in a non-residential school and taking place outside school premises could be regarded as within the course of employment. The key to this finding was the fact that the teacher's grooming of his victim was initiated in his office with offers to help the pupil get fit and leading to excursions outside school. Of further assistance here is the Scottish case of *K v. Gilmartin's Executrix*,[356] where the court applied the *Lister* 'connection test' to reach a finding of vicarious liability in the

---

[351] *Mary (M) v. City of Los Angeles* 814 P. 2d 1341 (Cal 1991).   [352] [2001] 5 WWR 6.
[353] *B(E) v. Order of the Oblates of Mary Immaculate in the Province of British Columbia* [2003] 7 WWR 421, upheld on appeal at [2005] 3 SCR 45.
[354] See P. Giliker, 'Rough Justice in an Unjust World' (2002) 65 *Modern Law Review* 269 at 277.
[355] *A v. Hoare* [2006] EWCA Civ 395 at [132].   [356] [2002] SLT 801.

context of abuse by a teacher in a day school. The necessary 'connection' was supplied by the 'daily physical and mental control over the pursuer as pupil, with power and authority to instruct and discipline; all arising from Mr Gilmartin's special position of trust as the pursuer's form teacher'.[357] In *L(H) v. Canada*, the employer of a school administrator who ran a boxing programme for youths in the local community was also held vicariously liable for the sexual assaults committed upon a pupil at the boxing club.[358] The environment of the boxing club meant that a 'significant measure of emotional intimacy was inevitable'. Wearing team jackets and attending team events led to bonded emotional relationships of familiarity, interdependence and emulation. Job-related power and opportunity and the vulnerability of the children sufficed to fulfil the 'increased risk' test.

These cases can be contrasted with the case of *H(SG) v. Gorsline*,[359] the abuser in this case being the claimant's physical education (PE) teacher. The claim of vicarious liability failed as the abuser's position of teacher in a non-residential school did not materially enhance the risk of abuse. No intimate or extended contact was required between PE teachers and their pupils. Further, the power of the abuser was 'tempered' by being only one of many teachers, including counsellors and a female PE teacher. Similarly, in *G(ED) v. Hammer*,[360] the abuse of a pupil by the school janitor did not trigger vicarious liability as the janitor's actions were not sufficiently connected to his employment; janitors had no direct duties relating to the care or instruction of pupils.

## Adult victims of abuse

Although it is tempting to view the rulings in *Lister* and *Bazley v. Curry* as applicable only to cases of abuse against minors, Lord Hobhouse in *Lister* indicated that this was not the case:

> The classes of persons or institutions that are in this type of special relationship to another human being include schools, prisons, hospitals and even, in relation to their visitors, occupiers of land. They are liable if they themselves fail to perform the duty they consequently owe. If they entrust the performance of that duty to an employee and that employee fails to perform the duty, they are still liable ... The liability of the

---

[357] [2001] 6 WWR 132 (Alta QB).  [358] [2003] 5 WWR 421.
[359] [2004] 23 CCLT (3d) 65.
[360] [2001] 5 WWR 80, specifically approved by the Supreme Court in *Jacobi v. Griffiths* [1999] 2 SCR 570 and not disturbed on appeal [2003] 11 WWR 244.

employers is a vicarious liability because the actual breach of duty is that of the employee.[361]

Clearly, the reasoning in *Lister* is not intended to be restricted to cases of child abuse, but may apply in any case where the relationship between claimant and defendant is such that the claimant can be regarded as being dependent upon or at the mercy of the other.

### The English and Canadian approaches compared

The Canadian risk-based approach and the English connectedness test both share a causal flavour but differ in their emphasis on culpability. The Canadian approach imposes vicarious liability for sexual abuse more readily and so caution must be exercised before seeking to transpose Canadian authorities into English law. Nevertheless, both approaches reject the proposition that creating the opportunity for the wrong is sufficient for the wrong to fall within the course of employment, and it can be difficult to distinguish the opportunity test from the 'sufficient connection' and the 'increased risk' tests, particularly as the risk referred to in *Bazley* is such a generalised risk as opposed to a specific reasonably foreseeable risk.

### Public policy objections to vicarious liability

An intriguing means of denying the application of vicarious liability for abuse was offered by Binnie J in *Jacobi* (albeit *obiter*). He argued that imposing strict liability on employers for the sexual deviance of their workers could result in over-deterrence and the withdrawal of personnel from childcare facilities: 'Children's recreation is not a field that offers monetary profits as an incentive to volunteers to soldier on despite the risk of personal financial liability.' The weight of Canadian authority is now against the 'not for profit' defence. In *Bazley v. Curry* the argument had been rejected. The risk creator rather than the innocent victim ought to bear the burden of the risk.[362] 'Given that a choice must be made [between two faultless parties] it is fairer to place the loss on the party that introduced the risk and had the better opportunity to control it.'[363]

The public policy arguments against liability were raised again in the context of the liability of the established Church. The Supreme

---

[361] [2001] UKHL 22; [2002] 1 AC 215 at 789.   [362] (1997) 30 BCLR 3d 1 at [54].
[363] (1997) 30 BCLR 3d 1 at [54], *per* MacLachlin J. This was followed in *B (M) v. British Colombia* [2001] 5 WWR 6 at [46].

Court in *John Doe v. Bennett* declined to find that non-profit employers should be exempt from the doctrine of vicarious liability, rather the non-profit status of the defendant may impact on the policy reasoning which forms the rationale for vicarious liability. Thus, where the defendant was a non-profit organisation, the imposition of vicarious liability was compatible with fairness and public policy provided there was a 'strong connection' between the enterprise risk and the abuse.[364]

It is worthy of note that the institution in *Lister* (Hesley Hall) was a commercial enterprise, although their Lordships' statements regarding prisons and mental patients suggest that English courts would not preclude vicarious liability against public/'not for profit' defendants.

## Insurance coverage

A number of issues may arise in relation to the construction of the defendant's insurance policy and whether coverage extends to the harms occasioned by child abuse, particularly when that abuse takes the form of intentional wrongs. An insurer owes essentially two duties to the insured: the duty to defend (to pay for the cost of defending litigation) and the duty to indemnify (to absorb the cost of liability, if established). The duty to defend is generally broader than the duty to indemnify as it applies wherever the claim, if proven, would fall within the wording of the policy, therefore the duty to defend can apply even though the claim against the insured turns out to be groundless. The duty to indemnify applies only where the claim proves to be a valid one. Many of the issues outlined below relate to the coverage of the policy (e.g. whether coverage extends to claims for psychiatric injury or intentional wrongs) and are therefore potentially of relevance to both duties.

### 1. Construction of the policy

#### 'Bodily injury'

First, many insurance policies restrict cover to claims relating to 'bodily harm' or 'bodily injury', which raises the question of whether coverage will extend to psychiatric harm where the policy is silent on the matter.

---

[364] [2004] SCC 17 at [24].

On the one hand, it can be argued that 'bodily injury' should be construed so as to include psychiatric harm unless the policy indicates otherwise. This might follow from the suggestion by the House of Lords in *Page v. Smith* that psychiatric harm is to be treated as equivalent in importance to physical harm.[365] There are also a number of rulings which interpret statutory references to 'bodily injury' or 'bodily harm' as embracing psychiatric harms.[366] On the other hand, there is a distinction between the sentiment expressed in English law that claims for psychiatric and physical damage are to be treated as of equal merit[367] and assertions that psychiatric harm is in fact a type of physical or bodily harm. There is Scottish authority to suggest that the courts will look to the specific psychiatric condition in order to decide the issue. In *Connelly v. New Hampshire Insurance Co Ltd*,[368] the court was satisfied that post-traumatic stress disorder could be described as a 'bodily *injury*', as opposed to a disease, as it was a specific condition triggered by specific factors as opposed to a diffuse illness, and it qualified as 'bodily' because it was a psychological and physiological reaction to violent shock. The court indicated, however, that depression would not have qualified as an 'injury'.

## 'Accidental'

References to 'accidental' harm, damage or injury in insurance policies unless otherwise defined will generally include those occasioned by an 'unlooked for mishap or untoward event which is not expected or designed'.[369] A broad view is taken of the term 'accidental'. Where the policy indicates that injuries must be 'accidental' from the assured's perspective, injuries which were intended by another will still qualify as 'accidental'.[370] Furthermore, just because the injury in question is sustained in the workplace in the course of traumatic work (therefore exposure to the trauma might be regarded as anticipated or intended

---

[365] Per Lord Lloyd of Berwick [1996] 1 AC 155, 188. See also *Victoria General Hospital v. General Accident Assurance Co of Canada* [1995] 8 WWR 106, finding that bodily injury in an insurance policy extended to psychiatric harm.
[366] *R v. Ireland (Robert Matthew); R v. Burstow (Anthony Christopher)* [1998] AC 147; *R v. Chan Fook* [1994] 1 WLR 689 – 'The body of the victim includes all parts of his body, including his organs, his nervous system and his brain. Bodily injury therefore may include injury to any of those parts of his body responsible for his mental and other faculties' (*per* Hobhouse LJ at 152).
[367] *Page v. Smith* [1996] AC 155, discussed in Chapter 4.      [368] 1997 SLT 1341.
[369] *Fenton v. Thorley* [1903] AC 443 *per* Lord MacNaghten at 448.
[370] *Trim Joint District School Board of Management v. Kelly* [1914] AC 667.

by the injured party) does not mean that the consequent injury is not accidental.[371] This has implications for a claim by an employee seeking compensation from an employer for allegedly exposing workers to traumatic cases of child abuse without proper training or support.

### 2. The insured perpetrator

Even where the wording of the policy appears to leave room for the insured to seek indemnity for intentional wrongs, the courts are likely to find that public policy will not allow such an indemnity to be enforced. Generally speaking, liability insurance will not extend cover to a third party for the intentional criminal act of the insured for public policy reasons.[372] In *Gray v. Barr*, the insured, who was found by the civil courts to have been guilty of manslaughter, was not permitted to enforce his insurance policy in respect of the victim's widow. It seems that this applies even where the harm occasioned by the insured's intentional wrong was accidental or not meant. The decision in *Gray* was reached on grounds of public policy and quite independently of construction of the policy concerned. Although the subject of criticism, the effect of *Gray v. Barr* has been recently confirmed in the Court of Appeal in *Churchill Insurance v. Charlton*.[373] The insured deliberately reversed his vehicle into a parked car, injuring its passenger. The insured was convicted of criminal damage although there was no evidence to suggest that he had intended harm to the claimant. The Court of Appeal applied the principle that a person may not stand to gain an advantage arising from the consequences of his own iniquity.[374] This was applied by construing the insurance contract as if it were worded so as 'not to apply to damage arising from the insured's own deliberate criminal act'. As the English courts have determined that sexual abuse is not actionable against the perpetrator as negligence,[375] this prevents claimants or defendants arguing that the wrong is not an intentional one, in order to evade the public policy rule expressed in *Gray* and *Charlton*.

If, for any reason, the courts were persuaded that public policy did not prevent enforcement of the insurance contract by an insured who had

---

[371] *Connelly v. New Hampshire Insurance Co Ltd* 1997 SLT 1341.
[372] *Gray v. Barr* [1971] 2 QB 554.  [373] [2001] EWCA Civ 112; [2002] QB 578.
[374] Following *Beresford v. Royal Insurance Co Ltd* [1938] AC 586, 595, per Lord Atkin – an assured cannot recover under an insurance contract for the consequences of his own deliberate wrongdoing.
[375] *Stubbings v. Webb* [1993] AC 498 (HL).

committed an intentional wrong, the position of the insured would depend upon construction of the terms of the policy. A policy which excludes coverage for intentionally caused harms (e.g. by providing cover only for 'accidental harms' or specifically excluding intentional harms) might meet the objection that whilst the defendant *intended* the acts constituting the abuse, they did not *intend* (i.e. desire) the harm which has eventuated. Such an argument is unlikely to be successful as the law's construction of intention is usually of the objective variety so that the relevant intention is inferred from obviously harmful conduct.

The case of *Non-Marine Underwriters, Lloyds of London v. Scalera*,[376] although Canadian, points to a similar fate for perpetrators attempting to trigger the duty to defend by arguing that their tort of the damage was not intentional. *Scalera* concerned the duty to defend and whether a homeowner's policy which excluded coverage for claims for intentional harm could be triggered by a claim brought against the perpetrator of sexual abuse in battery and in the alternative as a negligence or breach of fiduciary duty claim. The Supreme Court of Canada ruled that alternative pleadings in negligence or breach of fiduciary duty should not be allowed to trigger the duty to defend if the alternative claim was purely derivative (i.e. if it relied on the same facts and harms as the intentional tort claim). In other words, attempts to disguise intentional tort claims as negligence claims would not provide access to the insurer's funds. As to the battery claim, an intent to injure was inferred using an objective approach. Criticism of *Scalera* followed on the grounds that it denied the victim of abuse access to the insurance funds therefore often depriving them of an effective compensation award. In deciding that sexual battery necessarily involved an intention to injure, it has been argued that the decision misapplied the concept of battery as it was developed in Canadian law. In Canada, a battery can be committed either intentionally or negligently, therefore it should not be assumed that the insured who committed a battery intended injury.

### 3. The insured non-perpetrator

Where the insured party is not the perpetrator of the abuse but is alleged to have been negligent in their failure to prevent the abuse or prevent its continuance, any exclusion of coverage for intentional harms in the wording of the policy may also deny coverage to the insured depending

---

[376] [2000] SCC 24; (2000) 50 CCLT(2d) 1.

upon the precise wording of the policy. Where the policy states that the exclusion applies to 'intentional harms caused by the insured' or something similar, it would not normally prevent indemnity against the insured who was merely negligent.[377] Thus, where a claim is brought in negligence against the non-perpetrator and it is not regarded as an attempt to dress up a battery claim as an alternative form of action, the duty to defend should still arise. On the other hand, where the policy refers simply to coverage for intentional acts, then it may exclude coverage whoever the perpetrator in fact is.[378] If the policy is not clear on whether accidental damage is to be regarded as accidental from the perspective of the insured or the perpetrator the *contra preferentum* rule requires that ambiguities should be construed against the author of the policy (i.e. the insurance company).

Where an insurer seeks to avoid indemnification following a finding of the insured's liability the precise wording of the policy and that of the judgment of liability are crucial. In the *Bryn Alyn* litigation[379] the insurer sought to rely on an exception clause in the policy excluding the duty to indemnify loss caused by deliberate acts and omissions of the company or those with senior management roles in the company. Although the insured had been found liable for acts of child abuse by some of its managerial staff, Simon J found that the exception did not apply as liability had been phrased in terms of negligence by the company in its oversight of its residential facility and supervision of staff and not deliberate managerial torts. If this decision is correct many such exclusion clauses will be ineffective in abuse claims, as the limitation periods will mean that the majority of child abuse cases will be framed as negligence claims and not as deliberate acts.

Where the insured's liability is vicarious, coverage which only extends to 'accidental harm' to a third party may be forfeited if the damage was inflicted intentionally by the insured's employee. Again, whether the insured is covered depends firstly on the wording of the policy. In *Hawley v. Luminar Leisure Ltd*,[380] the policy extended to liabilities arising out of 'accidental bodily injury to any person'. The insurer argued that the deliberate and violent assault of the insured's doorman for which the

---

[377] *Midland Insurance Co. v. Smith* (1881) 6 QBD 561 – fact that insured's wife had deliberately caused the damage did not invalidate the insurance.
[378] See Grace and Vella, *Civil Liability for Sexual Abuse and Violence in Canada*, at 304–5, discussing *W v. (T) v. W (KRJ)* (1996) 29 OR (3d) 277.
[379] [2006] EWHC 48; 2006 WL 421839.   [380] [2006] EWCA Civ 18; (2006) 150 SJLB.

insured was vicariously liable did not constitute 'accidental' injury. The Court of Appeal took a different view saying that, unless otherwise stipulated, coverage extended to incidents which were accidental from the perspective of the assured not that of the perpetrator. As vicarious liability did not attribute the state of mind of the perpetrator to the employer but merely extended liability from the employee to the employer, the deliberately inflicted injury remained 'accidental' for the purposes of the insurance contract.[381]

## Alternative routes to compensation: criminal injuries compensation

Since 1964, a scheme has existed for compensating the victims of crime from state funds. The evolved scheme has been criticised for resting on 'shaky intellectual foundations',[382] in part because the precise rationale for offering preferential terms of compensation to the victims of crime is not clear (although it appears to rest upon a mixture of symbolic expression of public sympathy and condemnation of criminal acts[383]). There are currently three schemes in operation; the original scheme of 1964, under which a number of claims are still 'live';[384] the statutory scheme introduced in 1996, which applies to applications made on or after 1 April 1996; and the revised statutory scheme of 2001, which applies to claims received on or after 1 April 2001.[385] It should be noted that the current scheme is under review following allegations that the existing regime failed victims of the 7 July bombing of the London Underground.[386] It is proposed that the scheme should undergo major simplification with speedier resolution of claims and increased support for victims of the most serious crimes.

---

[381] This is effectively the same result as that obtained in the Canadian case of *Bluebird Cabs v. Guardian Insurance Co of Canada* (1999) 173 DLR (4th) 318.

[382] P. Duff, 'The Measure of Criminal Injuries Compensation: Political Pragmatism or Dog's Dinner?' *Oxford Journal of Legal Studies* 18 (1998) 105.

[383] Duff, 'The Measure of Criminal Injuries Compensation'. For further criticism of the scheme, see D. Meiers, *State Compensation for Criminal Injuries* (Blackstone Press, 1997) and A. Ashworth, 'Punishment and Compensation: Victims, Offenders and the State' (1986) 6 *Oxford Journal of Legal Studies* 86.

[384] See A. Tettenborn, *The Law of Damages* (Butterworths, 2003) at Chapter 32 for details of the old scheme and the 1996 scheme.

[385] For an excellent potted history of the scheme, see Duff, 'The Measure of Criminal Injuries Compensation'.

[386] See *Rebuilding Lives – Supporting Victims of Crime*, Cm 6705 (HMSO, 2005).

The Criminal Injuries Compensation Act 1995 placed on a statutory footing what had previously been an administrative scheme operated under the Crown's prerogative powers. The pre-1996 scheme afforded *ex gratia* compensation to applicants who had suffered personal injury directly attributable to a 'crime of violence'. Compensation was assessed according to the usual principles applied to awards in tort claims, albeit with some restrictions (for example, no exemplary damages were available and awards for loss of earnings were capped at one-and-a-half times the average earnings of an industrial worker). The scheme was administered by the Criminal Injuries Compensation Board ('the Board') and applicants could seek judicial review of an unfavourable decision.

Under the 1995 Act, the Board was replaced by the Criminal Injuries Compensation Authority ('the Authority'). Since the introduction of a statutory scheme, awards have been payable for 'criminal injury', that is, personal injury which is attributable to:

(a) a crime of violence;
(b) an offence of trespass on the railway;
(c) the apprehension or attempted apprehension of an offender or a suspected offender;
(d) the prevention or attempted prevention of an offence; or
(e) the giving of help to any constable who is engaged in any such activity.[387]

For the purposes of examining abuse claims, the only relevant category of the above is that of para. (a), 'crimes of violence'. The meaning of this term is explored later, but it is worth mentioning now that the term 'violence' has the effect of excluding recovery for many cases of child abuse. Neglect and emotional abuse are generally a poor fit for crimes of violence,[388] which explains why criminal injuries compensation may prove to be an inadequate alternative remedy in child abuse cases. The application is heard by a claims officer, with a right of review and, subsequently an appeal to the Authority. The other main distinction between the old and the new regimes is that awards under the statutory scheme are fixed according to a tariff system. The 2001 scheme

---

[387] Para. 8.
[388] C. Keenan, 'A Plea Against Tort Liability for Child Protection Agencies in England and Wales' (2003) 42 *Washburn Law Journal* 235 at 249.

incorporates a detailed tariff system,[389] providing for over 400 types of injury and with detailed provisions for injuries caused by sexual offences. The shift to a tariff system was motivated by an attempt to control the spiralling costs of the criminal injuries compensation scheme and also to ensure consistency in awards for the same injuries. The tariff system works by looking to the severity of the injury and not the impact on the particular applicant, therefore the circumstances of the victim (employment status, age, gender) are irrelevant to the award. The tariffs are frequently criticised for the fact that awards generally turn out to be less favourable than where the same injury was the product of a civil as opposed to a criminal wrong and compensation is secured through the courts. Duff suggests that such criticism is misplaced. Whilst it is discomforting at the symbolic level to see the victim of a crime of violence receive less than a victim of a road traffic accident, such criticism ignores the fact that the difference is to be explained by reference to the source of the payment. In the case of the criminal wrong, the claim is funded by the innocent taxpayer and must therefore be subject to financial limits.[390]

Under s. 1 of the 1995 Act, the Secretary of State was empowered to establish a scheme for criminal injuries compensation. The current scheme was published in 2001 and applies to all applications made on or after 1 April 2001. The 2001 scheme provides compensation for criminal injuries, that is, personal injury which is directly attributable to a crime of violence with a maximum award of £500,000.[391] This ceiling applies to all claims arising out of the same injury. In other words, if an application were made to the scheme regarding a serious injury, following which the applicant died and a relative made further claims arising out of the death of a family member, both claims would be regarded as arising out of the same injury and when combined they would be subject to the £500,000 limit.[392] 'Personal injury' is defined so

---

[389] The first tariff system was introduced in 1994 under the prerogative powers. This scheme was declared an abuse of power by the House of Lords in *R v. Secretary of State for the Home Department, ex parte Fire Brigades Union and others* [1995] 2 WLR 464, as it was inconsistent with the provision made for introducing a new scheme under the Criminal Justice Act 1988. A new improved tariff scheme was swiftly introduced under the Criminal Injuries Compensation Act 1995. The new scheme provided for compensation for lost earnings and medical care in serious cases in addition to the one-off tariff award.
[390] Duff, 'The Measure of Criminal Injuries Compensation', at 131.
[391] Para. 24. This cap on awards applies to the award made before any reductions under the scheme.
[392] Para. 24.

as to include mental injury, further defined as temporary mental anxiety, medically verified, or a disabling mental illness confirmed by psychiatric diagnosis.[393] Such conditions may result directly from physical injury or from a sexual offence or may occur in the absence of physical injury.[394]

Paragraph 10 of the Criminal Injuries Compensation Scheme requires applications to be made within two years of the incident which caused the injury. A decision is made at first instance by a claims officer, and appeals can be made from the officer's decision to the Criminal Injuries Compensation Appeals Panel, which adopts an inquisitorial approach to proceedings. There is no right of appeal from a decision of the Panel. Any challenge of the Panel's decision must be launched by way of judicial review.

### 1. Awards for non-parasitic mental injury

Despite the inclusion of psychiatric harm within the definition of 'personal injury', the general rule is that psychiatric harm which is not accompanied by either physical injury or a sexual offence, is not recoverable according to para. 9 of the scheme, unless:

(a) the applicant was put in reasonable fear of immediate physical harm to his own person; or
(b) the applicant had a close relationship of love and affection with another person at the time when that person sustained physical and/or mental injury (including fatal injury) directly attributable to a criminal injury AND
　(i) that relationship still subsists (unless the victim has died) and
　(ii) the applicant either witnessed and was present on the occasion when the other person sustained the injury, or was closely involved in its immediate aftermath; or
(c) the claim arises out of a sexual offence, or the applicant was the non-consenting victim of that offence (which does not include a victim who consented in fact but was deemed in law not to have consented); or
(d) the applicant is or was employed in the business of a railway company, and either witnessed and was present on the occasion when another person sustained physical (including fatal) injury

---

[393] Para. 9, *Criminal Injuries Compensation Scheme* 2001, available at http://www.cicap.gov.uk.
[394] Other exclusions from the scheme, not relevant to claims relating to sexual abuse, are detailed. Readers are directed to texts such as Tettenborn, Wilby and Bennett, *The Law of Damages*.

directly attributable to an offence of trespass on a railway, or was closely involved in its immediate aftermath.

Thus, non-parasitic psychiatric harm is only recoverable under the scheme where the claimant qualifies as a primary or secondary victim,[395] where it is the result of a non-consensual sexual offence or where mental injury is suffered as a result of the physical injury of a trespasser on a railway line.

### 2. Awards for parasitic mental injury

Where mental injury accompanies physical harm, that mental injury can attract a separate award where the mental harm would justify an award at the same tariff level or higher than the associated physical injury. In the case of sexual abuse, however, the tariffs are designed so as to reflect the mental injury flowing from such abuse and no further award is permitted.

### 3. 'Directly attributable to'

The requirement that the injury be directly attributable to a crime of violence imports not only a causation requirement but is also regarded as a limiting device, much in the same way as the remoteness rules operate at common law.[396] A number of cases have addressed the meaning of this phrase in relation to bystanders of the abuse (see below).

### 4. Direct attribution and bystander claims

The meaning of this phrase has been addressed in relation to the claims of those who would be regarded as secondary victims under the common law *Alcock* framework. In *R v. Criminal Injuries Compensation Board, ex p Johnson*,[397] the applicant had discovered the body of her murdered friend at her home and suffered a shock-induced psychiatric illness. The Board had rejected her application on the grounds that under the *Alcock* rules she did not have a sufficiently proximate

---

[395] As defined in *White v. Chief Constable of South Yorkshire* [1999] 2 AC 455 and *Alcock v. Chief Constable of South Yorkshire* [1992] 1 AC 310.
[396] See *R v. Criminal Injuries Compensation Board, ex p Kent and Milne* [1998] 1 WLR 1458 below.
[397] [1994] PIQR P469.

relationship to the deceased. The High Court allowed her appeal. Only two elements needed to be established: that the applicant had suffered a recognised psychiatric illness and that it had been caused by finding the body. The court stated further that foreseeability was not a test for the award of compensation,[398] although it might be relevant to the causation enquiry as the less foreseeable psychiatric injury was in the circumstances, the more difficult it would be to prove that discovering the body had caused the mental trauma. Note that the case was heard in 1994, before the introduction of a statutory scheme which now defines personal injury so as to exclude the claims of secondary victims. *Johnson* is therefore largely of academic importance. In any case, the decision in *Johnson* must be treated with care, given the later decision in *R v. Criminal Injuries Compensation Board, ex p Kent and Milne*.[399] The applicants suffered reactive depression as a result of discovering that their child had suffered serious sexual assaults at the hands of the second applicants' father. Applying the *Alcock* criteria, the court regarded the injury as not 'directly attributable' to the assaults as the applicants lacked 'direct perception' of the crimes of violence.[400] The word 'directly' was intended to perform a restrictive function. Again, adopting the rhetoric of *Alcock*, the court thought that it might have been different if the applicant had been told by their daughter in graphic detail of one of the assaults whilst in a distraught condition, as this might have been equivalent to witnessing the crime herself. There is a lack of congruence between the decisions of *Johnson* and *Kent*. There is clear recognition in *Johnson* that the issue of 'direct attribution' is one of simple causation and there is a reluctance to import common law limits into the criminal injuries compensation scheme. By contrast, the court in *Kent* assumes that the common law restrictions ought to be applied without expressing a rationale for such a conclusion. Direct attribution therefore seems to have acquired the meaning of 'attributable to direct perception of a crime of violence' in the context of psychiatric injury. Such reasoning is an unwelcome echo of the outmoded remoteness

---

[398] See also *O'Dowd v. Secretary of State for Northern Ireland* [1982] 9 NIJB. It is submitted that the court in *Johnson* erred in treated the closeness of relationship as an aspect of foreseeability.
[399] [1998] 1 WLR 1458.
[400] This raises the question of whether had the applicants' injury been caused by the belief that they had brought their child and the abuser together (e.g. for baby-sitting) would the Board have been more easily convinced that their injury was directly attributable to crimes of violence having regard to *W v. Essex CC* [2001] 2 AC 592.

reasoning employed in *Coultas*[401] and, it is submitted, represents an inappropriate fusing of proximity and causation considerations. The issue of entitlement (mirroring the function of duty of care at common law) in criminal injuries compensation is resolved by a finding of a crime of violence affecting the applicant; therefore direct attribution should be treated going purely to causation and not entitlement.

Should the policy restrictions in *Alcock* apply to criminal injuries compensation claims? On the one hand, the criminal injuries compensation scheme is a limited fund paid for by taxpayers and therefore there is sense in attempting to limit claims to those regarded as the most deserving, after all it is not directly financed by the culpable party's assets or insurance policies. Is the taxpayer to be compared to the negligent defendant whose liability should be confined within strict limits to prevent an explosion of claims? On the other hand, the scheme already contains design limits relating to the maximum award, the restriction on damages for non-physical injuries, etc. The ruling in *Johnson* that common law limitations should apply also seems difficult to reconcile with the fact that, under the scheme, train drivers are identified as having a claim for mental harm suffered as a result of a trespasser throwing themselves onto the train tracks, yet it is far from clear that such a claim would be successful at common law against the trespasser's estate.[402] Where Parliament has already designed limits to compensation, is it really necessary for the courts to import additional safeguards against a flood of claims? Given that this is a statutory scheme, it is Parliament that ultimately bears responsibility for restricting entitlement if the fund looks as though it will not meet all valid claims. It might be counter-argued, however, that claims should not succeed against the state where they would have been unsuccessful against the negligent and therefore culpable defendant at common law and so, *Alcock* criteria ought to be applied. It is important not to forget that the schemes of tort liability and that of criminal injuries compensation have different working rationales. Whilst tort exists in part to compensate those injured, it must constantly strive to achieve a balance between the culpability of the defendant and the need of the claimant. In the context of criminal injuries, the state fund does not pay out because of its culpability, but purely

---

[401] *Victorian Railway Commissioners v. Coultas* (1888) LR 13 App Cas 222.
[402] Whilst the case of *Dooley v. Cammell Laird & Co Ltd* [1951] 1 Lloyd's Rep 271 would seem to accept the legitimacy of such a claim, this decision is now in doubt since the definition of primary victims utilised in *White v. Chief Constable of South Yorkshire* [1999] 2 AC 455.

because of the need of the applicant triggered by their injury. There is, therefore, less need to balance the claimant's need against the impact on a defendant who, whilst negligent, is not a villain deserving of punishment.

## 5. 'A crime of violence'

In 1969 the scope of the old scheme was narrowed from 'personal injury directly attributable to a criminal offence' to 'personal injury directly attributable to a crime of violence'. No definition of 'crimes of violence' is provided in the schemes themselves or in the case law.[403] Whilst most crimes of violence will include the infliction of force or threat of force, such elements are not a necessary requirement. This is confirmed by the fact that the scheme recognises that injuries occasioned by the offences lacking a requirement of force such as arson and poisoning can be regarded as personal injuries within the scheme. The Court of Appeal in *R v. Criminal Injuries Compensation Board, ex p Webb* regarded it as inappropriate to provide a definition, preferring to say that the Board would 'recognise a crime of violence when they hear about it'.[404] In *Webb*, the claim of four train drivers who suffered psychiatric harm as a result of witnessing trespassers on the railway fall under the train they were driving, was rejected as not involving a crime of violence. The offence to which the train drivers were victim prohibited endangering the safety of any person on the railway but did not constitute a crime of violence.[405] It was the nature of the crime and not its consequences which was to be assessed to determine its violence; therefore, it seems that it is not sufficient that the offence involves a possibility of violence,[406] rather there must be some intention or recklessness as to that violence. It was certainly not sufficient that the trespassers met a violent end and that the applicant's personal injury was directly attributable to that violence.[407] The term 'crime of violence' has, it seems, a fairly specialised meaning. There can be no list of crimes of violence, rather

---

[403] Although a definition was attempted by s. 109 of the Criminal Justice Act 1988, which was never brought into force. The definition included offences listed in a separate schedule and those offences which required intent or recklessness as to personal injury or death.
[404] [1987] QB 74 at 80.   [405] S. 34 of the Offences Against the Person Act 1861.
[406] Disapproving the guidance offered by Wien J in *R v. Criminal Injuries Compensation Board, ex parte Clowes* [1977] 1 WLR 1353.
[407] Note, however, that the scheme was since extended to include the claims of train drivers such as those in *R v. Criminal Injuries Compensation Board, ex p Warner; R v. Criminal Injuries Compensation Board, ex p Webb* [1987] QB 74.

the Authority/Panel must make a decision as to whether the events which actually occurred constituted a crime of violence.[408] The degree of force used in the commission of a sexual offence could therefore result in a finding that the applicant was the victim of a crime of violence notwithstanding their consent.[409]

The 'crime of violence' requirement does not require a conviction, and if a defendant is acquitted because their mental state means that they did not have capacity for *mens rea* of the relevant offence, that does not negate the existence of a crime of violence for the purposes of the scheme.[410] Where the 'offender' and the applicant were living as members of the same family[411] at the time the injury was inflicted, compensation will generally be withheld unless the offender has been prosecuted (or not prosecuted with good reason) and where the injury occurred by way of violence between adults in the family, the parties are no longer living together and are unlikely to resume cohabitation.[412]

### 6. Abuse claims

In 2001–02, 505 claims relating to sexual abuse were listed with the Criminal Injuries Compensation Authority.[413] Under the 2001 scheme, there are now 16 descriptions of sexual abuse of children, the most serious being at level 19, with an award of £33,000. There is also now provision for awards in respect of sexually transmitted diseases.[414]

Where the injury is a consequence of a sexual offence, although the consent of the applicant may not be relevant to guilt, such consent is relevant to the Authority's assessment of whether the injury was the result of a 'crime of violence'. The ultimate question in such cases appears to be whether the applicant can be described as a 'victim' of the particular crime in question[415] and if the applicant lacked the capacity to consent to the acts in question he should be regarded as a

---

[408] *R (August) v. Criminal Injuries Compensation Appeals Panel* [2001] QB 774 at 783.
[409] [2001] QB 774 at 803.   [410] [1987] QB 74 at 80.
[411] This includes a man and woman living together as husband and wife, although no mention is made of whether homosexual couples can be regarded as living together as a family.
[412] Para. 17, Criminal Injuries Compensation Scheme 2001, available at http://www.cicap.gov.uk.
[413] *Annual Report and Accounts 2001–2* (Criminal Injuries Compensation Authority, 2002).
[414] Tettenborn, Wilby and Bennett, *The Law of Damages*, at 32.47.
[415] *R (on the application of E) v. Criminal Injuries Compensation Appeals Panel* [2003] EWCA Civ 234; (2003) 153 NLJ 403 at [21].

victim.[416] In *R (August) v. Criminal Injuries Compensation Appeals Panel*,[417] the injuries alleged were the result of offences of buggery and gross indecency.[418] Although the consent of the applicants, minors at the time of the offences, did not negate criminal liability of the offenders,[419] the Court of Appeal concluded that the Board was entitled to find that such consent precluded the defendant's acts from constituting crimes of violence in this particular case. It would not, however, be open to a panel to decide that the presence of consent precluded a finding of a crime of violence.[420] Of course, where the claim relates to a sexual offence and is for psychiatric trauma alone, the scheme itself rules out compensation to consenting persons, albeit that the law deems that they have not given consent.[421] It was argued unsuccessfully in *August* that the Panel ought to have taken into account the public policy dimension of sexual abuse compensation (i.e. that a child ought to be regarded as a victim of such crimes and not a consensual participant). Certainly, those who drafted the Sexual Offences Act 1956 are unlikely to have had in mind the need to protect children from sexual exploitation leading to long-term psychological disorder. Nevertheless, the court in *August* concluded that the mischief which the Act sought to prevent was offensive behaviour rather than the exploitation of children. The court regarded the public policy argument as ultimately a complaint about the terms of the scheme, something which it was not in the court's power to rectify. It is important to view the decision in *August* as one particular to its exceptional facts, in that the court was told that at the time of the offence the first applicant, aged 13, had been actively seeking out adults with a view to them paying for his sexual services.[422] The later case of *R (on the application of JE) v. Criminal Injuries Compensation Appeals Panel*,[423] involving acts of indecent assault of a mental defective[424] by his cell mate, appears to have been distinguished from *August*. Although the complainant had been an active participant in later acts of indecency, the applicant bore little responsibility for the events which occurred as

---

[416] [2003] EWCA Civ 234 at [30].   [417] [2001] QB 774.
[418] Ss. 12 and 13 of the Sexual Offences Act 1956 respectively.
[419] S. 7(2)(c) of the Sexual Offences Act 1956.   [420] At 777.   [421] Para. 9(c).
[422] It is worthy of note that a claim at common law for battery as against the offender in this case may have been precluded by the principle of *ex turpi causa non oritur*.
[423] [2003] EWCA Civ 234.
[424] A term used in the Sexual Offences Act 1956, s. 45 as meaning 'a person suffering from a state of arrested or incomplete development of mind which includes severe impairment of intelligence and social functioning'.

compared with *August*, who had been equally responsible for the prohibited conduct. The case was remitted to be re-heard by a different Panel. The Court of Appeal suggested that in future cases where the issue of consent was not clear it might be more appropriate for the Panel to rely upon para. 13(d) of the scheme, which allows regard to be had to the conduct of the applicant to modify an award, as opposed to deciding that consent in fact was either present or not present, the former leading to the conclusion that the claim must fail outright.

## Conclusion

Although the award of damages at the conclusion of civil litigation has little capacity to 'remedy' the wrong done to the abused, the curative effect of litigation and public vindication of the victim should not be underestimated.[425] The civil claim has the potential to provide not only compensation for the pecuniary and non-pecuniary harm caused by another's wrong, it also provides a valuable mechanism of accountability for determining responsibility for that wrong.[426] Moreover, it has been argued that when regard is had to the psychological impact of litigation, civil action against the perpetrator of abuse is preferable to criminal prosecution, as it places the abused in a position of equal or greater power than the abuser who takes the defensive role.[427]

In the jurisdiction of England and Wales there are many features of the case law which undermine both the therapeutic and compensatory capacities of tort litigation, in particular the paucity of actions available against the perpetrator of abuse. The law's insistence on doctrinal tidiness by maintaining a rigid separation of intentional and unintentional wrongs has had a devastating effect on the coherence of civil remedies available for abuse so that the perpetrator of the abuse is better protected from liability than the non-perpetrator who is accused of not doing enough to prevent it (for more on this see Chapter 5). The action under the principle of *Wilkinson v. Downton* might be looked to in order to overcome some of the obstacles until the statutory framework on limitation is changed, but is currently under-utilised as far as abuse

---

[425] CF *Trear v. Sills* 69 Cal App 4th 1341 (Cal Act App 1999) at 1358, *per* Sills PJ: 'The judicial system most assuredly does not exist to provide a venue for cathartic confrontation.'
[426] *Z v. United Kingdom* [2001] 2 FLR 612 – the negligence action was regarded as fulfilling the need for a remedy which included compensation and the determination of liability.
[427] Nabors, 'The Statute of Limitations' at 159.

claims are concerned. Our courts also lack the flexibility of the breach of fiduciary duty action which has been applied with notable generosity to the abuse claimant in Canada. Although bringing its own problems of arbitrary parameters (i.e. the relationships which can be described as fiduciary ones), it has served the abuse claimant well in terms of providing more generous rules in relation to limitation of actions and causation.

Are the effects of these restricted litigation options limited to leaving the abuse claimant dependent upon forms of action which are ill-suited to the peculiarities of the abuse claim or are there more far reaching effects? The reader can judge whether it is far-fetched to suggest that the fact that litigation in this area is characterised by claims against the non-perpetrator is due in part to the law's obstruction of remedies against the perpetrator. Thus, ironically, what the courts perceive as a rising tide of litigation against local authorities and child protection professionals may be the result in part of blocking the claimant's other options. Moreover, the lack of judicial exposure to claims against perpetrators has left this area of law stunted and underdeveloped.

All this is to be contrasted with the litigation opportunities created by the 'close connection' test now applied in the context of vicarious liability which facilitates claims against the employer of the abuser for deliberate assaults and interference. Thus, as compared with the relative inaccessibility of the perpetrator of historical abuse, the employer of those involved in caring for children has become a frequently sought out alternative defendant who is at least as accessible as the individual directly responsible for the abuse. Whilst insured employers are good sources of compensation, the therapeutic effects of such litigation as compared with those of litigation against the perpetrator are questionable and the trade-off of actionability against the perpetrator and actionability against the non-perpetrator employer is of little use where abuse occurs in the family home.

Before turning to the claims of those wrongly accused of abuse, a little should be said about the contrast between the judgments in *Stubbings v. Webb* and *Lister v. Hesley Hall*. In the case of *Stubbings*, Lord Griffiths appears to be struck by the extreme nature of sexual abuse allegations and finds it difficult to conceptualise a duty not to abuse a fellow citizen. Here the uniqueness of sexual abuse finds expression in a refusal to accommodate the claim of such a heinous wrong within the existing tort rules, even if the effect is to deny the victim of the heinous wrong a remedy. Yet in *Lister*, great strides are made in the liberalisation of the law of vicarious liability so that incidents of sexual abuse can potentially be conceptualised as 'within the course of employment' and compensated. Why is this? The fact that *Lister* concerned a non-perpetrator defendant and *Stubbings* was an action brought against the perpetrator is not the only significant difference between these two cases. In *Lister*, the abuse by the warden had been the subject of a police investigation and the fact that it had occurred was accepted by all parties to the proceedings, including the defendants. In *Stubbings*, the allegations were denied by both father and stepbrother and Lord Griffiths commented that it would be a matter of grave difficulty for a court to determine where the truth lay. His Lordship clearly had little confidence in the ability of the courts to determine contested allegations of abuse. In such circumstances it is perhaps more convenient for the courts to dispose of cases on a technicality than to deal with the substance of the claim.

# 3

## Litigation Against the Accuser

> It is indisputable that being labelled a child abuser is one of the most loathsome labels in society and most often results in grave physical, emotional, professional, and personal ramifications ... Even when such an accusation is proven to be false, it is unlikely that social stigma, damage to personal relationships, and emotional turmoil can be avoided. In fact, the harm caused by misdiagnosis often extends beyond the accused parent and devastates the entire family. Society also suffers because false accusations cast doubt on true claims of abuse and thus undermine valuable efforts to identify and eradicate sexual abuse.[1]

### Introduction

Those accused of child abuse, but who maintain their innocence, may seek compensation from those who have initiated the allegations or acted upon them (e.g. medical professionals or those working in social welfare or child protection services). The damage for which compensation is sought may vary from psychiatric injury or distress to damage to reputation or economic losses in the form of lost remuneration or forfeited career opportunities. To this end, the alleged abuser may consider bringing proceedings asserting, for example, that doctors have provided an inadequate standard of therapeutic care or that local authorities have negligently or maliciously conducted their investigations into the alleged child abuse.[2] Such claims may sound in malicious prosecution, defamation or the tort of negligence. Whichever route of redress is pursued, the exoneration of the claimant prior to a claim does not

---

[1] *Hungerford v. Jones*, 143 NH 208, 211 (1998).
[2] *B(D) v. Children's Aid Society of Durham* (1996) 30 CCLT (2d) 310 – liable for economic losses consequent upon public authority's bias and lack of good faith in pursuing a trial despite no longer considering the accused to be a risk to children, but because the accused had refused to waive legal costs incurred so far.

guarantee the success of such litigation; the malicious prosecution action carries a formidable burden of proof, the negligence action is fraught with difficulties of establishing a duty of care towards a potential abuser given the courts' wariness of undermining the primary duty to the potential victim of the abuse, and the defamation action is hampered by a generous application of the qualified privilege defence in abuse cases.

As the extract from *Hungerford v. Jones* above indicates, the US courts are more inclined to view erroneous and negligent allegations of abuse as a wrong which inflicts a multitude of harms on the accused, the child, the family unit and society as a whole and which therefore merits compensation and deterrence. As will become evident, this portrayal of erroneous allegations is in stark contrast to the jurisdiction of England and Wales, where the judiciary have chosen to regard allegations made in error as the necessary price of effective child protection procedures. In the pages that follow the potential liability of local authorities, social workers and medical practitioners engaged in child protection cases are examined separately, despite the overlap on issues such as the justice, fairness and reasonableness of imposing a duty of care on these parties. This separation is purely for convenience of exposition in order that considerations specific to the medical practitioner as defendant (such as the scope of the doctor:patient relationship and duties of confidentiality) can be dealt with discretely. As with Chapter 2, the reader is referred to Chapter 4 for discussion of issues of causation, remoteness and quantum. The potential for liability to the wrongly accused must also be viewed against the caveat of witness immunity discussed below.

## Claims against social services/local authorities

### 1. The tort of negligence

In order to bring a successful negligence claim, the accused must first demonstrate that they are owed a duty of care by the defendant. To this end, the alleged abuser must demonstrate that harm to the subject of erroneous abuse allegations (usually psychiatric harm) was reasonably foreseeable, that a proximate relationship existed between the accused and the defendant and that the imposition of a duty of care is just, fair and reasonable.[3] The now questionable authority of *X v. Bedfordshire*

---

[3] *Caparo Industries plc v. Dickman* [1990] 1 All ER 568.

CC, although concerned with a claim by abused children, initially shaped the judicial response to claims by the alleged abuser on the issue of justice, fairness and reasonableness.[4] Lord Browne-Wilkinson had said in X that, on the grounds of justice, fairness and reasonableness, a common law duty of care should not be superimposed on the local authority's statutory duties concerning children in peril if its effect would be inconsistent with, or would have a tendency to discourage, due performance of these statutory duties. As the risk of litigation at common law was assumed to lead to defensive and excessively cautious performance of child protection responsibilities, it was better that a common law duty towards the child was not imposed. After this ruling in X it was assumed that the same result would obtain if the question had been one of whether local authorities involved in child protection work owed a duty of care to the alleged abuser.

## JD v. East Berkshire Community NHS Trust

Whilst the decision in X with regard to the duty of care owed to children at risk of abuse appears to have been displaced by a line of cases culminating in JD v. East Berkshire Community NHS Trust,[5] much of the X judgment remains good law with regard to the accused claimant. The case of JD raised directly the issue of liability to the wrongly accused in the context of three claims summarised below, the House of Lords finding that no duty of care was owed by medical practitioners towards those wrongly accused of abusing their children:[6]

- The '*Oldham* claim' – this case related to a child who was separated from her parents for almost nine months whilst suspicions of child abuse prompted by a diagnosis of non-accidental injury in hospital were investigated. The abuse allegations were dispensed with when the child was diagnosed as suffering from brittle bone disease, a

---

[4] [1995] 2 AC 633. Although the majority of the claims determined in X were those of children allegedly affected by the defendants' negligence, the claim of M v. Newham LBC concerned a claim brought by both mother and child who had been separated due to the defendant's mistaken belief that the mother's boyfriend was the child's abuser (for more discussion of this case see Chapter 2).

[5] JD v. East Berkshire Community NHS Trust [2005] UKHL 23; [2005] 2 WLR 993, see Chapter 2.

[6] With the exception of Lord Bingham dissenting. Their Lordships' ruling has since been applied by the Court of Appeal in D v. Bury Metropolitan Borough Council; H v. Bury Metropolitan Borough Council [2006] EWCA Civ 1; [2006] 1 FCR 148.

condition which was entirely consistent with the fractures which gave rise to the initial diagnosis of abuse.
- The *'East Berkshire* claim' – a case in which a child was placed on the 'at risk' register following a suggestion that the child's allergies were an invention of his mother who was exhibiting signs of Munchausen's Syndrome by Proxy (MSBP). When the true extent of the child's allergic reactions was discovered, the MSBP diagnosis was abandoned, but the child's mother claimed damages for psychiatric harm as a result of seeing a note of the MSBP diagnosis on her son's file.[7]
- The *'Dewsbury* claim' – this claim concerned a father wrongly accused of sexual abuse who had been separated from his daughter for ten days. In the presence of other hospital visitors from the claimant's community, he was prevented from seeing his daughter at the hospital with the result that news of the accusations quickly spread through the father's neighbourhood. The father was vindicated when his daughter was diagnosed as having Schamberg's disease, a skin condition resulting in patchy discolouration of the skin.

The finding against a duty of care in all these cases was due to successful arguments that both proximity and the justice, fairness and reasonableness requirement precluded a duty of care on these facts. This was because:

(i) reasoning by analogy with judgments in cases of 'secondary victims' who had witnessed tragic events occurring to their loved ones,[8] there was no proximity as there was no 'critical event' which could be regarded as triggering the harm to the claimant (Lord Rodger); and
(ii) a duty of care would not be just, fair and reasonable as it would cut across the duty owed to the child; in any case, reasoning by analogy

---

[7] In *JD v. East Berkshire*, at first instance ([2003] Lloyd's Rep Med 9), the alleged 'abuser' attempted to circumvent the anticipated ruling that no duty was owed to a non-patient by arguing that on the facts of this case, the clinician concerned had diagnosed her – a fact which created the necessary proximity. The court, however, regarded the conflict as identical to that in child abuse cases and therefore it was not just, fair and reasonable to impose a duty, although the court refused to offer a conclusion on whether proximity had been established ([2003] Lloyd's Rep Med 9 (Chester CC)). Cf. the contrary decision in *James W v. Superior Court* (1993) 17 Cal App 4th 246, where the 'family' was referred to a counsellor and a duty was owed to the parent.
[8] The leading authorities on secondary victim claims being *Alcock v. Chief Constable of South Yorkshire* [1992] 1 AC 310 and *McLoughlin v. O'Brian* [1983] 1 AC 410.

with claims brought by those wrongly accused of criminal acts by the police, a duty of care ought only to exist where there was an absence of good faith on the part of the defendant.[9]

The content of these rulings relies heavily on the 'reasoning by analogy' approach,[10] a technique of judicial reasoning based on an intuitive desire to avoid inequity between similar types of case by ensuring that claimants in such cases are bound for a similar outcome. It is also an approach which creates an undeserved appearance of objectivity: quite different conclusions could have been reached had different areas of law been selected for the analogising process.[11]

**Reasonable foreseeability and proximity** As to the foreseeability of harm to these parent claimants, proof of such foreseeability is surely unproblematic.[12] Such an individual is not only stigmatised by society, but suffers irreparable damage in their familial relationships, possibly resulting in divorce or loss of employment opportunities, and their rights of custody/access may be affected where young children are involved. The Court of Appeal in *JD* accepted the trial judge's conclusion that there was an arguable case of foreseeability of harm to the wrongly accused parents in the three cases before it and nothing further was said on foreseeability in the House of Lords. If support were needed for an argument that psychiatric and economic harm might result from child abuse allegations, reference could be made to Eady J's statement in libel proceedings based on such allegations: 'With the possible exception of murder, it is difficult to think of any charge more calculated to lead to the revulsion and condemnation of a person's fellow citizens than that of the systematic and sadistic abuse of children.'[13]

Only Lord Rodger dealt with the proximity aspect of establishing a duty of care in any detail. In his judgment, which treated the appeals as primarily concerned with the recovery of damages for psychiatric injury,

---

[9] [2005] UKHL 23; [2005] 2 WLR 993 at [77] and [136], relying on *Calveley v. Chief Constable of the Merseyside Police* [1989] AC 1228 and *Elguzouli-Daf v. Comr of Police of the Metropolis* [1995] QB 335.
[10] Promoted in *Caparo Industries plc v. Dickman* [1990] 1 All ER 568 for use alongside the tripartite test for establishing a duty of care in novel situations.
[11] See below.
[12] As noted above, the foreseeability of harm to the accused parent was accepted as arguable by the Court of Appeal in the *JD* litigation.
[13] *Lillie and Reed v. Newcastle City Council* [2002] EWHC 1600; (2002) 146 SJLB 225 at [1538].

proximity required something more than the fact that the claimants had taken their children to see doctors employed by the defendants. Proximity demanded proof of something along the lines of 'experiencing a critical event'.[14] Otherwise, a wrongly accused parent could sue for psychiatric damage whereas a 'secondary victim' parent who suffered psychiatric damage when their child was killed in a road accident could not sue the negligent driver unless they had witnessed a sudden traumatic event.[15] With respect, the analogy drawn between wrongly accused parents and 'secondary victims' is flawed, as it appears to assume that the recovery of damages for psychiatric harm at common law is confined to claimants who are either involved in or who witness a sudden traumatic event when this is blatantly not the case. If Lord Rodger's argument were taken to its logical conclusion there would be no such thing as a stress at work claim due to the absence of a 'critical event', and yet such claims have recently been given the House of Lords' seal of approval.[16] Notably, the proximity reasoning was absent from the later judgment in *D v Bury MBC*, where the Court of Appeal relied purely on policy to deny a duty of care was owed to a mother separated from her child during an abuse investigation.[17]

**Justice, fairness and reasonableness** The remainder of their Lordships' judgments in *JD* focused solely on the policy issues raised, concluding that it would not be just, fair and reasonable to impose a duty of care towards the accused on the defendants.[18] Lord Nicholls found the conflict of interest argument compelling and drew analogies not with 'nervous shock' claims but with case law governing the remedies available to those wrongly suspected of criminal conduct. These cases revealed that the only civil remedies for such claimants were the tort of misfeasance, defamation and malicious prosecution, all of which required malice or the absence of good faith for the claimant to succeed.[19] Lord Nicholls thus concluded that in the sphere of erroneous

---

[14] At [108].
[15] As *per* the rules set out for secondary victims in *Alcock v. Chief Constable of South Yorkshire* [1992] 1 AC 310.
[16] *Barber v. Somerset CC* [2004] UKHL 13; [2004] 1 WLR 1089.
[17] [2006] EWCA Civ 1; [2006] 1 FCR 148.
[18] Cf. the dissenting judgment of Lord Bingham.
[19] At [77]. Although malice is not a requirement of the defamation action, the defence of qualified privilege would invariably apply in such cases and can only be defeated by malice.

allegations of abuse, compensation should only be available where there was a lack of good faith on the defendant's part. As with the analogy drawn with secondary victims, the analogy employed by Lord Nicholls should not be accepted without further consideration. Those who, through no fault of their own, become the subject of false criminal allegations by the police have the protection of the exacting 'beyond reasonable doubt' standard of proof and have the benefit of legal representation during questioning and any court appearance. The same cannot be said of parents who are falsely accused of abuse, for the standard of proof applicable to justify intervention (e.g. the granting of a care order by the Family Proceedings Court) in suspected child abuse cases is one of a 'real possibility of harm' to the child and is more akin to the civil standard.[20]

Lord Brown thought that it would be impossible to conceptualise duties being owed to the child and to the potential abuser without these duties inevitably being in conflict. The denial of a duty of care also acted as a safeguard against vexatious litigation in an area which would probably be prone to retaliation by disgruntled families. Lord Rodger agreed that the imposition of a duty of care would not be 'just, fair and reasonable' because a duty of care to the wrongly accused would cut across the duty owed to the child. His acceptance of the conflict of interest argument is clearly predicated on defensive practice reasoning. He referred to 'the insidious effect that [the defendant's] awareness of the proposed duty would have upon the mind and conduct of the doctor (subtly tending to the suppression of doubts and instincts which in the child's interests ought rather to be encouraged)'.[21]

Incidentally, the paramountcy of professional duties towards the child has been used elsewhere as justification for the denial of a duty of care. In *A and another v. Essex CC* the conflict of interest rhetoric was central to the finding that adoption agencies owe no duty of care to prospective adoptive parents.[22] The result of this finding is that if the

---

[20] *Re H (Minors) Sexual Abuse: Standard of Proof* [1996] AC 563, where the term 'likely to suffer' in s. 31 of the Children Act 1989 was interpreted to mean that there was a 'real possibility' of suffering. Confirmed in *North Yorkshire CC v. SA* [2003] EWCA Civ 839; [2003] 2 FLR 849.
[21] [2005] UKHL 23; [2005] 2 WLR 993 at [137]. See Lord Bingham's (dissenting) scathing remark that to describe awareness of a legal duty as having an insidious effect on the mind of the defendant was to undermine the foundation of professional negligence liability [2005] UKHL 23; [2005] 2 WLR 993 at [33].
[22] [2003] EWCA Civ 1848; [2004] 1 FCR 660.

adoption agency decides to withhold information from the adoptive parents regarding the adopted child's propensity to violence or their mental state (and such decision was not so unreasonable as to fall outside the agency's statutory discretion), no remedy is available in negligence. Thus, it is not only in the investigation of abuse allegations that the child's interests preclude a duty of care being owed to adults involved in the caring process.

## Comment on *JD*

Ultimately, their Lordships chose to regard allegations made in error as the necessary price of effective child protection procedures, saying that though the wrongly accused parents in these cases had 'legitimate grievances' and had suffered 'every parent's nightmare', they were 'paying the price of the law's denial of a duty of care', but it was a price paid 'in the interests of children generally'.[23] The ruling in *JD* that no duty of care is owed to parents or other accused persons in cases involving the investigation of suspected child abuse, is replicated in judgments from Canada,[24] New Zealand[25] and Australia.[26] The pervasive acceptance of the rhetoric that a duty of care to the parent would undermine the paramountcy of the duty to the child and cause detrimental defensive practice should not, however, preclude analysis of its plausibility. Notably, the US courts have been more willing to embrace the notion of a duty to the accused parent, at least in the context of the liability of the alleged victim's therapist (see below). These authorities provide evidence that the logic of the conflict of interest rhetoric is not universally compelling.

The reasoning in *JD* directly endorses the assumption that a duty of care to the child's parents would inevitably be in direct conflict with the duty to the child. However, the Court of Appeal had expressly recognised that the duty of care owed to the child was not simply a duty to take reasonable care to protect the child from preventable abuse. It also encompassed a duty to take reasonable care to ensure that the child was not unnecessarily removed from its family. Therefore, in cases where the child's interests were best served by keeping the family together (e.g. unfounded allegations of abuse), the interests of the child and its parents

---

[23] [2005] UKHL 23; [2005] 2 WLR 993, *per* Lord Nicholls at [52] and Lord Brown at [138].
[24] *GA v. British Colombia* (1989) 61 DLR (4th) 136.
[25] *B v. Attorney General (No. 1 of 2003)* [2003] UKPC 61.
[26] *Sullivan v. Moody* (2001) 28 Fam LR 104.

would be mutually compatible. Furthermore, earlier case law recognises the harm that can be caused to a child by unnecessary or precipitate action to remove a child from its parents, 'however inadequate', and placing the child into foster care, 'however loving and skilled'.[27] Even the *X v. Bedfordshire CC* judgment recognises that the Children Act 1989 requires the local authority to have regard not only to the physical wellbeing of the child but also to the advantages of not disrupting the child's family environment.[28] Given the multidimensional nature of the duty of care owed to the child, it is difficult to see how recognising a duty of care to the parents would involve any additional burden or increase the risk of defensive practice: in other words, the responsibilities of the social worker do not change by recognising that the same duty is owed *additionally* to the parents.[29] Where the evidence suggests that abuse has occurred, or where there is a real and significant risk of abuse in the future, any perceived conflict between the duties owed to the parent and to the child can be resolved by reference to the paramountcy principle, thereby allowing the child's interests to take precedence. Moreover, where the evidence is equivocal as to whether there is a risk of abuse or not, a social worker who has erred on the side of caution in the child's interests is unlikely to be regarded by the courts as having breached their duty of care. Thus, the duty of care owed to the parents would only be enforceable insofar as it was compatible with the duty owed to the child.

The solution suggested above is not unique, but is merely a variation on other instances where the law employs a structuring or prioritising of duties of care and could therefore be reached by analogising with areas of law other than those which their Lordships in *JD* chose to focus upon. In the law governing the medical treatment of the pregnant woman, for example, it is acknowledged that doctors owe a duty of care to the pregnant woman *and* to the foetus, in so far as they are compatible, but that when the duties conflict, the rights of the pregnant woman must trump those of the unborn.[30] A solicitor drafting a will owes a duty of

---

[27] *Re H* [1991] FCR 736.
[28] See e.g. s. 17, which imposes a duty on the local authority to safeguard the welfare of children in need so far as is consistent with that duty to promote the upbringing of these children by their families.
[29] See discussion of *Hungerford v. Jones* 722 A 2d 478 (NH 1998) below.
[30] S. 1 of the Congenital Disabilities (Civil Liability) Act 1976, the therapeutic duty extends to the child, enforceable once born. The rights of the mother will, however, always prevail: *Re MB (Caesarean Section)* [1997] 2 FLR 426.

care to both the testator client and the intended beneficiaries, again only insofar as the duties are compatible.[31] The underlying policy rationale for recognising a duty of care to a non-client in this scenario was that otherwise the duty of care owed to the testator may be unenforceable once the testator had died. Equally, it can be forcefully argued that the duty owed to the child not to disrupt family life without good cause may be unenforceable in practice. The Court of Appeal in *D v. Bury MBC* clearly recognised that it would be almost impossible to prove that psychiatric damage had been caused to a young child due to being separated from its parents, as the limited language capability of a young child does not lend itself to psychiatric diagnosis.[32]

It is not only the conflict of interest assumption in the *JD* judgments which is precarious. The 'defensive practice' logic on which the judgments of Lord Nicholls and Lord Rodger in *JD* rest can also be refuted if reference is made to the case of Professor Southall. Professor Southall's peremptory allegations after watching a television documentary that a father had murdered two of his children is exactly the kind of case where civil action by the accused might be regarded as feasible and appropriate. In June 2004 Professor Southall was found guilty of serious professional misconduct by the General Medical Council ('GMC') and barred from child protection work for three years.[33] This finding by the GMC that irresponsible and unfounded allegations of child abuse can constitute serious professional misconduct signals the importance of fairness towards the accused in the child protection process. This message has important implications for the reasoning employed in *JD*. Given that fitness to practise proceedings can result in penalties which are devastating for the career of the individual practitioner, why is the risk of defensive practice and the impact of civil liability on the profession emphasised by their Lordships when the implications for the individual concerned are likely to be far less devastating than disciplinary proceedings? One possible answer may be that fitness to practise proceedings are insulated from vexatious complaints by the criminal standard of proof which attaches to such proceedings and the screening mechanisms applied before allowing a complaint to proceed to a full hearing (although

---

[31] *White v. Jones* [1995] 2 AC 207.     [32] [2006] EWCA Civ 1; [2006] 1 FCR 148.
[33] The High Court later refused to erase Professor Southall from the GMC's register but imposed tighter conditions on his future practise: *Council for the Regulation of Healthcare Professionals* v.*General Medical Council* [2005] EWHC 579; [2005] Lloyd's Rep Med 365.

the striking out procedures and the breach of duty stage in negligence litigation can be used to similar effect).

Others have argued in the alternative that a duty to the parents could usefully be recognised but that the task on which the defendant was engaged when the allegation was made is all important. Where the task is to treat the child, no third-party intervention should be tolerated, but where the task is to investigate with neutrality suspicions of abuse, standing to sue might sensibly be extended to affected third parties.[34] This would mean that, ordinarily, a defendant who stands in a professional client relationship with the allegedly abused person would not owe a duty of care to a third party accused. Furthermore, with reference to the discussion of *White v. Jones* above, the client is capable of enforcing the standard of care required of the defendant; therefore, the standard of care is adequately enforced. However, where the professional has been appointed by state agencies (e.g. welfare services) to investigate allegations of child abuse, there is a risk that the agency's mandate of the best interests of the child will unduly bias all concerned towards concluding that abuse has occurred, and that the child should be removed from their abusive environment. In such circumstances, a duty of care towards the parents and family of the child would serve as a useful check to ensure a measure of balance in the investigation and would reinforce the duty to the child to protect it from peremptory removal from its family.[35]

## Standard of care as a control device

It seems clear that the *Bolam* test will be applied to the standard of care expected of social workers and other professionals involved in work with children.[36] The *Bolam* test determines that the defendant will not be liable in negligence if they have acted in accordance with a 'responsible body of opinion' from the relevant profession. This standard affords defendants considerable latitude by acknowledging that a multitude of different practices may still meet the requisite standard. Thus, it is argued, the professional standard of care is sufficiently flexible to

---

[34] D. Partlett, 'Recovered Memories of Child Sexual Abuse and Liability' (1998) 4 *Psychology, Public Policy and Law* 1253.
[35] Partlett, 'Recovered Memories' at 1253.
[36] *Bolam v. Friern General Hospital Management Committee* [1957] 2 All ER 118. For its application to social workers, see *A v. Essex CC* [2003] EWCA Civ 1848; [2004] 1 FLR 749 at [57]–[58]; Lord Slynn of Hadley, in *Barrett v. Enfield LBC* [2001] 2 AC 550 at 568; *M v. Newham LBC* [1995] 2 AC 633, 666B, Sir Thomas Bingham MR describing social work as a profession.

accommodate the difficulties which a perceived conflict of interest may present to the professional defendant and there is no need to eliminate the possibility of a claim by ruling out a duty of care.

In further support of recognising a measured duty of care to those wrongly accused of abuse, counsel for the claimants in *JD* argued that the law on establishing a breach of duty could provide the necessary leniency to defendants engaged in difficult tasks of child protection. However, Lord Nicholls rejected counsel's suggestion of jettisoning the concept of duty of care as a means of controlling litigation in this field in favour of focusing on proof of breach of duty to accommodate the complexities of child protection work.[37] Lord Bingham's dissent spoke of such a strategy much more favourably and made reference to *Phelps v. Hillingdon LBC*,[38] where concerns were expressed about a flood of 'educational malpractice' claims being the result of recognising a duty of care on the part of local authority defendants towards children with unidentified dyslexia. Lord Clyde in *Phelps* had commented that any fear of a flood of 'educational malpractice' claims could be countered by the fact that the claimant must show that the standard of care fell below the *Bolam* standard, a 'deliberately and properly high standard' in recognition of the difficult nature of some of the decisions the defendant makes and 'leaving room for differences of view on the propriety of one course of action over another'. It is the author's view that this standpoint would have been equally apposite in litigation against professionals involved in cases of suspected child abuse. It is hard to fathom why particular types of work where it is acknowledged that the utmost care and sensitivity is needed, should effectively be excused from the legal requirement of the exercise of reasonable care. The law relating to standard of care enables attention to be paid to issues such as the need for quick action which abbreviates time for detailed consideration[39] and divergence of viewpoints as to best practice within a profession.[40]

## 2. An action for breach of statutory duty[41]

If the negligence route is unavailable to the wrongly accused claimant would it be possible in the alternative to bring a breach of statutory duty

---

[37] [2005] UKHL 23; [2005] 2 WLR 993 at [92]–[94].   [38] [2001] 2 AC 619.
[39] *Watt v. Hertfordshire CC* [1954] 1 WLR 835.
[40] *Bolam v. Friern General Hospital Management Committee* [1957] 2 All ER 118.
[41] For further detail on this cause of action see Chapter 2.

action? As to whether breach of a given statute gives rise to a civil remedy independent of the negligence action, the answer is always ultimately one of what Parliament intended.[42] Where the statute is silent as to whether Parliament intended a civil action for breach of this particular statutory provision to be available, the courts rely on a non-exhaustive set of presumptions in order to hypothesise as to Parliament's intentions in this regard. It seems unlikely that those wrongly accused of abuse could bring an action for breach of statutory duty where procedures under the Children Act 1989 or sibling legislation were not followed. For such an action to arise the claimant would need to demonstrate that they were one of the people whom the statutory regime was designed to protect, and that the damage suffered was of a type which the Act was designed to prevent.[43] It seems unlikely that a court would find that these pieces of legislation were designed to protect those suspected of abuse. Indeed, in *X v. Bedfordshire CC*, Lord Browne-Wilkinson described the Children Act 1989 as 'introduced primarily for the protection of a limited class, namely children at risk'.[44]

Further ammunition against the parents' claim for breach of statutory duty exists in the form of a presumption that the existence of statutory enforcement mechanisms or mechanisms for complaint will preclude a private law action.[45] Thus, in *X v. Bedfordshire CC*, the existence of the statutory complaints procedure[46] and the role of the Local Government Ombudsman[47] assisted the court in concluding that a tort claim for breach of statutory duty ought not to be available to children harmed by the local authority's failure to protect them. In claims brought by abused children, the ECtHR reached a contrary conclusion. A complaint to the ombudsman regarding the social services' inaction did not constitute an effective remedy under Article 13 of the ECHR, as the ombudsman had the power only to make recommendations and did not make a binding determination.[48] This ought to be persuasive in convincing a court

---

[42] *Cutler v. Wandsworth Stadium* [1949] AC 398.
[43] *Gorris v. Scott* (1874) 9 LR Exch 125.   [44] At 747.
[45] *Lonrho v. Shell Petroleum Co.* [1982] AC 173.
[46] S. 26(3) of the Children Act 1989 and the Local Authority Social Services (Complaints Procedure) Order 1990, SI 1990 No. 2244.
[47] These remedies should now be viewed in light of the Ombudsman for Children Act 2002, s. 8 of which provides that the post of ombudsman created by the Act may investigate complaints made against public bodies concerning action which appears to have adversely affected a child.
[48] *E v. UK* (2003) 36 EHHR 31 at H14.

that a breach of statutory duty action ought to be available to wrongly accused parents.

### 3. Claims brought under the Human Rights Act 1998

Violation of Article 8: the right to respect for family life

Where the conduct complained of occurred after October 2000, an action may be available against the public authority responsible under the Human Rights Act 1998.[49] The claim of the wrongly accused parent or family member is likely to be framed as one for breach of Article 8 of the Convention; a failure to afford 'respect for family life'. A fundamental element of 'family life' is the mutual right of both parent and child to enjoy each other's company; therefore, state intervention resulting in the separation of parent and child which is ostensibly on the grounds of suspected abuse must be the result of careful assessments which comply with Convention jurisprudence.

An interference with family life will not constitute a violation of Convention rights, provided it has been justified in accordance with the terms of Article 8(2), that is:

> ... [it is] in accordance with the law and is necessary in a democratic society in the interests of national security, public safety or the economic well-being of the country, for the prevention of disorder or crime, for the protection of health or morals, or for the protection of the rights and freedoms of others.

Judgments from the ECtHR on claims by separated families under Article 8 have focused on whether the separation was 'necessary in a democratic society'. Here, Convention jurisprudence has insisted on a degree of procedural fairness in decision making which involves an interference with family life.[50] It is acknowledged that action may need to be taken to protect the child in an emergency, in which case it will not always be practicable to afford the parent or guardian the opportunity to be involved in the decision-making process, as to do so may put the child at further risk.[51] However, once the emergency is over and the child is in a safe place, the state is under a duty to ensure that a careful assessment is made of the options for caring for the child,

---

[49] S. 7.
[50] *TP and KM v. UK* (2002) 34 EHRR 42; *Venema v. Netherlands* [2003] 1 FCR 153.
[51] *Venema v. Netherlands* [2003] 1 FCR 153.

including possible alternative arrangements for the child's care. Once the child is in a safe place, stricter scrutiny is called for with regard to steps which may curtail parental rights of access, and taking a child into care is to be regarded as a temporary measure to be discontinued as soon as possible.[52]

The procedural obligations of the state in this regard include legal representation of parents where court proceedings are employed to determine a child's future caring arrangements, not pursuing draconian steps such as adoption without thorough consideration of less severe options and involvement of parents in decision making, including an opportunity to respond to the evidence against them upon which the allegations are founded. These procedural requirements are well illustrated by two cases of enforced separation which occurred in the UK. In *P, C and S v. UK*,[53] the local authority took the applicant's child into care due to the concerns raised by a prior conviction of the mother in the US for deliberately administering laxatives to her first child (supposedly an expression of MSBP). The ECtHR heard that, in response to these concerns, the applicant's second child had been removed from her on the day of its birth and had shortly thereafter been freed for adoption. The judgment stated that removing a child from its mother at birth required 'exceptional justification' because of the traumatic impact of such a step on the physical and mental wellbeing of both mother and child, coupled with the fact that removal deprives the child of the health advantages of breast feeding. The procedural requirements of Article 8 were violated by the state's failure to ensure that the applicant was represented at legal proceedings to free the child for adoption (proceedings which were highly emotive and involved complex experts' evidence) and its peremptory action in moving straight for the draconian step of adoption without proper consideration of alternative care arrangements (e.g. long-term fostering).

In *TP v. UK*,[54] the ECtHR reviewed the decision of the English courts in *M v. Newham*.[55] The child concerned was suspected of being the victim of sexual abuse and was interviewed without the presence of her mother. In the interview, the child mentioned the name of the man responsible, a name which by sheer coincidence was shared by her mother's boyfriend. As a result of the interview, the child was removed from her mother to safeguard her from the threat of further abuse. After

---

[52] *P, C and S v. UK* [2002] 3 FCR 1.   [53] [2002] 3 FCR 1.   [54] [2001] 2 FLR 549.
[55] One of the cases heard on appeal in the case of *X (Minors) v. Bedfordshire CC* [1995] 2 AC 633 in the House of Lords.

a year's separation, the child's mother was permitted to view a video recording of the interview. Her response to the video shed new light on the abuse allegations and it became apparent that the person mentioned by her daughter as the abuser was not her mother's boyfriend at all, but a family friend/cousin of the same name. Mother and child were swiftly reunited. The ECtHR found that in the arena of child protection, states were to be given a wide margin of appreciation, but only insofar as emergency measures taken to safeguard the child from immediate danger were concerned. Therefore, whilst the initial decision to take the child into care was not criticised, the mother's Article 8 rights had been violated by the failure to provide her with adequate involvement in the decision-making process thereafter, for example, either by submitting the matter to the courts or promptly allowing her an opportunity to respond to the content of the video interview.[56] The state was obliged to ensure that the material on which they had decided to remove the child from the family home was made available to her mother at the earliest practicable opportunity, even in the absence of a specific request by the mother. In addition to the violation of Article 8, there had been no satisfaction of the right to a remedy under Article 13, as neither the ombudsman or statutory complaints regime afforded the opportunity for compensation. Damages were therefore awarded for distress and anxiety and feelings of frustration and injustice.

These cases demonstrate that in contrast to the common law position, the accused who is a close member of the child's family is afforded a remedy under the ECHR where the children of the accused have been removed unnecessarily. The common law now lacks symmetry in providing protection of the child claimant's Convention rights but not those of the parents. After all, it was recognised in the Court of Appeal in *JD* that the duty of care owed to the child included a duty not to remove the child from the family home peremptorily; therefore, whilst the child's Article 8 rights are reflected in the negligence remedy, the parents' rights under Article 8 are not. If, as appears to be the case, the courts are willing to extend a duty of care to the child claimant in the light of the Human Rights Act, why can it not carve a remedy for the parents in a similar fashion? On this point the Court of Appeal in *JD* merely stated that the law of negligence did not have to replicate the duty not to violate Article 8, and that a violation of Article 8 may occur where

---

[56] See also *Glass v. UK* [2004] 1 FCR 553, where the child's right to parental involvement in decision-making is emphasised.

the tort of negligence was not made out.[57] Presumably, therefore, the court is relying on the availability of an action brought specifically under the Human Rights Act to address any Article 8 issues affecting the wrongly accused parent. Such an action will, of course, be of no avail to the claimant seeking compensation for conduct which occurred pre-2000. In the House of Lords, Lord Nicholls again refused to extend the duty of care so as to mirror the protection provided by Article 8 on the grounds that it would create an unjustifiable distinction between allegations against a child's primary carers (e.g. parents who would be protected by the duty of care) and other victims of abuse allegations such as school teachers or child minders.[58]

Complaints under Article 8 are not confined to cases where the accused parent has been separated from the child or excluded from the family home. An allegation that the complainant may be abusing a member of the family may be enough. In *W v. Westminster CC*, a report prepared for a child protection case conference included the comment that a year previously concerns had been raised that the claimant may have been grooming his stepdaughter for prostitution. This disclosure to those invited to the conference was found to be unnecessary, humiliating and likely to have caused at least some temporary damage to the claimant's reputation. A violation of Article 8 was established, although no damages were awarded in light of the fact that the defendants had investigated the disclosure promptly and had since apologised for their conduct.[59]

### Violation of Article 6: the right of access to court

In *TP v. UK*,[60] the applicants argued that the House of Lords ruling in *X v. Bedfordshire CC* that no duty of care arose out of local authorities' statutory child protection functions effectively conferred a blanket immunity against liability and thereby violated the applicants' right to access to court under Article 6. This argument was based on the earlier ruling in *Osman v. UK*,[61] which had decided that an immunity afforded to the police from liability in negligence in their crime prevention function violated the claimant's right of access to court. In *TP* the

---

[57] At [85]. See also *K v. Secretary of State for the Home Department* [2002] EWCA Civ 983, where Arden LJ asserts that s. 7 of the Human Rights Act exists for the enforcement of ECHR rights where the common law does not reflect these rights.
[58] [2005] UKHL 23; [2005] 2 WLR 993 at [80].   [59] [2005] EWHC 102.
[60] [2001] 2 FLR 549.   [61] [1999] 1 FLR 193.

ECtHR distanced itself from its ruling in *Osman*, suggesting that it was based on a misunderstanding of the workings of English tort law and that the English court's decision that imposing a duty of care on the police in such cases would not be 'just, fair and reasonable' did not disclose an immunity engaging the right of access to court under Article 6.[62] There appear to be two elements to this depiction of the *Osman* ruling. First, the judgment of Lord Browne-Wilkinson in *X v. Bedfordshire CC* had clarified that the courts were obliged to consider both arguments supporting the justice and fairness of imposing a duty (including the consideration that a wrong deserves a remedy) and arguments suggesting that imposition of a duty of care in these circumstances would be unfair and unjust. Thus the court's conclusion was to be the result of a balancing process which considered both sides. Secondly, the Court stated that Article 6 did not guarantee the content of civil rights within any given Member State (e.g. the right to sue the police or social services in negligence), rather it guaranteed that there should be no disproportionate obstacles to the enforcement of those civil rights.

Having undermined the grounds on which the Article 6 argument in *TP* was based, this part of the claimant's case was doomed to failure. The Court added that as the *X* case had reached the House of Lords with the benefit of legal aid, there had been no practical obstruction hindering the applicant from litigating their case. Moreover, the fact that their case had been struck out as disclosing no reasonable cause of action without a full assessment of the facts did not constitute a violation of Article 6 either.

Complaints under Article 6 should essentially relate to the fairness of the hearing overall. Thus, in the context of a criminal trial, the Court found in *PS v. Germany*[63] that a conviction for sexual offences based on uncorroborated evidence of a witness with no opportunity for cross-examination of this witness constituted a violation of Article 6. Even in the context of a civil action, similar procedural unfairness may violate Article 6 given the seriousness of allegations of sexual offences against a child.

Given the ruling in *JD* that no civil redress is available to the subject of false allegations of abuse in the absence of bad faith, the torts of misfeasance, defamation and malicious prosecution assume fresh importance. The former of these is discussed immediately below, given its particular application to those working in local authority departments. For detail on actions in defamation and malicious prosecution see the discussion towards the end of this chapter.

---

[62] *Z v. United Kingdom* (2002) 34 EHRR 97.   [63] (2003) 36 EHRR 61.

## 4. Misfeasance in public office

Two forms of the tort of misfeasance in public office have been identified.[64] The first form involves targeted malice and applies when a public officer engaged in conduct intended to injure the claimant, whereas the second form involves implied malice and requires proof that the public officer knew he had no power to do the act complained of and that the act would probably injure the claimant. A successful misfeasance action requires proof of material physical, psychiatric or economic damage suffered as a result of the public officer's act.[65]

Prior to demonstrating the necessary malice, it must be shown that the tortfeasor is a 'public officer'. In the New Zealand case of *E v. K*,[66] a father wrongly accused of abusing his daughter sued the social worker who had informed the police of the allegations. The court found, however, that the social worker was not a public officer: the statutory principle of ensuring that the child's interests were paramount did not disclose a duty owed towards the public. It seems unlikely that an English court would have reached the same conclusion. In *W v. Essex CC*,[67] the claimant alleged that a social worker was guilty of the tort of misfeasance and that the council were vicariously liable for that tort. The court did not take issue with the assumption relied upon by the claimant that a social worker was a public officer. Furthermore, in *X v. Bedfordshire CC*, Lord Browne-Wilkinson described the Children Act 1989 as a statute intended to create an administrative scheme designed to protect the welfare of the community.[68] This would seem to support the suggestion that a social worker carrying out the remit of the local authority is a public officer.

It is highly unlikely that a claimant will be able to demonstrate proof of either targeted or implied malice against a social worker. In *W v. Essex CC* in the Court of Appeal, the fact that whilst acting in pursuance of statutory powers the officer negligently or even deliberately gave misleading information did not mean he knowingly exceeding his powers for the purpose of demonstrating implied malice.

---

[64] As set out by Lord Steyn in *Three Rivers DC v. Governor and Company of the Bank of England* [2000] 2 WLR 1220 at 1230–1236.
[65] *Watkins v. Secretary of State for the Home Department and Others* [2006] UKHL 17; [2006] 2 WLR 807, overturning the Court of Appeal's decision that where the tortious act amounts to a breach of the claimant's constitutional rights it is actionable per se.
[66] [1995] 2 NZLR 239.   [67] [1998] PIQR 346.   [68] [1995] 2 AC 633 at 747.

## 5. Witness immunity[69]

Even if a negligence or breach of statutory duty action were to be available to a wrongly accused party in English law, the defendants may raise witness immunity either as a defence or as an attempt to negate suggestions that they owe a duty of care to those affected by an abuse investigation. The immunity applies equally to honest and dishonest witnesses,[70] although this is subject to what is said below about referral to disciplinary bodies. In *Darker v. Chief Constable for the West Midlands Police*,[71] it was confirmed that public policy did not justify extending witness immunity to things said or done which could not be fairly said to be part of their participation in the judicial process.[72] This distinction is not always easy to apply, and the limits of the immunity are drawn by balancing the public interest in the administration of justice and the competing policy that a wrong should not be without a remedy.[73] Case law establishes that, whereas the drafting of documents in anticipation of court proceedings attracts immunity,[74] the immunity does not apply to work which is done primarily to advise a client of their litigation prospects.[75] The limits of witness immunity will apply equally to claims by the accused claimant. The case of *L (A Minor) v. Reading BC*[76] might, however, be usefully referred to, involving as it did the raising of the witness immunity argument in a case brought by a vindicated father. The Court of Appeal refused to strike out actions in negligence and misfeasance in public office on the grounds of witness immunity, given that the allegations against the defendant amounted to little short of perjury. As witness immunity was not absolute and was to be applied proportionately, it was not to be used to defend an abuse of power such as that alleged on these facts.[77]

Witness immunity will also preclude disciplinary proceedings where the content of the complaint relates to a professional's conduct as an expert witness in a court of law.[78] This immunity was expressed in *Meadow*

---

[69] The issue of witness immunity has been dealt with in some detail in Chapter 2 with regard to the abused claimant.
[70] *Meadow v. General Medical Council* [2006] EWHC 146; [2006] 2 All ER 329 at [13].
[71] [2000] 4 All ER 193.   [72] [2000] 4 All ER 193, per Lord Hope of Craighead at 197.
[73] *Darker v. Chief Constable for the West Midlands Police* [2000] 4 All ER 193.
[74] *Taylor v. Director of the Serious Fraud Office* [1999] 2 AC 177.
[75] *Palmer v. Durnford Ford* [1992] 2 All ER 122.   [76] [2001] PIQR 29.
[77] Misuse of video evidence and pressurising the child in interview to accuse her father of abuse.
[78] *Meadow v. General Medical Council* [2006] EWHC 146; [2006] 2 All ER 329.

*v. General Medical Council* as subject to the possibility that the court may itself make a referral to the relevant disciplinary body where it is felt that the expert's conduct falls so far below professional standards that the expert's professional status ought to be reviewed.[79] According to the *Meadow* judgment, a witness who acted honestly and in good faith is extremely unlikely to be the subject of a court referral; incompetence or overconfidence in one's own abilities will not suffice. Whilst it may appear that the courts are arrogating to themselves a new power here, this statement was presumably made on the grounds that standing is not generally required for making complaints to disciplinary bodies.

## Claims against the medical profession

### 1. Confidentiality obligations[80]

The medical profession may become involved in abuse allegations either by identifying a patient who may be the subject of abuse (in which case they are under a quasi-statutory obligation to report their suspicions to social services),[81] by having a potential victim of abuse referred to them for assessment, or by being invited to give evidence to the police or the courts. In the former instance, the doctor's ethical obligations comprise an intricate mix of confidentiality, beneficence (acting to ensure the protection of those at risk), non-maleficence (not taking peremptory action which would cause harm) and protecting the public interest.

The legal duty of confidence can be viewed as attaching to the relationship shared by confider and confidee (e.g. the doctor/patient relationship[82]). Alternatively, the duty of confidence arises where it can be said that the confidee has notice that the information is confidential with the effect that it would be just in all the circumstances that he

---

[79] *Ibid*. At [22]–[23].
[80] The issue of breach of confidence may well be raised in the context of a social worker's conduct but is more readily associated with the duties of the medical profession and is discussed in this section for the sake of convenience.
[81] See para 5.6 of *Working Together to Safeguard Children* (DoH, Home Office, DfEE, 1999), the government's guidance to doctors and social workers issued under s. 7 of the Local Authority Services Act 1970: 'If somebody believes that a child may be suffering, or may be at risk of suffering significant harm, then s/he should always refer his or her concerns to the local authority social services department.'
[82] *Attorney General v. Guardian Newspapers (No. 2)* [1990] 1 AC 109, *per* Lord Keith at 255.

should be precluded from disclosing the information to others.[83] For example, if the confidee received information that the confider was the subject of abuse, they would surely be taken to have notice that such information must be kept confidential.[84] The legal duty of confidence 'depends on the broad principle of equity that he who has received information in confidence shall not take unfair advantage of it'.[85] For the purposes of bring an action in equity for breach of confidence, it seems that it is not necessary to prove that the subject of the confidential information suffered any detriment from its disclosure,[86] or at least if proof of detriment is necessary, the requirement is a rather hollow one, requiring only that the disclosure was unwanted.[87] The duty of confidence can also be enforced according to the ordinary principles of contract law where a contract exists between the parties[88] (of course, a contract would not exist where the doctor concerned is working for the NHS[89]), or via the tort of negligence where it can be demonstrated that the defendant negligently breached confidence and that breach has occasioned harm to the claimant.[90]

Where allegations of abuse are made to a doctor, or the doctor suspects abuse to be occurring, the paramount duty is to protect the child. Disclosure of the confidential information can lawfully be made with the consent of the subject(s) of the information. If the child as patient refuses to consent to disclosure, the GMC advises that if the doctor feels disclosure is in the patient's medical interests they may disclose their suspicions to the relevant authorities, having first tried to persuade the parent to agree to disclosure.[91] Seeking parental consent (whether the parent is the suspected abuser or not) before reporting suspicions to social services is regarded as good practice, although where

---

[83] *Ibid.*, per Lord Goff at 658.
[84] *Attorney General v. Guardian Newspapers (No. 2)* [1988] 3 All ER 545, per Lord Goff at 658, or, alternatively, applying the test applied in *R v. Department of Health, ex parte Source Informatics* [2000] 1 All ER 786 (CA), disclosure without justification would affect the reasonable doctor's conscience.
[85] *Attorney General v. Guardian Newspapers (No. 2)* [1990] 1 AC 109, per Bingham LJ (approved in the House of Lords' judgment at 215–216).
[86] Rose J in *X v. Y* [1988] 2 All ER 648 at 657.
[87] Lord Keith in *Attorney General v. Guardian Newspapers (No. 2)* [1990] 1 AC 109 at 256.
[88] *Ackroyd v. MerseyCare NHS Trust* [2003] EWCA Civ 663; [2003] Lloyd's Rep Med 379; *Cornelius v. De Taranto* [2001] EMLR 12 (QBD), confirmed by the Court of Appeal ([2002] EMLR 6).
[89] *Reynolds v. Health First Medical Group* [2000] Lloyd's Rep Med 240.
[90] *C v. Cairns* [2003] Lloyd's Med Rep 90; *Furniss v. Fitchett* [1958] NZLR 396.
[91] *Protecting and Providing Information* (GMC, 2004) para 28.

involving the parents would increase the risk to the child, such involvement can be avoided.[92]

If both the child and the alleged perpetrator are the doctor's patients, the duty to protect the child may conflict with the duty of confidentiality owed to the suspected abuser and it must be decided whether the public interest principle justifies disclosure. The duty of confidence may be displaced by the 'public interest' defence, which applies where it can be said that the public interest in reporting the allegations outweighs the public interest in maintaining the confidence. It is well established that the public interest principle will permit disclosure where maintaining the patient's confidence presents a real risk of serious physical harm.[93]

### Conflicting duties: the duty of confidence and the duty to report suspected abuse

A frequent source of confusion is the uncertainty surrounding the precise fit between the *permitted instances* of disclosing confidential information and the apparent *duty* to disclose suspicions of abuse to social services.[94] In the context of confidentiality, the GMC refers to 'the risk of death' or of 'serious harm' as justifying disclosure.[95] On the other hand, professional guidance from the Royal College of Paediatricians and Child Health ('RCPCH') on the duty to report cases of children who are suffering or are likely to suffer significant harm states:

> ... it is important for all parties to consider the possibility that any form of harm may be *significant* in any seriously abusive relationship with a child. This is irrespective of whether the child is at the time suffering or seems likely to suffer significant physical injury in the immediate future (given that an abusive relationship may suddenly spin out of control).[96]

Whilst on the face of it the duty of confidence and the duty to report abuse appear to produce conflicting responsibilities (i.e. a duty to

---

[92] *Responsibilities of Doctors in Child Protection Cases with regard to Confidentiality* (RCPCH, February 2004) at 2.7.
[93] *W v. Edgell* [1990] 1 All ER 835. In addition to arguments based on the public interest principle, it has recently become clear that confidence may be breached on the alternative grounds that it is in the best interests of the child patient (or presumably in the best interests of the incompetent adult patient): *C v. Cairns* [2003] Lloyd's Rep Med 90: 'Thus though it is agreed that on (rare) occasions duties of confidence would have to give way to the "best interests" of the patient those "best interests" would have to be assessed according to the level of knowledge prevailing at the time', per Stuart Brown QC.
[94] See note 81 above.   [95] *Protecting and Providing Information*, para 27.
[96] *Responsibilities of Doctors* at 4.8 (emphasis added).

maintain confidence unless there is a *serious risk* of harm and a duty to report cases of suspected *significant* harm), a court would probably take the view that there is no meaningful distinction between the risks of *significant* and *serious* harm in the context of child abuse. In other words, any reasonable suspicion of abuse equates to a risk of 'serious harm'. Therefore, whether the doctor's disclosure of suspected abuse is viewed from the perspective of the doctor's confidentiality obligations or the quasi-statutory obligation to inform social services where child abuse is suspected, there is probably little difference between the threshold of risk required to justify disclosure in the former case and that which demands disclosure under the latter. There seems little objection, therefore, to the proposition that the public interest would justify breach of a patient's confidence where the objective is to protect a child from a real risk of physical or sexual abuse. This conclusion is consistent with the soundings of the recent Climbié Inquiry, which endorsed the principle that child protection required professionals and others to share information, as it was precisely the failure to share information, which was regarded as responsible for the preventable death of 8-year-old Victoria Climbié at the hands of her carers.[97]

Whilst the general framework of the duty of confidence and the exceptions which allow lawful disclosure are clear, the exact scope of the circumstances in which disclosure will be permitted are less than clear. Interestingly, in the case of *TP v. UK*,[98] one of the doctors involved in the case expressed the opinion that the video-taped interview in which it was purported the child had identified her mother's boyfriend as her abuser should not be disclosed to the mother on the grounds of confidentiality! Professional guidance to the medical profession resonates with the sentiment of safeguarding the child's best interests, but different sources of guidance do not express the duty in identical terms. For example, British Medical Association ('BMA') guidance focuses on the patient who is capable of consenting and provides that:

> In any case where abuse is suspected, the vulnerable person's wellbeing is paramount, and the promotion of such should be the motivating factor in any decision to disclose. Wherever possible, doctors should discuss disclosure with the individual concerned and seek consent ... However, in

---

[97] *The Victoria Climbié Inquiry: Report of an Inquiry by Lord Laming.* (Stationery Office, 2003) at 7.28 citing in particular the confusion amongst professionals as to the legal restrictions on disclosure.
[98] [2001] 2 FLR 549.

some circumstances disclosure will be urgently required to avert serious harm. In such cases doctors will have to weigh up the benefits of taking time to involve and inform patients and the risks associated with delaying.[99]

The current guidance from the GMC differs from that of the BMA by focusing on patients who are unable to consent to disclosure (e.g. young children). In such circumstances, the doctor must make a judgment as to what is in the patient's best interests:

> If, for any reason, you believe that disclosure of information is not in the best interests of an abused or neglected patient, you should discuss the issues with an experienced colleague. If you decide not to disclose information, you must be prepared to justify your decision.[100]

Note that, according to the GMC's guidance on confidentiality, the doctor is under no explicit duty to involve an experienced colleague if they decide that disclosure *is* in the patient's best interests. The guidance therefore enshrines a presumption that disclosure of suspicions of abuse is to be preferred, and that a contrary course of action must be supported and justified.

## 2. The tort of negligence

The courts are generally opposed to imposing liability on the medical profession towards non-patients, a major obstacle to the assertion that a third party to the therapeutic relationship between doctor and child patient, and who is accused or suspected of committing child abuse, is owed a duty of care.

### Proximity considerations: the accused as non-patient

Once again, to establish that a duty of care is owed by the doctor as defendant, the alleged abuser must demonstrate foreseeability of harm, proximity with the defendant and that the imposition of a duty of care is just, fair and reasonable.[101] Establishing foreseeability of psychiatric harm to the alleged abuser is fairly unproblematic (see above). In the case of the therapist or treating clinician who has played a role in accusing the claimant of abuse, litigation is hampered by the fact that the clinician's patient is generally the suspected victim of the abuse and

---

[99] *Confidentiality and Disclosure of Health Information* (BMA, 1999).
[100] *Protecting and Providing Information*, para 29.
[101] *Caparo Industries plc v. Dickman* [1990] 1 All ER 568.

the alleged abuser is outside that therapeutic relationship. That being so, proof of proximity between the parties is unlikely. The issue of whether proximity can be demonstrated depends upon the relationship between the defendant and alleged abuser, and in many cases is precluded because the defendant's client or patient is the potential victim of the abuse, and this relationship does not automatically extend to the parents or family of the patient.

To clarify the traditional English position with regard to therapeutic duties to third parties generally, and to the child patient's parents in particular, it is useful to refer to the pre-*JD* decision in *Powell v. Boldaz*.[102] Here, the parents of a deceased child sued a number of defendants, including general practitioners and an NHS trust, for causing psychiatric damage by allegedly forging documents relating to the medical treatment and subsequent death of their child. The Court of Appeal held that the doctor's duty was to the patient and none other, and did not extend to the parents of a patient unless the doctor had undertaken to treat the parents (e.g. for depression following their son's death). Similarly, in *A B and others v. Leeds Teaching Hospital NHS Trust*,[103] Gage J found that doctors owed no duty of care to the parents of deceased child patients when conducting post-mortems on their child's body without consent. The only exceptions were cases where the purpose of the post-mortem was to advise the parents on the risks of complications in future pregnancies, and the parties could therefore be described as in a doctor/patient relationship.

It is submitted, however, that these cases place undue emphasis on whether there was a duty to heal owed to the parents, suggesting that unless the claimant could be described as a 'patient', they could not be owed a duty of care by the defendant doctor. Yet, for the purposes of the claims in *Powell* and in *AB*, the claimants were not alleging negligent medical treatment, so why would a finding that they were 'patients' be a prerequisite to a claim? These cases can also be criticised as being out of line with rulings in relation to other professions such as solicitors. If solicitors can share a special relationship giving rise to a duty of care to non-clients, why cannot a doctor owe a duty of care to a non-patient? As indicated above, the duty owed by solicitors to the beneficiaries of their client's will is now well established.[104] The key to these judgments

---

[102] (1998) 39 BMLR 116 (CA).   [103] [2004] EWHC 644; [2005] 2 WLR 358.
[104] *White v. Jones* [1995] 2 AC 207; *Carr-Glynn v. Frearsons* [1998] 4 All ER 614.

appears to be the fact that the courts in those cases were convinced of the complementarity of the duties to the client and the non-client, *and* the fact that the client was deceased and so full recompense for the consequences of the harm (e.g. via an action in contract by the client) was not otherwise possible.

### Policy considerations: justice, fairness and reasonableness

Their Lordships in *JD* ruled out a duty of care being owed by defendant medical practitioners to parents wrongly accused of abusing their children largely on the grounds of justice, fairness and reasonableness. A duty of care would cut across the duty owed to the child, and, in any case, reasoning by analogy with claims brought by those wrongly accused of criminal acts by the police, a duty of care ought only to exist where there was an absence of good faith on the part of the defendant. Authorities across most jurisdictions are similarly against the doctor or therapist owing a duty of care to the parents of a child alleged to have been abused on policy grounds. This position has recently been confirmed in Scotland in *Fairlie v. Perth and Kinross Healthcare NHS Trust*.[105] Here, the Outer House held that, in the absence of very clear circumstances to indicate that a consultant psychiatrist was acting outside the doctor/patient relationship with the child and had assumed a duty of care towards her parent(s), no duty of care would arise. Such a duty of care would, in any case, be problematic in conflicting with the public duty of psychiatrists to disclose to the relevant authorities their suspicions of abuse.[106] Even if a duty of care had been proved in *Fairlie*, there was the further issue of what damage had been suffered. The pursuer was seeking damages for loss of reputation which were traditionally recovered in defamation and not otherwise. Suing for loss of reputation using another form of action would usurp the strict time limit of one year imposed in a defamation action. (This particular reasoning is unlikely to be followed by English courts.[107])

---

[105] [2004] ScotCS 174.  [106] Based on the case of *W v. Edgell* [1990] 1 All ER 835.
[107] Where economic loss flowing from a statement concerning the claimant can be demonstrated, an action in either negligence or defamation may be available: *Spring v. Guardian Assurance plc* [1995] 2 AC 296. Although in *JD*, with regard to the East Berkshire claim, the Court of Appeal added that this particular claim had the appearance of a claim for defamation and allowing a negligence claim would involve bypassing the qualified privilege defence which ought not to be tolerated.

## Standard of care

Members of the medical profession are required to exercise the degree of skill of an ordinary person exercising and professing to possess the skills of that profession.[108] A defendant doctor will not be liable in negligence provided his or her conduct is supported by a responsible body of medical opinion.[109] Following professional guidance will usually suffice to demonstrate to the court that the defendant's conduct was supported by a 'responsible body' of professional opinion. It is, therefore, of some importance that in the context of suspected abuse, the BMA advises that doctors should not promise to keep information about child abuse confidential[110] and that if a doctor 'has a reasonable belief that a child is at serious risk of immediate harm, he or she should *act immediately* to protect the interests of the child'.[111] Furthermore, where both the potential abuser and potential abuse victim are registered with the same doctor, the BMA advises that the doctor's primary responsibility is to the child as the more vulnerable party.[112] Good practice publications in this area emphasise the importance of information sharing and multidisciplinary assessments of potential child abuse. The multidisciplinary nature of assessment is in part a legacy of the Cleveland scandal,[113] after which it became regarded as unsafe to rely solely on medical diagnosis to determine whether a child had been abused.[114] In cases where the doctor has concluded that the child is at risk of serious harm they should inform the local authority's social services department,[115] discuss their concerns with the mother/parent and inform them that they will be informing social services, consult a senior child protection professional and possibly refer the child to a consultant paediatrician if it is practicable to do so.[116] The professional duty will also require the defendant to keep abreast of published research and ethical guidance on issues pertaining to the treatment and management of patients who are suspected victims of abuse either by use of

---

[108] *Bolam v. Friern General Hospital Management Committee* [1957] 2 All ER 118.
[109] *Ibid.*
[110] *Doctors' Responsibilities in Child Protection Cases: Guidance from the Ethics Department* (BMA, 2004), p. 4.
[111] *Doctors' Responsibilities* (emphasis added), p. 6.     [112] *Doctors' Responsibilities*, p. 4.
[113] See discussion of the Cleveland scandal in Chapter 1.
[114] M. Bannon and Y. Carter (ed.), *Protecting Children from Abuse and Neglect in Primary Care* (OUP, 2003) at 163.
[115] *Working Together*, para 5.6.
[116] Bannon and Carter, *Protecting Children from Abuse and Neglect* at 155.

professional journals or taking up training opportunities.[117] Having said that it, has been reported that there is a general lack of undergraduate or postgraduate training of general practitioners in child maltreatment and, consequently, an underutilised role in preventing abuse and protecting children from abuse.[118]

One potential problem in articulating the appropriate standard of care would be that imposing a duty of care on the medical profession towards the accused implies that the defendant must not simply accept his patient's revelations as truth, but must engage in some form of investigation to seek corroboration of his patient's allegations. Yet the doctor's powers of investigation are severely limited, and it is difficult to see how the doctor could conduct such non-clinical investigations.[119]

### Defendant liability for implantation of false memories in the US

The liability of doctors, therapists and counsellors for revealing or implanting 'false memories' of abuse is, and is likely to remain, an unexplored avenue of complaint in English law.[120] There are, however, a number of US decisions addressing this type of legal action and the cases generated by this type of complaint provide evidence that the conflict of interest rhetoric used to deny a professional duty of care to those wrongly accused of abuse is not universally compelling.

The first hurdle for a claimant accused of abuse seeking damages for the harm caused by negligent implantation of false memories is to demonstrate that the therapist owes them a duty of care. Attention to this issue was heightened by the seminal litigation in the unreported

---

[117] *Crawford v. Board of Governors of Charing Cross Hospital* (1953) *The Times*, 8 December.
[118] *The Role of Primary Care in the Protection of Children from Abuse and Neglect: A Position Paper for the Royal College of General Practitioners* (2002). This was followed by the publication by the Royal College of General Practitioners offering guidance on the protection of children from abuse and neglect (Carter and Bannon, *Protecting Children from Abuse and Neglect*).
[119] Partlett, 'Recovered Memories of Child Sexual Abuse' at 1253.
[120] This is largely due to the Brandon Report (Brandon et al., 'Reported Recovered Memories of Child Sexual Abuse'). The report condemns practices which are used to elicit recovered memories of abuse (e.g. hypnosis and drug-induced abreaction). See further discussion of the Brandon Report in Chapter 4. The tone of the Brandon Report should reduce the incidence of therapeutic practices which could result in implantation of false memories of abuse. It also means that where implantation has occurred in the course of therapy, proof of breach of the therapeutic standard of care should be more straightforward than in the US.

Californian case of *Ramona v. Isabella*.[121] In *Ramona* a jury awarded damages of $500,000 to a father for emotional distress and the loss of his job, both caused by allegations of abuse arising out of his daughter's therapy. His daughter, Holly, began seeing therapists because of her bulimia and was told by the defendant therapist (Marche Isabella) that 70–80% of bulimia sufferers had suffered childhood sexual abuse. After several months of therapy, Holly began to recall memories of sexual abuse, including acts of bestiality, by her father. Holly was later offered sodium amytal, a barbiturate used as a relaxant which was once believed to facilitate the recovery of memories, and was told that she could not lie under the influence of this drug. The sodium amytal interview was not recorded but, according to Holly and her therapist, it confirmed Holly's memories of abuse by her father. The success of Mr Ramona's claim in negligence appears to have hinged on the fact that the defendants arranged a session during which Mr Ramona would be confronted with Holly's allegations, thereby involving the accused father in their therapeutic scheme and bringing him under the mantle of the therapeutic duty of care.

The outcome of *Ramona* can be contrasted with *Doe v. McKay*,[122] where the Illinois Supreme Court found no duty of care was owed to a third-party accused father despite his involvement in the therapy. His daughter had been receiving psychological treatment under the defendant's care during which she retrieved false memories of abuse by her father. A session was arranged with her father present so as to confront him with the allegations and allegedly to force a confession. The trial judge had decided for the father on the grounds of 'transferred negligence' – a doctrine which allowed a malpractice claim brought by a third party to succeed where the claimant was a quasi-patient (e.g. by virtue of being involved in the treatment of the defendant's patient). The Supreme Court rejected this reasoning, finding that transferred negligence did not apply where the interests of the patient and quasi-patient were conflicting, and that imposing a duty of

---

[121] *Ramona v. Isabella* (No C61898 Cal Sup Cr May 13, 1994). See also the Ingram case: *Ingram v. Chase Riverland and Robert Snyder* (1995), in which allegedly a man convicted of raping his daughters was interrogated by authorities in such a way that Ingram was effectively in a state of hypnosis which induced the creation of pseudo-memories of the abuse resulting in a false confession by an innocent man. (Note K. Olio and W. Cornell, 'The Façade of Scientific Documentation: A Case Study of Richard Ofshe's Analysis of the Paul Ingram Case' (1998) 4 *Psychology Public Policy and Law* 1182, which casts doubt on the validity of what has become the urban legend of *Ingram*'s case).

[122] 700 NE 2d 1018 (Ill 1998).

care would result in divided loyalties on the part of the therapist, thereby compromising the treatment of the patient. Furthermore, in order for a therapist to defend litigation by the third party, the therapist would need to breach the patient's confidence despite the importance of confidentiality to the therapeutic relationship.

### Other authorities denying a duty of care to the third-party accused

Amongst the US cases which, like *Doe v. McKay*, have ruled against a third party to the therapeutic relationship being owed a duty of care, the conflict of duty reasoning has been accompanied by a number of other arguments against liability to non-patients.

**Defensive practice/undermining therapeutic duties** The policy restrictions cited in *X v. Bedfordshire CC*, are, it seems, equally applicable to negligence claims in the US against the psychotherapist who uncovers the alleged abuse. The spectre of negligence liability may unduly inhibit the work of psychotherapists and may prevent genuine cases of abuse being identified. This reasoning was employed by the Connecticut Supreme Court in *Zamstein v. Marvasti*.[123] The allegations of abuse in this case arose out of divorce proceedings rather than therapy, but were supported by a psychiatrist who was asked to interview the children concerned. Mr Zamstein was charged with abuse offences but, after his acquittal, sued the psychiatrist alleging that he had edited the videotapes so as to increase the appearance of guilt and had failed to fulfil the required standard of care by neglecting to interview him in addition to the children. The court ruled that the importance of encouraging professionals to work in this field without fear of liability to third parties outweighed Mr Zamstein's need for redress. English case law would seem to support such an approach. Similarly, in *Flanders v. Cooper*,[124] the court refused to impose a duty on the grounds that it would prove a disincentive to the detection and treatment of sexual abuse;

**Interference with patient autonomy** In *JAH v. Wadle Associates*,[125] the court refused to find that a third party had standing to challenge therapeutic care on the grounds that it would interfere with the patient's right to decide for themselves whether the treatment was beneficial.[126]

---

[123] 692 A 2d 781 (Conn 1997).    [124] 706 A 2d 589 (1998).    [125] 589 NW 2d 256 (1999).
[126] See also *Althaus v. Cohen* 756 A 2d 1166 (2000).

**Inexactitude of therapist's skill** In *Trear v. Sills*,[127] a remedy was denied to an accused parent on the grounds that, by way of analogy, a lawyer is not expected to owe a duty to protect the interests of his client's adversary. The inexactitude of the therapeutic enterprise was also influential, along with the suggestion that an enforceable duty to the alleged abuser would deprive the patient of the 'unquantifiable aspects' of the therapist's judgment. The court in *Trears* reconciled its decision with *Tarasoff v. Regents of University of California*[128] (where a duty of care to a third party was found), on the grounds that the stated intention to murder a third party in *Tarasoff* was an objectively verifiable fact, therefore consequentially, T was a foreseeable victim. The field of repressed memory, on the other hand, did not permit such verifiability:

> There is a huge difference between, on the one hand, a specific identifiable patient who announces an intention to kill a specific identifiable human being, and a matter of great academic and practical controversy within a profession which is itself not subject to easy verification.[129]

**Preservation of confidentiality** In *Johnson v. Rogers Memorial Hospital Inc*,[130] the patient confronted her parents during a therapy session with recovered memories of abuse. The Wisconsin Court of Appeals ruled that the need to maintain confidentiality of the patient's medical records precluded such an action, although this dismissal was held to be premature by the Wisconsin Supreme Court.[131] It seems likely, therefore, that confidentiality obligations will generally prevent actionability by alleged abusers, unless the patient waives confidentiality by perhaps joining the alleged abuser as co-claimant. Certainly such an action would conflict with the doctor's fiduciary duty towards their patients or the duty to act in the best interests of their patient.

**Middle ground** The court in *PT v. Richard Hall Community Mental Health Care Centre*[132] adopted a middle ground by rejecting a duty of care as owed to non-custodial parents but recognising a duty of care

---

[127] 69 Cal App 4th 1341 (Cal Ct App 1999). See also *Doe v. McKay* 700 NE 2d 1018 (Ill 1998) to the same effect.
[128] (1976) 551 P 2d 334 131 Cal R 14.
[129] *Per* Sills PJ at 1354–5. Such arguments seems to miss the point. The proposition is not that if therapists get it wrong they will be liable in damages, but that negligence must be proved first.
[130] (2000) WI App 166. [131] *Ibid*. [132] 364 NJ Super 561, 837 A 2d 436 (2002).

owed by mental health specialists towards custodial parents of the child patient, albeit that the duty of care was derivative of that owed to the child. Therefore, a custodial parent could sue where the interests of the parent and the child were the same (e.g. could sue therapists for failure to identify signs of abuse exhibited by their child).

## Authorities supporting a duty of care to the third-party accused

Equally, there are a number of authorities where the US courts have come out in favour of a duty of care being owed to an accused family member by defendant therapists. These cases tend to explicitly recognise the arguments regarding conflicts of duties and defensive practice but refer additionally to competing public interest considerations which dictate that a duty of care ought nevertheless to be imposed. They are of value to the general discussion of the judgment in *JD* in adding weight to the argument that the 'conflict of interests' rhetoric used to deny that persons involved in child protection work owe a duty of care to accused parents is not unassailable:

**Potential for harm** In *Caryl S v. Child and Adolescent Treatment Serv Inc*,[133] the court regarded accused grandparents, who were temporarily the subject of a court order prohibiting contact with the child, as being owed a duty of care by the child's therapist. This was because the potential harm to the alleged abuser arising from such therapy was equally as great as the potential harm to the child if the therapy were performed negligently.

**Parallel with other professionals** Similarly, in *Montoya v. Bebensee*,[134] the court emphasised that imposing a duty towards accused parents who would foreseeably be harmed by negligent therapy would involve no more liability than that imposed on any other professional.

**Additional duty does not heighten standard of care** In *Hungerford v. Jones*,[135] the court rejected authorities refusing to recognise a duty of care to parents on the grounds that they overlooked the fact that such a duty did not increase the onus on the defendant. In cases where the therapist took public action regarding the accusations (e.g. encouraging

---

[133] 238 AD 953, 661 NYS 2d 168 (Ct App 1997).
[134] 161 Misc 2d 563 (1994); affd at 761 P2d 285 (Colo Ct App 1988).
[135] 722 A 2d 478 (NH 1998).

the patient to contact the police), the social utility in keeping the duty exclusive to the patient was outweighed by the potential harm to family members from false allegations.

**Specific undertaking**  In *Tuman v. Genesis Associates*,[136] it was found that the therapeutic duty of care extended to the parents on the grounds that a specific written undertaking had been made to them whereby the parents paid for the sessions and the defendants undertook to perform therapy to an acceptable standard of care.

**Patient deceased**  *Sawyer v. Midelfort*[137] shows a court accepting in principle that a therapist owed a duty of care to a third-party accused not to negligently implant false repressed memories of abuse. The patient's recovered memories of abuse concerned her parents, boyfriend, two priests, her uncle, brother and grandfather, and it was the sheer number of alleged abusers which formed the basis of allegations that the therapy was negligent and that the recovered memories were false. After the defendant's patient confronted her parents with her recovered memories of abuse, she moved away, cut off all contact with them and changed her surname to prevent discovery. (The issue of confidentiality had not dominated in *Sawyer*, as the defendant's patient had died before the action was brought.)

### The merits and demerits of third-party liability

Bowman and Mertz regard third-party liability to the alleged abuser as objectionable in the therapeutic context, primarily because the extension of liability to a non-patient corrupts the doctor/patient relationship, but also because such litigation against the therapist by a non-patient with no direct involvement of the patient, denies the abuse victim a voice, thereby robbing them of personhood and agency.[138] (It might be added that few therapeutic relationships are likely to survive the intrusion of litigation, therefore third-party liability will in all probability destroy the relationship of trust and confidence between therapist and patient.) Furthermore, they add that the doubt which third-party liability casts in the judiciary's mind on the effectiveness of therapy in recovering memories of abuse may result in the legal pendulum swinging in a dangerous direction towards scepticism with regard

---

[136] 894 F Supp 183 (1995).   [137] 595 NW 2d 423 (Wis 1999).
[138] Bowman and Mertz, 'A Dangerous Direction'.

to the civil claim of the victim against their abuser. In their view, the appropriate defendant in such cases is the person alleging the abuse, and the appropriate form of action would be either defamation or malicious prosecution.[139] Greer raises a number of objections to the suggestion that liability imposed on the therapist is misplaced and ought to be directed at their patient.[140] This is, first, because a caring father would not wish to launch civil litigation against his own psychologically damaged child; secondly, because a child who genuinely believes they were the subject of abuse is unlikely to have the necessary malice for litigation in defamation or malicious prosecution to be successful,[141] and, thirdly, because the therapist is far more likely to be insured than their patient.

### 3. Claims brought under the Human Rights Act 1998

Where the medical practitioner concerned works for the National Health Service, the relevant health authority may be the subject of a Human Rights Act action under s. 7. The reader is referred to the discussion above as to the possible content of such a claim.

### 4. Disciplinary proceedings

An aggrieved party wrongly accused of abuse may be more interested in seeking disciplinary action against their accusers than in seeking compensation. For the purposes of illustration, this section focuses on the disciplinary procedures for registered medical practitioners (doctors), although the procedures for allied professions are broadly similar.[142]

---

[139] See also Biesterveld, who argues that avoidance of the problem could often be achieved by an emphasis on informed consent in the use of psychotherapy, informing patients of the risk of false memories (K. Biesterveld, 'False Memories and the Public Policy Debate: Toward a Heightened Standard of Care for Psychotherapy' (2002) *Wisconsin Law Review* 169).

[140] Greer, 'Tales of Sexual Panic in the Legal Academy'.

[141] Malice being necessary to defeat the defences of qualified privilege in most cases (see below).

[142] For example, the Nursing and Midwifery Council deals with alleged impairment of fitness to practise for nurses, midwives and specialist community public health nurses (health visitors). Social work is regulated by the General Social Care Council which issues codes of conduct for the profession and investigates conduct-related complaints. The Council was created by the Care Standards Act 2000, which for the first time introduced broadly comparable conduct procedures to those used in the medical professions.

There are presently five grounds upon which a registered medical practitioner's 'fitness to practise' might be alleged to be 'impaired' and duly investigated by the GMC, the profession's regulatory body:

- misconduct;
- deficient professional performance;
- a conviction/caution in the British Isles for a criminal offence, or a conviction elsewhere for an offence which, if committed in England and Wales, would constitute a criminal offence;
- adverse physical or mental health; or
- a determination by a body in the UK responsible under any enactment for the regulation of a health or social care profession to the effect that his fitness to practise as a member of that profession is impaired, or a determination by a regulatory body elsewhere to the same effect.[143]

Most of these terms have been left without precise definition. Modern accounts of professional misconduct acknowledge the futility of seeking to exhaustively set out its parameters. In particular, they admit that despite the needs of the profession for certainty in the crucial concept of 'professional misconduct', its meaning fluctuates with shifting values in wider society.[144] In any given case of alleged misconduct, the GMC's Investigation Committee decides whether the complaint is of sufficient gravity to merit consideration by its Fitness to Practise Panel ('FTP'). Once referred to the FTP, the registered practitioner may, if it is found that their fitness to practise has been 'impaired', be the subject of an order erasing their name from the register,[145] suspending them from the register or attaching conditions to their future practise.

The standard of proof applied by the FTP, is, as a matter of custom and practice, that of proof 'beyond reasonable doubt'. The GMC's decision on this and the courts' endorsement of it, appear to be grounded in the protectionist arguments that a finding of professional misconduct has dire consequences for a doctor's livelihood.[146] Not all

---

[143] Medical Act 1983, s. 35(2)(a)–(e) respectively as revised by the Medical Act 1983 (Amendment) Order 2002.
[144] *Good Medical Practice* (2nd edn., GMC, 1998) – accepts that its definition of good medical practice is not exhaustive and that it cannot explicitly identify all the forms of misconduct which might bring registration into question.
[145] This option is not available where fitness is questioned on the grounds of health.
[146] *Per* Lord Tucker in *Bhandari v. Advocates' Committee* [1956] 3 All ER 742 at 745: in cases of moral turpitude or deceit '... we cannot envisage any body of professional men

the protections of the criminal justice system are extended to the accused practitioner. Rules on admissibility of evidence, for example, are far less stringent than those which apply in the criminal courts.[147] Clearly, however, this demanding burden of proof, rightly or wrongly, protects many practitioners from sanction and has led to recent calls for the burden of proof to be lowered to something approximating the 'balance of probabilities'.[148]

The Commission for Healthcare Regulatory Excellence ('CHRE') has the power to launch a public interest appeal in the High Court against rulings of regulatory bodies, including the GMC, where it regards the sanction applied as 'too lenient'.[149] The courts have upheld public interest appeals where, for example, the penalty applied allows a practitioner to return to practice before any sentence imposed by the criminal courts has been served.[150]

## Negligence claims against social services/local authorities and medical practitioners in other jurisdictions

### 1. Liability in Australia

Australian law on the duties of those involved in child protection work towards accused parents is still shaped by the now discredited ruling in *X* v. *Bedfordshire CC*, and, given that subsequent English case law only changes the law with regard to the child's claim, the ruling is unlikely to unsettle the position regarding the abuser. Three cases (*Hillman*, *Connon* and *Sullivan*) all endorse the conflict of duty reasoning which precludes a duty of care to accused claimants in English law.

---

[sic.] sitting in judgment on a colleague who would be content to condemn on a balance of probabilities'.

[147] Rule 50 of the GMC Preliminary Proceedings Committee and Professional Conduct Committee (Procedure) Rules 1988, SI 1988 No. 2255.

[148] This was one of the main recommendations of the *Inquiry into Quality and Practice within the NHS Arising from the Actions of Rodney Ledward*. (2000). A preliminary feasibility report on the proposal can be found at 'Establishing the appropriate standard of proof for GMC hearings into conduct, performance and health' (King's Fund, 2001).

[149] S. 29 of the National Health Service (Regulation of Health Care Professionals) Act 2002.

[150] *Council for Healthcare Regulatory Excellence v. General Dental Council* [2005] EWHC 87 (practitioner's penalty of suspension for 12 months 'too lenient' given that his sentence for having pornographic images of children on his computer, included a three-year community rehabilitation order).

*Hillman v. Black*[151] was one of the first Australian cases to examine the issue. The accused father sued the Department of Community Welfare and two medical practitioners in negligence for their conduct in assessing his 3-year-old daughter as being at risk of sexual abuse and causing him to be separated from his family. The Supreme Court of South Australia determined that it was not just, fair and reasonable to impose a duty of care to the wrongly accused father for the reasons expressed in *X v. Bedfordshire CC*.[152] To hold otherwise would inhibit the proper performance of the defendants' statutory powers and duties where the prime consideration was the welfare of the child. The court also agreed with the trial judge that the claimant father did not enjoy proximity with the doctors as their only patient was the three-year-old child.

Although factually very similar to the case of *Hillman v. Black*, *CLT v Connon*[153] is another crucial case, as it was decided after a High Court of Australia ruling,[154] in which the concept of proximity as it relates to duty of care appears to have been rejected.[155] If proximity was no longer a prerequisite for duty, did this mean that the outcome in *Hillman v. Black* would change? In *Connon*, Doyle CJ in the Supreme Court of South Australia regarded injury to a vindicated father resulting from allegations of sexual abuse as 'readily foreseeable'.[156] He considered, however, that no duty of care was owed to the father because the harm was an indirect result of the defendant doctors' suggestions of abuse. It was the reliance of others on these suggestions that had triggered the allegations.[157] Further, a duty to alleged abusers would not sit easily with the duty to treat the child's interests as paramount.

In the later case of *Sullivan v. Moody*,[158] the High Court of Australia considered a case concerning two children examined by medical practitioners who concluded that the children were the victims of sexual abuse. Both claimants (the fathers of the children) faced criminal charges as a result of these findings, although neither was convicted. The court, following *Hillman v. Black*, decided that the alleged abusers

---

[151] (1996) 67 SASR 490.
[152] At that time, justice, fairness and reasonableness were construed as part of proximity, as compared with the English courts' treatment of them as separate criteria.
[153] (2000) 77 SASR 449.   [154] *Perre v. Apand Pty Ltd* (1999) 198 CLR 180.
[155] F. Bates, 'Policy, Bureaucracy, Tort Law and Child Sexual Abuse: Stirring the Miasma' (2001) 9(3) *Tort Law Review* 183 at 184.
[156] At 451.
[157] Surely this reasoning is relevant to proof of causation rather than establishing a duty of care?
[158] (2001) 28 Fam LR 104.

were third parties to the therapeutic relationship, having not sought treatment for themselves, and were therefore not owed a duty of care. Although the claimants sought to argue that a duty should be owed to parents of the child-patient if they were the subjects of the allegations, the court rejected such a contention on the grounds that it would create indefensible distinctions between, for example, the accused parent and the accused teacher. Further, the imposition of a duty of care would be inconsistent with the doctors' statutory responsibilities under the Community Welfare Act 1972 (SA), which provided that medical practitioners, *inter alia*, were under a legal duty to report suspicions of child abuse to the relevant authorities.[159] Recognition of a common law duty to the alleged abuser would involve a conflict of duties, in particular, colliding with the duty to treat the child's interests as paramount – 'the interests of the children and those suspected of causing their harm are diverse and irreconcilable'.[160] The same considerations would preclude an action in negligence by the proprietor of a childcare facility for psychiatric harm caused by mismanagement of an inquiry into the safety of the children cared for there.[161] The observation was made in *Sullivan* that the alleged abuser would, in any case, have an alternative remedy of a defamation suit, an option which was far more suited to resolving the conflicts of interest between disclosure of suspicions and the claimant's reputation in the form of the defence of qualified privilege. Authorising a negligence suit in such cases would have the further deleterious effect of undermining the careful balance achieved in the law of defamation.[162]

### 2. The Canadian position

In Canada, the issue of whether a duty of care may extend to those suspected of abuse has not been dealt with in any detail, although there are first instance rulings suggesting that it is very unlikely that a doctor involved in the treatment of an abused child would owe a duty of care to her parents.[163] Where the essence of a claim is essentially an allegation

---

[159] S. 91(1).  [160] (2001) 28 Fam LR 104.
[161] *Hood and another v. State of Queensland and others* [2002] QSC 169.
[162] This argument does not appear to have been persuasive in English law: see, for example, the House of Lords judgment in *Spring v. Guardian Assurance* [1995] 2 AC 296.
[163] *H(RL) v. H(M)* 1998 ACWS (3d) 831.

that the authorities or their personnel were negligent in the exercise of their statutory powers or discretion, the courts apply a special threshold of liability based on *Home Office v. Dorset Yacht Co Ltd*.[164] An action in negligence will not be made out where there is a want of the degree of care normally required by the tort of negligence. Rather there will only be liability if there was a failure to consider the matter at all, or the opinion reached or action taken was so unreasonable as to show a failure to carry out the duty or there was a lack of good faith.[165] Negligence in the performance of operational matters (e.g. a failure to follow procedure or to follow a superior's instructions) could, however, lead more readily to liability.[166] Thus, in *GA v. British Colombia*,[167] the court found that the social worker, who had removed children from their family home on what were later found to be false allegations of sexual abuse, was not negligent despite a number of errors of judgment. Further, the statute in question explicitly conferred an immunity from civil action upon the defendants, provided the court was convinced that they were acting in good faith. Therefore, as the social worker had an honest belief that the well-being of the claimant's children was at risk, she had acted in good faith and would not be liable in negligence for her errors of judgment.[168]

## 3. New Zealand

The issue of liability towards the alleged abuser in New Zealand has arisen in a recent appeal to the Privy Council where the conflict of interests rhetoric was sanctioned yet again. In *B v. Attorney General (No. 1 of 2003)*,[169] two children had been put into foster care following a report that one of the children had told a school friend that she was sexually abused by her father. The family was separated for six months before being reunited on the grounds that the children were not at risk. Both children and the father brought a claim for mental trauma in negligence against the Department of Social Welfare on the grounds, *inter alia*, that the child had withdrawn her allegations two weeks after she had made them, but no action had been taken to reassess the case against her father. The Privy Council concluded that a duty of care was

---

[164] [1970] 2 All ER 294.  [165] *GA v. British Colombia* (1989) 61 DLR (4th) 136.
[166] *Home Office v. Dorset Yacht Co Ltd* [1970] 2 All ER 294.
[167] (1989) 61 DLR (4th) 136.
[168] Supported in *D (B) v. British Colombia* [1997] 4 WWR 484.  [169] [2003] UKPC 61.

owed to the children in the exercise of powers under the now repealed Act to arrange a prompt inquiry where there was reason to believe a child was at risk. Further, the duty was not limited to the initiation of the inquiry but extended throughout the duration of the inquiry.[170] No such duty was owed to the father, however, as: 'In an inquiry into an abuse allegation the interests of the alleged perpetrator and of the children as the alleged victims are poles apart.'[171] Whilst those conducting the inquiry must act in good faith throughout the investigation, 'to impose a common law duty of care on the department and the individual professionals in favour of the alleged victims or potential victims and, at one and the same time, in favour of the alleged perpetrator would not be satisfactory'.

In the earlier case of *E v. K*,[172] a social worker was found to owe no duty of care to the accused father, although the court did note that this did not mean that all claims by wrongly accused parents against social workers would fail.[173] The court found that there was indeed a proximate relationship between the parties but that the negligence claim must fail on policy grounds; namely the conflict of interest argument and the fact that a duty of care to the parents would undermine the paramountcy principle. It was also noted that actions in defamation and malicious prosecution would be available to the accused as alternative remedies.

## General claims against the accusers

In the following section, consideration is given to the other forms of action apart from the negligence claim which might be used to obtain compensation from those who have wrongly accused the claimant of abuse, including the alleged victim. There is also the further possibility of a judicial review action against, for example, decisions to put a child on the child protection register, although review is only to be granted rarely.[174] As this is an administrative remedy rather than a civil remedy, this avenue is not explored further here.

---

[170] Reversing the Court of Appeal's decision in this respect. The case of *Prince v. Attorney General* [1996] 3 NZLR 733 (High Court of Auckland) had already established a duty of care existed in relation to the decision of whether to launch an investigation.
[171] Although the case was decided on the basis of now superseded legislation, it is tempting to assume that the same outcome would be achieved on the basis of current legislation, as the general statutory principle that the child's interests are paramount is unchanged.
[172] [1995] 2 NZLR 239.   [173] At 249.
[174] *R v. Harrow LBC, ex parte D* [1990] 1 FLR 79.

## 1. Actions in defamation

There are now a number of alternative means by which a statement might be regarded as 'defamatory'. The following might be of relevance in a claim brought by someone who has been wrongly identified as a possible abuser. A statement which 'tends to lower a person's reputation in the estimation of right-thinking people generally',[175] 'tends to cause a person to be shunned or avoided'[176] or 'exposes a person to hatred, contempt or ridicule'[177] is capable of being defamatory. There is little doubt that an allegation that the claimant is the perpetrator of sexual or physical abuse would be capable of being defamatory under all three of these definitions. Whilst libel (publications in a permanent form, e.g. reports, newspaper articles, recordings) is actionable without proof of damage, slander (spoken defamation) generally requires proof of some 'special damage'. In the case of allegations of abuse, the requirement of special damage is unlikely to prove problematic, for any slander which imputes that the claimant is guilty of a criminal offence which is punishable by imprisonment in the first instance does not need to demonstrate special damage.[178] Offences of child abuse would undoubtedly qualify as such offences. Furthermore, as the court in *G(R) v. Christison* remarked: 'society is so shocked by disclosures of sex abuse of children by parents that there is almost a presumption that the allegations are true.'[179] The courts also appear to regard allegations of child abuse as being 'the worst kind' of defamation[180] and involving 'one of the most loathsome labels in society'.[181] In *W v. Westminster CC*,[182] the court commented that a statement that concerns had been raised that the claimant might be grooming his stepdaughter for prostitution were capable of being defamatory. This was the case even though a fair-minded person would not necessarily have assumed the claimant to be guilty of such wrongdoing,

---

[175] *Sim v. Stretch* [1936] 2 All ER 1237.
[176] *Youssoupoff v. Metro-Goldwyn Mayer* (1934) 50 TLR 581.
[177] *Parmiter v. Coupland* (1840) 6 M & W 105 at 108.
[178] *Ormiston v. Great Western Rly Co.* [1917] 1 KB 598.
[179] [1997] 1 WWR 641 at [59].
[180] *Amalgamated Television Services Pty Ltd v. Marsden* [2002] NSWCA 419, para 1410.
[181] *Hungerford v. Jones*, 143 NH 208, 211 (1998). See also *W v. Westminster CC* [2005] EWHC 102; [2005] 4 All ER 96 (Note), where the judge noted that such remarks were 'damaging indeed, even if made to one person . . .' at [112].
[182] [2005] EWHC 102; [2005] 4 All ER 96 (Note).

it was sufficient that they would 'have had reservations about him until the matter was resolved'.[183]

Clearly, therefore, the statement made of the claimant does not need to be unequivocal in its allegation that the claimant is guilty of child abuse. Even if the publication contains reference to the claimant's denial of the allegation or there are words supporting an inference which is inconsistent with the allegation of abuse, this will not necessarily be enough to neutralise the bane of the defamatory statement.[184] In *Klason v. Australian Capital Territory*,[185] local authority records contained notes to the effect that allegations that the claimant had abused his daughter had been substantiated by child protection services, but that a judge in the family court had found the allegations to be unsubstantiated. Reference to the judge's ruling was not enough to neutralise the defamatory statement as the publication as a whole still conveyed to the reasonable reader the impression that the defendants regarded the claimant as guilty of child abuse. Furthermore, if such allegations are proved to have been made unlawfully, they are capable of attracting general damages close to the ceiling of £200,000 reserved for the most serious cases.[186] Therefore, if an accused claimant was ever called upon to demonstrate special damage occasioned by the allegations, they would likely have little difficulty in doing so.

The defamatory statement must 'refer to the claimant', that is, it must be understood by the right-minded reader as implicating the claimant in particular.[187] Where the defendant's publication reports allegations of abuse within particular institutions without naming suspected perpetrators, it is unlikely that individual employees of such institutions would have a right of action in defamation, as it could not usually be said that any particular employee had been referred to.[188] There are, however, exceptions. Where it can be said that the institution or department referred to employs only a small number of employees, it might be said that any defamatory statement was published of all those employed

---

[183] This comes very close to conflicting with earlier rulings that a fair minded reader would not infer that the claimant was guilty of wrongdoing after reading a report that the claimant was being investigated by the fraud squad: *Lewis v. Daily Telegraph* [1964] AC 234 (otherwise 'it would be almost impossible to give accurate information about anything', *per* Lord Devlin at 286).
[184] *Mark v. Associated Newspapers* [2002] EMLR 38 at 42.     [185] [2003] ACTSC 104.
[186] *Lillie and Reed v. Newcastle City Council* [2002] EWHC 1600; (2002) 146 SJLB 225.
[187] *Hulton and Co v. Jones* [1910] AC 20.
[188] *Knuppfer v. London Express Newspapers* [1944] AC 116.

there. Further, if the claimant occupies a prominent role in the institution (e.g. Chief Executive) so that it can be said that any defamatory statement of the organisation implicates them in particular, an action may succeed.[189] In *Butler v. Southam*,[190] a series of newspaper articles reported widespread child abuse in five institutions over a period of fifty years. The court ruled that these stories were not generally capable of referring to any employees in particular, but that as one of the later articles identified two employees by name, the defamatory sting in the earlier articles could be regarded as referring to them individually. As to whether a statement of a class referred to the claimant, the gravity of the imputation, the number of persons in the class and other relevant circumstances could affect the court's decision.[191]

In order to establish a defamation action, the claimant must also demonstrate that the statement was 'published'. A publication occurs when the defamatory statement is communicated to someone other than the defamer and the defamed, even if that communication is unintended (e.g. if it is overheard by a third party).[192] The originator of the defamatory statement is liable for all intended or foreseeable publications of the statement, with foreseeable repetitions being defined as any publication which is likely or foreseeable as a significant risk.[193] A defendant will have a defence where they have merely passed on the defamatory statement, rather than having played any active part in the defamation, provided they can bring themselves within the terms of the defence of 'innocent dissemination' under s. 1 of the Defamation Act 1996. This defence requires that the defendant must be either a 'mere distributor' (e.g. bookshop, newsagent or library) a broadcaster of live programmes or an internet service provider. Once within the terms of the defence, the defendant must further demonstrate that they took reasonable care in relation to the publication and that they had no reason to believe that what they did caused or contributed to a defamatory publication.

One issue which has arisen in the context of publication and the liability of the therapist who first uncovers allegations of abuse is

---

[189] Both these exceptions were recognised by Lord Atkin in *Knuppfer v. London Express Newspapers* [1944] AC 116.
[190] [2001] NSCA 121.
[191] Ibid. Following B. Neill and R. Rampton, *Duncan and Neill on Defamation* (2nd edn, Butterworths, 1983) at 6.13.
[192] *White v. J F Stone* [1939] 2 KB 827.
[193] *McManus v. Beckham* [2002] EWCA Civ 939; [2002] 1 WLR 2982.

whether the therapist could be liable for causing defamatory statements uttered by their patient because they encouraged her to believe that she was abused (as appears to have happened in the *Ramona* case). In such a case there may be no publication by the defendant therapist themselves, but nevertheless they may be regarded as having caused or materially contributed to the making of a defamatory statement. In *Tuman v. Genesis Associates*,[194] the issue was raised but the court rejected the possibility of the therapist being liable in defamation on the grounds that a defamation action requires publication by the defendant.[195]

### The qualified privilege defence

Qualified privilege operates as a defence to the defamation action. The privilege is 'qualified', in the sense that the defence will fail if the defendant is found to have been actuated by malice. The defence applies where the defendant's statement was made because the defendant had a duty or interest in communicating the information or suspicion, and the person to whom the information was communicated also had a duty or interest in receiving the information.[196] In other words, the defendant was 'duty bound' to make this statement. The courts have refused to go further and extend the defence of absolute privilege to such communications.[197] Thus, an allegation by a defendant parent, teacher, doctor or nurse would likely be covered by qualified privilege, provided the allegation was reported to the proper authorities (social workers, the police or the NSPCC) and provided the occasion of privilege was not abused. Communications from these authorities to the claimant's employer with regard to the suitability of the claimant for commencing or continuing work with children would likewise be occasions of qualified privilege.[198] The qualified privilege defence would probably also extend to a child reporting allegations of abuse to the non-offending parent.[199]

It might be thought that material which is not strictly relevant to the performance of the duty which attracts qualified privilege would fall

---

[194] 894 F Supp 183 (1995).
[195] Cf. Partlett, 'Recovered Memories', at 1253, where it is argued that the therapist's liability may be based on the parallel of *Theaker v. Richardson* [1962] 1 WLR 151, where the defendant wrote a letter to C which was then foreseeably distributed to others.
[196] *Adam v. Ward* [1917] AC 309.
[197] *W v. Westminster City Council* [2004] EWHC 2866; [2004] All ER (D) 130 (Dec).
[198] *PH v. Chief Constable of H* [2003] EWCA Civ 102.
[199] *C(LG) v. C(VM)* [1996] BCJ no. 1585.

outside the defence. Nevertheless, this is not the case, otherwise the protection afforded by qualified privilege would be illusory, given the subjectivity which attaches to the enquiry as to what is 'relevant'.[200] Irrelevant information or unnecessary embellishment can, however, be factors which lead the court to infer that the defendant was actuated by malice. For example, implied malice may be proved where a defendant makes 'graphic use of word and gesture' which is unnecessary to fulfil the duty to communicate the allegation.[201]

### Qualified privilege and publications to the world at large

A distinct form of qualified privilege emerged in relation to publications made to the world at large in the case of *Reynolds v. Times Newspapers*.[202] The availability of the qualified privilege defence in such circumstances depends upon 'responsible' publication by the defendant: in other words, unless the defendant is acting responsibly, the defence of qualified privilege cannot arise.[203] Factors to be weighed in the balance to determine whether the defendant acted responsibly in publishing the allegation include:

- the seriousness of the allegation (the more serious the charge, the more the public is misinformed and the individual harmed, if the allegation is not true);
- the nature of the information, and the extent to which the subject matter is a matter of *public concern*;
- the *source* of the information;
- the steps taken to *verify* the allegation;
- the *status* of the information (the allegation may have already been the subject of an investigation which commands respect);
- the *urgency* of the matter;
- whether *comment or response was sought from the subject of the allegations*; and
- the *tone of the publication*.

---

[200] *Horrocks v. Lowe* [1975] AC 135 at 151, *per* Lord Diplock, applying *Adam v. Ward* [1917] AC 309 at 326–7 and applied in *PH v. Chief Constable of H* [2003] EWCA Civ 102 in the context of suggestions of physical child abuse.

[201] *Widenmaier v. Jarvis* [1981] 9 ACSW (2d) 364 – administrator's explanation to staff of colleague's dismissal for sexual abuse of residents at old people's home involving superfluous and unnecessarily explicit detail.

[202] [1999] 4 All ER 609.

[203] *Loutchansky v. Times Newspapers* [2001] EWCA Civ 1805; [2002] QB 283.

The legal distinction between the traditional form of qualified privilege and the *Reynolds* form of privilege is that for the purposes of the latter, malice is relevant to whether there is a *prima facie* case for qualified privilege, as proof of malice will negate the defendant's assertion that they have published 'responsibly'. Thus, rather than there being a two-stage inquiry as to whether qualified privilege arises and then whether malice vitiates its operation, the *Reynolds* form of privilege necessarily involves consideration of any suggestions of malice in the course of determining whether qualified privilege arises at all. This can be demonstrated by reference to the apposite case of *Lillie and Reed v. Newcastle City Council*.[204] Here, *Reynolds* privilege was discussed in the context of a local authority independent review panel's report concerning allegations that two of the nursery nurses it employed had been abusing the children in their care. Eady J found that the review panel would have been protected by the defence of qualified privilege, but that the defence was not applicable on the facts as the final report left no doubt in the reader's mind that the panel regarded the claimants as guilty of child abuse, despite the fact of an earlier Crown Court acquittal of the same charges. Hundreds of copies of the report were distributed and excerpts appeared in the local press. The defence of qualified privilege was vitiated as the panel members were acting with express malice. A cavalier approach had been taken to the evidence before the panel and the facts had been misrepresented so as to support the panel members' belief that the claimants had been involved in child abuse. The liabilities of the panel encompassed the publication of excerpts of the report in the newspapers,[205] except to the extent that the newspapers had engaged in a frolic of their own in publishing information which did not originate from the report.

## Malice: express or implied

Express malice can only be proved where the defendant's desire to comply with the relevant duty played no significant part in his motives for publishing what he believed to be true.[206] In other words, the malicious motive must be the dominant motive for the defence to fail due to express malice. Thus, in the *Klason* case discussed above, even though the entries in local authority records were motivated in part by an obdurate refusal to admit that the defendant's initial assessment of

---

[204] [2002] EWHC 1600.  [205] Following *Speight v. Gosnay* (1891) 60 LJQB 231.
[206] *Horrocks v. Lowe* [1975] AC 135 at 151.

child abuse may have been wrong, coupled with resentment towards the claimant, the defence of qualified privilege was not defeated, as these were not the dominant motives of the publication.[207] In *G(R) v. Christison*,[208] a mother distributed reports of alleged abuse by her child's stepmother to social services, the police and the stepmother's employer. The court found that the defendant's parental duty to protect her child was strong enough to give rise to *prima facie* qualified privilege. However, a bitter divorce and ongoing battle for custody of the children, during which the defendant had repeatedly attempted to discredit the claimant, served as evidence of malice defeating qualified privilege. A social worker or other professional may be found to be actuated by malice if they are over-zealous in their pursuit of child protection proceedings or allegations where it is concluded that they were acting to protect their own reputation or to convince others that they were right rather than acting to protect the child.[209]

Generally speaking, if the defendant publishes defamatory allegations which he or she does not believe to be true, this is conclusive evidence of implied malice, and here again the defence of qualified privilege will fail. In the context of communications of allegations of child abuse contained in a report prepared for a child protection conference, it seems that a more robust version of the qualified privilege defence applies: the public interest requires some latitude for honest mistakes.[210] The court in *W v. Westminster CC*[211] heard that a report prepared for a child protection conference stated that professionals had previously raised concerns that the claimant was grooming his stepdaughter for prostitution. The conference members included the mother of the child concerned, the child's headteacher, school nurse and social workers. The High Court ruled that, as the report was confidential and published to a very small group of people, the defendant did not need to have an honest belief in the truth of the allegation in order to claim the defence of qualified privilege.[212] Provided the defendant has acted in good faith (i.e. with the motive of discharging his or her duty of child protection), the defence would apply. It is only when the defendant's desire to protect the child from possible abuse played no significant part in his motives

---

[207] [2003] ACTSC 104.   [208] *G (R) v. Christison* [1997] 1 WWR 641.
[209] [1997] 1 WWR 641.
[210] *W v. Westminster CC* [2005] EWHC 102; [2005] 4 All ER 96 (Note).
[211] [2004] EWHC 2866; [2004] All ER (D) 130 (Dec).
[212] The court distinguished reports which were published to the world, such as that in *Lillie and Reed v. Newcastle City Council* [2002] EWHC 1600.

for publishing the allegation that qualified privilege would fail. The reason for the liberal application of the defence in such circumstances is that social workers and other professionals involved in the preparation of such reports are likely to be dealing with families at loggerheads, and whilst a social worker may suspect that the accusing parent is lying, they may still be under a duty to take the matter further, such is the potency of the duty to ensure that the child is protected from the risk of abuse.[213]

Although a defamation suit might be regarded as the most appropriate remedy where the complaint is directed at statements made by the defendant, the fact that a claim in defamation would fail because of the liberal application of the qualified privilege defence will not be a barrier to other actions, such as a negligence action[214] or an action under the Human Rights Act 1998.[215]

## 2. Malicious prosecution

Malicious prosecution is a tightly controlled tort, with the courts eager to ensure that its availability does not stymie the willingness of genuine complainants seeking enforcement of the law in good faith. This form of action is available where the defendant initiated proceedings for which there was no reasonable and probable cause, and the proceedings were resolved in the claimant's favour (for example, by acquittal, discontinuation of proceedings or the quashing of a conviction). It must also be demonstrated that the defendant had acted maliciously and that the claimant suffered damage. The requirement of 'malice' entails that the defendant was motivated by a desire other than to bring a criminal to justice,[216] and 'damage' may take the form of loss of liberty or pecuniary damage (e.g. the expenses incurred in defending the proceedings).

The action is available against both private persons and law enforcement agencies (e.g. the police and Crown Prosecution Service ('CPS')), provided it can be said that the defendant 'initiated' the relevant proceedings. Indeed, an action for malicious prosecution against the police or CPS may be the only available option as these bodies do not owe a

---

[213] [2004] EWHC 2866; [2004] All ER (D) 130 (Dec); confirmed in [2005] EWHC 102.
[214] *Spring v. Guardian Assurance* [1995] 2 AC 296.
[215] *W v. Westminster CC* [2005] EWHC 102; [2005] 4 All ER 96 (Note).
[216] *Glinski v. McIver* [1962] AC 726.

general duty of care with regard to the conduct of criminal proceedings, therefore an action in negligence would not usually be available.[217]

A broad meaning is given to 'initiating'. For example, where the falsely alleged facts are not capable of independent verification, a defendant who provides false information to the police in the knowledge that it will likely result in the initiation of criminal proceedings against the claimant will suffice. In such circumstances, the prosecution is to be treated as procured by the defendant.[218] It is unlikely that the parents of a child who falsely alleged sex abuse against the claimant would be regarded as having initiated proceedings.[219] This is consistent with the fact that parents are not vicariously liable for the torts of their children. In the Canadian case of *Wood v. Kennedy*, the court also refused to hold the parents liable in negligence for allowing their child's unfounded allegations to proceed to a prosecution as this would circumvent the malice requirement in a malicious prosecution action. (Note that in English law, this would probably not be the decisive factor in rejecting a negligence action.[220] Courts in England and Wales would be more likely to say that it would not be 'just, fair and reasonable' to impose a duty of care on the parents in such cases given that such a duty would conflict with their overwhelming duty to protect their child.)

In *Savile v. Roberts*,[221] the court did not appear to regard the malicious prosecution action as confined to criminal proceedings but as extending to *any* proceedings which inflict damage to a man's fame, person (including loss of liberty) or property (including the cost of expense to ensure his acquittal). The tort of malicious prosecution has been ruled as inapplicable to initiation of disciplinary proceedings,[222] but has occasionally been used in the context of malicious institution of civil proceedings.[223] It has been argued that such an action should only

---

[217] *Elguzouli-Daf v. Metropolitan Police Comr* [1995] QB 335; *A v. Children's Aid Society* 1996 ACWS (3d) 435.
[218] *Martin v. Watson* [1995] 3 All ER 559.
[219] *Wood v. Kennedy* (1998) 165 DLR (4th) 542.
[220] *Spring v. Guardian Assurance* [1995] 2 AC 296 – action available in negligence notwithstanding that it might be regarded as circumventing the qualified privilege defence in defamation.
[221] (1698) 1 Ld Raym 374.
[222] *Gregory v. Portsmouth City Council* [2000] 1 All ER 560.
[223] *Savile v. Roberts* (1698) 1 Ld Raym 374. See also *Rawlinson v. Purnell Jenkison and Roscoe* [1999] 1 NZLR 479 – action would be available against firm of solicitors for continuing civil proceedings despite knowledge that they were affected by a serious error of law.

be exceptionally available as the alleged abuser's victory (as defendant) in civil proceedings repairs the damage to his reputation and he is entitled to recover the costs of the proceedings against the unsuccessful claimant.[224] This is perhaps a naïve view of society's perceptions of civil proceedings. A finding in favour of the defendant does not necessarily vindicate them in the eyes of the public.

### 3. Intentional infliction of psychiatric harm

The case of *Wilkinson v. Downton*, albeit an English High Court decision, provided the foundations of an independent cause of action in torts for wrongfully caused physical or psychiatric harm.[225] Under the rule applied in this case, the defendant was liable for wilful acts calculated to cause harm to the claimant which in fact caused harm where there was no justification for the act. Thus it seems that there does not need to be proof of a 'wrong', but rather conduct without justification.[226] The widely perceived merits of the rule are in providing recovery where a claim of assault may not be available due to a lack of a threat of force, lack of immediacy of the threat of force or uncertainty as to whether words alone can constitute an assault.[227] Availability of the action is, however, limited by the requirement that damage be proved.

Somewhat surprisingly, the rule has been applied to protect a convicted abuser from the harm caused by deliberate publication of his misdeeds. In *Tucker v. News Media Ownership*,[228] a case with very unusual facts, the New Zealand court accepted that an interim injunction ought to be granted to restrain publication of the claimant's history of indecency convictions, given the fact that he was awaiting a heart transplant. Adverse publicity could have triggered a possibly lethal deterioration in the claimant's already frail health. The court relied on the principle in *Wilkinson v. Downton*[229] to reach this decision, fashioning it so as to fill a lacuna in personal privacy protection in New Zealand law. Although not explicitly stated in the judgments, intention to cause harm would have been relatively easy to prove as the claimant's doctor

---

[224] *Quartz Hill Consolidated Gold Mining Co v. Eyre* (1883) 11 QBD 674.
[225] [1897] 2 QB 57.
[226] See Witting, 'Tort Liability for Intended Mental Distress' for further discussion of the extent to which this is a requirement of liability.
[227] See *R v. St George* (1840) 9 Car & P 483. Although note that *R v. Ireland* [1998] AC 47 would suggest that words alone can constitute an assault, at least in criminal law.
[228] [1986] NZLR 716.  [229] [1897] 2 QB 57.

had telephoned the editor of the defendant publication to warn him of the potential consequences of publication.[230] It is important to note that this new privacy remedy was available, notwithstanding the truth of the threatened publication, and this was therefore a case where a defamation action would not have been available. As the publication concerned the claimant's wrongful conduct, it might also be queried whether a plea of *ex turpi causa non oritur* might have succeeded.[231] The court in *Tucker* considered the need to prevent interference with the torts of defamation and the rights to freedom of speech and freedom of information, but took the view that interference with these rights was justifiable on the facts as 'life potentially is at risk'. It was also noted that the New Zealand definition of homicide included wilfully frightening a sick person and accelerating a fatal disease.[232] A very different outcome would have been likely if the portended impact of the publication had not been life-threatening.[233]

## Conclusion

The legal remedies available to the wrongly accused claimant are severely restricted, generally by appeals to the importance of child protection work necessitating that it should be untrammelled by obligations to the subjects of resulting abuse allegations. The rhetoric that a duty of care cannot be owed by local authorities or medical practitioners towards the alleged abuser due to the irreconcilable interests of the child and the accused has proved popular in the highest courts in the UK, Canada, Australia and New Zealand. In spite of this widespread endorsement, the logic of this rhetoric is by no means incontrovertible as the cases from the US on therapist liability demonstrate. It might be argued that judicial insistence that a duty of care to the abuser conflicts with the duty to the child appears to treat the alleged abuser, unfairly, as a *de facto* abuser. Clearly, the interests of an abused child and their abuser are

---

[230] At 723.
[231] *Revill v. Newbery* [1996] 2 WLR 239 – would depend on whether the denial of a remedy was proportionate to the claimant's wrong, a question which would likely be answered in the negative as the purpose of the action is to protect health not seek compensation.
[232] At 719. See also *R v. Dawson (Brian)* (1985) 81 Cr App R 150 to this effect.
[233] It might be argued that publication which is likely to trigger depression may ultimately be life threatening if suicide ideation occurs, particularly if the claimant has a history of such symptoms. Issues of caution and remoteness would need investigating before liability could be determined.

diametrically opposed. However, given that at the time the negligence complained of was committed, the claimant is not proven to be the child's abuser, surely the presumption of innocence should operate in the accused's favour? If this were the case, where the alleged abuser is a close family member or is a carer of the child, the conclusion that their interests are in direct conflict with those of the child is far from inevitable.[234] Their Lordships in *JD* used reasoning by analogy (with secondary victim cases and wrongly arrested claimants) to bolster their conclusions. Yet, as we have seen, reasoning by analogy with other areas of law (e.g. the law on treatment of the pregnant woman and foetus and the duty of care owed by solicitors to beneficiaries under the wills they draft) would have produced quite different conclusions.

Rather than adopting a position which vetoes a duty of care ever being owed to an accused parent, justice would be better served if the law accommodated a duty of care being owed to the accused once action has been taken to safeguard the child in question from further abuse. For example, once emergency steps have been taken to ensure that the child is in a safe environment by removing the accused from the family home or removing the child, conduct of the investigation beyond that point ought to be on the basis of a duty of care being owed to the child *and* to the accused parent. Such a duty might include an obligation to ensure that the case is properly investigated, and that the parent is given the opportunity to see the evidence against them and to present their side of events. This approach would be compatible with ECtHR rulings on Article 8 protection and has been suggested as the way forward for the tort of negligence.[235]

Whether or not the assumption that a duty to parents will inevitably undermine the duty towards the child is flawed, the sentiments expressed in *X (Minors) v. Bedfordshire CC*[236] and by Lord Rodger in *JD v. East Berkshire Community NHS Trust*[237] regarding the risk of defensive practice ought not to be dismissed too eagerly. It is probably

---

[234] Bates has also argued that the interests of the child and accused parent are not necessarily in conflict – consider, for example, the accused parent who commits suicide after being accused of abuse as the result of incompetence on the part of social services: Bates, 'Policy, Bureaucracy, Tort Law and Child Sexual Abuse' at 194.

[235] B. Atkin and G. McLay, 'Suing Child Welfare Agencies – a Comparative View from New Zealand' (2001) 13 *Child and Family Law Quarterly* 287 at 310. See also the dissenting judgment of Lord Bingham in *JD v. East Berkshire Community NHS Trust* [2005] UKHL 23; [2005] 2 WLR 993.

[236] [1995] 2 AC 633.   [237] [2005] UKHL 23; [2005] 2 WLR 993.

no coincidence that many of the stress claims against employers which have come to court have concerned employees working in social services, often with child protection case loads.[238] Further, when the standard of proof for intervention in suspected cases of child abuse under the Children Act 1989 is such a 'low level risk' standard, it becomes clear that the probability of error inherent in the statutory regime is exceedingly high.[239] That does not, however, of itself provide justification for any special harbour from liability, but it does require that the law handles the issue of whether there has been a breach of that duty with particular sensitivity. Dealing with issues of professional liability as standard of care issues still provides the courts with sufficient latitude to manage child abuse allegations sensitively, and also delivers more in terms of the torts regime's function of setting standards outlined in Chapter 1. The current position in denying a duty of care pre-empts debate and discussion of good practice in this field, whereas shifting the focus to the standard of care and application of the *Bolam* standard to social workers, health visitors, doctors involved in suspected child abuse cases gives the courts the opportunity to hand down clear precedents to the effect that given conduct is a breach of local authority's/professional's duty of care and provides a mechanism of specific deterrence for future conduct. It also provides the opportunity for the court to resolve issues pertaining to conflict between different sources of professional guidance. Whilst it might be argued that recognising a duty of care being owed to the child should suffice in providing opportunities for the court to delve into issues of professional standards and enabling the torts regime to perform its standard setting function, such cases will be exceedingly rare given the difficulties of establishing psychiatric damage to a young child. Furthermore, surely a claim brought by the wrongly accused, if brought fairly contemporaneously with the negligence, would be preferable to a claim brought by the child once they have reached adulthood,[240] given the difficulties of resolving disputes after the passage of many years.

This chapter reveals that in the context of both negligence and defamation actions the vindicatory capacity of torts litigation for the

---

[238] See particularly the cases of *Walker v. Northumberland CC* [1995] 1 All ER 737; *State of New South Wales v. Seedsman* [2000] NSWCA 119; *Green v. Argyll Bute Council* (OH) (2002) GWD 9; and *Gogay v. Hertfordshire CC* [2001] FCR 455.
[239] See note 20 above.
[240] As is the case in *D v. Bury MBC* [2006] EWCA Civ 1; [2006] 1 FCR 148.

wrongly accused claimant is denied on the grounds of the primary status of the child. Yet, ironically, the two previous chapters have demonstrated that the therapeutic and compensatory capacities of tort litigation for the abused claimant (i.e. the 'child' in the wrongly accused judgments) are undermined by the law's insistence on doctrinal tidiness and under-utilisation of non-traditional causes of action such as *Wilkinson v. Downton* and breach of fiduciary duty. To these difficulties can be added the formidable barriers presented by limitation statutes discussed in Chapter 5. Increased actionability for both these groups of claimants would still mean that they face the formidable problems of establishing damage caused by the tort; a subject to which we now turn.

# 4

# Damage, Causation and Quantum

## Introduction

It has been suggested that in the United States, the preferential legal treatment accorded to abuse claimants has resulted in the courts applying a 'broad brush' approach to proof of damage and causation.[1] Once the wrong has been proved, the courts tend to assume that the abuse is responsible for all of the claimant's psychological problems without applying the strict rules of causation which would often otherwise spell the end of the claimant's case. Whatever the experiences of the US, the requirements pertaining to the proof of damage and causation may very well constitute insurmountable obstacles for the abuse claimant in England and Wales. It should be noted, however, that matters pertaining to proof of damage and causation in this type of litigation have rarely surfaced in our courts because the claim has been disposed of on prior issues of limitation or liability, leaving other issues unexposed and unexplored. The potential concerns arising out of the damage/causation inquiry are myriad, and the lack of legal authority on these issues specific to abuse claims makes reference to the experiences of other similar jurisdictions expedient for the purposes of speculating how these issues might be played out in the future. For example, it is frequently the case that abuse claimants have suffered a number of traumatic events apart from the abuse which is the subject of the litigation, and such complexity causes intractable problems when assessing causation and quantum. These problems are particularly thorny, given that the litigation is generally brought many years after the abuse, making it increasingly impossible to disentangle the abuse from other traumagenic events which have affected the claimant's life since the defendant's wrong. These difficulties raise the following legal questions:

1. With regard to the burden of proof in abuse claims, how is the 'balance of probabilities' threshold to be applied?

[1] Wilson, 'Suing for Lost Childhood'.

2. Can claimants rely on evidence arising from recovered memories to discharge this burden?
3. In claims brought in tort when must the claimant prove a 'recognised psychiatric disorder' in order to recover damages for the psychological consequences of the abuse (and when, if ever, does distress falling short of such recognised disorders qualify for compensation)?
4. Where proof of a recognised disorder is required, how can a court be convinced that such a disorder is suffered and are there 'signature diseases' or particular diagnoses which a court will more readily accept as having been caused by the abuse?
5. In the case of a child who has been abused in care, how is it possible to disentangle the psychological consequences of abuse from the psychological consequences of that child being removed from its family and placed in care?[2]
6. How is quantum to be dealt with when it becomes clear that the abuse is one of a number of contributory factors at work in the aetiology of mental disorders?
7. To what extent would a perpetrator or non-perpetrator defendant be liable in damages for the consequences of alcoholism, drug taking or criminal activities which were allegedly caused by the abuse?

## Burden of proof

In civil child protection cases, the courts have taken the view that, given the seriousness of allegations of abuse, cogent evidence is required before the courts will be satisfied that the case has been proved on the balance of probabilities: 'the more improbable the event, the stronger must be the evidence that it did occur before, on the balance of probabilities, its occurrence will be established.'[3] This statement does not

---

[2] *W v. Attorney General* [1999] 2 NZLR 709 – the child in this case having been removed from her home due to parental neglect was then abused by her foster parents.

[3] *Re H (Minors)* [1996] AC 563 at 586, *per* Lord Nicholls and also *Halford v. Brookes* [1992] PIQR P175. For the same sentiment expressed in Canadian judgments see *Continental Insurance Co. v. Dalton Cartage Co. Ltd et al.* (1982) 131 DLR (3d) 559 at 563, *per* Laskin CJC: 'The more serious the allegations the greater the care that must be exercised when considering the evidence' (also *Blackwater v. Plint* (2001), 93 BCLR (3d) 228 at paras 10–12; *B(M) v. British Columbia* (2001) 87 BCLR (3d) 12 (CA) at para 25) and in Australia, see *M v. M* (1988) 166 CLR 69 at 76, where the High Court of Australia said that the Family Court should not make a positive finding that an allegation of sexual abuse is true unless the court is so satisfied according to the civil standard of proof, with due regard to the factors mentioned in *Briginshaw v. Briginshaw* (1938) 60 CLR 336 at

appear to be referring to a third standard of proof but rather indicates that the judiciary will take steps to examine the evidence with particular care, given the serious implications that allegations of abuse have for an individual's social standing.[4] Of course, actions in negligence against non-perpetrator defendants are less likely to be affected by such strictures on the burden of proof as the implications for such defendants of a finding of liability are far less severe. Thus, in civil claims for compensation arising out of child abuse, the usual burden of proving the case on the balance of probabilities becomes more difficult to satisfy. An exception exists where the defendant has been previously convicted of abuse-related offences against the claimant and the claimant subsequently brings civil proceedings on the basis of the facts upon which the conviction is based. In such a case the usual burden of proof is reversed and it is for the defendant to disprove the claimant's case on the balance of probabilities.[5]

If the standard of proof as applied in abuse claims is particularly exacting, it might be assumed that courts in England and Wales will approach controversial types of evidence in a conservative manner. How, for example, have the courts dealt with claimants whose case is built upon recovered memories of the abuse?

### 1. English law and repressed memories

> As all litigation is perforce about the past, and virtually all litigation involves witnesses who are testifying about memories of the past, issues of the accuracy of memory lie at the very core of the legitimacy of litigation as a means for the resolution of interpersonal and social conflict.[6]

Whilst the above statement does have some resonance in the context of abuse claims, particularly as the perpetrator defendant usually vehemently denies the allegations, the judiciary of England and Wales are generally astute to require something more than the affidavit evidence of

---

362, per Dixon J: 'The seriousness of an allegation made, the inherent unlikelihood of an occurrence of a given description, or the gravity of the consequences flowing from a particular finding are considerations which must affect the answer to the question whether the issue has been proved to the reasonable satisfaction of the tribunal').

[4] See discussion to this effect in Chapter 3.
[5] S. 11 of the Civil Evidence Act 1968.
[6] R. Zoltek-Jick, 'For Whom Does the Bell Toll? Repressed Memory and Challenges for the Law,' in P. S. Appelbaum, L. A. Uyehara and M. R. Elin, *Trauma and Memory: Clinical and Legal Controversies* (OUP, 1997) at 472.

the parties before being convinced that the claim is made out on the 'balance of probabilities'. Debates about the fallibility of memory have, however, been played out exhaustively in the courts of the US and Canada. Abuse litigation in those jurisdictions has been dominated by concerns pertaining to the phenomenon of repressed and recovered memories, where the claimant retrieves forgotten memories of abuse many years after the alleged abuse took place and relies on these 'recovered' memories in litigation against the abuser. This retrieval process is typically alleged to occur during the therapeutic process, and is widely regarded as a necessary step towards resolving the patient's psychological problems. The need for judicial determination of the credibility of repressed memory evidence seems to have been pre-empted for the purposes of our jurisdiction by the publication of the Brandon Report, a paper based on a small working group's review of the literature on the subject. The report concluded that: 'when memories are recovered after long periods of amnesia, particularly when extraordinary means were used to secure the recovery of memory, there is a *high probability* that the memories are false.'[7] The report goes on to describe memory enhancement techniques generally (including drug-induced abreaction, hypnosis, dream interpretation and age regression) as 'powerful and dangerous methods of persuasion',[8] and says of the theory of repressed memory that it is not supported by evidence and literature on the subject lacks reference to well-corroborated cases of repressed/recovered memories.[9]

The Brandon Report, originally commissioned by the Royal College of Psychiatrists but published as an independent paper, has the status of professional guidance for the profession of psychiatry, and therapists who deviate from this guidance may be subject to disciplinary proceedings before the General Medical Council. The result of this guidance is that the English courts have heard extremely little about repressed memory and far more about late onset psychiatric disorders in the context of arguments that the usual limitation periods should be extended to accommodate the claimant. This notable absence of argument pertaining to repressed memory is likely due to lawyers' assumptions that the courts would not look favourably on such evidence given that the Brandon Report amounts to a strongly worded presumption against both the validity of recovered memories and the techniques used

---

[7] Brandon, *Reported Recovered Memories* (emphasis added).
[8] *Ibid.* at 301.   [9] *Ibid.* at 303.

to elicit them. For example, in the *Bryn Alyn* litigation one of the claimants, known as DEJ, was described as having 'successfully blocked' his memories of the abuse for 15 years, hence his delay in coming to court. Another claimant was described as 'burying these painful features' until 1992.[10] This terminology of 'blocking' and 'burying' differs from the theory of recovered memories because, in both instances, there is no allegation that the claimant has forgotten the abuse, rather that he has put the abuse to back of his mind and chosen not to think about it.

The objections mounted to repressed memory evidence by the Brandon Report guidelines relate to the fallibility of memory generally and the risk of therapeutic implantation of false memories:

### Reliability of repressed memory evidence

Aside from the Brandon Report's scepticism regarding the concept of recovered memory, acceptance of the principle of recovered memory in the wider international scientific community is far from unanimous. The American Medical Association[11] takes the view that the issue of the existence of repression is controversial and that the reliability of recovered memory is inherently suspect and requires corroborative evidence. The reports of the Australian Psychological Society[12] are similarly equivocal about the existence of repressed memory. Notably, all of these statements contain variations on the placatory assertion that 'sexual abuse is to be taken seriously'.

Concerns regarding the reliability of recovered memory evidence are due in part to the means by which such memories are recovered. Whilst some individuals report suddenly recovering memories of abuse after a visual trigger, those who recover memories during therapy may have been the subject of hypnosis or the use of barbiturates which lower inhibitions to induce abreaction (defined as 'the expression and consequent release of a previously repressed emotion, achieved through hypnosis or suggestion').[13]

---

[10] *KR v. Bryn Alyn Community (Holdings) Ltd (In Liquidation)* 2001 WL 753345 at [111].
[11] *Report on Memories of Childhood Abuse* (American Medical Association Council on Scientific Affairs) (reprinted in (1995) 43 *International Journal of Clinical and Experimental Hypnosis* 114).
[12] *Guidelines Relating to the Reporting of Recovered Memories* (Australian Psychological Society, 1994).
[13] *Oxford English Dictionary* (www.oed.com). The most common drug used to achieve abreaction is sodium amytal.

The Brandon Report concludes that the most credible abuse allegations are those which are made spontaneously by children of contemporary or recent abuse. Conversely, there are three classes of memories which should not be regarded as credible: memories of satanic abuse or other bizarre events, memories from before the age of four years and memories of reported abuse over many years forgotten until recovered during therapy.[14] In the case of the latter, the theory of recovered memories is predicated on a flawed assumption that human memory works very much like a video recorder producing accurate replays of past events, whereas most modern conceptions of memory accept that memory is fallible and is subject to revision, reappraisal and reorganisation over time. Focused remembering will also subject the memory to reinterpretation; therefore, the more often recall is consciously performed for the purposes of therapy or litigation, the more unreliable the memory becomes. Note that whilst the Brandon Report is sceptical about the reliability of recovered memories to such a degree that litigation which requires acceptance of recovered memory evidence is highly unlikely to be successful, it does not reject the possibility of such recovery being genuine in any given case.

### The risk of therapeutic implantation of false memories

Memories of abuse which are allegedly repressed and then recovered typically surface when a psychiatrist's patient presents with psychological problems in adulthood which have no obvious trigger but which may be consistent with abuse during childhood. The psychiatrist may inadvertently or deliberately raise sexual experiences during childhood in the course of therapy and begin a line of inquiry which leads to suggestions of forgotten trauma. The patient may regard the suggestion of forgotten trauma as offering a plausible explanation for otherwise inexplicable psychological problems and may unwittingly embellish their memories in the pursuit of the legitimation of this theory. Thus, the suggestion of forgotten abuse may serve a therapeutic function for the patient who uses it to make sense of their predicament (and possibly shift blame away from themselves for their problems[15]). The risk of suggestibility and of false implantation of memories is not just theoretical. There is some empirical research supporting the potential for

---

[14] Brandon, *Reported Recovered Memories*, at 304.
[15] See e.g. A. Brown and D. Barrett, *Knowledge of Evil: Child Prostitution and Child Sexual Abuse in Twentieth Century England* (Willan Publishing, 2002).

implantation which concludes that false memories are generally recalled in less detail than true memories.[16]

The liability of the therapist has been dealt with earlier in Chapter 3, but for now it is worth stating that there are at least two potential victims suffering harm in cases of therapeutic intervention causing false memories of abuse: *the alleged abuser* (who may suffer a crisis in familial relations, the stigma attached to paedophilia and consequent legal action such as prosecution, all of which may conceivably result in psychological harm requiring treatment) and the *therapist's patient* (who may be further traumatised by the erroneous belief that someone close to them has abused them).[17]

If the implicit or explicit suggestions of therapists create a risk of implanting false memories of abuse, the techniques associated with retrieving forgotten memories only enhance this risk. Whilst there is general acceptance of hypnosis as a therapeutic tool, there is no such widespread acceptance of its value as a forensic tool,[18] although recent research suggests that jurors tend to assume that evidence procured by hypnosis is reliable and credible.[19] A number of issues cast doubt on the reliability of testimony based on hypnotically enhanced memories:

- the suggestibility of witnesses whilst under hypnosis to cues given by the hypnotherapist (e.g. the known purpose of the hypnotism, a desire to please the therapist or confabulation to fill in gaps in the witnesses' memories);
- the fact that the purpose of hypnosis in the context of therapy is not to uncover past events but to uncover the subject's perceptions of past events;[20]
- the phenomenon of 'memory hardening' (i.e. excessive confidence in the truth of memories uncovered by hypnosis); and
- the creation of pseudo memories.

---

[16] Loftus and Ketcham, *The Myth of Repressed Memory and Allegations of Sexual Abuse* (St Martins, 1996).
[17] 'Patients who are mistakenly diagnosed as having been abused, frequently end up as mental health casualties': Brandon et al., *Reported Recovered Memories*, at 304.
[18] T. Fleming, 'Admissibility of Hypnotically Refreshed or Enhanced Testimony' (1990) 77 ALR 4th 927.
[19] B. L. Coleman, M. J. Stevens and G. D. Reeder, 'What Makes Recovered Memory Testimony so Compelling to Jurors?' (2001) 25(4) *Law and Human Behaviour* 317.
[20] Kisch, 'From the Couch to the Bench'.

The Brandon Report says of hypnosis as a means of recovering memories that it 'increases the confidence with which the memory is held while reducing its reliability'.[21] For the purposes of criminal proceedings, the Crown Prosecution Service is similarly negative about the reliability of memories retrieved by hypnosis, stating that there is a strong likelihood that evidence obtained under hypnosis is unreliable and inadmissible in court and that it is impossible to distinguish truth and confabulation in such cases unless there is independent corroborative evidence.[22] Consequently, witnesses who have been hypnotised are only to be used in exceptional circumstances.

On the few occasions in which the criminal courts have been presented with evidence retrieved by hypnosis, they have rejected such evidence as inadmissible where Home Office guidelines have not been followed.[23] In *R v. Browning*, for example, a murder conviction was quashed in part because the retrieval of hypnotically refreshed evidence from the witness for the prosecution had not complied with the requirements that the hypnotherapist must take a memoir of witness recollections before hypnosis, that the hypnotherapist must make a witness statement and that any information obtained under hypnosis must be made the subject of a witness statement within twenty four hours.

### 2. Admissibility of recovered memory evidence in the US

Given the unequivocal rejection of the reliability of recovered memories and the techniques applied to retrieve such memories by the Brandon Report, issues pertaining to admissibility of such evidence in civil claims are unlikely to be raised for judicial consideration in the courts of England and Wales. Nevertheless, a brief summary of the position in the US is given here to demonstrate the further problems which have been encountered.

---

[21] Brandon et al., *Reported Recovered Memories*, at 300. See also *R v. Mayes* [1995] CLY 930 (CC Portsm) – claimant's evidence identifying his attackers and obtained by hypnotherapy was not inadmissible but was unreliable because of the suggestibility of patients under hypnotherapy. The witness had false confidence in his recollections which had been cemented by hypnosis. Court was particularly concerned that after the first hypnosis session C admitted he could not distinguish things experienced by him and things related to him by third parties.

[22] www.cps.gov.uk/legal/section13/chapter_p.html#_Toc44657871, accessed 22 February 2005.

[23] *R v. Browning* (1994) (CA); [1995] Crim LR 227. The guidelines can be found in *The Use of Hypnosis by the Police in the Investigation of Crime* (Home Office Circular 066/1988).

A shift has been observed in US abuse litigation from a reliance on procedural (limitation) strategies by defendants to an emphasis on challenging the substance of the claim by questioning the validity of recovered memory evidence. This can be achieved by impugning either the methods used to retrieve memory or the validity of the theory of recovered memory itself. The case law has focused on whether repressed memory accounts are admissible according to the rules on the admissibility of scientific evidence in the court room. State courts subscribe to the standard of either *Frye v. US*[24] (general acceptance in the field) or the more flexible *Daubert v. Merrell Dow* standard,[25] which requires that the expert opinion supporting the evidence is both 'reliable' and 'relevant'. As it cannot be said that repressed memory is a generally accepted construct in psychiatry, it is the *Daubert* standard which is more likely to lead to a finding that repressed memory evidence is admissible. Guidance on the application of the *Daubert* standard to the theory of recovered memory was provided in *State of New Hampshire v. Hungerford*.[26] For the purposes of determining the reliability of such evidence under the second arm of the *Daubert* test, the following factors were to be considered:

1. the level of peer review and publication;
2. whether the phenomenon has been generally accepted in the psychological community;
3. whether it has been empirically tested;
4. the potential/known rate of false recovered memories;
5. the age of the witness at the time of the alleged abuse;
6. the length of time between the event and recovery of memory;
7. the presence of verifiable corroborative evidence; and
8. the circumstances surrounding the recovery (e.g. therapy or otherwise).

The earlier case of *Shahzade v. Gregory*[27] had found repressed memory evidence to be in principle admissible under the *Daubert* test, as the theory had attained general acceptance, had been subjected to peer review and publication and, although it could not be tested empirically, the theory had been validated in various studies. The court in *State of New Hampshire v. Hungerford*,[28] however, decided against the reliability

---

[24] 293 F 1013 (DC Cir. 1923).    [25] 113 S Ct 2786 (1993).
[26] 142 NH 110, 119 (1997).    [27] 923 F Sup at 286 (D Mass 1996).
[28] 142 NH 110, 119 (1997).

of recovered memory evidence, despite the existence of peer review, the profession was 'extremely divided, at best' on the validity of the phenomenon. Furthermore, empirical evidence of repression was lacking, due to the ethical problems of trials involving traumatic memories and there was no way of determining the rate of false memories masquerading as recovered memories.

Most US cases in which the courts have accepted the admissibility of repressed memory evidence require some corroborative evidence of the abuse and would not allow a prosecution/civil action to succeed on the basis of recovered memories alone. A typical example of the tenor of such judgments is *Moriarty v. Garden Sanctuary Church of God*,[29] where the South Carolina Court of Appeals dealt with the case of emotional injuries occasioned by alleged abuse revealed after 20 years of repression. The court accepted the validity of the principle of repressed memory, although it made cautious soundings regarding the potential inaccuracy of such evidence and the risk of implantation caused by poor therapeutic practices. The defendant would, however, be adequately protected against such risks by requiring expert evidence as to the existence of memory repression for the purposes of arguments of delayed discovery and objective verifiable evidence of the abuse for the purposes of proving the claim. Such corroborative evidence could include contemporaneous letters, diaries, accounts of siblings, medical records, a conviction consistent with child abuse or evidence of abuse of others.[30] Given the lapse of 20 or 30 years since the abuse occurred, it is often impossible to summon this sort of corroborative detail.

## Damage

### 1. Physical damage

In the tort of negligence, the label applied to the type of harm suffered by the claimant is crucial in determining the rules of actionability. Implicit in the matrix applied by the courts to determine the existence of a duty of care, there exists a taxonomy of types of harm, thus the ease of proving a duty of care is owed varies with the nature of the harm inflicted. Within this taxonomy, physical harm is the least contentious form of harm in the sense that the duty of care owed by defendants to prevent physical harm is usually regarded as axiomatic; consequently,

---

[29] 334 SC 150 (Ct App 1999).   [30] 511 SE 2d 699 (Ct App 1999), *per* Judge Hall at 710.

there are relatively few rules standing in the claimant's way when they are suing the defendant for negligently inflicted physical harm. In the context of physical abuse cases litigated when the victim is an adult, there is less scope for arguing that the damage did not manifest itself or that the cause of action was not discovered until years after the abuse and therefore that the usual limitation periods ought to be extended (although there may be a case for asking the court to exercise its discretion in this regard[31]). By contrast, where the damage claimed is psychiatric in nature, rules abound as to the circumstances in which that harm must be inflicted and the thresholds of harm which must be suffered for the case to be actionable. There is, however, more scope for arguing that the damage did not emerge or did not become known to the claimant until years after the tort was committed and that the claimant should be excused significant delay in airing their grievances before the courts.

## 2. Psychiatric damage

The once rigidly maintained distinction between disorders of the body and of the mind is melting away but is not yet extinct. Since 1994 the *Diagnostic Statistical Manual of Mental Disorders* has openly acknowledged an overlap between concepts of mental and physical illness, saying that there is much that is 'physical' in mental disorders and much that is 'mental' in physical disorders.[32] Progress in neuroscience promises to reveal further evidence of the overlap; for example, there is emerging evidence that PTSD has biochemical and neurological characteristics which distinguish it from other mental disorders.[33] The courts have demonstrated some sympathy with the view that unyielding legal distinctions between physical and psychiatric harms are no longer sustainable in the light of current clinical knowledge. The ruling from the House of Lords in *Page v. Smith*[34] that psychiatric harm is a type of personal injury alongside physical harm, has been taken by many as suggesting that claims for psychiatric harm are to be treated as equivalent in merit to those for physical harm:[35]

---

[31] S. 33 of the Limitation Act 1980.  [32] At xxi, 1994.
[33] G. Mezey and I. Robins, 'Usefulness and Validity of Post-traumatic Stress Disorder as a Psychiatric Category' (2001) *British Medical Journal* 561.
[34] [1996] AC 155.
[35] *Per* Lord Lloyd of Berwick in *Page v. Smith* [1996] 1 AC 155 at 188.

[i]n an age when medical knowledge is expanding fast, and psychiatric knowledge with it, it would not be sensible to commit the law to a distinction between physical and psychiatric injury which may already seem somewhat artificial, and may soon be altogether outmoded.[36]

*Page* was not the first case expressly to emphasise the likeness as opposed to the distinctions between physical and mental harm in the context of compensation. In *Bourhill v. Young*, Lord Macmillan observed that:

The distinction between mental shock and bodily injury was never a scientific one, for mental shock is presumably in all cases the result of, or at least accompanied by, some physical disturbance in the sufferer's system . . . But in the case of mental shock there are elements of greater subtlety than in the case of an ordinary physical injury, and these elements may give rise to debate as to the precise scope of liability.

Thus, in *Bourhill*, the sentiment is one of recognising parallels between physical and mental harm, rather than equivalence, whilst also acknowledging that different considerations may apply so as to restrict liability in the case of the latter. The courts' assimilation of this ideal whereby physical and mental harm are placed on an equal footing has, however, been patchy and inconsistent.[37]

### 3. Damages for 'pure' psychiatric harm in tort

Whilst there has traditionally been little difficulty in recovering damages for 'parasitic' psychiatric harm in tort (i.e. that which is accompanied by some associated physical harm), the circumstances in which 'pure' psychiatric harm has been recovered (i.e. that which is not attendant upon some physical injury), as is the case with most sexual abuse claims, are characterised by restrictive thresholds of entitlement. Generally speaking, recovery for 'pure' psychiatric harm is excluded from the torts regime, unless it can be categorised as a recognised psychiatric illness or disorder.[38] (Of course, where distress accompanies physical

---

[36] [1943] AC 92 at 108. See also Lord Wilberforce in *McLoughlin v. O'Brian* [1982] 2 All ER 298 at 301 and Taylor JA in *Rhodes v. Canadian National Rly* (1990) 75 DLR 4th 248, 296.
[37] See P. Case, 'Secondary Iatrogenic Harm: Claims for Psychiatric Damage Following a Death Caused by Medical Error' (2004) 67(4) *Modern Law Review* 561.
[38] 'The plaintiff must have suffered psychiatric injury in the form of a recognised psychiatric illness. The function of this principle is to exclude claims in respect of normal emotions such as grief or distress.' Per Lord Goff in *White v. Chief Constable for South*

harm as a result of the defendant's actions it can be accounted for in general damages for pain and suffering.)

### Actions against the perpetrator: intentional wrongs

Where the harm is classified as being the result of 'intentional' wrongs, as for example in a tort claim against the perpetrator of childhood abuse, psychiatric damage may be recovered as a stand alone head of damage. These intentional wrongs might be actioned as:

- a trespass to the person (assault or battery);[39]
- a course of conduct which amounts to harassment;[40] or
- a criminal injury giving rise to compensation under the Criminal Injuries Compensation Schemes.

In the case of these 'intentional' harms there is less need for the 'recognised psychiatric disorder' requirement as a means of stemming the tide of litigation. The floodgate considerations which are often relied upon in negligence claims to restrict recovery to recognised psychiatric disorders are less pressing in cases of intentional harm, as, generally speaking, we live in a society where incidents of intentional harm are relatively rare. Further, given the malice or bad faith on the part of the defendant which often characterises intentional wrongs, there is little perceived imperative to balance the interests of the defendant against those of the claimant.[41] Thus, in cases where the claimant is suing for stand alone psychiatric harm caused by an intentional wrong, the rule

---

*Yorkshire* at 10. See also *Kerby v. Redbridge Health Authority* [1994] PIQR Q1 (no damages for 'dashed hopes' when pregnancy ended in the death of the claimant's child, *Bagley v. North Hertfordshire HA* (1986) NLJ 1014 not followed) and *F v. Wirral BC* [1991] 2 All ER 648 at 674: ('The negligent killing of a child gave no cause of action for the loss by a parent of the custody and of the delight in the company of a child or for the grief and loss suffered.' Note, however, that the court did not rule out such damages where the death of a child was caused by a deliberate wrong such as deceit or misfeasance in public office, *per* Ralph Gibson LJ at 676 and Stuart Smith LJ at 687.) In Australia see *Mount Isa Mines Ltd v. Pusey* (1970) 125 CLR 383; [1971] ALR 253: generally the law requires 'some lasting disorder of body or mind' (at 394).

[39] *R v. Ireland (Robert Matthew); R v. Burstow (Anthony Christopher)* [1998] AC 147, finding that psychiatric harm was sufficient to establish an assault occasioning actual bodily harm (although note this is a criminal case and therefore only of persuasive value for torts).

[40] Protection from Harassment Act 1997, ss. 1 and 3.

[41] It has been observed that in relation to torts other than negligence, the recognised psychiatric disorder requirement may not apply as the potential for a flood of litigation is only made out in the tort of negligence. Law Commission, *Liability for Psychiatric Illness* (Law Com No. 249, 1998) at 1.10.

requiring a recognised psychiatric illness seems inapplicable.[42] In addition to actions against the perpetrator, any action relying on the vicarious liability of a non-perpetrator for the intentional tort of an employee will also be subject to the more liberal rules as to the types of psychiatric damage which are recoverable:[43] in other words, such an action will be treated as an action for an intentional wrong for the purposes of assessing the types of damage which are recoverable.

### Actions under *Wilkinson v. Downton* and the recognised disorder requirement

The *Wilkinson v. Downton*[44] action for intentional interference with the person was recommended in Chapter 2 as being beneficial to abuse claimants in possibly giving rise to more generous limitation periods. A further beneficial aspect of this cause of action is the possibility that, as with other intentional wrongs, the recognised disorder threshold of damage does not apply. Appearing to confirm this, Lord Hoffmann in *Hunter v. Canary Wharf*[45] stated:

> I see no reason why a tort of intention should be subject to the rule which excludes compensation for mere distress, inconvenience or discomfort in actions based on negligence. The policy considerations are quite different.[46]

Although later cases have not eliminated the possibility of damages for distress falling short of a recognised disorder in *Wilkinson v. Downton* actions, they have made it increasingly difficult to envisage where Lord

---

[42] For the purposes of the Protection from Harassment Act 1997, damages are available for anxiety caused by harassment (s. 3) and in the context of criminal injuries compensation, damages are available for temporary anxiety which is medically verified (para. 9, Criminal Injuries Compensation Scheme 2001), see Chapter 2.

[43] For example, at first instance in *KR v. Bryn Alyn Community (Holdings) Ltd (In Liquidation)* 2001 WL 753345, the claimant known as MK recovered damages of £5,000 for the significant distress she suffered following the Waterhouse Inquiry revelations, despite the absence of any proven recognised disorder.

[44] [1897] 2 QB 57.   [45] [1997] AC 655 at 706.

[46] This is supported by Lord Steyn in *Smith New Court Securities Ltd v. Scrimgeour Vickers (Asset Management) Ltd* [1997] AC 254 at 279: 'The exclusion of heads of loss in the law of negligence, which reflects considerations of legal policy, does not necessarily avail the intentional wrongdoer.' This was because the more stringent remedies against an intentional wrongdoer reflected the policy of the law of torts in first serving as a deterrent and, second, compensating the claimant.

Hoffmann's *obiter* might apply.[47] In *Wainwright v. Home Office*,[48] Lord Hoffmann was faced with what he had said in *Hunter* and elaborated by saying that distress may be actionable where the 'defendant acted in a way which he knew was unjustifiable and intended to cause harm or at least acted without caring whether he caused harm or not'. Nevertheless, he was mindful that Parliament had chosen to restrict the tort of harassment to a 'course of conduct,' and therefore the courts ought to be reluctant to encroach on Parliament's territory by fashioning rules which would enable distress damages to be recoverable in incidents of single intentional acts. Moreover, Article 8 of the ECHR (the right to respect for private and family life) did not require the courts to develop a remedy for distress on these facts, as the right implicated did not necessarily justify a damages award regardless of whether the harm was caused intentionally, negligently or accidentally.

The outcome of the above is that it remains open whether, in an extreme case of intentionally caused harm (such as sexual abuse) actioned under the principle of *Wilkinson v. Downton*, damages for distress falling short of a recognised disorder would be available. In any case, such an action would also have open to it the argument that psychiatric harm was a result of an invasion of physical integrity comparable to physical injury, and therefore consequential damages for distress would be payable as part of the pain and suffering award.[49] In *Wainwright v. Home Office*, Lord Hoffmann's judgment is ambiguous on the separate issue of whether the required intention must be to cause distress or an intention to cause a recognisable psychiatric illness, although it is the author's view that intention to cause humiliation and/or distress would probably suffice for an action under *Wilkinson* to lie.

In the Canadian version of the *Wilkinson* action, claimants must convince the court that they have suffered a 'visible and provable illness'.[50] Although the terminology is slightly different from the recognised psychiatric illness requirement in English law, the requirement is for most purposes the same, although there is less emphasis on identifying a label for the claimant's illness and on expert psychiatric evidence.

---

[47] In *C v. D* [2006] EWHC 166 at [94], Field J appears to assume that liability under *Wilkinson v. Downton* can never yield damages for distress falling short of a recognised disorder, although leaving open the possibility that Lord Hoffmann intended to create a new category of liability for mere distress.
[48] [2003] UKHL 53; [2003] 3 WLR 1137.
[49] *Parkinson v. St James and Seacroft University Hospital NHS Trust* [2001] EWCA Civ 530; [2002] QB 266, *per* Hale LJ likening an invasion of physical integrity to a physical injury.
[50] *Rahmetulla v. Vanfed Credit Union* (1984) 29 CCLT 78 (BCSC).

For example, in *Rahemtulla v. Vanfed Credit Union*,[51] the court was satisfied that the claimant had suffered a visible and provable illness in the form of 'severe emotional distress' requiring brief hospitalisation twice, notwithstanding the absence of expert medical evidence. A more liberal approach is adopted in the parallel 'tort of outrage' in the US, where only 'severe emotional distress' needs to be shown: '... one who by extreme and outrageous conduct intentionally or recklessly causes severe emotional distress to another is subject to liability for such emotional distress.'[52]

### Claims against the non-perpetrator: negligence claims

Where compensation is sought from the non-perpetrator who allegedly failed to prevent the abuse (e.g. social services, the abused's doctor, the medical profession), the claim will generally be brought in negligence. The use of the 'primary'/'secondary' victim distinction for psychiatric damage claims brought in the English tort of negligence has produced fragmentation in the categorisation of claims so that the law is not easily stated. 'Primary' victims are those who are physically endangered by the alleged negligence of the defendant and are thereby involved directly in some traumatic experience which triggers psychiatric harm (e.g. the car passenger who suffers trauma as the result of a collision caused by a negligent driver), whereas the label of 'secondary' victim is generally reserved for those whose involvement with the traumatic incident or experience is limited to witnessing or hearing of the imperilment of others. Until recently, the courts appeared to be suggesting that primary victims must suffer injury as a consequence of a sudden traumatic event involving imminent harm.[53] Since *Donachie v. Chief Constable of the Greater Manchester Police*,[54] however, it seems that an 'event' as such is not a requirement, although often a feature of primary victim cases.[55] It is rather that where negligence by the defendant would result in reasonably foreseeable physical harm, the duty of care extends to both physical and psychiatric harm, but if the only foreseeable harm is psychiatric then a sudden event is required if the claimant is to qualify as a primary victim. These definitions should present little difficulty for most abuse claims. The victim of physical abuse would usually be regarded as a primary victim as he/she will generally fit the definition of being

---

[51] (1984) 29 CCLT 78 (BCSC). [52] Restatement (Second) of Torts 1977, para 46(1).
[53] *A B and others v. Leeds Teaching Hospital NHS Trust* [2004] EWHC 644; [2005] 2 WLR 358.
[54] [2004] EWCA Civ 405, (2004) SJLB 509. [55] At [23].

either physically endangered or harmed by the defendant[56] (including negligence which exposed the claimant to bullying by a third party[57]) or will have been placed in the position of reasonably believing they were physically endangered.[58] Similarly, the victim of sexual abuse may fit the definition of a primary victim, even if the abuse occurs without the explicit threat of physical danger, for the claimant's physical integrity has been violated and there are *dicta* to suggest that such a violation ought to be treated in law as equivalent to physical injury.[59] Where the claimant's allegations concern emotional abuse, the primary victim nomenclature is no longer apposite, as there is no physical endangerment or compromising of physical integrity. Notably, in the leading cases on compensating child abuse there is no mention of primary or secondary victim status even though psychiatric damage forms the substance of the claim[60] and the courts may simply be willing to assume that a victim of child abuse deserves to be treated as a primary victim in the same way that a stressed employee apparently does.[61]

Whether the claimant is characterised as a primary or secondary victim or otherwise, in a negligence claim, the courts have applied a common threshold to the recovery of damages for pure mental trauma: the claimant must demonstrate that they have suffered a 'recognised psychiatric disorder'. This threshold has the effect of precluding claims for 'lesser' psychological suffering caused by the defendant's tort, namely distress, emotional upset, grief, anger, anxiety, stress or worry.[62] The recognised disorder requirement is generally applied to claims for pure psychiatric damage in contract,[63] and also to statutory rights of action.[64]

---

[56] *Page v. Smith* [1996] AC 155.
[57] *Bradford-Smart v. West Sussex CC* [2002] EWCA Civ 7; [2002] 1 FCR 425.
[58] *Page v. Smith* [1996] AC 155; *Dulieu v. White & Sons* [1901] 2 KB 669.
[59] Per Butler-Sloss LJ in *McLoughlin v. Jones* [2001] EWCA Civ 1743; [2002] 2 WLR 1279 and *Parkinson v. St James and Seacroft University Hospital NHS Trust* [2002] QB 266, per Hale LJ. Note also that the aetiological criterion for post-traumatic stress disorder insists on actual or threatened injury or a threat to physical integrity (see below).
[60] *X (Minors) v. Bedfordshire CC* [1995] 2 AC 633; *Barrett v. Enfield LBC* [1999] UKHL 25; [2001] 2 AC 550; *Lister v. Hesley Hall Ltd* [2001] UKHL 22; [2002] 1 AC 215.
[61] *Barber v. Somerset CC* [2004] UKHL 13; [2004] 1 WLR 1089.
[62] *D v. Bury MBC; H v. Bury MBC* [2006] EWCA Civ 1; [2006] 1 FCR 148; *Hinz v. Berry* [1970] 2 QB 40 and per Lord Goff in *White v. Chief Constable of South Yorkshire* [1999] 2 AC 455.
[63] *Gogay v. Hertfordshire CC* [2001] FCR 455.
[64] See e.g. *R v. Ireland (Robert Matthew); R v. Burstow (Anthony Christopher)* [1998] AC 147 at 156.

## 4. The recognised psychiatric disorder requirement

The general common law requirement of a recognised psychiatric disorder raises the further question of how and by whom must the disorder be 'recognised'? The common law's use of the passive term 'recognised' endorses what some would regard as the myth of modern psychiatry, that mental disorders are 'discovered' rather than 'invented'. Any diagnostic label which is included in the *Diagnostic and Statistical Manual of Mental Disorders* (4th edn)[65] ('DSM IV') would surely qualify as 'recognised' for the purposes of the common law, although that is not to say that common law 'recognition' and inclusion in the manual are mutually extensive. Inclusion in the manual, for example, does not necessarily represent a consensus as to the validity of the diagnosis.[66] This fact is unlikely to provide room for argument that an included diagnosis is not 'recognised' given that, by way of analogy, the standard of care required of the medical profession in English law does not require consensus by medical practitioners.[67]

The Australian case of *State of New South Wales v. Seedsman*[68] offers a salutary example of judicial pragmatism in cases where there is a lack of fit between the claimant's psychiatric disorder and DSM IV criteria.[69] The claimant sought damages for PTSD caused by her exposure to cases of child abuse in her work as a police officer. It was argued that her illness could not be described as PTSD, because DSM IV required either direct personal endangerment, witnessing the physical endangerment of others first hand, or hearing of the physical endangerment of a loved one. The claimant had not directly perceived the perpetration of abuse but only its aftermath and the children concerned were only known to her through her work. The judge regarded DSM IV as offering 'guidelines rather than strict boundaries', and accepted a diagnosis of PTSD notwithstanding that the claimant's condition failed to mirror DSM

---

[65] Washington DC, American Psychiatric Association, 1994.
[66] See e.g. in relation to dissociative disorders, Pope et al., 'Attitudes Towards DSM IV Dissociative Disorders Diagnoses'.
[67] *Bolam v. Friern Hospital Management Committee* [1957] 1 WLR 582; *Bolitho v. City and Hackney HA* [1997] 4 All ER 771.
[68] [2000] NSWCA 119.
[69] A pragmatic approach was also emphasised by Brennan J in *Jaensch v. Coffey* (1984) 155 CLR 549 at 560: 'compensation is awarded for the disability from which the plaintiff suffers, not for its conformity with a label of dubious medical acceptability.'

descriptors.[70] The *Seedsman* approach is likely to appeal to the English judiciary if the Court of Appeal cases of *Calascione v. Dixon*[71] and *Vernon v. Boseley*[72] are anything to go by. Both judgments accept a diagnosis of pathological grief disorder without adverse comment, yet the condition has still to be accepted for inclusion in the manual in its own right.[73] More recently, in *A v. Archbishop of Birmingham*,[74] the High Court did not require definitive proof that an abuse victim's trauma fitted a specific classification, rather that the severity of suffering merited compensation. Specific mention was made of the fact that the DSM criteria were 'dated and ripe for revision' and, in any case, clinical practice did not rely solely on DSM classifications to make diagnoses. This pragmatism is laudable, and indeed necessary, when it is remembered that DSM IV classifications are widely regarded as outdated, based as they are on received wisdom of the 1980s and early 1990s.

The lack of fit between DSM categories and medico-legal terminology has not only been recognised judicially, but also in DSM IV itself in the form of a rider which warns against over-reliance on its classifications in legal contexts:

> The clinical and scientific considerations involved in categorisation of these conditions as mental disorders may not be wholly relevant to legal judgments, for example, that take into account such issues as individual responsibility, disability, determination and competency.[75]

Further, the manual notes that the inclusion of diagnostic categories such as 'pathological gambling' or 'paedophilia' does not imply that the condition meets legal or non-medical criteria for what constitutes a mental disorder.[76]

---

[70] This pragmatism may be reserved for strong cases, given the court's emphasis of the unique features of the claimant's injury: it involved occasions of 'exceptional human depravity', a significant number of deaths and intense suffering of young children and the frequent observation of dead and mutilated bodies.
[71] (1991) 19 BMLR 97.   [72] [1997] 1 All ER 577.
[73] See, however, the proposals for change which were not adopted: S. J. Marwit, 'DSM III-R, Grief Reactions and a Call for Revision' (1991) 22 *Professional Psychology: Research and Practice* 75. For a similar example from Canada, see *A(TWN) v. Clarke* [2004] 3 WWR 11 – the court did not regard a diagnosis that fit DSM IV criteria as crucial. Rather the question was whether the impact of the abuse was such as to have significantly interfered with the claimant's life.
[74] [2005] EWHC 1361 (QB).   [75] American Psychiatrists Association, 2000, p. xxxvii.
[76] American Psychiatrists Association, 2000, p. xxxvii.

## 5. The role of expert evidence

Whatever reservations are expressed in DSM IV about the profession of psychiatry's manual being used to determine legal issues, where the 'recognised psychiatric disorder' requirement applies the parameters of liability in the tort of negligence are to a large extent determined by what psychiatry currently defines as pathological degrees of psychiatric symptoms.[77] It is arguably, therefore, the discipline of psychiatry and its representatives in the role of expert witnesses, that has the last word on actionability and not the courts, at least where the law requires a 'recognised' condition. Having said that, the purpose of expert evidence is to assist the court and not to usurp the decision-making role of the judge:

> ... Judges are not expected to suspend judicial belief simply because the evidence is given by an expert. An expert is not in any special position and there is no presumption of belief in a doctor however distinguished he or she may be. It is, however, necessary for a judge to give reasons for disagreeing with experts' conclusions or recommendations.[78]

Provided the courts have expert evidence before them which suggests that the claimant is suffering from a recognised, labelled psychiatric disorder, they are unlikely to regard conflict in the choice of label as fatal to the claimant's case, but rather to see the conflict as evidence of a disagreement over the severity of the claimant's disorder.[79]

## 6. Classifications of mental illness

It should be borne in mind that the therapeutic and legal uses to which clinical diagnoses are put are very different; a fact which can lead to significant tension between therapeutic and legal applications of clinical concepts. In clinical contexts the functions of diagnoses include facilitation of professional debate, discussion and research with a view to improving and developing the available treatments.[80] By contrast, the

---

[77] Where damages are available for distress falling short of a recognised disorder, it seems that no expert evidence is needed to convince the courts that distress has been suffered: *Aldersea and others v. Public Transport Corp; Chandler v. Public Transport Corp* (2001) 3 VR 499; [2001] VSC 169, although a psychologists' report of observed distress may be relevant in determining the existence or extent of psychiatric injury.

[78] *Re B (A Minor) (Rejection of Expert Evidence)* [1996] 3 FCR 272, per Butler Sloss LJ at 280.

[79] *KR v. Bryn Alyn Community (Holdings) Ltd (In Liquidation)* 2001 WL 753345 at [96].

[80] Mezey and Robins, 'Usefulness and Validity of Post-traumatic Stress Disorder'.

use of these diagnoses in a legal context determines the legitimacy of the claim (i.e. vouching for the severity of the claimant's injury). It also serves as a factor to be considered when deciding which claims ought to be excluded from the realms of actionability when the courts are applying rules to define limits on liability and control the flow of claims.

Whilst there is no signature disorder associated with child abuse, it has been judicially observed that borderline personality disorder ('BPD') and PTSD, both of which would be regarded as recognised psychiatric disorders, are typical manifestations of abuse-related trauma.[81] The particular category of disorder alleged to have been suffered can therefore be relevant to the credibility of the claim, because a court is more likely to accept that abuse was the cause of these disorders.

## PTSD

The PTSD diagnosis is not uncontroversial and, without denying that those diagnosed with PTSD are often genuinely suffering trauma-related distress and disability, there are a number of authors who regard the PTSD diagnosis itself as an invention of psychiatry.[82] The origins of PTSD can be traced to the work in the 1860s of John Erichsen, who identified psychological symptoms emanating from physical trauma to the spine caused by railway accidents ('nervous shock'). Under the new label of 'shell shock' traumagenic injury was later regarded as triggered by psychological stimuli, a finding which emanated from research on the impact of the trauma suffered by soldiers who fought in World War I. It was not, however, until 1980 that the PTSD diagnosis appeared in the *Diagnostic Statistical Manual of Mental Disorders* following the work of activists who campaigned for recognition and compensation for Vietnam War veterans.

The diagnostic criteria for PTSD as currently set out in DSM IV T-R are as follows:[83]

---

[81] *W v. Attorney General* [1999] 2 NZLR 709.
[82] 'It originates in the scientific and clinical discourses of the nineteenth century; before that time, there is unhappiness, despair and disturbing recollections, but no traumatic memory, in the sense we know it today': A. Young, *The Harmony of Illusions – Inventing Post-Traumatic Stress Disorder* (Princeton University Press, 1995) at 141.
[83] *Diagnostic Statistical Manual Fourth Edition, Text Revision* ('DSM IV (T-R)'). (American Psychiatric Association, 2000), 309.81.

A. The person has been exposed to a traumatic event in which both of the following are present:
   1) The person experienced, witnessed, or was confronted with an event or events that involved actual or threatened death or serious injury, or a threat to the physical integrity of self or others;
   2) The person's response involved intense fear, helplessness or horror.
B. The traumatic event is persistently re-experienced in one (or more) of the following ways:
   1) Recurrent and intrusive distressing recollections of the event, including images, thoughts or perceptions;
   2) Recurrent dreams of the event;
   3) Acting or feeling as if the traumatic event were recurring (includes a sense of reliving the experience, illusions, hallucinations and dissociative flashback episodes, including those that occur on awakening or when intoxicated);
   4) Intense psychological distress at exposure to internal or external cues that symbolise or resemble an aspect of the traumatic event;
   5) Physiological reactivity on exposure to internal or external cues that symbolise or resemble an aspect of the traumatic event.
C. Persistent avoidance of stimuli associated with the trauma and numbing of general responsiveness (not present before the trauma) as indicated by three (or more) of the following:
   1) Efforts to avoid thoughts, feelings or conversations associated with the trauma;
   2) Efforts to avoid activities, places or people that arouse recollections of the trauma;
   3) Inability to recall an important aspect of the trauma;
   4) Marked diminished interest or participation in significant activities;
   5) Feeling of detachment or estrangement from others;
   6) Restricted range of affect;
   7) Sense of a foreshortened future.
D. Persistent symptoms of increased arousal (not present before the trauma) as indicated by two (or more) of the following:
   1) Difficulty falling or staying asleep;
   2) Irritability or outbursts of anger;
   3) Difficulty concentrating;
   4) Hypervigilance;
   5) Exaggerated startled response.

The law's attachment to PTSD as a diagnosis has skewed society's perception of trauma-related disorders. There are many disorders which can result from traumatic experiences, yet the courts are routinely presented with only one – PTSD. The defining feature of this disorder is its etiological event (criterion A) and herein lies the secret of PTSD's success as a legal construct. The fact that the DSM explicitly connects PTSD with a traumatic event increases the credibility of the claimant's allegation that their psychiatric illness was caused by incidents of abuse as opposed to organic causes. Thus, there is an element of legal convenience in the PTSD diagnosis. In fact, it has been commented in clinical circles that evidence that the patient has experienced a credible etiological event transforms symptoms which would otherwise be diagnosed as depression or some other disorder into a case of PTSD; for example, mood disorder symptoms become 're-experiences' and phobic symptoms become 'avoidance'.[84] Judicial readiness to accept the PTSD diagnosis is evidenced in the *Bryn Alyn* litigation, where Connell J was satisfied that the claimants suffered PTSD on the grounds that the expert evidence was that the abuse recounted was serious and traumatic enough to trigger PTSD and the symptoms of suicidal tendencies, anxiety and particularly flashbacks were suggestive of PTSD.[85] Furthermore, PTSD is portrayed as a non-divisible injury (i.e. caused by a single event) and thus it is less likely that damage will be apportioned (see below).

There are, however, pitfalls for litigants whose claim is essentially that childhood abuse has caused PTSD. For example, one court in Australia assumed that where PTSD was alleged, the diagnostic criteria (particularly the flashbacks) necessarily meant that the claimant would be aware of the fact of her symptoms (i.e. that she was suffering from psychiatric injury) and that she would be aware of their connection to the abuse much earlier than she had alleged was the case.[86] This assumption had devastating consequences for any claim that limitation periods ought to be extended to take account of the claimant's delayed discovery of their injury. Had the claimant been suffering from depression or delusions, she would not necessarily have been aware that her symptoms indicated the presence of a psychiatric illness and a more liberal approach to limitation would have been possible. There is certainly a hint of contradiction between the law's association of PTSD with delayed discovery of the facts necessary to consider bringing a claim for the purposes of the limitation rules (see Chapter 5) and the fact that PTSD diagnostic

[84] Young, *The Harmony of Illusions* at 120.
[85] *KR v. Bryn Alyn Community (Holdings) Ltd (In Liquidation)* 2001 WL 753345 [110].
[86] *Hopkins v. Secretary of Queensland* [2004] QDC 021.

criteria require a form of re-living/re-experiencing the traumatic event (diagnostic criterion B). On the other hand, avoidance strategies whereby litigation has been delayed due to the claimant's instinct to avoid confronting his experiences and/or his abuser are perfectly consistent with the PTSD diagnosis given the references in criterion C to persistent avoidance of stimuli associated with the traumatic event.

## Borderline personality disorder

BPD was once considered to be a mild form of schizophrenia. The subject exhibits a pattern of instability in interpersonal relationships and self-image and impulsivity indicated by five or more of the following:[87]

- frantic efforts to avoid real or imagined abandonment;
- a pattern of unstable and intense interpersonal relationships;
- identity disturbance: markedly and persistently unstable self-image or sense of self;
- impulsivity in at least two areas that are potentially self-damaging (e.g., spending, sex, substance abuse, reckless driving, binge eating);
- recurrent suicidal behaviour, gestures, or threats, or self-mutilating behaviour;
- affective instability due to a marked reactivity of mood (e.g., intense episodic dysphoria, irritability, or anxiety usually lasting a few hours and only rarely more than a few days);
- chronic feelings of emptiness;
- inappropriate, intense anger or difficulty controlling anger (e.g. frequent displays of temper, constant anger, recurrent physical fights);
- transient, stress-related paranoid ideation or severe dissociative symptoms.

As mentioned above, this diagnosis is often associated with sexual abuse during childhood, although the aetiology of BPD is likely to include several factors, including an organic predisposition to the disorder, as well as psychosocial and environmental factors. Due to the characteristic instability and pervasive anger of BPD patients, there is perceived to be an increased risk that these individuals will make false accusations, a fact which can be seized upon by defendants in abuse

---

[87] DSM IV (T-R) at 301.83. It might be observed that as with many of the classifications there is a certain arbitrariness in these criteria – why five traits and not four or at least six?

claims as a means of attacking the claimant's credibility. Thus, unlike PTSD, a BPD diagnosis can be regarded as potentially impugning the claimant's case.

It has been noted that the diagnostic criteria for PTSD and BPD are exceedingly similar, the main difference being reference to exposure to a traumatic event prior to onset of the condition in the case of PTSD.[88] BPD sufferers are regarded as frequently having a predisposition to personality disorder which would likely pre-date any traumatic event for which the defendant is responsible. Therefore, not only does the BPD diagnosis lend itself to suggestions that the claimant is making false or embellished claims, it may also lead to allegations that the claimant has a susceptibility to psychiatric disorder. Although this should not affect the success of a claim which is brought by the claimant suing the perpetrator of abuse or suing a non-perpetrator as 'primary victim' of the defendant's negligence, it may affect the award of damages for it can easily be argued that the onset of BPD was likely for this individual notwithstanding the abuse or that other factors clearly contributed to the diagnosis.

## Substance abuse (alcoholism/drug dependency)

Accepting that there is a correlation between abuse and later alcoholism is a far cry from fulfilling the legal causation requirement of proving that the abuse made a 'material contribution' to the claimant's alcoholism in a particular case. In the Canadian case of *D(P) v. Allen*, the central issue was whether childhood sexual abuse by a Catholic priest was a contributory factor to the claimant's alcoholism.[89] The court found in the negative, saying that the abuse had ended 12 years before the claimant began using alcohol and there were only a few occasions when the claimant could say that she had had a drink because of thoughts of the abuse. It was not necessary for there to be an explicit connection between the abuse and the motive to drink, but there must be some evidence linking the alcohol use to the abuse. In any event, as with BPD, claims alleging that alcoholism is the damage suffered as a result of the defendant's wrong are high risk, as alcoholics are often assumed to make unreliable and untruthful witnesses.

---

[88] P. K. Sutherland and D. J. Henderson, 'Expert Psychiatrists and Comments on Witness Credibility' available at www.smith-lawfirm.com/Sutherland_article.html.
[89] (2004) 132 ACWS (3d) 1098.

## Other disorders

Whilst an association is thought to exist between schizophrenia and the trauma caused by child abuse, little is known about the precise mechanisms causing the onset of this disorder and there is as yet no convincing evidence that child abuse of itself causes schizophrenia. Nevertheless, the High Court has recently demonstrated its willingness to award damages to a claimant whose suffering was symptomatic of schizophrenia or something very close to it.[90] This was on the basis of an acknowledged lack of precision and fluidity in diagnostic criteria and also that the central question for the court in determining damage was to assess the impact of the illness caused by abuse, however it was to be labelled. It is not sufficient to plead that negligence causing parent and child to be separated for some time has caused harm to the child resulting from separation anxiety because such separation is bound to cause developmental problems in the future. The Court of Appeal in *D v. Bury MBC*[91] was invited to draw the inference that separation of a child from its mother caused harm to the child even if psychiatry was currently unable to definitively apply a label to that harm. The court declined, preferring to reinforce the general rule that a recognised disorder must be shown and evidence must be submitted as to its existence notwithstanding the difficulties of diagnosing mental problems in very young children due to their inability to communicate.

Whilst some link can be found between many neuroses and childhood abuse, there are a number of myths in this regard which have now been dispelled. In the infamous *Ramona* litigation, it was revealed that Holly Ramona's therapist had told her that 80% of cases of bulimia were associated with childhood sexual abuse, thus planting in her mind suspicions of forgotten abuse. There is, however, no empirical evidence supporting such a claim, and in fact any specific link between abuse and eating disorders is currently regarded as tenuous at best.[92] Likewise, diagnoses of multiple personality disorder (MPD) alongside recovered memories of abuse are condemned by the Brandon Report as likely to be iatrogenically produced.[93]

---

[90] *A v. Archbishop of Birmingham* [2005] EWHC 1361 (QB).
[91] [2006] EWCA Civ 1; [2006] 1 FCR 148.
[92] C. M. Vize and P. J. Cooper, 'Sexual Abuse in Patients with Eating Disorders, Patients with Depression and Normal Controls – a Comparative Study' (1995) 167 *British Journal of Psychology* 80.
[93] Brandon et al., *Reported Recovered Memories*.

## 7. Mental illness and credibility

The court's conclusion as to the claimant's credibility ought not to be based simply upon the individual's performance in the witness box, but also whether their evidence is in accordance with the preponderance of probabilities.[94] When the claimant presents to court seeking compensation for psychiatric illness, there is a risk that their injury will undermine their credibility either as a witness or as a reasonable claimant. In the past, many sexual assault claims were defended by assertions that the claimant suffered from a pre-existing mental illness which was responsible for producing the 'false' allegations of rape or assault.[95] Thus, claiming that psychiatric illness has resulted from abuse which is denied by the defendant can be a double-edged sword. As indicated above, a claimant presenting with BPD, a condition which can include symptoms of exaggeration and fabrication, may be regarded as an unreliable witness and the truth of their allegations may be brought into question. In the *Bryn Alyn* litigation, Connell J had agreed that one of the claimants could give his evidence wearing his baseball cap, as it was a source of comfort to him. Nevertheless, he went on to observe that, because the court could not see his face above the mouth and his eyes, it was more difficult in this case for the court to say that the claim advanced was proved to the required standard.[96]

## Causation and remoteness

### 1. Proving 'causation in fact'

Whether an abuse claim is brought in negligence, trespass or intentional interference with the person, it must be demonstrated that the wrong has caused the damage for which the claimant seeks compensation. First, the court must be convinced that the defendant's wrong constituted a 'cause in fact' of the damage. The 'but for test' is used as a filter to eliminate irrelevant factors; thus, if it can be said that 'but for' the defendant's wrong the harm would not have been suffered, then the wrong is *a* cause, although not necessarily *the* legal cause of the

---

[94] *HF v. Canada (Attorney General)* [2002] BCJ No 436 following *Faryna v. Chorny* [1952] 2 DLR 354.
[95] T. Wilkinson-Ryan, 'Admitting Mental Health Evidence to Impeach the Credibility of a Sexual Assault Complainant' (2004) 153 *University of Pennsylvania Law Review* 1372.
[96] *KR v. Bryn Alyn Community (Holdings) Ltd (In Liquidation)* 2001 WL 753345 at [168].

damage.[97] However, if it can be said that the harm would have been suffered even absent the abuse, or that the abuse would have been suffered absent the defendant's negligence, then the defendant is not liable. In *C v. Cairns*,[98] the court concluded that even if the 1970s general practitioner who did nothing when confronted by a case of child abuse was to be regarded as negligent, a claim against him would probably fail on causation grounds. This was because, even if the defendant had referred the case to another doctor, it was not clear that there was enough evidence to justify raising the alarm with the police, or that reporting the abuse would result in the claimant being removed from the family home. This case illustrates well the difficulties caused by the diffused lines of accountability where child protection is concerned. Proof that the negligence caused the abuse is problematical when it does not lie within the negligent defendant's power to prevent the damage occurring. This is generally the case when the negligence alleged is a failure to prevent a third party from inflicting the harm, but the position becomes even more complex when prevention of the harm also depends on the action of further agencies, such as social workers, the non-offending parent or the police. In *C v. Cairns*, however, the issues of breach of duty and causation are interlinked, as it is likely that a finding that a failure to act was negligent would also prompt a finding that in all probability once other agencies were alerted to the fact of abuse, the child would have been removed from the danger.

The 'but for' test does not provide an exclusive test for factual causation. Even where the claimant cannot prove that they would not have suffered the damage if it were not for the defendant's wrong, causation in fact is generally satisfied where the court can be convinced that the defendant's wrong 'materially contributed' to the damage in question.[99] As the wrong must only make a 'material' or 'significant' contribution to the damage, it is clear that the law does not require the defendant's wrong to be the sole cause of the damage for compensation to be payable.[100] The contribution will be regarded as material or significant provided it cannot be described as *de minimis*.

---

[97] *Barnett v. Chelsea and Kensington Hospital Management Committee* [1969] 1 QB 428.
[98] [2003] Lloyd's Med Rep 90.
[99] *Bonnington Castings Ltd v. Wardlaw* [1956] AC 613; *Wilsher v. Essex Area Health Authority* [1986] 3 All ER 801; *Athey v. Leonati* [1996] 3 SCR 458.
[100] *Bonnington Castings Ltd v. Wardlaw* [1956] AC 613.

## 2. Relaxation of the 'material contribution' test

In complex cases of psychological trauma, establishing that the defendant's wrong materially contributed to the sum of the claimant's neuroses may be extremely difficult. As the causation in fact inquiry is ultimately performed with the objective of finding where responsibility for the damage *ought* to rest,[101] there is room for considerations of justice and fairness even at this stage of the litigation. Recent years have seen the English courts adopt a more pragmatic approach to causation in a small number of cases where the courts have taken the view that proving the defendant's wrong materially contributed to the damage would have been impossible, but justice and fairness indicate that the defendant *ought* to be liable. The circumstances in which the courts will tolerate departures from the material contribution test appear, however, to be very narrowly defined and do not admit of a general principle of relaxing the burden of proving causation where the claimant would otherwise be the subject of a harsh decision. The House of Lords first recognised a departure from the material contribution test in *McGhee v. NCB*,[102] accepting that proof that the defendant's negligence had materially increased the risk of harm sufficed on the facts. Thirty years later, in *Fairchild v. Glenhaven Funeral Services*,[103] the House of Lords dealt with a case of mesothelioma, a disease about which little is known except that it is caused by exposure to asbestos and its severity is not determined by the level of exposure (i.e. it may possibly be caused by the inhalation of a single asbestos fibre). Given that the claimants had worked for a number of employers who had negligently exposed them to asbestos in their workplace, it was impossible to show which employers had materially contributed to the harm. Their Lordships agreed that, in exceptional cases such as this, proof that the defendant's wrong had materially increased the risk of harm would satisfy the claimant's burden of proof because it could be treated as equivalent to proof of a material contribution to the harm.[104] According to Lord Bingham, it would be easier to find equivalence between a material increase in the risk and a material contribution to the damage

---

[101] Jones, *Textbook on Torts* at 224. [102] [1982] 3 All ER 1008.
[103] [2002] UKHL 22; [2002] 3 All ER 305.
[104] For criticism of the causation point in *Fairchild* see T. Weir, 'Making it More Likely v. Making it Happen' (2002) 61 *Cambridge Law Journal* 519.

where the facts concerned a single noxious agent attributable to different sources than where there were a number of noxious agents involved.

The *Fairchild* approach to causation raises several questions in the context of proving an abuse claim. For example, given the difficulties of proving the source of psychiatric injury generally,[105] will *Fairchild* have any application in cases where the claimant seeks to prove that psychiatric damage was caused by abuse? How should the approach to causation differ (if at all) between negligence claims against non-perpetrators and battery claims against perpetrators?

### 3. Future application of Fairchild

There was little agreement between their Lordships in *Fairchild* as to when the more liberal 'material increase in the risk' approach might be applied. Lord Bingham's approach was the most prescriptive as he envisaged it only applying in cases of employer liability for negligent exposure of workers to asbestos where there was more than one employer whose negligent exposure might have been the source of the harm (in other words, cases which mirrored the facts of *Fairchild*). At the other end of the spectrum was Lord Rodger, who appeared to anticipate that the material increase of the risk approach could be applied wherever it was inherently impossible for claimants to prove how their injury was caused (e.g. where the current state of scientific knowledge is uncertain on the issue of how the injury is caused). Lord Rodger did, however, express uncertainty as to how far the principle might apply (e.g. could it apply where the other possible cause of the harm was a natural event or the act of a third party rather than the act or omission of the defendant?). Lord Rodger's *obiter* might be relied upon to argue that it is 'inherently impossible' to prove the aetiology of psychiatric illness, therefore proof of causation will be satisfied if the claimant can demonstrate that the abuse materially increased the risk of suffering the particular disorder experienced by the claimant.

*Fairchild* left uncertainty in its wake as to whether the principle applied would have more general application or would be isolated by later judgments consigning it to its particular facts (as happened with

---

[105] 'It will never be possible to determine with any kind of certainty the precise origin of a psychiatric injury. This is particularly true when the injury develops over a long period of time and is influenced by numerous different factors.' *D(P) v. Allen* (2004) 132 ACWS (3d) 1098 at 272.

*McGhee* before it). It seems, however, that the courts are more willing to embrace and extend the *Fairchild* principle of causation, but to date are proceeding cautiously and incrementally. The *Fairchild* approach to causation has since been applied in *Barker v. Corus (UK) plc*,[106] where damages were sought for mesothelioma caused by exposure to asbestos which occurred during the deceased's employment with the defendant and during a period of self-employment. Despite the deceased worker not being entirely 'innocent', the *Fairchild* principle was regarded as applicable. The approach in *Fairchild* has also been commented on with approval by the House of Lords in *Chester v. Afshar*,[107] with Lord Steyn commenting that the liberal approach could not be confined to the facts in *Fairchild* and that the judgment demonstrated that 'where justice and policy *demand* it a modification of causation principles is not beyond the wit of a modern court'.[108] It might be argued that in cases against the perpetrator where commission of the intentional wrong has been established, justice (to the claimant) and policy may dictate that a *Fairchild* approach should be adopted. In other jurisdictions there are examples of judges concluding that intentional wrongs as heinous as sexual abuse should deprive the defendant of arguments that the limitation rules should be strictly adhered to.[109] Surely some flexibility could be incorporated at the causation stage of litigation to reflect a policy that intentional torts should tip the balance in favour of the claimant insofar as negotiating a line of liability through uncertainties of causation are concerned.

## 4. Causation in law

### Novus actus interveniens

**Claimant's criminality: The *Clunis* argument** The issue referred to here as the '*Clunis* argument' is that of whether the defendant can be liable in damages for the consequences of criminal acts (e.g. violent assaults or drug taking) which it is alleged the claimant would not have committed 'but for' the defendant's wrong in committing or failing to prevent sexual abuse of the claimant. The issue is essentially one of *novus*

---

[106] [2006] UKHL 20, [2006] 3 All ER 785.  [107] [2004] UKHL 41; [2005] 1 AC 134.
[108] At [23].
[109] 'The patent inequity of allowing these individuals to go on with their life without liability, while the victim continues to suffer the consequences, clearly militates against any guarantee of repose.' *M(K) v. M(H)* [1992] 3 SCR 6, *per* La Forest J at [22].

*actus interveniens* – does the claimant's criminal act break the chain of causation? In *Clunis v. Camden and Islington HA*,[110] the Court of Appeal struck out a claim for damages by a man detained under mental health legislation who, after his release, had killed a stranger on an underground tube station. The substance of his claim was that neglect in the performance of aftercare services had constituted lost opportunities to prevent the crime occurring by readmitting him to hospital or procuring his agreement to be a voluntary patient. The Court of Appeal regarded the claim as bound to fail on two grounds:

1. It was founded on the claimant's own illegal act (*ex turpi non causa oritur*). The killing had resulted in a conviction for manslaughter due to the plea of diminished responsibility, indicating that the claimant retained some responsibility for his actions.
2. The health authority's statutory powers regarding after care of released patients did not give rise to a duty of care. Whilst this point is confined to the facts of the case, the first reason deserves further analysis.

It may seem anomalous for the court to accept that, on the one hand, abuse may be proved to have caused the claimant to indulge in criminal behaviour and yet on the other to refuse to compensate the claimant for the consequences of this criminality (e.g. time spent in prison, effect of drug abuse on health). It is to be remembered, however, that proving such a link in law requires only proof that the abuse made a material contribution to the criminality, the inference being that other factors may have had a role to play in turning the claimant to crime. This conclusion leaves room for the assumption that the claimant's self-determination played a part in the criminal conduct – sufficient justification for the court withholding damages on public policy grounds despite proof of a causal nexus between the claimant's criminality and the abuse.

The *Clunis* case raises a number of questions as to future possibilities. Where the claim was for the defendant's intentional wrongdoing as opposed to negligence, would the *ex turpi* principle have any application? The court in *Clunis* indicated that if the claimant could be said to lack voluntariness so that he did not know the nature and quality of his act was wrong, the *ex turpi* principle may not have applied. Does this leave any scope for a successful *Clunis* argument in the context of victims of sexual abuse?

---

[110] [1998] QB 989.

The *Clunis* argument was dealt with, if only briefly, in the *Bryn Alyn* litigation. At first instance, Connell J ruled that the court would not 'as a matter of public policy provide aid to claimants relying on a criminal or immoral act', therefore no damages for imprisonment or loss of earning during imprisonment would be awarded. In any case, the causal link between the claimant's convictions and the abuse had not been proved. In the Court of Appeal, the issue was raised again in the context of GM's claim, which included a claim for compensation for the costs of treatment for his opiate dependency. The court regarded this as distinguishable from *Clunis*: the claimant did not base this part of his claim on his own criminal act, but on the defendant's negligence in failing to prevent the abuse.[111] 'An argument may survive that damages are recoverable in respect of tortious acts that have resulted in a law abiding citizen becoming a criminal.'[112] This tends to suggest that the courts have not closed the door entirely on allegations that damages are payable for the consequences of the claimant's criminal behaviour where a causal nexus with abuse can be made out.

## 5. *Remoteness of damage*

Claims against the perpetrator defendant and non-perpetrator defendant must be distinguished again when considering the topic of remoteness of damage. For the purposes of intentional torts, 'an intention to injure the claimant disposes of any issue of remoteness'.[113] Thus, the defendant perpetrator is liable for all the direct consequences of his conduct, notwithstanding that they may be unforeseeable, unexpected or extraordinary.[114] In other words, no consideration is given to whether the harm to be compensated could have been anticipated by the defendant. This still raises issues of what may be regarded as 'direct'. How is directness established? Can alcoholism, drug taking or poor educational achievement be easily described as the direct result of abuse?

The test for remoteness of damage as applied to unintentional torts is based on foreseeability of the type of damage suffered and is derived from the *Wagon Mound* case.[115] Provided the type of harm suffered by the claimant was a foreseeable consequence of the wrong, it does not

---

[111] At [38]. [112] [130]. This aspect of the case was not appealed to the Court of Appeal.
[113] *Quinn v. Leatham* [1901] AC 495, *per* Lord Lindley; *Scott v. Shepherd* (1773) 2 Bl R 892.
[114] *Re Polemis and Furness, Withy & Co* [1921] 3 KB 560.
[115] *The Wagon Mound* [1961] AC 388.

matter that either the extent of that damage or the manner of its occurrence was unforeseeable.[116] In the case of personal injuries, it seems to suffice that personal injury of some kind was foreseeable,[117] for even though the courts have not gone so far as to say that only broad foreseeability of some personal injury is required to satisfy the rules of remoteness, this is often the effect of the thin skull rule (as to which see below).[118]

Will the courts distinguish between physical and psychiatric harms as different 'kinds' of damage? The ruling in *Page v. Smith* to the effect that the law ought not to distinguish between physical and psychiatric harms was made in the context of whether road users owed a duty of care to safeguard other road users from psychiatric harm. It has since been decided that this ruling does not have direct implications for the resolution of issues of remoteness of damage where the claimant must demonstrate that the type of harm they have suffered is of a foreseeable type. The court in *R v. Croydon HA*[119] refused to accept that *Page* prevented it from distinguishing between physical and psychiatric harms as different types of damage for the purposes of remoteness. It is also possible that the courts could bar recovery by drawing fine distinctions between different 'kinds' of psychiatric damage. The *Wagon Mound* test for remoteness prevails in Australia,[120] where more jurisprudence has evolved on remoteness of psychiatric damage due to Australian law's less convoluted approach to duty.[121] Evidence from that jurisdiction is that the courts may all too readily distinguish between the different means by which psychiatric damage is suffered. For example, it might be held that depression caused by the abuse is different in 'kind' from depression triggered by the litigation pursued to obtain compensation for the physical injury, making the latter too remote from the negligence.[122] This example not only encroaches on the principle that the manner of occurrence of the harm need not be foreseeable, but, if followed in English law, would also undermine the value of equivalence

---

[116] *Hughes v. Lord Advocate* [1963] AC 837.
[117] Cf. *Tremain v. Pike* [1969] 3 All ER 1303 and *Doughty v. Turner Manufacturing Co Ltd* [1964] 1 QB 518.
[118] Jones, *Textbook on Torts* at 270.   [119] [1998] PIQR Q26.
[120] *Chapman v. Hearse* (1961) 106 CLR 112.
[121] See e.g. the judgments in *Annetts v. Australian Stations Pty Ltd* (2002) 191 ALR 449 where the lattice of requirements applied to secondary victims of psychiatric injury is largely rejected as not being part of Australian law.
[122] *AMP v. RTA and others* [2001] NSWCA 186.

expressed in *Page*. A 'broad brush' approach appears to be taken to questions of remoteness where tangible physical injury is at stake;[123] therefore, it would surely not be acceptable if the courts followed the Australian example of separating out different kinds of psychiatric harm according to the precise way in which the harm was triggered.[124]

Allegations that the defendant ought to pay compensation for what might be regarded as 'lifestyle' damage caused by the abuse (e.g. alcoholism, drug dependency, prostitution and other criminal activities) raise further interesting questions as to whether these might be considered to be foreseeable 'types of damage' for the purposes of the remoteness rules. Whilst alcoholism and drug dependency are listed in DSM IV T-R as mental disorders, and therefore might generously be regarded as a type of psychiatric harm which foreseeably arises from abuse, the same cannot generally be said of delinquency leading to fines and/or imprisonment.

## 6. The thin skull (and crumbling skull) rules

The 'thin skull' rule establishes that the tortfeasor is liable for the claimant's injuries even if the injuries are unexpectedly severe due to a pre-existing condition or susceptibility which the defendant could not have known about.[125] In the case of PTSD, as with most psychiatric disorders, the claimant may be predisposed to suffer a pathological reaction to traumatic events which may cause their injury to be more severe than would ordinarily have been foreseen.[126] The thin skull rule is similar in effect to, and overlaps with, the above stated principle of remoteness that the extent of the damage need not be foreseeable.[127]

The thin skull rule can be contrasted with the rule that the defendant need not compensate the claimant for the debilitating effects of a pre-existing condition which had already manifested itself at the time of the tort. (This is referred to in some jurisdictions other than England and Wales as the 'crumbling skull' rule and is an expression of the general principle that the claimant should not be compensated so as to put them

---

[123] Jones, *Textbook on Torts* at 270–271.
[124] Although see to the contrary: *Pratley v. Surrey CC* [2003] EWCA Civ 1067; [2003] IRLR 794.
[125] *Page v. Smith* [1996] AC 155.
[126] Mezey and Robins, 'Usefulness and Validity of Post-traumatic Stress Disorder' on predisposition to PTSD.
[127] Jones, *Textbook on Torts* at 273.

in a better position than they would have been absent the tort.)[128] Furthermore, if there is a measurable likelihood that the claimant's condition would have affected the claimant in the future apart from the abuse (e.g. because of a susceptibility or, in the case of schizophrenia, because of cannabis use), this can be used to discount the award against the defendant. This last principle is one of quantum rather than liability,[129] as it involves speculation as to events that might have happened in the future. The distinction between the thin skull and crumbling skull rules is thought to be whether the pre-existing condition was manifest at the time of the tort.[130] The application of both rules is more difficult in cases of psychiatric as opposed to physical injury.

The crumbling skull argument is likely to be raised in any case where the defendants are alleged to have caused or allowed abuse to occur when the claimant was in local authority care. Unfortunately, the courts can assume too readily that a child who has spent any time in care would have suffered some lasting psychiatric problems in adulthood notwithstanding the defendant's wrong, caused by whatever incident prompted the removal of the claimant from the family home. For example, in *C v. Flintshire CC*,[131] Scott Baker J remarked of the claimant: 'The writing was already on the wall when she went into care that there were likely to be ongoing problems. She was drinking, staying out late and leading what looked like becoming, and later did become, a promiscuous lifestyle.'[132] Surely the charges of 'drinking and staying out late' could be made of many adolescents without any suggestion that such behaviour was a harbinger of psychiatric illness.

## 7. Breach of fiduciary duty

Once breach of a fiduciary duty is proven to the court's satisfaction, there are some authorities which suggest that the usual common law rules of causation do not apply. If it can be demonstrated that 'but for' the breach, the damage would not have occurred, the damage is recoverable from the defendant notwithstanding that the immediate cause of the damage is the dishonesty or failure of a third party (a *novus actus*

---

[128] *Whitfield v. Calhoun* (1999) 242 AR 201.   [129] Jones, *Textbook on Torts* at 275.
[130] *Pryor v. Bains and Johal* (1986) 69 BCLR 395.
[131] [2001] EWCA Civ 302; [2001] 2 FLR 33.
[132] [2001] EWCA Civ 302; [2001] 2 FLR 33 at [49].

*interveniens*).[133] Furthermore, a defence of contributory negligence may also be unavailable in breach of fiduciary duty actions, at least where the breach involves conscious disloyalty.[134]

## Quantum

### 1. Apportionment and the workings of the 'material contribution' test: divisible or non-divisible injury?

The general rule in relation to apportionment of damages is that there is no apportionment for a single, indivisible injury once it is proved that the defendant's act materially contributed to the harm (but not where the defendant is proved only to have increased the risk of harm).[135] This has been termed the 'all or nothing' approach to damages.[136] An indivisible injury is one such as mesothelioma in *Fairchild*, which it is thought may be caused by a single fibre of asbestos, as compared with cumulative diseases like asbestosis, where the severity of the injury is increased by cumulative exposure to asbestos fibres. Thus, in cases of non-divisible injury the claimant is entitled to seek damages representing 100% of his loss, despite the fact that the defendant may not be the

---

[133] *Target Holdings Ltd v. Redfern* [1996] 1 AC 421, *per* Lord Browne-Wilkinson at 434, approved in *Maguire v. Makaronis* (1997) 188 CLR 449 (although see *Swindle v. Harrison* [1997] 4 All ER 705 suggesting that the less stringent approach only applies where the breach is the equivalent of fraud and *Equitable Life Assurance Society v. Bowley* [2003] EWHC 2263; [2003] BCC 289 where doubt was expressed on this point altogether). Australian authorities similarly suggest a less restrictive approach to causation (*Re Dawson (dec'd)* [1966] 2 NSWR 211; *Hill v. Rose* [1990] VR 129, and in Canada, if the abuse is shown to be related to the breach, it is for the defendant to prove that the damage would have occurred regardless of the breach (*Hodgkinson v. Simms* [1994] 3 SCR 377 at 446).

[134] *Nationwide Building Society v. Various Solicitors (No. 3)* [1999] PNLR 606. See also *Brickenden v. London Loan & Savings Co* [1934] 3 DLR 465; *Hill v. Rose* [1990] VR 129 at 142.

[135] *Fairchild* as applied in *Athey v. Leonati* [1996] 3 SCR 458. See also *Rahman v. Arearose Ltd* [2001] QB 351 to the effect that the 1978 Act only applies to indivisible injuries to divide responsibility between concurrent tortfeasors and not to cases where different tortfeasors or other events had caused different aspects of the damage. In the latter instance, the court apportions liability according to the extent to which the defendant's wrong contributed to the damage. With contribution under the Act, the court arrives at an apportionment of damages according to what is just and equitable according to the extent of the defendant's responsibility.

[136] A. Porat and A. Stein, 'Indeterminate Causation and Apportionment of Damages: An Essay on *Holtby, Allen, and Fairchild*' (2003) 23 *Oxford Journal of Legal Studies* 667.

sole cause of his injuries.[137] The defendant is, however, entitled to seek contribution from other parties who had a role to play in causing the claimant's damage under the Civil Liability (Contribution) Act 1978[138] or to seek reduction of damages on the grounds of contributory negligence by the claimant. But what if the other causes of the injury are natural causes? It seems that the law effectively defines justice as requiring that the defendant should bear the burden of the whole loss in such cases rather than the innocent claimant who has been injured by tortious and non-tortious causes through no fault of their own.[139]

Where the injury is divisible, that is, where the harm is apparently attributable to a number of cumulative events, the courts are willing to depart from the 'all or nothing' approach and apportion the loss, discounting the level of damages payable by the defendant according to the contribution made to the harm by sources outside the defendant's responsibility.[140] This apportionment exercise must be conducted even if the available evidence makes it impossible to be precise about the respective contributions to the damage.[141] In cases of uncertainty there are *dicta* to suggest that 'fullest allowances should be made in favour of the plaintiffs for the uncertainties known to be involved in any apportionment',[142] although other authorities suggest that fairness to both claimant and defendant ought to be weighed equally.[143] The use of judicial intuition to make a fair apportionment[144] is not without its critics, many of whom point to the arbitrariness of the resulting apportionment.[145] It should, however, be remembered that, in abuse cases, the

---

[137] *M(M) v. F(R)* [1999] 2 WWR 446.   [138] Jones, *Textbook on Torts* at 240.
[139] For criticism of this aspect of *Fairchild* see S. Green, 'Winner Takes All' (2004) 120 *Law Quarterly Review* 566.
[140] *Holtby v. Brigham & Cowan (Hull) Ltd* [2000] 3 All ER 421; *Athey v. Leonati* [1996] 3 SCR 458; *A(TWN) v. Clarke* [2004] 3 WWR 11.
[141] *Allen v. British Rail Engineering* [2001] EWCA Civ 242; [2001] ICR 942.
[142] *Thompson v. Smith Ship Repairers Ltd* [1984] 1 QB 405, *per* Mustill J at 433.
[143] *Holtby v. Brigham & Crane (Hull) Ltd* [2000] 3 All ER 421: '... the court must do the best it can to achieve justice not only to the claimant but to the defendant and amongst defendants', *per* Stuart Smith LJ.
[144] The Court of Appeal did not criticise Connell J in *KR* for not using percentages to arrive at apportionment, provided he had in mind a global figure before assessing the proportion of the defendant's responsibility: *KR v. Bryn Alyn Community (Holdings) Ltd (In Liquidation)* 2001 WL 753345 at [120].
[145] Porat and Stein, 'Indeterminate causation' at 689. See also *C v. Flintshire CC* [2001] EWCA Civ 302; [2001] 2 FLR 33 for a discussion of arbitrariness in this context where the experts were divided as to whether the abuse suffered whilst in care had contributed to the claimant's pain and suffering to the tune of 80% or 20%.

courts will make assessments of the relative causal influence of various traumas on the claimant's disorder with the assistance of expert evidence, and whilst that evidence involves a guesstimation on the part of informed practitioners limited by the bounds of current knowledge, the whole process of fixing a monetary value on physical and psychiatric harms can be argued to be arbitrary and flawed. Recognition of the speculative nature of judgments on the relative impact of traumatic events does not therefore warrant abandonment of any attempt to apportion the loss.

A useful example of judicial apportionment in an abuse case is *C v. C*,[146] where 60% of damages representing the full extent of the claimant's pain and suffering was awarded against the claimant's father as the perpetrator of abuse despite the fact that the claimant had been a victim of 12 other perpetrators. This apportionment was deemed appropriate because the abuse by her father had had a major impact on her due to her age at the time of the abuse (14 to 18 years), the betrayal of trust which his abuse had involved and the aggravating factor that, at the time of the abuse by her father, he knew that she had already been the victim of sexual abuse.[147]

The principle of apportioning damages according to the extent of the contribution where the injury is divisible is equally applicable to psychiatric damage.[148] An advantage of the PTSD diagnosis for the claimant to add to those detailed above is that the diagnostic criteria cast this illness as a non-divisible injury. The DSM IV criteria suggest that the disorder is caused by a single traumatic event, therefore, according to *Fairchild*, the defendant's liability to pay damages for the PTSD can only be reduced by claiming that other tortfeasors were partly responsible for the event which triggered the PTSD under the Civil Liability (Contribution) Act 1978. Depression is, however, a divisible injury therefore damages are discountable according to the contribution made to the damage by other sources. Similarly, in the Canadian case of *D(P) v. Allen*, the court regarded alcoholism as a divisible injury, therefore damages would likely be discountable without proof of the liability of other tortfeasors.[149]

---

[146] (1994) 114 DLR (4th) 151.
[147] Without this aggravating factor the court would have awarded 50% damages against the father.
[148] See guidelines in *Hatton v. Sutherland* [2003] EWCA Civ 76; [2002] 2 All ER 1, as approved in *Barber v. Somerset CC* [2004] UKHL 13; [2004] 1 WLR 1089 and also *A(TWN) v. Clarke* [2004] 3 WWR 11; *Rahman v. Arearose Ltd* [2001] QB 351.
[149] (2004) 132 ACWS (3d) 1098.

Usually, a claimant presents with a cluster of psychiatric illnesses; therefore, deductions can be made from the defendant's liability on the grounds that, even if the defendant is wholly responsible for the PTSD, others bear responsibility for the claimant's further neuroses. Moreover, as psychiatric illnesses often overlap, even sole responsibility for PTSD may result in a small damages award, as the PTSD may not have added significantly to the total disability suffered. In the *Bryn Alyn* litigation at first instance, where issues of causation and quantum were dealt with, Connell J accepted that all the claimants had suffered a traumatic series of damaging experiences before being placed in the care of the defendants and therefore would have had difficulties in coping with day to day existence in any event. Therefore, in KM's case, despite the court being convinced that PTSD was suffered as a result of the abuse, damages of only £5,000 were awarded on the grounds that the disorder would have had only a modest impact on the claimant given that he already suffered antisocial personality disorders and other problems anyway.

### 2. *Supervening traumatic events or incidents*

Quantum may be affected by the occurrence of a supervening traumatic event, that is, an event which occurs after the defendant's wrong, inflicting damage on the claimant which is so devastating that it effectively wipes out the injury caused by the abuse. An example of a supervening traumatic event from outside the abuse context is to be found in *Baker v. Willoughby*.[150] In *Baker*, the defendant's tort caused an injury to the claimant's leg. Some years later, the same leg was shot during an armed robbery (the supervening traumatic event). This later injury to the same leg necessitated amputation thus obliterating the future effects of the first injury. Usually, a supervening traumatic event will bring an end to the defendant's liability so that damages representing the continuing impact of the defendant's wrong cease to be available beyond the point of the supervening trauma.[151] Thus, if the abuse victim suffers later psychiatric harm caused by bereavement or some other form of tragedy for which no-one is legally responsible and this trauma overwhelms their abuse-related injuries, the liability of the defendant responsible for the abuse ceases. This rule also applies if, exceptionally, it can be proved that a future supervening traumatic incident is likely (e.g. where the claimant is employed in a particularly perilous or stressful

---

[150] [1970] AC 167.   [151] *Jobling v. Associated Dairies* [1982] AC 794.

vocation).[152] However, where the supervening trauma is attributable to the tort of a third party (i.e. the claimant has been doubly wronged, e.g. by later abuse or neglect), *Baker* suggests that this will not impact on the damages payable by the original tortfeasor.[153] Whilst the defendant will not be liable for the additional damage inflicted by the later wrongdoer, the second wrongdoer, if held liable in damages, takes his victim as he finds him, and therefore extinguishing the first tortfeasor's liability would leave the doubly wronged victim under-compensated. The justifiability of the distinction the law appears to draw between the 'doubly wronged claimant' whom the law attempts to compensate fully and the claimant who is 'doubly unfortunate' (by being the victim of a tortious wrong and bad luck) who is deliberately left under-compensated is not immediately apparent.

### 3. General and special damages

For the purposes of ordinary personal injury claims, the law distinguishes between general damages (those items of loss which cannot be precisely calculated such as pain and suffering, loss of amenity and predicted loss of earnings for the future) and special damages (those items for which a precise figure can be calculated such as medical expenses and past loss of earnings).[154] The same is theoretically true in claims for abuse, although it is more difficult to demonstrate the link between abuse and medical expenses or loss of earnings for the purposes of proving an entitlement to special damages. For the future it might be suggested that a pragmatic approach is taken to the division between general and special damages, as is the case in defamation claims. This would be one way of dealing with the intractable problems of proving a causal link between abuse and the psychological and economic sequelae for the claimant. In defamation cases where the jury often fixes the amount of damages to be awarded, due to the difficulty of proving a link between loss of earnings and the defamatory statement, the jury takes into account lost earnings as part of general damages but adopts a moderate approach to the amount awarded. In other words, 'the strict requirements of proving causation are relaxed in return for moderation in the overall figure awarded'.[155] Such pragmatism could easily be applied in compensation claims arising out of child abuse.

---

[152] *Heil v. Rankin* [2000] 2 WLR 1173.   [153] *Baker v. Willoughby* [1970] AC 167.
[154] Jones, *Textbook on Torts* at 660.
[155] *Gleaner Co. Ltd v. Abrahams* [2003] UKPC 55; [2004] 1 AC 628, *per* Lord Hoffmann at [56].

With regard to the calculation of general damages, it seems arguable that a less restrained approach might be adopted towards levels of compensation in actions against perpetrator defendants for intentional wrongs than in cases against non-perpetrator defendants. This suggestion arises from oblique judicial references to a distinction between cases where the defendant is likely to meet the award and those where the compensation is likely to be provided by insurance cover. With regard to the latter, Lord Hoffmann, in the course of a Privy Council judgment, counselled that considerations of equity between victims who are successful in tort and those who are left with financial support provided without litigation ought to be taken into account:

> Compensation, both for financial loss and general damages, goes only to those who can prove negligence and causation. Those unable to do so are left to social security: no general damages and meagre compensation for loss of earnings. The unfairness might be more readily understandable if the successful tort plaintiffs recovered their damages from the defendants themselves but makes less sense when both social security and negligence damages come out of public funds. So any increase in general damages for personal injury awarded by the courts only widens the gap between those victims who can sue and those who cannot.[156]

Support for a similar approach being applied to abuse litigation can be found in Canadian case law. In *Y(S) v. C(FG)*,[157] the court refused to apply the cap usually applied to personal injury damages to damages for sexual abuse in a case against the perpetrator. This was because the latter involved intentional torts and criminal behaviour and, further, there was no evidence that this type of case against the perpetrator of the abuse had any impact on the public purse. A cap on damages was therefore not necessary to protect the general public from enormous insurance premiums.

### 4. *Aggravating and exemplary damages*

Aggravating features of the abuse may inflate the award made to the claimant on the grounds that these features have compounded the impact

---

[156] *Gleaner Co Ltd v. Abrahams* [2003] UKPC 55; [2004] 1 AC 628, *per* Lord Hoffmann at [51]. See also Lord Woolf MR on the topic of general damages in personal injury cases: 'Awards must be proportionate and take into account the consequences of increases in the awards of damages on defendants as a group and society as a whole' (in *Heil v. Rankin* [2001] QB 272 at 297).

[157] [1997] 1 WWR 229.

of the abuse on the claimant's psychological and/or economic prospects. Such aggravating factors might include the defendant's knowledge of the claimant's pre-existing vulnerability (for example, those running a care facility who exposed the claimant to the risk of abuse despite knowledge that the claimant had already been the victim of damaging abuse) or where the perpetrator of the abuse is someone in whom the claimant trusted as a child.[158] Whilst aggravating features of the abuse may be taken into account in assessing compensation, they should not be confused with punitive or deterrent components of damages awards. A finding that the claimant was the victim of an intentional as opposed to an inadvertent wrong can affect the calculation of damages to be awarded. In addition to the usual compensatory award, exemplary damages may be available, although it seems that this will only be in limited categories of case as set out by Lord Diplock in *Rookes v. Barnard*.[159] This case confines exemplary damages to cases of: (a) oppressive, arbitrary or unconscionable action by government servants; and (b) cases where the defendant has calculated that their wrongful act will probably make a profit which could exceed any compensation payable.

In other jurisdictions, 'punitive' damages are more freely awarded,[160] a fact which has directed criticism towards the prescriptive nature of the *Rookes*' categories. It has been suggested that exemplary damages ought to be available wherever the defendant's conduct is so outrageous that damages exceeding those necessary to compensate the claimant are required to show that the law will not tolerate such behaviour,[161] as is broadly the case in New Zealand.[162] In the New Zealand courts, intentional wrongdoing or conscious recklessness is not 'an essential prerequisite to an award of exemplary damages and so, in exceptional and rare cases, inadvertently negligent conduct which was so outrageous as to call for condemnation and punishment' could trigger an exemplary

---

[158] Both these factors feature in the case of *C v. Flintshire CC* [2001] EWCA Civ 302: 'the worse the horror story was at home ... the more critical it was that she was not treated the way she was when in care' at [39], *per* Scott Baker J.
[159] [1964] AC 1129.
[160] The proposal in Law Commission Rep No 247, *Aggravated, Exemplary and Restitutionary Damages* (1997) is to rename them punitive damages in line with most commonwealth jurisdictions.
[161] *Kuddus v. Chief Constable of Leicester Constabulary* [2001] UKHL 29; [2001] 3 All ER 193, *per* Lord Hutton.
[162] *A v. Bottrill* [2002] UKPC 44; [2003] 1 AC 449. For detail on the assessment of such damages, the reader is referred to H. McGregor, *McGregor on Damages* (Sweet & Maxwell, 2003), *Munkman on Damages* (2004) at Chapter 11 and Tettenborn, *The Law of Damages* at 32–50.

award.[163] Inevitably, therefore, exemplary damages will often be available against the perpetrator of abuse, but also possibly against the negligent non-perpetrator defendant. In Canada, punitive damages are awarded on the basis of the guidance set out in *Vorvis v. Insurance Corpn of British Colombia*:[164] they should be awarded where the conduct is deserving of punishment because of its 'harsh, vindictive, reprehensible and malicious nature'. Whilst this is not meant to be an exhaustive list of descriptors of cases where punitive damages may be appropriate, the conduct must be extreme in nature and deserving of full condemnation and punishment.[165] Unintentional wrongs which involve inadvertence rather than an intention to harm or malice are unlikely to fulfil either the *Rookes'* criteria or the broader approach adopted in other jurisdictions.[166]

There is authority to suggest that exemplary damages will not normally be imposed where the defendant has already been fined for the conduct in question, otherwise the defendant is being punished twice over.[167] It has been recommended that this approach should be extended to any case where the defendant has been convicted of criminal offences for the conduct complained of and a sentence has been imposed.[168]

## Conclusion

Issues of damage, causation and remoteness have been left largely unexposed by litigation thus far in the arena of abuse claims, thus necessitating a speculative approach to a number of questions addressed in this chapter. What is clear is that the principles of causation and remoteness and the ease of discharging the burden of proof are likely to differ depending on whether the claim is brought against the perpetrator defendant or a non-perpetrator defendant. The case of *Fairchild* has paved the way for modifying the traditional principles of causation

---

[163] *A v. Bottrill* [2002] UKPC 44; [2003] 1 AC 449, *per* Lord Nicholls at [50].
[164] (1989) 58 DLR (4th) 193.
[165] See e.g. *T(L) v. T(RW)* (1997) 36 BCLR (3d) 165, where punitive damages were awarded against the defendant father because he had deeply wronged the claimant and also society.
[166] *British Midland Tool Ltd v. Midland International Tooling Ltd and others* [2003] EWHC 466 (Ch).
[167] *Archer v. Brown* [1984] 2 All ER 267.
[168] *Aggravated, Exemplary and Restitutionary Damages* (1997).

where justice to the claimant demands it. It is vital that the courts recognise the particular difficulties that the abuse claimant faces in terms of proving that psychological scars were inflicted by abuse as opposed to either other external events in the claimant's life or internal predispositions to develop psychiatric problems. Moreover, they should be made aware that abuse can take an individual down a particular path which is strewn with other traumagenic factors (e.g. an unhealthy lifestyle or the possibility that the claimant will choose a spouse who is abusive), thereby exacerbating or compounding the damage in a way which is not susceptible to proof in a court of law. Given that these factors are typical characterisations of abuse claims, an overtly sympathetic approach to causation is merited.

# 5

# Limitation Periods

> ... delay will make it more difficult for the legal procedures themselves to vouchsafe a just conclusion – evidence may have disappeared and recollections become increasingly unreliable. Speedy rough justice will, therefore, generally be better justice than justice worn smooth and fragile with the passage of years.[1]

## The limitation framework

At the time of writing, the law of limitation as it affects abuse claims is poised for reform. If reform occurs, it will most likely take the form of a House of Lords ruling in an appeal from the *A v Hoare* judgment[2] or Parliament's overdue enactment of a Bill implementing the Law Commission's recommendations of 2001.[3] If reform has been effected by the time of publication, much of the discussion surrounding *Stubbings v. Webb* which follows will be of largely historical interest, but much of what is examined under the heading 'non-battery claims' will become equally relevant to actions in battery against the perpetrators of abuse.

Whatever the current state of the law, the popularity and potency of the limitation 'defence' to child abuse litigation has profound implications for claims in this area. It is undoubtedly the effectiveness of our limitation regime in pre-empting most civil litigation concerning abuse from ever reaching a full hearing that is responsible for the stunted development of the law covered in this book. The limitation issue disposes of a substantial number of civil claims for sexual abuse in favour of the defendant, with the result that issues central to the feasibility of abuse claims (such as, which is the most appropriate cause of

---

[1] *Central Asbestos Co. v. Dodd* [1973] AC 518 (HL), *per* Lord Simon of Glaisdale at 547.
[2] [2006] EWCA Civ 395.
[3] *Limitation of Actions* Report No 270 (Law Commission, 2001).

action, the scope of any duty of care, culpability, causation and quantum) may be dealt with only in summary or not at all. The impact of the limitation 'defence' on child abuse claims is also felt at the ideological level of judicial decisions. Arguments of limitation redirect the judicial spotlight from the defendant's wrong to the claimant's failure to act promptly and the unreasonableness of their delay.[4]

Rules applying limitation periods to civil actions will, by their very nature, produce arbitrary results in many cases. One decision which highlights the ruthless effects of this arbitrariness is the Scottish case of *K v. Gilmartin's Executrix*.[5] The psychological illness allegedly inflicted on the pursuer by his teacher's abuse had not been triggered until 1995, many years after the abuse had occurred. Ironically, it was the pursuer's assistance in a police investigation, resulting in the conviction and imprisonment of the perpetrator, which had triggered the onset of his illness. Applying the statutes of limitation, the court found that K's civil action had been extinguished in 1982. This result prompts the comment that if a criminal conviction can be obtained despite the passage of so many years, why cannot the civil claim of the pursuer be similarly tolerated, particularly given that it was the criminal process itself which had caused K's trauma to resurface.

The twin rationales underlying limitation statutes concern the protection of potential defendants from the uncertainty associated with an otherwise perpetual threat of litigation and the difficulty of ensuring a fair trial based on stale evidence (the longer the period of time that has elapsed between the wrong and the resulting litigation, the less likely it will be that witness evidence will be reliable or that documentary evidence will have survived). Thus, statutory bars protect the defendant from frivolous litigation which cannot be proven due to the passage of time. This also protects the justice system from the wasted resources taken up by stale claims which have little prospect of success. In cases of child abuse where the defendant's guilt has already been established, it has been argued that many of the underlying policy rationales for time limits fall away given the intentional nature of the defendant's conduct, accompanied by society's condemnation of child abuse; in other words, a defendant abuser is not deserving of the shield of limitation periods.[6] However, for the most part, limitation defences will be

---

[4] Zoltek-Jick, 'For Whom Does the Bell Toll?' at 452.   [5] 2004 SLT 1014.
[6] See *M(K) v. M(H)* [1992] 3 SCR 6, discussed later in this chapter.

raised at the outset of civil proceedings, in which case, the defendant must be accorded the presumption of innocence.

## 1. Limitation of actions and procedure

A Limitation Act defence bars the claimant's remedy, not their right (and does not even have this effect unless and until pleaded).[7] This means that the court will not consider issues of limitation unless they are specifically raised by the defendant. However, once the defendant has raised the Limitation Act, the legal burden of proving that the litigation has been brought within the applicable limitation period, or that the court's discretion ought to be exercised to extend time, falls on the claimant.[8]

Where limitation is addressed at a full hearing and after determination of liability, particularly against the perpetrator of the abuse, prejudice to the defendant is unlikely to feature greatly in the court's deliberations.[9] It is more common for limitation issues to be dealt with at the outset of civil proceedings. The defendant may, for example, plead the limitation defence and seek trial of limitation as a preliminary issue. Indeed, the Court of Appeal has recently suggested that in the context of abuse cases, judges should attempt to deal with limitation at a preliminary hearing wherever possible[10] (although a preliminary hearing has been rejected in such cases where it was felt that it would require the claimant to experience the discomfort of litigation on such sensitive matters twice over[11]). One further consequence of the rule that limitation periods do not extinguish the claimant's rights is that where the defendant may have a limitation defence, that will not generally permit the action to be struck out on the grounds that the claim discloses no reasonable cause of action unless it is clear that there are no possible arguments for permitting the claimant to proceed.[12] It may, however, be

---

[7] *Royal Nowegian Government v. Constant & Constant and Marine Engineering Co. Ltd* [1960] 2 Lloyd's Rep 431; *Ronex Properties Ltd v. John Laing Construction Ltd* [1983] QB 398, *per* Donaldson LJ at 405.

[8] *Cartledge v. E Jopling & Sons Ltd* [1963] AC 758; *Driscoll Varley v. Parkside Health Authority* (1995) Med LR 345.

[9] *M(K) v. M(H)* [1992] 3 SCR 6; *W v. Attorney General* [1999] 2 NZLR 709.

[10] *KR and others v. Bryn Alyn Community (Holdings) Ltd (In Liquidation), Royal & Sun Alliance plc* [2003] EWCA Civ 85; [2003] 1 FCR 385 at [74].

[11] *Ablett v. Devon CC* (2000) (Court of Appeal, unreported); *W v. Attorney General* [1999] 2 NZLR 709.

[12] *Ronex Properties Ltd v. John Laing Construction Ltd* [1983] QB 398.

possible to have the claimant's action struck out as an abuse of process.[13] In either event, the recent shift away from striking out in areas of law which are uncertain and developing should be borne in mind.[14]

In cases where limitation is dealt with as a preliminary issue, the courts must not be seen to allow a preliminary, and therefore relatively uninformed, assessment of the merits of the case to influence the finding on limitation. The trial judge in *Bryn Alyn*[15] had extended time on the grounds that the recently published Waterhouse Inquiry provided detailed evidence on which the court could rely, and therefore staleness of evidence was not a significant problem. The Court of Appeal regarded this as 'putting the cart before the horse'. The persuasiveness of the evidence supporting the claimant's allegations should not decide the issue of limitation – time bars and the merits of the case were entirely separate matters.[16] Further, the Waterhouse Inquiry had not been conducted with civil proceedings in mind and much of its conclusions were generalised and speculative. Its existence could not therefore be said to resolve issues of stale evidence.

## 2. Limitation Act 1980: a two-tier system

For the purposes of actions in tort there exists a two-tier limitation regime. First, subject to what is said below, s. 2 of the Limitation Act 1980 provides that an absolute limitation period of six years from the date on which the cause of action accrued is to be applied to tort actions. If the wrong complained of is actionable without proof of damage (e.g. an assault, battery or libel) the action will accrue on the date of the defendant's wrong. Although the mental harm caused by a battery may be continuing, that does not render the battery a continuing tort; therefore, the cause of action will still have accrued on the date of the wrong.[17] Alternatively, where proof of damage is a necessary prerequisite to the claimant's cause of action (e.g. negligence or slander) it is the date of damage which starts

---

[13] Under the Civil Procedure Rules 1998, 3.4, although this again is unlikely: T. Prime and G. Scanlan, *The Law of Limitation* (OUP, 2001) at 345, based on the unreported case of *Newall v. Therm-A-Stor Ltd* (17 January 1990) (CA).

[14] *Per* Lord Browne-Wilkinson in *Barrett v. Enfield LBC* [2001] 2 AC 550 at 557, saying that it was preferable that legal developments should occur on the basis of facts proved at trial rather than assumed hypothetical facts (approving his earlier judgment in *X (Minors) v. Bedfordshire CC* [1995] 2 AC 633 at 740–741).

[15] *KR and others v. Bryn Alyn Community (Holdings) Ltd (In Liquidation), Royal & Sun Alliance plc* [2003] EWCA Civ 85; [2003] 1 FCR 385.

[16] [2003] EWCA Civ 85; [2003] 1 FCR 385 at [61].  [17] *T v. H* [1995] 3 NZLR 37.

time to run.[18] There is, however, provision for delay in time starting to run by reason of minority or disability on the part of the claimant or deliberate concealment on the part of the defendant (see below).

An exception to the six-year limitation period is created by s. 11 of the Limitation Act. In cases of 'personal injury'[19] arising out of negligence, nuisance or breach of duty a three-year extendable limitation period applies. Whilst at first sight the general six-year limitation period is more generous to the claimant, it is the three-year limitation period applicable to personal injury claims which is the more liberal, due to the means by which it may be extended. In addition to the possibility of extending time on the grounds of disability or deliberate concealment, this shorter limitation period may be extended in two further ways:

- limitation periods can be suspended until such time as the claimant knew or ought to have known of their injury and its cause (delayed discovery)[20]; or
- the court can be invited to exercise its discretion to allow the case to proceed, notwithstanding the delay.[21]

The rationale usually given for the more generous grounds of extension being available where a personal injury has been caused by negligence, nuisance or breach of duty is that where the defendant has committed a deliberate wrong, the claimant is assumed to immediately know that they have been injured. Where, however, the injury is inflicted by negligence, the fact of injury and its attributability to the defendant's conduct may not be immediately apparent, therefore more flexibility in the rules of limitation is appropriate. In this respect, the limitation rules are at odds with the reality of many abuse victims' experiences. In the context of child abuse, realisation of the fact of psychological injury and its attributability to the abuse may take many years to emerge, whether or not that abuse is ultimately actioned as negligence or a deliberate wrong.

### Application of the Limitation Act to civil actions against perpetrators of abuse: *Stubbings v. Webb*

The application of the above provisions to allegations of sexual abuse was assessed by the House of Lords in *Stubbings v. Webb*.[22] Ms Stubbings'

---

[18] *Pirelli General Cable Works Ltd v. Oscar Faber & Partners* [1983] 2 AC 1.
[19] Defined as some disease or impairment of the claimant's physical or mental state (s. 38(1) of the Limitation Act 1980).
[20] Ss. 11 and 14.   [21] S. 33.   [22] [1993] AC 498.

claim was based on abuse perpetrated by her father and stepbrother during childhood, but civil litigation was not initiated until she was in her thirties. Actions against the perpetrators of sexual abuse were held to be subject to the absolute six-year period under s. 2 of the Limitation Act[23] (although, of course, time does not start to run until the child victim reaches 18).[24] The three-year limitation period with the benefit of extension on the grounds of delayed discovery or at the courts' discretion was not available to claimants suing the perpetrator(s) of child abuse. Thus, the *Stubbings* claim fell on the wrong side of the limitation period as it was outside the six years from the claimant reaching the age of maturity.

Lord Griffiths, delivering the only reasoned judgment (which, given this fact, was surprisingly short), relied on the recommendations of the Tucker Committee, which were implemented by the predecessor of s. 2.[25] The Tucker Committee had clearly stated that it did not regard actions for 'breach of duty' as encompassing actions for battery.[26] Therefore, any claim for sexual abuse brought in battery must be brought within the non-extendable six-year limitation period.[27]

### 1. Finding fault with Stubbings v. Webb

Although there are a number of cases in which the courts have rejected suggestions in which the ruling in *Stubbings* could be elided, these cases have expressed dissatisfaction with the law on limitation as it now stands.[28] Whilst Lord Griffiths' finding that a 'breach of duty' for the purposes of the Limitation Act did not include deliberate acts of battery

---

[23] Compare the High Court and Court of Appeal, which both accepted that they were bound by the majority decision in *Letang v. Cooper* [1965] 1 QB 232, which established that 'breach of duty' encompassed both intentional and unintentional inflicted personal injuries.

[24] S. 38(3).  [25] *Report of the Committee on the Limitation of Actions* 1949 (Cmd 7740).

[26] See 'Post *Stubbings* Developments' in Chapter 2 for judicial responses to the argument that sexual battery could be actioned as a breach of duty under the more flexible limitation provisions.

[27] Followed in *KR and others v. Bryn Alyn Community (Holdings) Ltd (In Liquidation), Royal & Sun Alliance* [2003] EWCA Civ 85; [2003] 1 FCR 385; *C v. Middlesbrough Council* [2004] EWCA Civ 1747; [2004] All ER (D) 339 (Dec) and *A v. Hoare* [2006] EWCA Civ 395; 2006 WL 901084.

[28] *Seymour v. Williams* [1995] PIQR 470 describing the law as 'illogical and surprising' (see below) and Auld LJ in *KR and others v. Bryn Alyn Community (Holdings) Ltd (In Liquidation), Royal & Sun Alliance plc* [2003] EWCA Civ 85; [2003] 1 FCR 385 at [100] described the divide between trespass and negligence claims for limitation purposes as 'turning on a distinction of no apparent principle or other merit.'

derives unambiguous support from the Tucker Committee's conclusions, there are a number of arguments that can be raised to suggest that the decision in *Stubbings* is flawed on many counts. Such flaws are all the more pertinent given that at the time of writing, the issues raised in *Stubbings* are due to be reviewed by the House of Lords.[29]

- First, the *Stubbings* ruling does not take account of the fact that, in 1949, when the Tucker Committee's report was written, the issue of sexual abuse was rarely broached in public and would have been far from the minds of the authors of that report.
- Furthermore, it might be argued that *Stubbings* ignores earlier English authority which clearly recognises the potential for a trespass action and an action on the case arising out of the same facts.[30] There are also provisions in the Limitation Act itself concerning fraudulent concealment which refer to a 'deliberate commission of a breach of duty' – terms which might be used to suggest that the draftsmen of the Act did not regard deliberate wrongs and breach of duty as mutually exclusive concepts.[31]
- In cases of intentional harm or battery which cause the death of the victim, the dependants' claim under the Fatal Accidents Act 1976 would have the benefit of a three-year limitation period extendable on the grounds of delayed discovery or at the court's discretion. This is hard to reconcile with the insistence in *Stubbings* on the six-year time limit where the battery is non-fatal.[32]
- Finally, there is also evidence in Lord Griffiths' judgment that in addition to statutory interpretation aided by the Tucker Committee's report, his Lordship was influenced by a strongly held view that claims such as that of Ms Stubbings were unprovable. At the outset of his speech, he noted that the allegations were denied by the defendants and that it would be a matter of great difficulty to determine where the truth lay with respect to events of 20 to 30 years ago. Such considerations should not figure in the application of limitation periods, otherwise the court may stand accused of confusing the application of limitation rules with the court's view of the merits of the case.[33] The issue of

---

[29] In the appeal from the Court of Appeal's decision in *A v. Hoare* [2006] EWCA Civ 395.
[30] The earlier English authority being *Leame v. Bray* (1803) 3 East 593 (102 ER 724).
[31] See s. 32(2) of the Limitation Act 1980.
[32] D. Di Mambro, *Butterworths Law of Limitation* (Butterworths, 2000) at C[132].
[33] A practice disapproved in *KR and others v. Bryn Alyn Community (Holdings) Ltd (In Liquidation), Royal & Sun Alliance plc* [2003] EWCA Civ 85; [2003] 1 FCR 385 (see below).

limitation should surely not be determined by whether the claimant should succeed in this case, but whether they should have the opportunity for their case to be heard?

Dissatisfaction with the ruling in *Stubbings* has led to indications of judicial willingness to forge exceptions to it, although none which has been of any great assistance to claimants thus far. In *KR v. Bryn Alyn Community Holdings*, the Court of Appeal stated that: 'The House of Lords did not decide in *Stubbings v. Webb* that deliberate assault was not capable of amounting to negligence, nuisance or breach of duty causing personal injury.'[34] In other words, there was nothing to prevent abuse being actioned as something other than a battery. Provided that the circumstances in which the abuse occurred could be described as a 'breach of duty,' the flexible s. 11 limitation period could be applied to an action against the perpetrator.[35] It is hard to imagine exactly what alternative cause of action the Court of Appeal could have had in mind. An action for breach of fiduciary duty would certainly fit the bill, but it seems unlikely to be successful in this jurisdiction,[36] an action for intentional interference with the person is no more likely to be regarded as founded on a breach of duty than a battery action would be and the Court of Appeal in the *Bryn Alyn* case rejected vicarious liability as a mechanism which could be used to circumvent *Stubbings* (see below).

The result of the above is that, until *Stubbings* is elided by case law or overturned by Parliament, a civil action against the perpetrator of abuse must generally be brought within six years of the abuse, whereas an action against a non-perpetrator (e.g. in the tort of negligence) will be subject to the more flexible three-year limitation period under s. 11. The *Stubbings* judgment, therefore, creates the absurdity that where there is a choice of suing the abuser or the potentially negligent employer of the abuser, there is an incentive to pursue the latter, even where the abuser has significant resources. Such a position is intolerable and precludes any meaningful relationship between culpability and liability.[37]

---

[34] At [99] and citing as support Lord Justice Salmon in *Morris v. CW Martin* [1966] 1 QB 716, where the overlap of an action in negligence and in conversion was considered a possibility.
[35] As happens in other jurisdictions. See e.g. in Australia, *Williams v. Milotin* (1957) 97 CLR 465, in Canada *B(M) v. British Colombia* [2001] 5 WWR 6 and, in New Zealand where the issue has been left open, *S v. Attorney General* [2003] NZLR 450.
[36] See Chapter 2 on this.
[37] The ruling in *Stubbings* was unsuccessfully challenged in Strasbourg (see Chapter 2 on *Stubbings v. UK* (1996) 23 EHRR 213).

## 2. Extending time for battery claims

Notwithstanding the ruling in *Stubbings* that the more rigid time limit applies to action against the perpetrators of sexual abuse, there remain two means by which the limitation period can be extended in such cases: (1) where the claimant is under a disability or is a minor at the time the cause of action accrues; or (2) where the defendant has fraudulently concealed information which would prevent the claimant from discovering their right of action. Apart from the general stalling of limitation periods until six years after the claimant's eighteenth birthday, these provisions will rarely be of much assistance to the abuse victim.

### Extension on the grounds of disability: s. 28

In English law, if the claimant is suffering from a disability at the time the cause of action accrued, their claim may be brought within six years from the end of their disability or their death. This mechanism applies to all civil cases, whether the injury is caused by a breach of duty or otherwise. A person is under a 'disability' if he is a minor or is a person who, by reason of mental disorder, is incapable of managing and administering his property and affairs, and time will not run until the end of the minority/disability or the death of such a claimant.[38] Lesser disabilities or ill health which merely limit the claimant's capacity to initiate legal proceedings on the matter concerned will not qualify under the current definition, although where the action is brought in negligence, the court may in theory exercise its discretion to extend time on the grounds of the claimant's ill health (although see the *Bryn Alyn* judgment below).

Where the claimant's general incapacity to manage his own affairs is proved, for example, where the abused has a long-term or permanent mental disorder, it may be that any cause of action founded on that abuse will survive for fifty years or more.[39] Note, however, that the disability provisions are not engaged when the onset of the claimant's disability occurs *after* the accrual of the cause of action.[40] The disability provisions are therefore of limited assistance to claimants whose disability

---

[38] S. 38(3).
[39] M. A. Jones, 'Limitation Periods and Plaintiffs under a Disability – a Zealous Protection?' (1995) 14 *Civil Justice Quarterly* 258.
[40] *Purnell v. Roche* [1927] 2 Ch 142. See similarly *Smith v. Advanced Electrics P/L* [2002] QSC 211 – PTSD suffered a few weeks after physical injuries inflicted by electric shock at

is intermittent, as a remission of the disability will cause time to run but a recurrence will not trigger a further suspension.[41] Where the claim is for personal injuries arising out of a breach of duty, the Limitation Act 1980 provides that the court can take this into account when exercising its discretion to extend time.[42] This definition of disability in requiring a general incapacity on the part of the claimant to manage their own affairs, together with the unhelpful approach to intermittent disorders, implements a high threshold of disability which most abuse claimants are unlikely to fulfil.

In other jurisdictions a concept of disability which extends beyond minority and incapacity to manage affairs is embraced, so that, for example, until the victim of abuse is equipped with full knowledge of the psychiatric harm and its causal nexus with the abuse, they might be classed as under a 'disability'. In New Zealand, disability is distinguished from being unable to face up to the process of suing and requires unsoundness of mind inhibiting the capacity to sue and that the alleged unsoundness results from a recognised mental illness or disability.[43] Thus, fear of the defendant making the claimant feel unable to sue is not to be regarded as a qualifying disability. The argument that repressed memories of the abuse qualify as a disability suspending time bars has been successful in some states of America.[44]

### Extension on the grounds of fraudulent concealment/estoppel: s. 32

Where the claimant's right of action is deliberately concealed by the defendant, the limitation period will not begin to run until the claimant has discovered the fraud or should reasonably have discovered it.[45] In *Cave v. Robinson Jarvis and Rolf*,[46] the fraudulent concealment provisions were regarded as applying where it would be 'unconscionable' for the defendant to rely on limitation arguments to defeat a claim. Therefore, in the case of a negligent defendant (e.g. a non-perpetrator

---

work. Although the PTSD caused aversion from anything to do with the accident, it did not count as a 'disability' affecting limitation periods as it was not present at the time the cause of action accrued.

[41] *Kirby v. Leather* [1965] QB 367.   [42] S. 33(3)(d).
[43] *T v. H* [1995] 3 NZLR 37. *W v. Attorney General* [1999] 2 NZLR 709 at [87]–[92] requiring only that the claimant is incapable of instructing a solicitor or commencing proceedings for a clearly established psychological reason. See also in Canada, Neeb and Harper, *Civil Action for Sexual Abuse* at 124.
[44] *Jones v. Jones* 242 NJ Super 195 (1990); *Leonard v. England* 115 NC App 103 (1994).
[45] S. 32(1)(b) of the Limitation Act 1980.   [46] [2002] UKHL 18; [2003] 1 AC 384.

employer of the abuser) who took active steps to conceal their breach of duty the limitation period would not run. Alternatively, where the defendant had committed a deliberate wrong (e.g. the perpetrator of abuse), time would not run where the defendant concealed their wrong or failed to disclose it in circumstances where it was likely to remain undiscovered for some time.[47] Unlike the provisions set out in relation to disability, fraudulent concealment does not have to be contemporaneous with the wrong for the limitation period to be extended. In effect, a subsequent act of fraudulent concealment will suspend time.[48]

Canadian courts have once again been characteristically flexible in their application of the notion of fraudulent concealment to extend limitation periods.[49] In *M(K) v. M(H)*, La Forest J stated that in actions at common law for battery or equitable actions for breach of fiduciary duty, the acts of the abuser in concealing the wrongfulness of the abuse from the victim could be regarded as fraudulent concealment which would operate to delay limitation periods. Such concealment could take the form of the abusers' enforcement of secrecy, using threats of force or blackmail (e.g. persuading the victim that disclosure would cause breakdown of the family unit/parent's marriage) or, as in *M(K) v. M(H)* itself, bribery by rewarding the child victim with money and sweets. La Forest J categorised abuse as a 'double wrong', by virtue of the fact that the abuse itself coincided with the defendant's 'abuse of the child's innocence to prevent recognition or revelation of the abuse'.[50]

Broadly the same concept appears in the guise of equitable estoppel in the US cases.[51] The courts take the view that if the reasons for the claimant's delay beyond usual limitation periods are attributable to the defendant's despicable and intentional act (as opposed to negligence), they should not afford a defence strategy to the defendant. The notion of equitable estoppel has suffered some setbacks in this field, such as the ruling in *Smith v. Smith*,[52] that the wrong which prevented the claimant from litigating must be an independent wrong from the act of abuse which forms the basis of the claim. This ruling can, however, be circumvented by pleading separate compounding incidents of abuse.[53]

---

[47] [2002] UKHL 18; [2003] 1 AC 384 at [25].
[48] *Sheldon v. RM Outhwaite (Underwriting Agencies) Ltd* [1995] 2 All ER 562.
[49] At para. 56.   [50] At para. 65.
[51] See A. Rosenfeld, 'The Statute of Limitations Barrier in Childhood Sexual Abuse Cases' (1989) 12 *Harvard Women's Law Journal* 206.
[52] 830 F 2d 11, 12 (2d Cir 1987).   [53] Nabors, 'The Statute of Limitations' at 165.

## 3. Application of Stubbings *elsewhere in the UK*

Although the House of Lords is the final appellate court for Scotland, Neeb and Harper have argued that the ruling in *Stubbings* would not apply in Scotland, as the limitation provisions are so different as to render *Stubbings* distinguishable.[54] The Prescription and Limitation (Scotland) Act 1973 applies a reasonable discoverability qualification to *all* claims for personal injuries, without regard to whether such injury was caused by breach of duty or was intentionally or unintentionally caused.[55] The test of discovery remains objective, but takes into account the circumstances particular to the specific pursuer and suspends the limitation period until knowledge of facts such as the injury, its causal nexus with the wrong and the identity of the defendant can reasonably be discovered. Further, s. 19A of the Scottish Act provides the court with a discretionary power to override limitation periods. The provisions for Northern Ireland under the Limitation (Northern Ireland) Order 1989,[56] are broadly the same as for England and so the judgment in *Stubbings v. Webb* is likely to be applied.

## 4. *Utilising alternative forms of action to circumvent* Stubbings v. Webb

The finding in *Stubbings* that claims against the perpetrator of the abuse are subject to the strict six-year limitation period is a grave disadvantage to many abuse claimants. It is, however, possible that in some cases, the limitation rule in *Stubbings* can be circumvented by utilising another form of action. The main opportunity to do this arises where the claim can be framed in negligence against a non-perpetrator (e.g. the employer of the perpetrator). The application of limitation provisions to such claims is dealt with later below. There are also a number of other possibilities which can be mentioned briefly, namely breach of fiduciary duty and wrongful interference claims. Either of these causes of action, if viable, may trigger a more liberal approach to limitation and will be dealt with first.

### Breach of fiduciary duty

Although the potential for a breach of fiduciary duty action based on sexual abuse seems an unlikely prospect in English law, the slim

---

[54] At 155.   [55] S. 17.   [56] SI 1989/1339 (NI II).

possibility of such a claim is worthy of brief exploration. If abuse triggering psychiatric harm could be actioned as a breach of fiduciary duty in English law, it would arguably open up the s. 11 extendable limitation period because the action would then be for personal injury based on a 'breach of duty'. Launching a civil claim as a breach of fiduciary duty by the perpetrator of the abuse rather than as a battery could assist the claimant in avoiding the effect of *Stubbings*. Such an action would, however, face two major obstacles in the form of *Sidaway v. Governors of Bethlem Royal Hospital*[57] and *Bryn Alyn*.[58] Whilst English law recognises that parents have a legal duty to act in their children's best interests,[59] fiduciary obligations in English law have generally only been recognised in the context of the protection of economic interests, rather than physical integrity (compare this with the much more liberal application of fiduciary duties in Canada discussed in Chapter 2). Consequently, the House of Lords' judgment in *Sidaway* rejected the proposition of the doctor/patient relationship being defined as a fiduciary one,[60] despite its currency in other jurisdictions.[61] Lord Scarman regarded the doctor/patient relationship as being 'a very special one – the patient putting his health and his life in the doctor's hands',[62] although not a fiduciary one. His reasoning was that fiduciary duties existed to provide redress where a right recognised in law would otherwise have no protection. This judgment does not appear to envisage the fiduciary duty action as *only* being available for the protection of economic interests, but in order to extend its ambit to sexual abuse

---

[57] [1985] AC 871.

[58] *KR and others v. Bryn Alyn Community (Holdings) Ltd (In Liquidation), Royal & Sun Alliance plc* [2003] EWCA Civ 85; [2003] 1 FCR 385.

[59] *Re C (HIV)* [1999] 2 FLR 1004; *Re R (A Minor) (Blood Transfusion)* [1993] 2 FLR 757.

[60] Most other Commonwealth jurisdictions do portray doctor/patient relations as fiduciary: e.g. *Taylor v. McGillivray* 110 DLR (4th) 64, which illustrates that a consenting sexual relationship between physician and patient gives rise to an actionable breach of fiduciary duty in Canadian law. The refusal to recognise such in English law seems to have a lot to do with the common law's determination that patients are not entitled to all available information regarding their medical treatment, rather that such a right is subject to therapeutic privilege – a concept which would be at odds with the fiduciary relationship.

[61] E. g. *Taylor v. McGillivray* (1993) 110 DLR (4th) 64 (Canada) and *Norberg v. Weinrib* (1992) 92 DLR (4th) 449, where McLachlin J stated that fiduciary obligations were capable of protecting 'not only narrow legal and economic interests, but can also service to defend fundamental human and personal interests' at 499. See also *Breen v. Williams* (1996) 138 ALR 259, which suggests that the doctor owes fiduciary obligations to the patient, although not giving rise to a right of equitable compensation for personal injury.

[62] [1985] AC 871 at 884.

victims, it would seem that the court would at the very least need convincing that the battery action does not provide the claimant with adequate protection. Further problems arise out of the *Bryn Alyn* judgment in deciding that an action for intentional harm such as sexual abuse could not be actioned alternatively as breach of a non-delegable duty in order to avoid the effect of *Stubbings*. By analogy, a similar fate may meet a breach of fiduciary duty claim.

In addition to opening up the extendable three-year limitation period, if abuse could be treated as a breach of fiduciary duty (although only applicable to certain categories of abuser[63]), limitation periods could theoretically be overridden altogether as complaints in equity are not necessarily constrained by statutory limitation periods. Section 36(1) of the Limitation Act provides that the time limits set out in the 1980 Act do not apply to claims for equitable relief, except insofar as the court *may* apply these time limits by analogy with the common law position. The Act, therefore, leaves the matter of limitation to the courts in cases where the claimant is seeking equitable relief. Thus, until recently, it seemed that an action for breach of fiduciary duty would not be trammelled by the usual limitation periods. The cases which support such a conclusion were, however, first instance cases[64] and were disapproved in *Cia de Seguros Imperio v. Heath (REBX) Ltd*.[65] The court in *Cia de Seguros* preferred to say that, at least where there was a concurrent jurisdiction at common law and in equity, the statutory limitation periods were to apply to the equitable jurisdiction 'by analogy'.[66] The policy justifications for limitation periods were still extant in actions for breach of fiduciary duty.

Thus, it seems that as abuse articulated as a breach of fiduciary obligation can alternatively be actioned at common law as a battery, the limitation periods must apply by analogy to the fiduciary action. It is therefore quite possible that the limitation periods would have no

---

[63] See Chapter 2.
[64] See *Nelson v. Rye* [1996] 2 All ER 186 and *Kershaw v. Whelan (No. 2)* (1997) *The Times*, 10 February (although these were cases against a solicitor rather than an abuser).
[65] [1999] 1 All ER (Comm) 750.
[66] Relying on the House of Lords decision in *Knox v. Gye* (1872) LR 5 HL 656. See also the Australian decision in *Woodhead v. Elbourne* [2000] QSC 42, where the court condemned the use of a plea of breach of fiduciary duty as a means of circumventing limitation periods, the New Zealand case of *S v. G* [1995] 3 NZLR 681 and *H v. H* [1997] 2 NZLR 700. For the Canadian position see *Butler v. Nash* 2003 126 ACWSJ (3d) 140, where the court ruled that equitable claims ought to be brought promptly (following *Louie v. Lastman* (2001) 199 DLR (4th) 741 (Ont Superior Ct of Justice).

application at all if the wrong were actioned as a breach of fiduciary duty. Even if the statutory limitation periods were found not to be applicable by analogy, it would still be open to the court to find that it would be inequitable to allow the case to proceed on the grounds of laches or prejudice to the defendant.[67] The end result would therefore probably be the same whether the Limitation Act provisions were applied or not.

### Wrongful interference with the person

According to the principle in *Wilkinson v. Downton*, the defendant is liable for wilful acts without justification which are calculated to cause physical harm to the claimant and which in fact cause physical harm.[68] Under this cause of action, the right to sue accrues upon damage, therefore, as the courts have recognised that the 'damage' is the psychiatric injury which forms the substance of the claim,[69] this would ultimately provide access to a longer limitation period than the six years from the incidence of the abuse. This remains a relatively untested route for compensating abuse in English courts, but there seems to be no reason why it may not be utilised instead of battery in an action against the perpetrator, although the Court of Appeal has expressed a preference that abuse claimants should not utilise this 'obscure tort whose jurisprudential basis remains unclear'.[70] Such a form of action would not enable the claimant to access the delayed discovery and discretion provisions, but would still be preferable to the battery claim where the cause of action accrues on the occurrence of the wrong complained of.

## Application of limitation periods to civil actions against non-perpetrator defendants

### 1. Vicarious liability

In the *Bryn Alyn* litigation[71] (discussed in more detail Chapter 2), it was argued that an employer's vicarious liability for acts of abuse by

---

[67] *Smith v. Clay* (1767) 3 Brown CC 639; *Re Pauling's Settlement* [1962] 1 WLR 86; *Williams v. The Minister, Aboriginal Land Rights Act 1983 and Anor* [1999] NSWSC 843; *S v. G* [1995] 3 NZLR 681.
[68] [1897] 2 QB 57.
[69] *KR and others v. Bryn Alyn Community (Holdings) Ltd (In Liquidation), Royal & Sun Alliance plc* [2003] EWCA Civ 85; [2003] 1 FCR 385 (discussed below).
[70] *A v. Hoare* [2006] EWCA Civ 395 at [136].
[71] [2003] EWCA Civ 85; [2003] 1 FCR 385.

employees of an institution involved in childcare was based on the employee's breach of the duty delegated to them to care for the children and, therefore, entitled the claimant to the extendable three-year limitation period under s. 11.[72] The Court of Appeal rejected this argument, saying that any claims for compensation arising out of a deliberate wrong, whether relying on the principle of vicarious liability or otherwise, would fall under the absolute six-year limitation period.[73]

With respect, this decision is at odds with the conclusion in the same judgment that there was nothing to prevent abuse being actioned as something other than a battery. Provided that, on the facts, the circumstances in which the abuse occurred could be described as a 'breach of duty', the flexible s. 11 limitation period could be applied to an action against the perpetrator. Moreover, in two vicarious liability cases, including the House of Lords case of *Lister* (another case concerned with child abuse), the deliberate wrong of the employee is described as a breach of the non-delegable duty of care which the employer owes to the claimant.[74] The judgment in *Bryn Alyn* failed to explain convincingly why the vicarious liability of an employer for the perpetration of child abuse by an employee cannot similarly be regarded as an action for a 'breach of duty' for the purposes of limitation.

Having said all this, if the decision in *Bryn Alyn* can be defended, it is on the grounds that a contrary decision would have produced a perverse outcome; the deliberate conduct of the perpetrator would have benefited from the absolute limitation period of six years, but the 'innocent' employer's conduct would not. This would once again turn the notion of attaching liability to moral responsibility, a core rationale of the tort regime, on its head. It would, however, have provided some claimants with a means of avoiding the perversity in *Stubbings*.

## 2. Non-battery claims

The following discussion explores how time can currently be extended in cases actioned in negligence, although, as indicated above, it may be that at the time of reading these mechanisms for extending time have

---

[72] This argument was based on the judgment of Lord Diplock and Lord Hobhouse in the House of Lords decision in *Lister v. Hesley Hall Ltd* [2002] 1 AC 215, discussed in Chapter 2.
[73] Followed in *C v. Middlesbrough Council* [2004] EWCA Civ 1747; [2004] All ER (D) 339 (Dec).
[74] *Lister v. Hesley Hall Ltd* [2002] 1 AC 215; *Morris v. CW Martin* [1966] 1 QB 716.

been made available to battery claimants. As few such cases have reached the English courts, cases from other jurisdictions are used by way of illustration. Where a civil claim is brought against a non-perpetrator in the tort of negligence, the limitation period can be extended according to the principles of (1) disability or (2) fraudulent concealment, as outlined above, or, additionally, under (3) the doctrine of delayed discovery or (4) by inviting the court to exercise its discretion to extend time. (Of course, the same avenues for extending time would be available in assault/battery claims if the ruling in *Stubbings* that deliberate wrongs must be actioned under the inflexible three-year rule were to be overturned.)

## The delayed discovery doctrine: s. 14

Limitation provisions can be tolled in many jurisdictions until such time as the claimant knew or should have known of their injury and its cause. This principle is often known as delayed discovery or the principle of reasonable discoverability. Whilst Canada and many other jurisdictions recognise a common law doctrine of delayed discovery,[75] English common law recognises no such doctrine.[76] There is, however, a statutory version under s. 11 of the Limitation Act 1980 which, as explained above, applies in cases of personal injury caused by 'negligence, nuisance or breach of duty'.[77]

These statutory provisions of delayed discovery were introduced to deal with concerns arising out of workers injured by slow acting workplace hazards, such as asbestos, where discovery of the harm post-dated the wrongful exposure by many years.[78] The three-year limitation period runs from the date on which the cause of action accrued or the date of knowledge (if later) of the person injured.[79] Section 14 defines the

---

[75] *Kamloops City v. Nielson* [1984] 2 SCR 2.
[76] *Pirelli General Cable Works Ltd v. Oscar Faber & Partners* [1983] 2 AC 1, overruling *Sparham-Souter v. Town & Country Developments (Essex) Ltd* [1976] QB 858 (although these cases concerned with pure economic loss as opposed to personal injury). For the position relating to injury to the person at common law, see *Cartledge v. E Jopling & Sons Ltd* [1963] AC 758.
[77] The delayed discoverability provision applies retrospectively to wrongs which occurred before the provision came into force under the Limitation Act 1963. However, it only applies to claims to which a three-year limitation period applies, not to claims with any other period of limitation, whether or not they are for a 'breach of duty': *McDonnell v. Congregation of Christian Brothers Trustees* [2003] UKHL 63; [2003] 3 WLR 1627, following *Arnold v. Central Electricity Generating Board* [1988] AC 228.
[78] Following the injustice exposed by *Cartledge v. E Jopling & Sons Ltd* [1962] 1 QB 189.
[79] S. 11(4)(a) and (b).

relevant 'knowledge' as meaning knowledge that the injury in question was 'significant' AND that the injury was attributable to the wrong complained of. The knowledge required for s. 14 to operate can be actual or constructive, as 'knowledge' includes knowledge which the claimant might reasonably have been expected to acquire:

(a) from facts observable or ascertainable by him; or
(b) from facts ascertainable by him with the help of medical or other appropriate expert advice which it is reasonable for him to seek.[80]

Thus, insofar as the abuse related trauma causes the claimant to repress or deny the abuse and the extent to which the injury remained latent, these processes which inhibit discovery of the relevant facts may be raised in argument under s. 14, at least where the defendant is being sued for negligence or some other breach of duty. However, evidence that the claimant's defence mechanisms have caused him or her to avoid confronting the fact of the abuse is unlikely to be regarded as inhibiting the claimant's acquisition of the relevant knowledge,[81] and ought to be raised instead in the context of whether the court should exercise its discretion to extend time.

As the claimant will generally be seeking to demonstrate to the court that they did not in fact obtain the knowledge necessary to launch a claim until some time after the cause of action accrued, it will often fall to the defendant to convince the court that a reasonable claimant ought to have discovered the relevant facts earlier. The complex provisions of s. 14 raise a number of issues for determination:

1. Is s. 14 triggered when there is or ought to be knowledge of the initial assault, or only when there is knowledge of the psychiatric injuries caused by the abuse which might manifest themselves many years later?
2. Whichever is the case, when is such an injury to be regarded as 'significant'?
3. When is the claimant expected to have acquired knowledge of the causal nexus between their harm and the defendant's conduct?
4. In determining when the claimant ought to have acquired knowledge of these facts, to what extent are his/her personality traits, abilities and resources relevant?

---

[80] S. 14(3).   [81] *Hopkins v. Secretary of Queensland* [2004] QDC 021.

**What constitutes the 'injury'?** The knowledge required before the delayed discovery provisions trigger the limitation period is knowledge that they have suffered 'significant' injury. It has already been demonstrated that in English law, bizarrely, cases against non-perpetrators for failure to prevent the abuse can take advantage of the delayed discovery rules, but claims against the perpetrator cannot. In a now superseded part of Lord Griffiths' judgment in *Stubbings v. Webb*, he also considered whether, if he were wrong about the absolute six-year limitation period being applicable to a claim for sexual battery, would the claimant be able to extend the limitation period under s. 14 on the basis that she did not have knowledge that she had suffered a 'significant injury' until many years after the abuse ceased. Lord Griffiths responded:

> I have the greatest difficulty in accepting that a woman who knows that she has been raped does not know that she has suffered a significant injury ... Sexual abuse that goes no further than indecent fondling of a child raises a more difficult question, but some of the plaintiff's allegations are so serious that I should have had difficulty in regarding them as other than significant.[82]

Thus, for the purposes of establishing knowledge of significant injury, Lord Griffiths treated the psychiatric harm as a development of or a continuation of the *physical* assault, rather than as a separate harm.

Lord Griffiths' distinction between penetrative assault and indecent fondling, produced further absurdity. The victim of mere fondling or inappropriate touching would have easier access to the delayed discovery provisions of s. 14 because they could more easily convince the court that they did not reasonably regard the injury as 'significant' at the time of the abuse. This distinction, however, ignores the 'distorted perceptions'[83] that repeated abuse can cause. For example, the victim who is duped into assuming responsibility and blaming themselves for the abuse will not regard the abuser as a potential defendant, and a very young child is unlikely to regard litigation as an option. What is glaringly apparent from Lord Griffiths' judgment is a deep-rooted scepticism towards the claimant's argument that knowledge of her injury was not more or less contemporaneous with knowledge of her abuse.[84]

---

[82] At 506. See also *Gray v. Reeves* [1992] 89 DLR (4th) 315, following Lord Griffiths on this point.
[83] Discussed earlier in Chapter 2.   [84] See [1993] AC 498 at 506.

Ten years later in the *Bryn Alyn* litigation,[85] the Court of Appeal chose to depart from Lord Griffiths' view in *Stubbings* that a rape victim must be taken to have known that they have suffered 'significant injury' for the purposes of s. 14. The Court of Appeal regarded Lord Griffiths' judgment as flawed on two counts. First, it failed to distinguish between the immediate effects of the abuse and the long-term psychiatric damage which manifested itself much later and which formed the subject matter of the claim. As the claim was for the long-term psychiatric injury, it was that injury (as opposed to the assault itself and any physical injury and immediate distress) which the claimant must have knowledge of and must reasonably regard as significant.[86] Secondly, Lord Griffiths' judgment failed to take into account the partly subjective nature of the term 'significant'. The court should ask whether 'an already damaged child such as the claimant would reasonably turn his mind to litigation as a solution to his problems'.[87] After *Bryn Alyn*, it seems that the claimant must have actual or constructive knowledge of their psychiatric injury, rather than of the assault, before time will start to run against a claimant suing a non-perpetrator.

These statements from *Bryn Alyn* might be understood as suggesting that a claimant could action the same wrong twice; once for the battery and consequent distress and again for the later onset of psychiatric harm. However, if a claimant did bring proceedings regarding the initial abuse and the immediately apparent injuries of distress and humiliation, a later action for any psychological harm which manifested itself years down the line would surely be barred by the principles of *res judicata*[88] and also by the rule that damages are awarded on a 'once and for all' basis.[89]

---

[85] [2003] EWCA Civ 85; [2003] 1 FCR 385.
[86] Followed in *Hodges v. Northampton CC* [2004] EWCA Civ 526; [2005] PIQR P7. It seems that suggestions in *Stubbings* (HL) and *B (KL) v. British Colombia* [2001] 197 DLR (4th) 431 that lack of knowledge as to the extent of the injury does not prevent knowledge that the injury was significant are no longer good law in the English courts.
[87] [2003] EWCA Civ 85; [2003] 1 FCR 385 at [42].
[88] *Henderson v. Henderson* (1843) 3 Hare 100: 'the Court requires the parties to that litigation to bring forward their whole case, and will not (except under special circumstances) permit the same parties to open the same subject of litigation in respect of a matter which might have been brought forward as part of the subject in context, but which was not brought forward ...'
[89] McGregor, *McGregor on Damages* at 9–024, remarking that there is very little in the way of direct authority for this 'taken for granted' principle, but citing *Hodsoll v. Stallebrass* (1940) 11 A & E 301 as an illustration of the rule.

The same would seem to apply if the first claim was settled rather than decided by the courts.[90]

The *Bryn Alyn* judgment has not been followed by the Scottish courts, at least where the court is concerned with the application of prescription periods rather than limitation of actions.[91] In *K v. Gilmartin's Executrix*,[92] the pursuer argued that abuse gave rise to two separate obligations to compensate; first in respect of the assault itself and any immediate harm suffered and, secondly, with regard to the later onset of resulting psychiatric harm. The argument was rejected – abuse gave rise to a single obligation to provide reparation and time started to run as soon as there was a coincidence of injury and wrong (i.e. the initial assault).

The claimant does not need knowledge of the specific diagnosis of their mental disorder to be aware that they have suffered 'significant' injury. In *Nelson v. Commonwealth of Australia*, the claimant was regarded as having knowledge of the fact of injury and its extent even though he was not aware that his symptoms could be described as PTSD and he believed his problems to be an 'emotional' condition and not a 'medical' one:[93]

> It would be very strange if a person, aware of all the symptoms and in circumstances where there was no evidence that they would worsen, could say that he or she was not aware of their extent, merely because different doctors may describe them differently.

Thus, it is the effect on the claimant that must be known, not the precise label with which to describe the illness being suffered. Clearly, if it were otherwise, it could often be argued that, until the diagnosis provided by the claimant's expert witness, they did not know the nature and extent of their injuries and limitation periods would be regularly suspended until the claimant contemplated litigation. Crucial to the finding in *Nelson* was the fact that the claimant had been receiving counselling and visiting a consultant psychologist long before he read on his file that he had been diagnosed with PTSD.

**Knowledge that the injury was 'significant'**  Significance is given a specialised meaning in the context of s. 14. An injury is only to be

---

[90] *Bristow v. Grout* (1986) *The Times*, 3 November.
[91] The concept of prescription does not exist in English law. In Scottish law it comprises an absolute limitation period which cannot be waived by the parties. With regard to limitation, an admission of liability by the defendant may result in loss of the ability to claim a limitation defence: *Wright v. John Bagnall & Sons Ltd* [1900] 1 QB 240.
[92] 2004 SLT 1014.   [93] [2001] NSWCA 443.

regarded as 'significant' if the claimant would reasonably have considered it sufficiently serious to institute litigation (presuming that the defendant was solvent and did not deny liability).[94] This issue of whether the claimant's injury might reasonably be regarded as 'significant' is 'a highly judgmental question'.[95] The courts do, however, seem to confine their assessment of the significance of the injury to consideration of its severity rather than its cause or unusualness,[96] or even the prospects of obtaining compensation. Legal developments which enhance the claimant's prospects of success in court (e.g. the ruling in *Lister* that an employer could be vicariously liable for the sexual assault committed by their employee) are not relevant to whether the claimant had knowledge that the injury was significant under s. 14 (although they might be considered under the s. 33 provisions for the exercise of the court's discretion).[97]

There are no short-cuts to establishing whether claimants had the requisite knowledge. The relevant knowledge is not necessarily acquired merely because the claimant knew that the acts of abuse were 'disgusting' and 'wrong'.[98] Asking each claimant whether they knew at the time what had happened to them was 'wrong' would not be enough to establish constructive knowledge, although such an inquiry might be a step on the way to identifying whether they had the relevant knowledge.[99] The nature of the disorder suffered by the claimant may have a bearing on the courts' readiness to believe that the claimant's knowledge that she was suffering significant injury attributable to the abuse was inhibited for many years. In the context of an abuse victim suffering from PTSD, including nightmares and flashbacks of the abuse, the court in *Hopkins v. Secretary of Queensland*[100] refused to believe that the claimant did not realise the significance of her mental state and its cause for more than 15 years.

---

[94] S. 14(2).   [95] Per Bingham LJ in *Stubbings v. Webb* [1992] QB 197 at 208 (CA).
[96] *Dobbie v. Medway Health Authority* [1994] 4 All ER 450.
[97] *Rowe v. Kingston upon Hull City Council* [2003] EWCA Civ 1281; [2003] ELR 771.
[98] *Gray v. Reeves* [1992] 89 DLR (4th) 315. See also *Ross v. Garabedian* 742 NE 2d 1046 (Mass 2001) – belief that a consensual underage sexual relationship was 'wrong' and 'shameful' did not constitute sufficient knowledge of harm to trigger the statute of limitations.
[99] *KR and others v. Bryn Alyn Community (Holdings) Ltd (In Liquidation), Royal & Sun Alliance plc* [2003] EWCA Civ 85; [2003] 1 FCR 385 at [48].
[100] [2004] QDC 021.

**Delay in recognising the causal nexus**  For the purposes of s. 14 of the Limitation Act 1980, 'knowledge' includes cognisance that the injury is attributable to the defendant's wrong: 'The knowledge required . . . is a broad knowledge of the essence of the causally relevant act or omission to which the injury is attributable.'[101] This 'broad knowledge' requires only that the claimant recognises or ought to recognise that the relevant act or omission's causal nexus with the damage is a real possibility – it does not require that the claimant realised that the defendant's conduct was the probable cause.[102] It can be argued that, whilst the claimant had knowledge of their significant injury and knowledge of the defendant's wrong, knowledge of these facts does not necessitate knowledge of their connection. There are a number of different episodes in a claimant's life which may trigger awareness that prior abuse is responsible for mental problems, for example, the perpetrator being convicted of sexual offences, the claimant receiving therapy for their psychiatric illness, joining a group of persons who were also abused or working with abused children. Whilst the claimant may argue that they did not have the requisite awareness until after counselling/therapy, criminal investigations, meeting someone with similar experiences, any of these events may be seized upon by defendants to argue that the claimant ought to have discovered the potential for a claim earlier than they did. For example, it would be particularly difficult for a claimant to argue that they were unaware that they were not to blame for the abuse when the perpetrator was known to have been convicted of sexual offences involving children.

The psychiatric reports of the claimant's psychiatric condition will be of vital importance in cases where the claimant argues that they had not made the connection between the abuse and their injury sooner. For example, it is worth noting that in the New Zealand case of *W v. Attorney General*[103] expert evidence convinced the court that the claimant had not discovered the causal nexus between her mental condition/criminal tendencies and abuse suffered when she was 12 years old until she read a newspaper about a woman, similar to herself, whose criminal conduct was the result of the abuse she experienced as a child. Whilst W had undergone counselling, written a book about her experiences in care including her abuse and had made applications for the equivalent of

---

[101] *North Essex Health Authority v. Spargo* [1997] 8 Med LR 125, *per* Brooke LJ.
[102] *Nash v. Eli Lilly & Co* [1993] 1 WLR 782; *Davies v. City & Hackney Health Authority* [1989] 2 Med LR 366.
[103] [1999] 2 NZLR 709.

criminal injuries compensation, the court accepted that it was only the newspaper story that had awakened the claimant to the truth. W had not associated herself with stories of abuse and mental harm as, due to the abuse, she had always believed that her problems were due to her being 'bad'.

Given that the standard of discoverability extends to actual and constructive knowledge, it might be argued that the extent of sexual abuse and its impact on the victim's mental health are by now so notorious that a reasonable person would not take 10 or 20 years to make the connection between the injury and the wrong. Indeed, the judgment of Auld LJ in *Bryn Alyn*[104] indicates as much: 'increased public awareness is likely to usher in a generation more sensitive to its seriousness and "significance" in a s. 14 sense.'[105] If, as Auld LJ suggests, decisions on delayed discovery are dependent on the climate surrounding abuse claims at the time of the abuse, the courts have the perfect excuse for closing down abuse claims in the future due to the questionable view that now the social climate is more receptive to reports of sexual abuse,[106] and a related assumption that potential claimants should know immediately that their injury is significant and that litigation is a feasible prospect. As indicated above, the late 1980s is a crucial period for claims brought in England and Wales, coinciding, as it does, with the publication of the Cleveland Inquiry, but also because 1986 saw the first reported civil case seeking compensation for rape.[107]

However, in the context of abuse, the fact that society generally was aware of the causal nexus between abuse and long-term psychiatric trauma should not suffice to convince a court that the claimant ought to have made the causal connection immediately. Implicit in the application of s. 14 would surely be the requirement that the claimant must have knowledge that the defendant bore responsibility for the

---

[104] [2003] EWCA Civ 85; [2003] 1 FCR 385 at [43].
[105] See also Browne-Wilkinson V-C in *Stubbings v. Webb* [1992] QB 197 (CA) at 212. This argument also impressed Sosman J (dissenting) in *Ross v. Garabedian* 742 NE 2d 1046 (Mass 2001), given the barrage of media coverage in recent times on the issue. Such an argument should, however, be subject to consideration of the fact that any coping mechanisms of the victim which served to prevent such connection being made was caused by the abuse.
[106] See Bingham LJ in CA, *Stubbings v. Webb* [1992] QB 197: '... during the period in question [late 1970s] there was not that general awareness among the public of the psychological effects of child abuse which certain well-publicised events since then have caused.'
[107] *W v. Meah* [1986] 1 All ER 935. See also Chapter 2 on this.

abuse. This raises interesting issues regarding the previously mentioned distorted perceptions of the abuse encouraged by the abuser.[108] If the claimant is labouring under an 'illusion of responsibility' for the abuse, the connection between the injury and the defendant's 'wrong' can never be made. In such cases, useful reference might be made to the Canadian case of *H(G) v. Gorsline*.[109] The claimant, who knew that she had been the subject of wrongful abuse from the time it occurred, was not barred from bringing a claim 15 years later (13 years beyond the statutory limitation period), because the action did not accrue until the victim understood the true nature of the harm inflicted and that the abuser, not the victim, bore responsibility for it. On the facts, it was not until the claimant was working as a teaching assistant that she observed the vulnerability of children and realised that she was not the one responsible for the abuse.

**The role of medical/expert advice** As explained above, the knowledge required for s. 14 to operate can be constructive, as 'knowledge' includes knowledge which the claimant might reasonably have been expected to acquire from facts ascertainable by him with the help of medical or other appropriate expert advice which it would have been reasonable for him to have sought.[110] This provision enables the defendant to argue that the claimant's delayed discovery is due to their unreasonable failure to seek medical or other expert advice sooner, and that such advice would have revealed the significance of their injury and/or its causal nexus with the defendant's conduct. Familiarity with the medical profession due to a number of physical ailments does not necessarily strengthen arguments that the claimant ought to have sought assistance for her psychological problems promptly.[111] The courts may distinguish a reasonable claimant's ability to recognise that physical discomfort is an illness requiring treatment and the reasonable person's capacity to recognise that anxiety and difficulty in forming relationships may amount to a mental disorder which would benefit from therapy.

Alternatively, the defendant may raise evidence that the claimant did seek medical advice in order to argue that the claimant cannot therefore maintain that she did not discover the link between her trauma and the abuse until much later in time. The date at which the claimant first sought medical advice on issues connected to the abuse is therefore of vital importance and can be fatal to the argument that they did not

---

[108] See Chapter 1.  [109] [2001] 6 WWR 132 (Alta QB).  [110] S. 14(3).
[111] *Calder v. Uzelac* [2003] VSCA 175.

appreciate the causal nexus between the abuse and its psychological impact. Even where the adviser's notes do not reveal that advice to this effect was given, the courts often assume that medical advice would, in the ordinary course of events, have revealed the connection and the court may require the claimant to convince it that this did not happen in their case. The judicial assumption that medical advice will reveal the nexus between abuse and long-term trauma is not necessarily a safe one. The causal link between abuse and mental illness has, in fact, been a relatively recent revelation to the medical profession. Interestingly, the claimant's medical notes in *Stubbings v. Webb* confirmed that she had disclosed some details of her childhood sexual abuse to doctors and psychiatrists at a number of intervals almost ten years before a psychiatrist suggested that there might be a connection between the abuse and her psychiatric problems.[112] By contrast, it was doubted in *C v. Cairns* that a claimant receiving treatment for mental problems in the mid 1980s would not have been alerted by the medical profession to the likely connection between the mental problems and a disclosure of sexual abuse.[113] Thus, it appears that from the time when a claimant receives treatment for mental problems, provided such time occurs after the early 1980s, it will be very difficult for the claimant to argue that they did not appreciate the causal nexus between their abuse and their mental state.

The Australian case of *Carter v. Corporation of the Sisters of Mercy of the Diocese of Rockhampton*[114] is also notable in alerting us to the fact that courts sometimes expect claimants to be proactive in seeking the cause of their mental problems. McPherson J took the view that the claimant, who admitted to being aware of her mistreatment during her days at an orphanage and who knew that she was suffering depression, was unreasonable in not asking her psychiatrist what was causing her depression. In the author's view, if the therapist does not make the connection explicit, any requirement that the patient should make inquiries is expecting too much of the patient, after all the role of therapy is the pursuit of recovery not the allocation of blame.[115]

---

[112] [1993] AC 498.
[113] [2003] Lloyd's Med Rep 90. Cf. *W v. Attorney General* [1999] 2 NZLR 709, where the court accepted evidence that healthcare professionals were just beginning to become aware of a link between abuse and behavioural/personality disorders in 1984 (at [15]).
[114] [2001] QCA 335.
[115] Cf. the dissenting judgment of Atkinson J: 'While a reasonably well adjusted, ordinarily self-confident person might be able to make the requisite link and be prepared and able to take civil action for the wrongs done to them, typically, adults who have survived

An unqualified friend's diagnosis of the claimant's mental disorder would not usually suffice to fix the claimant with constructive knowledge of their injury. In *Sykes v. Commonwealth of Australia*,[116] the claimant convinced the court that although a friend had told him that he was probably suffering from PTSD, and he understood it had something to do with stress and anxiety, he did not appreciate that it was a mental disorder. This meant that time did not start to run until the following year, when a psychiatrist diagnosed PTSD and told the claimant that it was a psychiatric disorder.

**Section 14 – An objective test: relevance of the claimant's character and intelligence** Until recently, there existed conflicting authorities from the Court of Appeal on the issue of whether s. 14 demanded an objective or subjective approach to constructive knowledge – in other words, whether the character of the claimant (e.g. their shyness or reluctance to confide in others) could be taken into account when deciding at what point they ought to have recognised the fact of their injury and its attribution to the conduct of the defendant. This issue is important to the abuse claimant in terms of what kinds of explanation the courts will accept from the claimant for their delay in bringing the matter of their abuse to court. In the more recent of these authorities, *Forbes v. Wandsworth Health Authority*,[117] a patient whose leg had been amputated following an attempted bypass operation, had waited ten years before inquiring as to the reasons for the amputation. Whilst Stuart Smith LJ accepted that patients who trusted their doctors might not suspect that negligence might be the reason for the amputation, s. 14(3) required the application of a reasonable man standard with the personal characteristics of the claimant being disregarded. A reasonable man, if he had suffered a major injury, should and would take advice promptly. This can be contrasted with the judgment from a differently constituted Court of Appeal in *Nash v. Eli Lilly & Co*,[118] where Purchas LJ asserted that the test for constructive knowledge was a 'qualified objective' approach allowing the court to take into account the 'position, circumstances and *character* of the plaintiff'.[119] In *Adams*

such abuse are lacking in self-esteem and remain powerless' (at [86]) and relying on *R v. L(WK)* [1991] 1 SCR 1091 (Supreme Court of Canada).
[116] [2000] NSWSC 3.   [117] [1997] QB 402.   [118] [1993] 1 WLR 782.
[119] [1993] 1 WLR 782 at 799 (emphasis added). Followed by Henry LJ in *Ali v. Courtaulds Textiles Ltd* [1999] Lloyd's Rep Med 301, a case in which *Forbes* had not been included in the arguments.

*v. Bracknell Forest BC*, the House of Lords adopted the approach of *Forbes*, confirming that the test for delayed discovery for the purposes of s. 14 is essentially an objective test, which takes no account of the particular claimant's characteristics.[120] The 'character and intelligence' of the claimant were not to be taken into account when speculating on what a reasonable claimant would have done by way of inquiring as to the nature and cause of their injury. The courts should distinguish between the 'circumstances' of the claimant which were relevant to constructive knowledge provisions and 'personal characteristics' which were not.[121] Lord Hoffmann stated that, if the injury itself would inhibit a claimant from seeking advice, that fact should be taken into account (i.e. it qualified as a 'circumstance' rather than a 'characteristic'). Thus, if it can be said that the claimant's continued ignorance of their injury and its connection to the defendant is attributable to the trauma which the abuse caused (e.g. trauma-induced avoidance behaviours causing the claimant to delay seeking medical advice), then the court should be invited to take this into account as 'circumstances' which would have prevented a reasonable claimant from discovering the truth of their injuries and potential claim. If, however, the delay is due to inherent characteristics of the claimant's personality which are not attributable to the sequelae of the abuse, the court will conclude that the claimant ought to have discovered the relevant facts earlier.[122]

On the facts of *Adams*, a case brought by a claimant arguing that he had not discovered his dyslexia until the age of 27, Mr Adams was found to have acted unreasonably in not recognising his condition sooner. This was on the grounds that whilst the embarrassment and humiliation associated with reading difficulties were accepted as likely to cause the reasonable claimant to be reluctant to discuss the matter with his family, such 'circumstances' would not prevent a reasonable claimant from raising the issue of literacy with his doctor and thereby discovering his dyslexia. It is submitted that even if this distinction between disclosure

---

[120] [2004] UKHL 29; [2004] 3 WLR 89. See also *Collins v. Tesco Stores Ltd* [2003] EWCA Civ 1308, deciding that the degree of robustness and stoicism demonstrated by the claimant was not relevant to determining whether they ought to have perceived their injury as 'significant'.
[121] [2004] UKHL 29; [2004] 3 WLR 89, *per* Lord Walker at [77].
[122] It is submitted that the ruling in *Adams* would not affect the subjective approach in *Bryn Alyn* mentioned above, where the Court of Appeal stated that an already damaged child would not reasonably consider litigation as an option – the minority of the claimant would be a 'circumstance' and not a 'characteristic'.

to family and friends and disclosure to a general practitioner is a credible one, it ought not to be applied to the abuse victim. Persons who have been abused and develop avoidance behaviours are as unlikely to confide in their doctor as in their friends or family.

Again, echoing *Forbes*, their Lordships in *Adams* thought that any injustice against the claimant caused by adopting an objective approach to constructive knowledge could be resolved by resorting to the court's discretion to extend time under s. 33.[123] It is submitted that reliance on the existence of discretion to extend time as a reason for applying a very strict interpretation of constructive knowledge is unconvincing, as the courts' discretion to extend time is reserved for only the most compelling cases.[124] Moreover, as the Court of Appeal noted in *Adams*, there was significant prejudice to the defendant in allowing the claim to proceed given that the documents relating to Mr Adams had been destroyed over ten years ago.[125] It seems exceedingly unlikely, therefore, that a court would exercise its discretion in such a case, at least where the claim is one in negligence.

Thus, the *Adams* judgment is at once both encouraging and worrying to abuse claimants. On the one hand, the scepticism of their Lordships towards Mr Adams' reasons for not approaching the courts sooner would be offputting to the abuse claimant. Indeed, there are certain parallels between the individual with a condition such as dyslexia which is bound to affect confidence and expectation levels and the abuse victim whose confidence and trust in others is likely to be hampered by their experiences. Lord Hoffmann's judgment, however, offers some hope to abuse claimants who should seek to convince the court that any reticence to approach the courts is attributable to the 'circumstances' of their abuse or, in the words of the *Bryn Alyn* judgment, the court should look at the delay from the perspective of the already damaged child. Even this optimistic view of the significance of *Adams* is not without its pitfalls. What of those claimants whose personality is naturally reserved and unchallenging, making them ideal targets for abusing predators? Would their delay in litigating be regarded as attributable to circumstances or characteristics? 'Characteristics' and 'circumstances' will

---

[123] [2004] UKHL 29; [2004] 3 WLR 89, *per* Lord Scott at [73].
[124] In *Robinson v. St Helens MBC* [2002] EWCA Civ 1099; [2003] PIQR P9: 'courts should be slow to exercise their discretion in favour of a claimant in the absence of cogent medical evidence showing a serious effect on the claimant's health or enjoyment of life and employability' (at [33]).
[125] [2003] EWCA Civ 706; [2003] ELR 409.

often be intertwined in abuse cases, because abuse during childhood seems to have such a profound effect on the shaping of the adult psyche. This is why an emphatically subjective approach such as that described below is merited in these claims.

**The subjective approach (New Zealand): rejection of the 'reasonable child abuse victim' test** In New Zealand, the Court of Appeal railed against the use of a largely objective test in the context of delayed discovery and sex abuse victims. The judgment of Thomas J in *W v. Attorney General*[126] described the use of the objective test for delayed discovery, and the implication that the abuse claimant must act 'reasonably,' as a contradiction which 'will in due course be perceived as a grotesque invention of the law'.[127] It was beyond the courts' competence to speculate upon which of the claimant's idiosyncrasies were causally connected to the abuse and which were unconnected, the only fair solution was therefore to engage in a subjective inquiry as to when this claimant (rather than a reasonable person) ought to have acquired the relevant knowledge. There was no room for a test of discovery based on the conduct of a reasonable person in the position of the claimant as English law currently requires under *Adams*. Rather, the courts must recognise that, whilst psychiatrists have recognised patterns of post-abuse behaviour, 'the impact on each individual victim, and the reaction of each individual victim, will necessarily vary'.[128] A court may still be convinced that the claimant ought to have made the necessary connections earlier if it believed that the reason for the delay in discovery was unconnected with the psychological effects of the abuse.

**Canadian approach to delayed discovery** The Canadian case of *M(K) v. M(H)*[129] demonstrates the plethora of solutions an innovative judge might find to the limitation problem if sufficiently convinced of the injustice of blocking the claimant's case. The claim was one of child against father where the claimant only became aware that her psychiatric illness could be attributed to her father's abuse after joining a self-help group for incest victims (12 years after the abuse ended). It is also important to note that the jury in this case had already found the allegations of

---

[126] [1999] 2 NZLR 709.
[127] At [61], rejecting the objective test previously applied in the abuse case of *S v. G* [1995] 3 NZLR 681.
[128] At [62].  [129] [1992] 3 SCR 6.

abuse to be true; therefore, the usual presumption of innocence did not apply. La Forest J, sitting in the Supreme Court of Canada in tortious assault and battery proceedings against the father, rejected the rationales for limitation periods as applicable in this case as there was no public interest in protecting those responsible for deliberate and heinous wrongs such as incest.[130] Fashioning a liberal application of the delayed discoverability principle, La Forest J representing the majority asserted that there was a presumption in incest cases that discovery did not occur until therapy, which could be rebutted by defence evidence that the claimant had appreciated the connection between her/his abuse and subsequent illness earlier.[131] Notably, the Supreme Court relied upon the Court of Appeal's decision in *Stubbings v. Webb*,[132] where the court regarded the delayed discovery of the claimant's harm as reasonable, given that in the 1970s (but not the late 1980s) civil actions based on sexual abuse were unknown in the UK and it would not therefore have been reasonable for the claimant to consider her injuries sufficiently serious to justify litigation.

**Delayed discovery and types of repression** Also of note in the context of delayed discovery is the reference in US and Canadian case law to two distinct types of case where the limitation issue is complicated by the peculiarities of psychiatric harm triggered by abuse. Cases referred to opaquely as 'type 1' cases (causal repression) concern those claimants who have a clear recollection of the occurrence of abuse but who have experienced delayed realisation of the causal nexus between their psychiatric problems and the abuse. Such repression is hardly surprising given that the psychiatric damage may not present itself until years after the abuse ceases.[133] Lamm argues that total repression claimants could easily be recognised as having acted 'reasonably' in their late discovery of their claim, as the standards of what constitutes 'reasonable' conduct are

---

[130] 'While there are instances where the public interest is served by granting repose to certain classes of defendants, for example the cost of professional services if practitioners are exposed to unlimited liability, there is absolutely no corresponding public benefit in protecting individuals who perpetuate incest from the consequences of their wrongful actions.' ([1992] 3 SCR 6 at [22]). Cf. the approach in *H v. H* [1997] 2 NZLR 700, where the defendant denied the allegations and had the benefit of the presumption of innocence. The court in this case distanced itself from the pro-claimant stance expressed in *M(K) v. M(H)* (at 708).
[131] [1992] 3 SCR 6 at para. 48.
[132] [1991] 3 All ER 949, *per* Sir Nicholas Browne-Wilkinson VC at 960.
[133] Mullis, 'The abuse continues?' at 294.

routinely adjusted in the case of children and the mentally ill.[134] 'Type 2' cases refer to those claims where the repression is more complete and the claimant has blotted out any memory of the fact of the abuse itself for some time after the abuse occurred (total repression).[135] In the US, the concept of delayed discovery is a judicial creation and it was in cases of total repression that the limitation rules were first relaxed in this way.[136] The Washington court in *Tyson v. Tyson*[137] noted the absence of corroborating evidence of the abuse and refused to apply the rule to cases of repressed memory because the potential unfairness to the defendant which limitation statutes sought to avoid outweighed the need of the claimant for redress. With respect, the *Tyson* judgment appears to have conflated the issues of limitation with admissibility and allowed doubts about the substantive merits of the case to bar the claim on procedural grounds. Pearson J disagreed with the majority, stating that the majority had confused limitation issues with issues of provability, that they were unduly sceptical about mental health professionals as expert witnesses and that they did not appreciate the enormity of the problem of child sexual abuse. Pearson J's judgment that the rules of delayed discovery should be extended to adult survivors of child abuse who had blocked the abuse from their conscious memory proved influential, and has been followed in later cases.[138] The first extension of the rule to cases of causal repression came in *Hammer v. Hammer*,[139] on the grounds that: 'To protect the parent at the expense of the child works an intolerable perversion of justice.'[140] The rule of delayed discovery was also extended to cases against non-perpetrators in *Phinney v. Morgan*.[141]

---

[134] J. Lamm, 'Easing Access to the Courts for Incest Victims' (1991) 100 *Yale Law Journal* 2189 at 2199. See e.g. the court's adjustment of what was reasonable for a depressed person to do in *Montgomery v. Murphy* (1982) 136 DLR 3d 525, given that the defendant was the cause of that depression. Surely the same argument could be made here that as the defendant's conduct was responsible for the claimant's 'unreasonableness' it should not diminish their claim.

[135] The type 1 and type 2 distinction originates from *Johnson v. Johnson* 701 F. Supp. 1363 (N.D Ill. 1988). See Richardson, 'Missing Pieces of Memory' for criticism of the type 1 and 2 distinction.

[136] Applying the dissenting judgment of Pearson J in *Tyson v. Tyson* 727 P 2d 226 (Wash, 1986).

[137] 727 P 2d 226 (Wash, 1986).

[138] *Johnson v. Johnson*, 701 F. Supp. 1363 (N.D Ill. 1988), and *Mary D. v. John D.*, 264 Cal. Rptr. 633 (1989).

[139] 418 NW 2d 23 (Wis App 1987).

[140] At 27, cited in *M(K) v. M(H)* [1992] 3 SCR 6 at para. 39.

[141] 39 Mass Ct 202, 654 NE2d 77 (1995).

Acceptance of the delayed discovery rule in cases of either total repression or causal repression is by no means uniform across the US.[142] One particularly discreditable example of an American court undermining the delayed discovery argument is that of *Clay v. Kuhl*,[143] where the Illinois appellate court ruled that recovery of repressed memory did not trigger delayed discovery, but rather delayed *re*-discovery, and therefore the usual limitation period applied. Canadian courts have accepted delayed discovery in cases of both causal repression and total repression.[144]

### Judicial discretion to extend time: s. 33

A further means of extending the three-year limitation period applicable to negligence or breach of duty claims is to request the court to exercise its discretion to extend the limitation period where it would be equitable to allow the case to proceed notwithstanding the delay.[145] The Court of Appeal in *Bryn Alyn* adopted a very restrictive view of the court's discretion under s. 33, saying (*obiter*) that whereas the delayed discovery provisions under s. 14 conferred an entitlement on relevant claimants, s. 33 involved 'an exceptional indulgence to a claimant, to be granted only where equity between the parties demands it'.[146] The court must have regard to the prejudice to the claimant if the case is not allowed to proceed and the prejudice to the defendant if the limitation period is disapplied.[147] Factors to be considered when the court considers whether to exercise its discretion include: the length of, and reasons for, the claimant's delay; the effect of delay on the cogency of the cause of action; any disability suffered by the claimant after the cause of action accrued; and the conduct of the defendant after the cause of action accrued.[148] The court's discretion will not be exercised where the delay has been prejudicial to the defendant's ability to defend himself. In this regard, the defendant may argue that, during the course of the delay, his health has deteriorated so that his ability to defend himself is now impaired.[149] Additionally, delay may be regarded as causing evidential prejudice to the defendant on the grounds that where the alleged negligence occurred 20 or more years ago, 'with the best will in the world ...

---

[142] See e.g. *Kaiser v. Milliman* 747 P 2d 1130 (Wash App 1988). For a relatively recent summary of the position in the different States, see Reagan, 'Scientific Consensus on Memory Repression and Recovery'.
[143] 696 NE 2d 1245, 1250 (Ill App Ct 1998).
[144] *Gray v. Reeves* (1992) 64 BCLR (2d) 275 (SC).   [145] S. 33.
[146] [2003] EWCA Civ 85, [2003] 1 FCR 385 at [74].   [147] S. 33(1).   [148] S. 33(3).
[149] *H v. H* [1997] 2 NZLR 700.

it is not always easy for experts to put themselves back into the standards of the day'.[150] Such arguments can be countered by observations that the courts are frequently faced with the task of determining liability according to outmoded norms and practices of earlier times.[151] Besides, the protracted nature of litigation itself can produce a 20-year disparity between the time of the alleged wrong and the final determination of liability.

Section 33 instructs the court to have regard to all the circumstances of the case; therefore, the list of considerations outlined above is not exhaustive. Accordingly, the strength of the claimant's case may be another factor to be taken into account when balancing the hardship caused by allowing the case to proceed, notwithstanding the limitation period.[152] All other things being equal, applying the limitation period where the claimant otherwise has a strong case is regarded as unduly prejudicial to the claimant,[153] and conversely it will be regarded as unduly prejudicial to defendants to disapply the limitation period where the claimant has a weak case.[154] Where limitation is being dealt with as a preliminary issue, the court should be wary of taking into account the strength of the claimant's case, as it should not judge the merits of the case on affidavit evidence.[155] Despite the open-endedness of factors to be considered under s. 33, the fact that the defendant is insured and will not therefore pay directly for any damages awarded to the claimant, has been held not to be a relevant consideration.[156]

An issue has arisen concerning the meaning of 'delay' for the purposes of this particular provision. When the court is considering the reasons for the delay and the effect of delay on the cogency of the evidence, is it the delay in bringing the action after the limitation period had passed which is to be taken into account, or does it include the full period of time from when the cause of action accrued (including perhaps many

---

[150] *Forbes v. Wandsworth Health Authority* [1997] QB 402.
[151] *Roe v. Ministry of Health* [1954] 2 QB 66.
[152] *Forbes v. Wandsworth Health Authority* [1997] QB 402.
[153] *Forbes v. Wandsworth Health Authority* [1997] QB 402; *Carter v. Corporation of the Sisters of Mercy of the Diocese of Rockhampton* [2001] QCA 335. Cf. *Hartley v. Birmingham City DC* [1992] 1 WLR 968 at 979, per Parker LJ and *H v. H* [1997] 2 NZLR 700, where the view was taken that the strength of the claimant's case tips the balance in neither direction as applying the limitation period denies the claimant the opportunity to have their genuine grievance aired but also the defendant's ability to defend is blighted by the passage of time.
[154] *Nash v. Eli Lilly & Co* [1993] 1 WLR 782 at 804.
[155] *In the Dale Case* [1992] PIQR P373 at 380–381.
[156] *Kelly v. Bastible* [1997] 8 Med LR 15.

years during which the claimant did not have the relevant knowledge under s. 14)? It was argued, for example, in *T v. Boys and Girls Welfare Services*,[157] that the courts' discretion should be exercised where the claim was brought two years after the expiry of time on the grounds that such a marginal increase in the time taken to bring the action could not realistically be argued to significantly prejudice the defendant's ability to defend himself. Case law confirms, however, that Parliament intended the court to consider the full period of delay and its effect on the defendant's ability to defend.[158]

The issue of whether the court should exercise its discretion to disapply the limitation period should not be decided after the judge has determined the substantive issues of liability.[159]

**Discretion and the type of claim**   Even if an action against the perpetrator of abuse could be said to fall under the more flexible three-year period (e.g. by being the subject of proceedings for a breach of fiduciary duty or otherwise), it is likely that the discretion to extend time would be more likely to be exercised in a case against the intentional wrongdoer than in the case of an allegedly negligent failure to halt abuse. Although only *obiter*, the Court of Appeal's approach to the discretionary provisions in *Stubbings* is of interest on this point. Bingham LJ, who thought that abuse could be actioned as a 'breach of duty', was in favour of using the court's discretion to extend time. He rejected the defendant's argument that evidence from friends and family would have become stale over the 20 to 30 years since the alleged abuse and would prejudice the possibility of a fair trial. Rather, the case would likely be determined by the court's decision as to whom, the claimant or the defendant, was telling the truth; and on the issue of whether the abuse occurred or not, there was 'no room for forgetfulness or mistake'[160] – the abuse either occurred or it did not. Thus, where the evidence largely comprises one person's word against another, the further lapse of time is unlikely to render it more difficult for the defendant to defend himself. In the negligence claim of *C v. Cairns*, however, the reliability of the defendant's evidence 25 years after the defendant doctor's consultation with

---

[157] [2004] EWCA Civ 1747; [2004] All ER (D) 361 (Dec).
[158] *Donovan v. Gwentoys Ltd* [1990] AC 472; *T v. Boys and Girls Welfare Services* [2004] EWCA Civ 1747; [2004] All ER (D) 361 (Dec).
[159] *KR and others v. Bryn Alyn Community (Holdings) Ltd (In Liquidation), Royal & Sun Alliance plc* [2003] EWCA Civ 85; [2003] 1 FCR 385 at [74].
[160] [1992] QB 197 at 210.

the claimant was regarded as making a factual inquiry impossible. The court sensibly regarded the evidence surrounding a non-intentional omission as more likely to be lost in the mists of time.[161]

**Discretion and avoidance behaviour** As pointed out above, the courts' discretion to extend time is reserved for only the most compelling cases.[162] Avoidance behaviours demonstrated by abuse victims are described by Lamm as the persistent avoidance of 'any situation, such as initiating a lawsuit, that is likely to force them to recall and, therefore, to re-experience the traumas'.[163] A victim in full possession of the details of the abuse and attribution of psychiatric harm to it, may still be driven to avoid confronting and re-living their experiences by such direct means as litigation. Such factors could presumably be taken into account in an application to extend time under s. 33 of the Limitation Act 1980, because whether extension is equitable will depend in part on whether the claimant was 'reasonable' in delaying proceedings. English courts are beginning to show signs of recognising that the psychological impact of abuse has a direct effect on the willingness or ability of the litigant to come forward. In *Roland v. Tiso*,[164] Taylor LJ commented that 'offences involving sexual abuse within the family are by their very nature likely to remain undetected for substantial periods, partly because of fear, partly because of family solidarity and partly because of embarrassment'. Does this mean that the courts will be willing to exercise their discretion to extend time in cases of abuse featuring delay?

As noted above, issues of ill health or disability which explain the claimant's delay in coming to court can in theory be taken into account under s. 33, notwithstanding that onset of the 'disability' occurred after the accrual of the cause of action and/or that it does not meet the threshold of a mental disorder which renders the claimant incapable of managing and administering their property and affairs.[165] Note should, however, be taken of the *Bryn Alyn* judgment, where the fact that the claimant's delay could be explained by the fact that their trauma-induced state of mind had prevented them from bringing proceedings earlier did not necessarily give rise to a case for the court to exercise its

---
[161] [2003] Lloyd's Rep Med 90.
[162] In *Robinson v. St Helens MBC* [2003] PIQR P9: 'courts should be slow to exercise their discretion in favour of a claimant in the absence of cogent medical evidence showing a serious effect on the claimant's health or enjoyment of life and employability' (at 140).
[163] Lamm, 'Easing Access to the Courts for Incest Victims'.
[164] (1990) 12 Cr App R (S) 122, at 125.   [165] See s. 28.

discretion. Issues of disability were better dealt with under s. 14 rather than s. 33.

**Necessary therapeutic delay**   A possible ground for seeking the discretionary extension of limitation periods is that the claimant, whilst aware of the injury and its causal nexus with the defendant's conduct, avoided confrontation until the claimant had regained sufficient control over their illness to deal with the stress and anxiety that legal action involves. A similar argument was heard in the Canadian case of *Novak v. Bond*,[166] although concerned with physical injuries. The claimant successfully argued that it had not been in her best interests to litigate a delayed diagnosis of breast cancer earlier, as she had needed to concentrate her efforts on positive thinking and recovery. Undoubtedly, it was the claimant's mental state of preparation for facing litigation that was the subject of concern, rather than her physical capabilities, so could not the same argument be used to argue that time ought to be extended for the abuse victim?[167] There is some suggestion of such an argument in *Gray v. Reeves*, in the context of abuse where the court accepted that the victim must have reached a certain level of psychological healing and have sufficient social support before 'taking the potentially terrifying step of separation from and potential abandonment by her family that a lawsuit might precipitate'.[168]

## Other issues

### 1. Claims under the Limitation Act 1939

There is a group of claimants who suffered abuse prior to 1954 and who will not have the benefit of the delayed discovery provisions albeit that their actions are based on a breach of duty. The 1939 Act provides that tort claims can be brought up to six years after the accrual of the right of action and that in the case of minors the six years will start to run from the date of majority, provided the minor had not been in the custody of a parent at the time the cause of action accrued.[169] Although the Limitation Act 1954 introduced a three-year limitation period, it also provided that, in relation to claims where the limitation period had not

---

[166] (1998) DLR (4th) 577.
[167] *Novak* involved further delay of only a year and the action was allowed to proceed under a specific provision of the British Colombian limitation statute.
[168] [1992] 89 DLR (4th) 315, *per* Hall J at 330.   [169] Ss. 2(1) and 22.

already expired, the claimant would have the benefit of the limitation period which would expire last. In 1963 the limitation regime was amended again with the introduction of delayed discovery provisions with retrospective effect, but these reforms were only to apply to three-year limitation periods. In *McDonnell v. Congregation of Christian Brothers Trustees*,[170] the House of Lords heard with some sympathy the case of a man whose experience of sexual, physical and emotional abuse from 1941–51 at school had left him with chronic psychiatric injuries resulting in his being classed as a high suicide risk. The claimant, who had been in the care of the local authority, had still been a minor at the time the 1954 legislation came into force. He therefore remained subject to the six-year limitation period which started to run in his case in 1957 and expired in 1963. The House of Lords determined that, even though the claimant's claim may have been for a breach of duty, he could not take advantage of the delayed discovery provisions introduced in 1963 because these reforms were not intended to apply to six-year limitation periods. The claimant had effectively fallen between the various reforms and his limitation period had been frozen by the Limitation Act 1954.[171]

The *McDonnell* decision has direct implications for other claims frozen by the 1954 legislation, that is, where claimants had the benefit of the pre-1954 six-year limitation period.

## 2. Declaratory remedy

A novel solution to the limitation problem was that devised by Harman J in the New Zealand case of *H v. R*.[172] As the rules of limitation barred a claim, but did not 'destroy the underlying cause of action', it was therefore possible for the High Court to issue a declaration by way of alternative remedy in order that the wrong done to the claimant could be recognised and acknowledged, even if compensation could not be awarded: 'Too often common lawyers undervalue the therapeutic and restorative value of declaratory orders.' The therapeutic value of judgment for the claimant would at least afford some measure of justice to

---

[170] [2003] UKHL 63; [2003] 3 WLR 1627.
[171] This much had been previously decided by the House of Lords and their Lordships in *McDonnell* refused to depart from that earlier decision: *Arnold v. Central Electricity Generating Board* [1988] AC 228.
[172] [1996] NZLR 299.

the abuse victim who wanted 'justice' rather than money. Such a remedy would provide a means of compromise between the divergent goals of litigation and psychiatry.

### 3. Law Commission proposals for reform

Perversely, *Stubbings v. Webb* confirms that the intentional nature of the wrong has the effect of truncating the time available in which to make a claim and deprives the claimant of the opportunity to argue that knowledge of actionability accrued beyond the limitation period or to call upon the court to use its discretion to extend time. Yet, if the defendant had negligently failed to prevent the abuse occurring, the argument of delayed discovery, or the option of requesting the court to exercise its discretion, would theoretically have been available. The decision in *Bryn Alyn*, although far more sympathetic generally to the inhibiting factors affecting the decision of abuse victims to litigate, does little to undo the impact of *Stubbings* on claims against the perpetrator as opposed to the bystander who negligently failed to intervene. A large number of cases against the perpetrators of abuse for their intentional acts (and vicarious liability for the same) remain crippled by the non-extendable three-year limitation period.

The 'illogical and surprising' effect of *Stubbings* was noted in the Court of Appeal decision of *Seymour v. Williams*, where a claim in negligence against a mother who failed to prevent her husband's abuse of their daughter was allowed to proceed under the delayed discovery provisions, yet the battery claim against the father was regarded as out of time.[173] The Court of Appeal invited the Law Commission to review the law in this area. The Commission responded to the plea for a rethink with a report published in 2001, concluding that sexual abuse claims were not so unique as to be subject to no limitation period. The defendant still required the protection of limitation statutes because of the risk of false claims of abuse.[174] Instead, it recommended a general overhaul of limitation, one of the consequences of which would be to undo the effect of *Stubbings*. The Commission recommended a core regime where a three-year time limit started to run from the date of knowledge rather than the date of accrual of the cause of action. The three-year time limit would apply to *all* claims for personal injuries whether caused by breach of duty or trespass to the person, and the

---

[173] [1995] PIQR 470.  [174] *Limitation of Actions* (2001) (Law Com 270) at 4.25.

discretion to extend time would similarly be extended to all personal injury cases, whether caused by a breach of duty or otherwise. This would have the effect of avoiding the result in *Stubbings*, as the current six-year time limit, and limitations thereon would be abandoned, and would avoid 'much arid and highly wasteful litigation turning on a distinction of no apparent principle or merit'.[175]

*Reform of constructive knowledge provisions/delayed discovery* In the context of what the claimant ought to have known, the Law Commission disapproved the artificial distinction between the claimant's 'characteristics' and 'circumstances' which the House of Lords has recently confirmed.[176] The test for constructive knowledge should take into account the circumstances (including the financial resources of the claimant where, for example, expert advice at a price might have assisted the claimant in discovering the relevant facts) and abilities (including intellectual abilities) of the claimant.

*Reform of disability provisions* The Commission also recommended that the scope of the current disability provisions should be widened. A claimant who lacks capacity by reason of mental disability to make a decision for himself on the matter in question would have time extended for at least ten years from the onset of the disability. This extension of time would apply either where the disability was active at the point that time had started to run or in cases of 'supervening disability' where onset occurred after time had started to run.[177] Furthermore, with a view to facilitating the claims of sexual abuse victims, the new definition of 'mental disability' would include claimants suffering from dissociative amnesia (provided they could show that this was the cause of their inability to bring proceedings) or any other recognised mental disorder.[178] However, the potential for perpetual extension of time under the current law for claimants under a disability would be removed. Provided there was an adult carer who could act as the claimant's representative, time would start to run ten years from the date that the adult had the relevant knowledge in order to bring a claim.[179]

---

[175] *KR and others v. Bryn Alyn Community (Holdings) Ltd (In Liquidation), Royal & Sun Alliance plc* [2003] EWCA Civ 85; [2003] 1 FCR 385 at [100].
[176] *Limitation of Actions*, 3.45.  [177] *Ibid.*, 3.126.  [178] *Ibid.*, 3.123 and 4.28.
[179] *Ibid.*, 3.130.

In July 2002, the government announced that it accepted the Law Commission's recommendations in principle, but at the time of writing no steps have been taken to amend the limitation regime. There is, however, currently a campaign to change the law along the lines of the Law Commission's proposals being spearheaded by the Association of Child Abuse Lawyers.

## Conclusion

The tendency of limitation arguments to dominate abuse litigation encourages a focus on the claimant's behaviour, meaning that the claimant's credibility and motives are implicitly brought into question before the merits of the particular claim are assessed. The claimant may understandably feel that the procedural priority afforded to the limitation inquiry implies disbelief of the substance of their allegations, reinforcing the self-blame which often characterises abuse-related trauma and undermining the therapeutic potential of civil litigation. There are strong hints of such disbelief in Lord Griffiths' judgment in *Stubbings v. Webb*, exhibited by his Lordship's incredulity as to how the claimant could not have appreciated the significance of her injury sooner than she did. The tone of the judgment alludes to the possibility that either the substance of the allegations is false or that the assertion of delayed discovery by the claimant is fraudulent. Thankfully, in the *Bryn Alyn* case the Court of Appeal redefined the injury which the claimant must have knowledge of for the cause of action to accrue under s. 14, so that the claimant is now no longer portrayed as behaving unreasonably in not appreciating the significance of their injury contemporaneously with the assault. Having said that, Auld LJ clearly indicates that given a climate which is today more receptive to abuse allegations, delay will not be tolerated as readily in the future and, therefore, the claimant's explanation for their delay will not cease to be the subject of close scrutiny.

English law's continued focus on the reasonableness or otherwise of the claimant's behaviour in bringing a claim compares unfavourably with the approach advocated in New Zealand. The refusal to engage in assessments of the normalcy or reasonableness of the claimant's conduct in *W v. Attorney General* provides an example well worth considering if the law is to offer some therapeutic value to abuse litigants.

# Conclusion

Mirroring the pattern of civil litigation connected with child abuse, the majority of this text has dealt with compensation for the harms inflicted by sexual abuse. Many have asserted that this type of abuse is unique in causing such extraordinary psychological repercussions to the abused and in being an act of such extreme heinousness on the part of the abuser. This distinctiveness has led to an assumption that the claims derived from sexual abuse merit special treatment by the courts. Whether or not these assertions of uniqueness are exaggerated,[1] this perceived exceptionality has shaped the case law which emanates from claims for compensation. It seems that this real or perceived distinctiveness has found expression in two converse judicial responses: the 'pliable' and the 'exacting' responses.

Under the exacting response the courts tend to pronounce abuse claims as unworkable; their lack of fit with the templates of traditional tort actions may prompt the rejection of claims on procedural or doctrinal grounds. The courts express themselves as unwilling to accommodate this unfortunate victim and as not being prepared to distort principle to cater for an exceptional abhorrence. There are a number of examples of this approach in the jurisprudence of England and Wales, the most well known being *Stubbings v. Webb*, in refusing to accept that intentional abuse could be articulated as a 'breach of duty' in order to provide abuse victims with access to more generous and flexible limitation periods.[2] Even the graphic exposure of the preposterous effect of this ruling in *Seymour v. Williams*[3] (imposing liability on non-perpetrator defendants such as a bystanding mother whilst allowing the perpetrator to escape liability) was not enough to avoid its later reinforcement in the cases of *A v. Hoare*[4] and *Bryn Alyn*.[5] In both these

---

[1] See Chapter 1.   [2] [1993] AC 498.   [3] [1995] PIQR 470.
[4] [2006] EWCA Civ 395; [2006] 1 WLR 2320.
[5] *KR and others v. Bryn Alyn Community (Holdings) Ltd (in liquidation), Royal & Sun Alliance plc* [2003] EWCA Civ 85; [2003] 1 FCR 385.

cases, the courts were provided with opportunities to undo the effect of *Stubbings* with the assistance of later developments in the law, including the Human Rights Act and the articulation of sexual abuse as 'breach of a non-delegable duty' in the case of *Lister v. Hesley Hall Ltd*, but neither court was willing to innovate in these directions. Suggestions that the principle from the case of *Wilkinson v. Downton* could be utilised to the benefit of abuse claimants have also fallen on stony ground.[6]

In contrast, the pliable response to the distinctiveness of sexual abuse claims manifests itself in judgments characterised by flexibility and accommodation of the abuse victim's difficulties in meeting the requirements of bringing a claim. Existing remedies may be multiplied or rendered malleable by judicial innovation in order that the victim is afforded just compensation and that opportunities to eliminate sexual abuse are maximised. The Canadian jurisdiction, in particular, and to a lesser extent the jurisdiction of New Zealand, demonstrate this pliable response. In Canada and New Zealand, abuse claims may sound in equity as breach of fiduciary duty actions when brought against the perpetrator[7] and sometimes when brought against non-perpetrators.[8] This additional remedy for the abuse victim stems from an express recognition that assault and battery offer, at best, only a crude description of the wrongs of abuse given that the psychological harm is often only detected many years after the wrong took place. The potential benefits offered by the availability of the breach of fiduciary duty action include a more truthful representation of the wrong (due to the focus being on a relationship characterised by power, control, inequality or dependence and an abuse or betrayal of that relationship), a more relaxed approach to causation and the possibility of circumventing the ruling in *Stubbings* as the wrong could then be described as a 'breach of duty'. Whatever its virtues, neither England and Wales nor Australia appears to be receptive to the breach of fiduciary action in this area.[9]

Advances in the progressive jurisdictions of Canada and New Zealand have also been made in the reshaping of limitation law to facilitate the abuse victim's claim. The Canadian courts have described the perpetrator's

---

[6] *A v. Hoare* [2006] EWCA Civ 395 at [136], although see the lower court decision in *C v. D and another* [2006] EWHC 166.
[7] *M(K) v. M(H)* [1992] 3 SCR 6; *H v. R* [1996] NZLR 299.
[8] *J v. J et al.* (1993) 102 DLR (4th) 177; *M(FS) v. Clarke* [1999] 11 WWR 301; *H(SG) v. Gorsline* [2004] 23 CCLT (3D) 65.
[9] *Sidaway v. Board of Governors of the Bethlem Royal Hospital* [1985] AC 871; *Paramasivam v. Flynn* (1998) 90 FCR 489.

enforcement of secrecy with explicit or implicit threats and bribery as fraudulent concealment so as to enable the abused claimant to access another mechanism for extending time.[10] In New Zealand the courts allow time to be extended where the claimant is affected by a disability constituted by a mental illness which inhibits the claimant from suing.[11] This jurisdiction has also rejected the requirement that the abuse victim behaves 'reasonably' for the purposes of limitation as a 'grotesque invention of the law'.[12] Castigating the objective approach to assessing the claimant's reasons for delay in coming to court, the judiciary have embraced an overtly subjective approach, which makes generous allowance for the fact that claimants are often so profoundly affected by the abuse that it is meaningless to require them to function as 'reasonable' claimants. In a similar vein, the courts of England and Wales have suggested that an assessment of the claimant's behaviour in taking time before litigating was to be undertaken from the subjective standpoint of an already damaged child,[13] but the House of Lords' ruling in *Adams v. Bracknell BC*[14] (a case not concerned with abuse but with allegedly negligent failure to diagnose dyslexia) raises some concerns for abuse claimants. First, there is the difficulty of navigating the 'circumstances'/'characteristics' divide which permeates the judgments in *Adams*; secondly, the scepticism which their Lordships directed at Mr Adams' reasons for not coming forward sooner does not bode well for the abuse claimant.

The developments in Canada and New Zealand outlined above demonstrate that with the assistance of judicial innovation, tort (and equity) can make a positive contribution in terms of compensation, standard setting, vindication and accountability for abuse claimants. What has been said above regarding the exacting response of the courts of England and Wales to abuse claims, however, is by no means intended as an unqualified condemnation of this jurisdiction's approach to compensating abuse. It is merely a comment on the law's development thus far. There are encouraging signs that things are changing for the better, not least the Court of Appeal judgment in *A v. Hoare*,[15] which expresses deep dissatisfaction with the current restrictions on limitation in cases

---

[10] *M(K) v. M(H)* [1992] 3 SCR 6.
[11] *T v. H* [1995] 3 NZLR 37; *W v. Attorney General* [1999] 2 NZLR 709. Contrast the restrictive definition of disability under the Limitation Act 1980, which requires minority or incapacity to manage affairs.
[12] *W v. Attorney General* [1999] 2 NZLR 709.
[13] *KR and others v. Bryn Alyn Community (Holdings) Ltd (in liquidation), Royal & Sun Alliance plc* [2003] EWCA Civ 85; [2003] 1 FCR 385.
[14] [2004] UKHL 29; [2005] 1 AC 76.   [15] [2006] EWCA Civ 395.

against perpetrators. Indeed, there is recent case law which indicates a far more pliable approach to compensating abuse, namely *Lister v. Hesley Hall Ltd*[16] (in extending the mantle of vicarious liability so that abuse committed by employees can potentially fall within an employer's liabilities) and aspects of the *Bryn Alyn* judgment[17] (in deciding that the knowledge of injury required in the delayed discovery provisions meant knowledge of the psychiatric harm which flowed from the abuse as opposed to knowledge of the original assault). Unfortunately, both these developments concern litigation against non-perpetrator defendants and do little to assist claimants seeking vindication or therapeutic judgments against their abuser. The real common denominator of *Lister* and *Bryn Alyn* is, however, the fact that the abuse had already been proven; the truth of the claimant's allegations of abuse was not to be the subject of judicial inquiry. This observation is perhaps a symptom of a deep rooted discomfort on the part of the judiciary with the task of assessing the veracity of abuse allegations. Indeed, it may be that the exacting approach which the law directs to abuse claims is attributable to this discomfort with abuse allegations manifested by an avoidance of the real issue: are the allegations true? Whilst such concerns are not unreasonable, that does not excuse the courts in employing a strategy of displacement, using technicalities to avoid the task of deciding on the truthfulness of the allegations, and in so doing stultifying an area of law which might otherwise be of great vindicatory and therapeutic effect to victims of abuse. If, by the time of publication, the position on limitation has been amended by the House of Lords or Parliament so as to enable abuse victims to access the court's discretion to extend time or the delayed discovery provisions in actions against perpetrators or vicarious liability actions, the doors will be opened to a great many more litigants than have been allowed to air their cases fully before the courts to date. The resulting case law will give the courts ample opportunity to follow the progressive examples of Canada and New Zealand and fulfil the law's promise of recompense, vindication and therapeutic benefits to these greatly wronged claimants.

---

[16] [2001] UKHL 22; [2002] 1 AC 215.
[17] *KR and others v. Bryn Alyn Community (Holdings) Ltd (in liquidation), Royal & Sun Alliance plc* [2003] EWCA Civ 85; [2003] 1 FCR 385.

# BIBLIOGRAPHY

## Articles

### A

Abel, R., 'A Critique of Torts' (1990) 374 CLA L Rev 785
Adams, K., 'The High Court on Vicarious Liability' (2003) 16 *Aust J of Labour Law* 10
Alpert, J., Brown, L. S. and Courtois, C. A., 'First Report of the American Psychological Association Working Group on Investigation of Memories of Childhood Abuse: Symptomatic Clients and Memories of Childhood Abuse – What the Trauma and Child Sexual Abuse Literature Tells Us' (1998) 4 *Psych Pub Pol and L* 941
Asher, R., 'Munchausen Syndrome' (1951) 1 *Lancet* 339
Ashworth, A., 'Punishment and Compensation: Victims, Offenders and the State' (1986) 6 OJLS 86
Atkin, B. and McLay, G., 'Suing Child Welfare Agencies – a Comparative View from New Zealand' (2001) 13 CFLQ 287

### B

Bartlett, P., 'Doctors as Fiduciaries: Equitable Regulation of the Doctor-patient Relationship' (1997) 5 Med L Rev 193
Bates, F., 'Policy, Bureaucracy, Tort Law and Child Sexual Abuse: Stirring the Miasma' (2001) 9(3) *Tort Law Review* 183
Bennett, D., 'Employers' Vicarious Liability: Assaults at Work and Sexual Abuse Claims' [2002] JPIL 359
Berman, L. and Rabinowicz, J., 'Bullying in School Claims' [2001] JIPL 247
Biesterveld, K., 'False Memories and the Public Policy Debate: Toward a Heightened Standard of Care for Psychotherapy' (2002) *Wis L Rev* 169
Bowman, C. G. and Mertz, E., 'A Dangerous Direction; Legal Intervention in Sexual Abuse Survivor Therapy' 109 *Harv L Rev* 549

Brandon, S. et al. 'Reported Recovered Memories of Child Sexual Abuse' (1998) 172 *British Journal of Psychology* 296 ('The Brandon Report')

Brennan, C., Third Party Liability for Child Abuse: Unanswered Questions' (2003) 15 JSWFL 23

Brennan, T. A., 'An Empirical Analysis of Accidents and Accidental Law. The Case of Medical Malpractice Law' (1992) 36 *Saint Louis University Law Journal* 823

Brown, C. G. and Mertz, E., 'A Dangerous Direction: Legal Intervention in Sexual Abuse Survivor Therapy' 109 *Harvard Law Review* 549

Buckley, R. A., 'Negligence in the Public Sphere – Is Clarity Possible?' (2000) 51 NILQ 25

# C

Carlson, B. McNutt, L. and Choi, D., 'Childhood and Adult Abuse Among Women in Primary Health Care' (2003) 18(8) *Journal of Interpersonal Violence* 924

Case, P., 'Secondary Latrogenic Harm: Claims for Psychiatric Damage Following a Death Caused by Medical Error' (2004) 67(4) *Modern Law Review* 561

Coleman, B. L., Stevens, M. J. G. and Reeder, D., 'What Makes Recovered Memory Testimony so Compelling to Jurors'? (2001) 25(4) *Law and Human Behaviour* 317

Coleman, J. L., 'Tort Law and the Demands of Corrective Justice' (1992) 67 *Indiana Law Journal* 349

# D

D'Cruz, H., 'The Social Construction of Child Maltreatment – the Role of Medical Practitioners' (2004) 4 *Journal of Social Work* 99

Des Rosiers, N., Feldthusen, B. and Hankivsky, O., 'Legal Compensation for Sexual Violence' (1998) 4 *Psychology, Public Policy and Law* 433

Doyle, C., 'Emotional Abuse of Children: Issues for Intervention' (1997) 6 *Child Abuse Review* 331

Duff, P., 'The Measure of Criminal Injuries Compensation: Political Pragmatism or Dog's Dinner?' (1998) 18 OJLS 105

# F

Feldman-Summers, S. and Pope, K., 'The Experience of "Forgetting" Childhood Abuse: A National Survey of Psychologists' (1994) 62 *Journal of Consulting and Clinical Psychology* 636

Feldthusen, B., 'The Civil Action for Sexual Battery: Therapeutic Jurisprudence?' in D. Wexler and B. Winick, *Law in a Therapeutic Key: Developments in Therapeutic Jurisprudence* (Carolina Academic Press, 1996)

Finkelhor, D. and Browne, A., 'The Traumatic Impact of Child Sexual Abuse: A Conceptualisation' (1985) 55 *American Journal of Orthopsychiatry* 541

Fleming, T., 'Admissibility of Hypnotically Refreshed or Enhanced Testimony' (1990) 77 ALR 4th 927

Flannigan, R., 'The Fiduciary Obligation' (1989) 9 OJLS 285

Flannigan, R., 'Fiduciary Regulation of Sexual Exploitation' (2000) 79 Can Bar Rev 301

Furniss, C., 'Bullying in Schools – It's Not a Crime Is It?' (2000) 12(1) *Education and the Law* 9

# G

Garbarino, J., 'The Elusive "Crime" of Emotional Abuse' (1978) 2 *Child Abuse and Neglect* 89

Giliker, P., 'Rough Justice in an Unjust World' (2002) 65 MLR 269

Glaser, D. and Prior, V., 'Is the Term Child Protection Applicable to Emotional Abuse?' (1997) 6 *Child Abuse Review* 315

Gleaves, D. and Hernandez, E., 'Recent Reformulations of Freud's Development and Abandonment of his Seduction Theory' (1999) 2 *History of Psychology* 324

Goldberg, S., 'Boston Archdiocese Threatens Bankruptcy' *Guardian*, 3 December 2002

Gore-Felton, C. et al., 'Psychologists' Beliefs and Clinical Characteristics Judging the Veracity of Childhood Sexual Abuse Memories' (2000) 31 *Professional Psychology Research and Practice* 372

Grace, E. and Vella, S., 'Vesting Mothers With Power They Do Not Have: The Non-Offending Parent in Civil Sexual Abuse Cases' (1994) 7 *Canadian Journal of Women and the Law* 184

Green, S., 'Winner Takes All' (2004) 120 LQR 566

Greer, E., 'Tales of Sexual Panic in the Legal Academy: The Assault on Reverse Incest Suits' (1998) 48 *Case Western Reserve* 513

Griffiths, D. L. and Maynihan, J. F., 'Multiple Epiphyseal Injuries in Babies (Battered Baby Syndrome)' (1963) 11 BMJ 1558

# H

Hall, M., 'After Waterhouse: Vicarious Liability and the Tort of Institutional Abuse' (2000) 22(2) *Journal of Social Welfare and Family Law* 159

Hartshorne, J. et al. '*Caparo* Under Fire': A Study into the Effects upon the Fire Service of Liability in Negligence' (2000) 21 MLR 502

Holdsworth, L., 'Is it Repressed Memory with Delayed Recall or is it False Memory Syndrome?' (1998) 22 *Law and Psychology Review* 103

## I

Iwaniec, D., 'An Overview of Emotional Maltreatment and Failure to Thrive' (1997) *Child Abuse Review* 370

## J

Jones, M. A., 'Limitation Periods and Plaintiffs under a Disability – a Zealous Protection?' (1995) 14 CJQ 258

## K

Keenan, C., 'A Plea Against Tort Liability for Child Protection Agencies in England and Wales' (2003) 42 *Washburn Law Journal* 235

Kempe, R. S., Kempe, H. et al., 'The Battered Child Syndrome' (1962) 181 JAMA 17

Kidner, R., 'Vicarious Liability: For Whom Should the Employer be Liable?' [1995] 15 LS 47

Kisch, W., 'From the Couch to the Bench: How Should the Legal System Respond to Recovered Memories of Childhood Sexual Abuse?' (1996) 5 *American University Journal of Gender and the Law* 207

## L

Lamm, J., 'Easing Access to the Courts for Incest Victims: Towards an Equitable Application of the Delayed Discovery Rule' (1991) 100 YLJ 2189

Larzelere, R., 'A Review of the Outcomes of Parental Use of Nonabusive or Customary Physical Punishment' (1996) 98 *Paediatrics* 824

Linden, A. B., 'Tort as Ombudsman' (1973) 51 *Canadian Bar Review* 155

Lyon, C., 'Legal Developments Following the Cleveland Report in England – A Consideration of Some Aspects of the Children's Bill' (1989) JSWL 200

## M

Macmartin, C., 'Judicial Constructions of the Seriousness of Child Sexual Abuse' (2004) 36 *Canadian Journal of Behavioural Science* 66

McClure, R., Davis, P., Meadow, R. and Sibert, J., 'Epidemiology of Munchausen Syndrome by Proxy, Non-accidental Poisoning and Non-Accidental Suffocation' (1996) *Archives of Disease in Childhood* 57

McCullough, M., 'Freud's Seduction Theory and Its Rehabilitation: A Saga of One Mistake After Another' (2001) 5 *Review of General Psychology* 3

McNally, R. J., 'Progress and Controversy in the Study of Posttraumatic Stress, Disorder' (2003) 54 *Annual Review of Psychology* 229

Marwit, S. J., 'Reliability of Diagnosing Complicated Grief: A Preliminary Investigation' (1996) 64 *Journal of Consulting and Clinical Psychology* 563

Meadow, R., 'Munchausen Syndrome by Proxy: The Hinterland of Child Abuse' (1977) *Lancet* 343

Meiers, D., 'Criminal Injuries Compensation: The New Regime' (2001) JPIL 371

Mertz, E. and Lonsway, K., 'The Power of Denial: Individual and Cultural Constructions of Child Sexual Abuse' (1998) 92 NW UL Rev 1415

Mezey, G. and Robins, I., 'Usefulness and Validity of Post-traumatic Stress Disorder as a Psychiatric Category' (2001) BMJ 561

Miller, J., 'Compensation for Mental Trauma Injuries in New Zealand.' (1998) *Australian Journal of Disaster and Trauma Studies* 1

Mullender, R., 'Corrective Justice, Distributive Justice and the Law of Negligence' (2001) 17 PN 35

Mullis, A., 'The Abuse Continues? *Stubbings and Others* v. *UK* in the ECHR' (1997) 9 CFLQ 291

Myers, J., 'New Era of Skepticism Regarding Children's Credibility' (1995) 1 *Psychology Public Policy and Law* 387

## N

Nabors, K. L., 'The Statute of Limitations: A Procedural Stumbling Block in Civil Incestuous Abuse Suits' (1990) 14 *Law and Psych Rev* 153

## O

Olafson, E., Corwin, D. and Summit, R., 'Modern History of Child Sexual Abuse Awareness: Cycles of Discovery and Suppression' (1993) 17 *Child Abuse and Neglect* 7

Olio, K. and Cornell, W., 'The Façade of Scientific Documentation: A Case Study of Richard Ofshe's Analysis of the Paul Ingram Case' (1998) 4 *Psychology Public Policy and Law* 1182

## P

Partlett, D., 'Recovered Memories of Child Sexual Abuse and Liability' (1998) 4 *Psychology, Public Policy and Law* 1253

Persaud, R., 'Keeping Mum over Child Abuse' (2005) 330 BMJ 152

Pope, H. G. et al., 'Attitudes Towards DSM IV Dissociative Disorders Diagnoses Among Board-Certified American Psychiatrists' (1999) 156 *American Journal of Psychiatry* 321

Porat, A. and Stein, A., 'Indeterminate Causation and Apportionment of Damages: An Essay on *Holtby, Allen*, and *Fairchild*' (2003) 23 OJLS 667

# R

Raitt, F. and Zeedyk, S., 'Mothers on Trial: Discourses of Cot Death and Munchausen's Syndrome by Proxy' (2004) 12 *Feminist Legal Studies* 257

Reagan, T., 'Scientific Consensus on Memory Repression and Recovery' (1999) 51 *Rutgers Law Review* 175

Renner, K. E., Alksnis, C. and Parks, I., 'The Standard of Social Justice as a Research Process' (1977) *Canadian Psychology* 38

Richardson, L. B., 'Missing Pieces of Memory: A Rejection of the "Type" Classifications and a Demand for a More Subjective Approach' (1999) 11 *St Thomas Law Review* 515

Rind, B., Tromovitch, P. and Bauserman, R., 'A Meta Analytic Examination of Assumed Properties of Child Sexual Abuse Using College Samples' (1998) 124(1) *Psychological Bulletin* 22

Rogers, W. V. H., 'Tort Law and Child Abuse: An Interim View from England' (1994) 3 *Tort Law Journal* 17

Rosenfeld, A., 'The Statute of Limitations Barrier in Childhood Sexual Abuse Cases' (1989) 12 *Harvard Women's Law Journal* 206

# S

Schwartz, G., 'Reality in the Economic Analysis of Tort: Does Tort Law Really Deter?' (1994) 42 UCLCA L Rev 377

Soothill, K. and Francis, B., 'Moral Panics and the Aftermath: A Study of Incest' (2002) 24 JSWFL 1

Smart, C., 'A History of Ambivalence and Conflict in the Discursive Construction of the "Child Victim" of Sexual Abuse' (1999) 8(3) *Social and Legal Studies* 391

Sutherland, P. K. and Henderson, D. J., 'Expert Psychiatrists and Comments on Witness Credibility' available at www.smith-lawfirm.com/sutherland_article.html.

# T

Trenwith, A., 'The Empire Strikes Back: Human Rights and the Piccairn Proceedings' (2003) 7(2) *Journal of South Pacific Law* 1

Trindade, F. A., 'Intentional Infliction of Purely Mental Distress' (1986) 6(2) OJLS 219

## V

Vines, P., 'Schools' Responsibility for Teachers' Sexual Assault: Non-Delegable Duty and Vicarious Liability' [2003] *Melbourne University Law Review* 22

Vize, C. M. and Cooper, P. J., 'Sexual Abuse in Patients with Eating Disorders, Patients with Depression and Normal Controls – a Comparative Analysis' (1995) 167 *British Journal of Psychiatry* 80

## W

Wattam, C., 'The Social Construction of Child Abuse for Practical Policy Purposes' (1996) CFLQ 189

Weinrib, E., 'The Fiduciary Obligation' (1975) 25 UTLJ 1

Weir, T., 'Making it More Likely v. Making it Happen' (2002) 61 CLJ 519

Wilkinson-Ryan, T., 'Admitting Mental Health Evidence to Impeach the Credibility of a Sexual Assault Complainant' (2004) 153 *University of Pennsylvania Law Review* 1372

Williams, L., 'Recall of Childhood Trauma: A Prospective Study of Women's Memories of Child Sexual Abuse' (1994) 62 *Journal of Consulting and Clinical Psychology* 1167

Wilson, E., 'Suing for Lost Childhood: Child Sexual Abuse, the Delayed Discovery Rule and the Problem of Finding Justice for Adult Survivors of Child Abuse' (2003) 12 UCLA 145

Witting, C. 'Tort Liability for Intended Mental Distress' (1998) 21(1) UNSWLJ 55

Wright, J., 'Right, Justice and Tort Law' in D. G. Owen (ed.) *Philosophical Foundations of Tort Law* (OUP, 1995)

## Z

Zoltek-Jick, R., 'For Whom Does the Bell Toll? Repressed Memory and Challenges for the Law' in P. S. Appelbaum, L. A. Uyehara and M. R. Elin, *Trauma and Memory: Clinical and Legal Controversies* (OUP, 1997)

## Books/Reports

### A

Allsop, J. and Mulcahy, L. *Regulating Medical Work* (OUP, 1996)

Appelbaum, P. S., Uyehara, L. A. and Elin, M. R., *Trauma and Memory: Clinical and Legal Controversies* (OUP, 1997)

Ashenden, S., *Governing Child Sexual Abuse: Negotiating the Boundaries of Public and Private, Law and Science* (Routledge, 2004)

## B

Bagley, C., *Child Sexual Abuse and Mental Health in Adolescents and Adults* (Avenbury, 1995)

Bannon, M. and Carter, Y. (ed.), *Protecting Children from Abuse and Neglect in Primary Care* (OUP, 2003)

Bass, E. and Davies, L., *The Courage to Heal* (Harper Collins, 1998)

Briere, J., *Child Abuse Trauma: Theory and Treatment of Lasting Effects* (Sage, 1992)

Brown, A. and Barrett, D., *Knowledge of Evil: Child Prostitution and Child Sexual Abuse in Twentieth Century England* (Willan Publishing, 2002)

Brown, P. et al., *Memory, Trauma Treatment and the Law* (1998)

## C

Cane, P., *Atiyah's Accidents, Compensation and the Law* (Widenfield and Nicolson, 1990)

Cawsom, P. et al., *Child Maltreatment in the UK: A Study of the Prevalence of Child Abuse and Neglect* (NSPCC, 2000)

Corby, B., Doig, A. and Roberts, V., *Public Inquiries into Abuse of Children in Residential Care* (Jessica Kingsley Publishers, 2001)

## D

Department of Health, *Working Together to Safeguard Children* (Department for Education and Employment, 1999)

Di Mambro, L., *Butterworths Law of Limitation* (Butterworths, 2000)

## E

Exall, G., *Munkman on Damages for Personal Injuries and Death* (11th edn, Butterworths, 2004)

## F

Fleming, J., *The Law of Torts* (9th edn, LBC Infro Services, 1998)

## G

Garbarino, J., Guttmann, E. and Seeley, J., *The Psychologically Battered Child* (Jossey Bass, 1986)

Grace, E. and Vella, S., *Civil Liability for Sexual Abuse and Violence in Canada* (Butterworths, 2000)

Grubb, A., *The Law of Tort* (Butterworths, 2002)

## H

Hoyano, L., Davies, R., Margan, R. and Maitland, L. *The Admissibility and Sufficiency of Evidence in Cases of Child Abuse* (Home Office, 1999)
Hyams, O., *Law of Education* (Sweet & Maxwell, 1998)

## I

Ison, T. G., *The Forensic Lottery* (Staples Press, 1967)

## J

Janet, P., *L'Automise Psychologique* (Felix Alcon, 1989)
Jones, M. A., *Textbook on Torts* (OUP, 2002)
Jones, M. A. and Case, P., *Claims for Pychiatic Damage* (Tottel, 2006)

## K

Katz, A, Buchanan, A. and Bream, V., *Bullying in Britain: Testmonies from Teenagers* (Young Voice, 2001)
Kelly, L., Regan, L. and Burton, S., *An Exploratory Study of the Prevalence of Sexual Abuse in a Sample of 16–21 Year Olds* (University of North London, 1991)
Kempe, R. S., and Kempe, H., *The Common Secret: Sexual Abuse of Adolescents* (W. H. Freeman, 1984)
Kitzinger, J., *Framing Abuse: Media Influence and Public Understanding of Sexual Violence Against Children* (Pluto Press, 2004)

## L

Loftus, E. and Ketcham, K., *The Myth of Repressed Memory and Allegations of Sexual Abuse* (St Martins, 1996)
Lyon, C., *Child Abuse* (Jordans 2003)

## M

McGregor, H., *McGregor on Damages* (Sweet & Maxwell, 2003)
Marr, N. and Field, T., *Bullycide: Death at Playtime* (Success Unlimited, 2000)
Masson, J. M., *The Assault on Truth: Freud's Suppression of the Seduction Theory* (Pocket Books, 1984)
Meiers, D., *State Compensation for Criminal Injuries* (Blackstone Press, 1997)

## N

Neeb, J. W. W. and Harper, S. J., *Civil Action for Sexual Abuse* (Butterworths, 1994)
Neil, B. and Rampton, R. *Duncan and Neill on Defamation* (2nd edn, Butterworths, 1983)

## P

Palfreyman, D. and Warner, D. (eds), *Higher Education Law* (2nd edn, Jordans, 2002)
Parkes, C. M., Laungani, P. and Young, B., *Death and Bereavement Across Cultures* (1997) (Routledge, London)
Parton, N., *The Politics of Child Abuse* (Macmillan, 1985)
Prime, T. and Scanlan, G., *The Law of Limitation* (OUP, 2001)

## R

Ruff, A., *Education Law: Text, Cases and Materials* (Butterworths, 2002)

## S

Salmond, J., *Salmond on Torts* (1st edn, 1907)
Stapleton, J., *Disease and the Compensation Debate* (OUP, 1986)
Stephenson, G., *Torts Sourcebook* (Cavendish, 2002)

## T

Taylor, C., *Court Licensed Abuse: Patriarchal Lore and the Legal Response to Intrafamilial Abuse of Children.* (Peter Lang, 2004)
Tettenborn, A., Wilbey QC, D. and Bennet, D., *The Law of Damages* (Butterworths, 2003)

## W

Wexler, D. and Winick, B., *Law in a Therapeutic Key: Developments in Therapeutic Jurisprudence.* (Carolina Academic Press, 1996)

## Y

Yates, A., *Sex Without Shame* (William Morrow, 1978)
Young, A., *The Harmony of Illusions – Inventing Post Traumatic Stress Disorder* (Princeton University Press, 1995)

# INDEX

abuse of position of trust, 34
abuse of process, 247
abuse victims. *See* victims
access to justice
   false accusations of abuse, 160–161
   and limitation periods, 59–60
accountability, and tort litigation, 3, 43–45, 226
accused. *See* litigation by accused
admissibility of evidence
   disciplinary proceedings, 180
   hypnosis, 206
   recovered memories, 24
      English law, 201–206
      US law, 206–208
adoption, iatrogenic neglect, 88, 151
adult victims, vicarious liability, 124–125
adversarial process, effect, 47
alcoholism, 223, 231, 233, 237
Alpert, J. 18
American Medical Association, 203
Aristotle, 37
assault. *See* trespass to the person
Association of Child Abuse Lawyers, 284
Atiyah, Patrick, 43
Australia
   breach of non-delegable duties, 106
   employers' negligence, 84
   false accusations of abuse, 151, 180–182
      defamation actions, 186
   limitation periods, extension, 269–270
   post-traumatic stress disorder, 221
   pure psychiatric harm, compensation, 216–217

Australia (cont.)
   remoteness of damage, 232–233
   secondary victims, 71
   tort litigation, 49–50
   trespass or negligence, 57
   vicarious liability, 111, 118–120
Australian Psychological Society, 203
avoidance behaviours, 24, 279–280

bankruptcy, shield, 53
battered child syndrome, 2, 27
battery. *See* trespass to the person
belief, right to, 5, 6
Bichard Inquiry, 82
borderline personality disorder
   credibility of claimants, 225
   diagnostic criteria, 222–223
   effect of child abuse, 219
   generally, 222–223
   v post-traumatic stress disorder, 223
Bowman, C. G., 177
Brandon Report, 23, 202–206, 224
breach of confidence
   abuse accusations, 164–166
   public interest defence, 166
breach of fiduciary duty
   actions against non-perpetrators, 104–105
   actions against perpetrators, 54, 66–69
   and battery, 56–58, 60–61
   causation rules, 66, 234–235
   contributory negligence, 235
   limitation periods, 255–258
   meaning, 66–69, 256–257
   non-tortious action, 108
   quantum of damages, 66
   use of remedy, 286

breach of non-delegable duties, 105–107, 108
breach of statutory duty
  actions against non-perpetrators, 75–76
  false accusations of abuse, 155–157
  strict liability, 76
Briere, J., 22
British Medical Association, 167–168, 171
Browne, A., 18
bulimia, 173, 224
bullying
  beyond school premises, 95–96
  defendants, 11–12
  definition, 10
  form of physical abuse, 10–12
  identification, 10–11
  policies, 98
  standard of care, 96–99
burden of proof
  child abuse, 200–208
  civil v criminal actions, 45, 201
  previous convictions, 201
  recovered memories, 201–206
bystander claims
  criminal injury compensation, 135–138
  forms of actions, 69–71

Canada
  alcoholism, compensation, 237
  battery, 129
  breach of fiduciary duty, 104–105, 142
  Charter of Rights, 49
  criminal abuse trials, 48
  damages, 240
  employers' liability in negligence, 78
  false accusations of abuse, 151, 182–183
  fiduciary obligations, 68–69, 256
  iatrogenic neglect, 93, 100, 102
  insurance policies, 129
  legal responses to abuse, 286–287
  limitation periods, extension, 254, 260, 268, 273–275, 280, 286
  malicious prosecutions, 193
  punitive damages, 242
  recovered memories, 202
  sexual abuse discourse, 13
  substance abuse, 223
  tort litigation, 49–50
  trespass or negligence, 57
  vicarious liability, 108, 111, 117–118, 120–123, 124, 125–126
  *Wilkinson v. Downton* actions, 62, 64, 213–214
Canning, Angela, 44–45
categories of abuse
  emotional abuse, 4, 14, 20, 132
  generally, 3–15
  legal concepts, 3
  neglect. *See* neglect
  physical abuse, 4, 5–12, 19–20
  sexual abuse. *See* sexual abuse
Catholic Church
  proliferation of civil claims, 53
  vicarious liability, 108, 111
causation
  and claimants' criminality, 229–231
  breach of fiduciary duty, 66, 234–235
  'but for test,' 225–226
  bystander claims, 135–138
  *Clunis* argument, 229–231
  criminal injury compensation, 135
  crumbling skull rule, 233–234
  delayed recognition, 266–268
  diffused accountability, 3, 226
  *Fairchild* approach, 227–229, 235, 237, 242
  generally, 225–235
  legal approaches, 35
  material contribution test, 226–228
  *novus actus interveniens*, 229–231
  proving causation in fact, 225–226
  psychoanalytical approaches, 34–35
  remoteness of damage, 231–233
  thin skull rules, 233
child abuse
  categories, 3–15
  context, 25–27
  damage. *See* damage
  evolving social construction, 1–3
  extent of problem, 24–25
  false accusations. *See* false accusations of abuse

# INDEX

child abuse (cont.)
  judicial scepticism, 177, 262, 284, 288
  legal concepts, 3
  litigation. *See* civil litigation; tort litigation
child pornography, 12
child protection
  diffused accountability, 3, 226
  margins of appreciation, 159
  onslaught of regulatory reforms, 31–33
child protection registers
  categories of abuse, 4
  decline in registration, 30
  physical abuse statistics, 8
  sexual abuse statistics, 12
  sexual offenders, 81–82
childcare institutions
  abuse in, 26–27
  bankruptcy shield, 53
  inspection, 31–32
  last resort, 31, 42
  and paedophilia, 112
ChildLine, 27
childminding, regulation, 32–33
Children's Commissioner, 33
children's rights
  judicial recognition, 34
  UN Convention 1969, 4, 8
civil litigation
  adequacy of remedy, 74
  and child abuse, 52–54
  v criminal injury compensation, 53–54, 131–141
  escalation of claims, 35–36, 53–54
  functions, 36–47, 141–142
  issues in English system, 141–143
  judicial responses to abuse claims, 285–288
  judicial scepticism, 177, 262, 284, 288
Clark, Sally, 44–45
Cleveland case, 2, 28–31, 44, 58
Cleveland Inquiry, 27, 171
Climbié Inquiry, 167
*Clunis* argument, 229–231
Clwyd County Council, 47
Colwell, Maria, 27

Commission for Healthcare Regulatory Excellence (CHRE), 180
Commission for Social Care Inspection, 31–32
compensation
  apportionment, 235–238
  contributions, 236
  corrective justice, 37
  crumbling skull rule, 233–234
  distributive justice, 38–40
  and just satisfaction, 74–75
  'lifestyle' damage, 233
  physical damage, 208–209
  psychiatric damage, 209–210
  pure psychiatric harm, 210–215
    classification of illnesses, 218–224
    intentional wrongs, 211–212
    negligence claims, 214–215
    primary/secondary victim dichotomy, 214–215
    recognised disorder requirement, 212–214, 215–217
    role of expert evidence, 218
    *Wllkinson v. Downton* actions, 212–214
  purpose of tort litigation, 36–40, 198
  symbolic force, 37
  thin skull rules, 233
compensation culture, 52
confidentiality
  and accusations of abuse, 164–166
  medical profession, 164–166
    doctor/patient relationship, 91
    v duty to report abuse, 166–168
  psychiatrist/patient, 79
  United States, 175
contract, compensation, 215
contributory negligence, 235
Convention on the Rights of the Child, 4, 8
corporal punishment
  form of abuse, 5–8
  psychiatric injuries, 19
  reasonable chastisement, 6–8
corrective justice
  concept, 37–38
  v distributive justice, 39–40
  and duty of care test, 39

corroboration, recovered memories, 208, 275
credibility, claimants, 43–44, 225
Criminal Injuries Compensation Authority, 132
criminal injury compensation
   abuse claims, 139–141
   adequacy of remedy, 74
   appeals and reviews, 132, 134
   bystander claims, 135–138
   causation, 135
   ceiling, 133
   v civil actions, 53–54, 131–141
   and convictions, 139
   crimes of violence, 138–139
   intra-family crimes, 139
   law reform, 131
   mental injuries, 134–135
   pure psychiatric harm, 211
   quantum, 37, 132–133
   requirements, 132
   schemes, 131
   time limits, 134
criminal prosecutions
   burden of proof, 45, 201
   and criminal injury compensation, 139
   fines v civil damages, 242
   and recovered memories, 206
Criminal Records Bureau, 82
crumbling skull rule, 233–234

damage
   child abuse, 16–24, 208–225
   crumbling skull rule, 233–234
   foreseeability, 231–232
   'lifestyle' damage, 233
   physical damage, 208–209
   psychiatric damage, 209–210
      See also psychiatric injuries
   remoteness, 231–233
   thin skull rules, 233
damages. See compensation; quantum of damages
day care, regulation, 32–33
declaratory orders, and limitation periods, 281–282

defamation
   damages for abuse allegations, 186
   evidence of publication, 187–188
   false accusations of abuse, 145, 185–192
   innocent dissemination defence, 187
   libel, 185
   loss of earnings, 239
   malice, 178, 188, 189, 190–192
   qualified privilege defence, 188–190
   slander, 185
defensive practice
   and false accusations of abuse, 150, 152, 153–154, 196–197
   and tort litigation, 86–87
delay
   See also limitation periods
   delayed discovery doctrine, 260–276
   and public awareness of abuse, 28, 267, 284
   and right to fair trial, 75, 276–277
   therapeutic delay, 280
delegation
   breach of non-delegable duties, 105–107, 108, 257
   vicarious liability, 115–116, 123
depression, 237, 269
deterrence, and tort litigation, 40–42
disability
   dissociative amnesia, 21–23, 283
   and limitation periods, 252–253, 260, 279–280
   law reform, 283
   meaning, 252–253
disciplinary proceedings
   appeals, 180
   defective medical evidence, 36, 163–164, 178–180
   and malicious prosecutions, 193
   and recovered memories, 202
   and tort litigation, 41
disqualification from working with children, 80–82
dissociative amnesia, 21–23, 283
distorted perceptions, victims, 23, 268, 284
distributive justice
   compensation, 38–40

distributive justice (cont.)
  v corrective justice, 39–40
  and vicarious liability, 39
doctor-patient relationship, 67–68, 91, 256–257
drug dependency
  effect of abuse, 223
  remoteness of damage, 231, 233
Duff, P., 133
duty of care
  and corrective justice, 39
  false accusations of abuse, 145–146, 168–170, 196
  floodgate argument, 77, 88
  iatrogenic neglect, 84
  legal approach, 35
  local authorities, 89–90, 145–146
  medical profession
    accused as non-patients, 168–170
    repressed memories, 172–174
  negligence actions, 77
  non-delegable duties, 105–107, 115–116, 123
  pregnancies, 152
  tripartite test, 39
  to victims' relatives, 70
  will drafting, 152, 153–154
dyslexia, 287

eating disorders, 224
education
  bullying. See bullying
  educational neglect, 15, 87–88
  floodgates of educational malpractice, 155
  iatrogenic neglect, 94–99
  non-delegable duties, 106
  and remoteness of damage, 231
emotional abuse
  criminal injury compensation, 132
  nature, 14
  psychiatric injuries, 20
  statistics, 4
employers
  negligence liability for abusers, 77–79
  vetting standards, 79–84
  vicarious liability. See vicarious liability

employment status, 109–110
entrepreneur test, 109
equal treatment, and limitation periods, 59–60
Erichsen, John, 219
estoppel, and limitation periods, 253–254
European Convention on Human Rights
  See also specific rights
  and child abuse, 3
  corporal punishment, 5, 6–7
  use of jurisprudence, 72
*ex turpi non causa oritur*, 230
exemplary damages, 48, 241
exhibitionism, 12
expert evidence
  Cleveland Case, 44
  and compensation for pure psychiatric harm, 218
  defective evidence, disciplinary proceedings, 178–180
  distrust, 44–45
  and extension of limitation periods, 268–270
  witness immunity, 92, 163–164

fabricated or induced illness (FII), 8–10, 20
fair trial
  access to justice, 59–60, 160–161
  and delay, 75, 245
  false accusations of abuse, 161
false accusations of abuse
  breach of statutory duty, 155–157
  comparative law, 180–184
  damage, 144
  defamation actions, 185–192
  'East Berkshire claim', 147
  forms of actions, 144–145
  good faith, 150, 161, 183, 191
  Human Rights Act claims, 157–161, 178
    access to courts, 160–161
    respect for family life, 157–160
  intentional infliction of psychiatric harm, 194–195
  judicial approaches, 145, 195–196
  judicial review, 184
  legal representation, 158

false accusations of abuse (cont.)
  by local authorities, 145–164
  malicious prosecution actions, 192–194
  by medical profession, 164–180
  misfeasance in public office, 162
  negligence
    defensive practice reasoning, 150, 152, 153–154, 196–197
    'Dewsbury claim', 147
    foreseeability, 148–149
    implanting false memories, 172–174
    JD v. East Berkshire Community NHS Trust, 146–154
    justice, fairness and reasonableness, 149–151, 170, 181
    by local authorities, 145–155
    by medical profession, 168–178
    'Oldham claim', 146
    proximity, 148–149, 168–170, 184
    standards of care, 154–155, 171–172
  pandemics, 58
  and standard of proof, 150
  types of claims, 144
  witness immunity, 163–164
*false negatives*, 3
*false positives*, 2
family separation, 25–26
feminism, 17
fiduciary duty. *See* breach of fiduciary duty
Finkelhor, D., 18
Flannigan, R., 66
floodgate arguments, 77, 88, 155, 211
foreseeability
  and awareness of abuse, 27–28
  criminal injury compensation, 136
  damage, 231–232
  and false accusations of abuse, 148–149
  thin skull rules, 233
forms of actions
  against non-perpetrators. *See* third-party defendants
  against perpetrators, 54–71
  bystander family members, 69–71
  choice, 35
  and limitation periods, 24, 101, 255–258

litigation by accused, 144–145
  by victims, 54–131
foster parents
  iatrogenic neglect, 90, 101–104
  vicarious liability for, 110–111
fraud, and limitation periods, 253–254, 260
Freud, Sigmund, 16–17, 30

General Medical Council
  disciplinary proceedings, 179–180
  disclosure of sexual abuse, 91
  duty to report abuse, 166, 168
  and false accusations of abuse, 153
Greer, E., 46, 178

harassment, 65, 211
Harper, S. J., 55, 255
healthcare professionals. *See* medical profession
Higgs, Marietta, 28
home abuse
  division of families, 25–26
  and public policy, 25–26
hospital trusts, iatrogenic neglect, 93–94
House of Commons Home Affairs Committee, 116
Human Rights Act 1998
  and false accusations of abuse, 157–161, 178
  impact on abuse litigation, 49
  non-retrospectivity, 60
  statutory interpretation compatibility, 60
  third-party liability under, 72–75
hypnosis, 205–206

iatrogenic neglect
  abuse by children in need, 88
  adoption agencies, 88, 151
  educational neglect, 87–88
  floodgate argument, 88
  foster home abuse, 90, 101–104
  generally, 84–99
  heath care professionals, 91–92
  hospital/NHS trusts, 93–94
  human rights actions, 89
  limitation periods, 259–280

iatrogenic neglect (cont.)
  local authorities, 84–90
  meaning, 72
  non-intervening parents, 101–104, 282
  police and correctional services, 99–101
  pure psychiatric harm, compensation, 214–215
  schools and teachers, 94–99
  social workers, 91–92
  *X v. Bedfordshire County Council*, 85–90
incest
  and public opinion, 28
  public policy, 26
inhuman or degrading treatment
  ECHR, 6–7, 54, 73
  local authorities, 89
  misfeasance, 107
  positive obligations, 73
insurance
  'accidental injuries', 127–128
  and actions by victims, 126–131
  'bodily injuries', 126–127
  and choice of defendants, 54
  construction of policies, 126–128
  *contra proferentem* rule, 130
  and extension of limitation periods, 277
  insured non-perpetrators, 129–131
  insured perpetrators, 128–129
  public policy, 128
  and vicarious liability, 130–131
intentional infliction of psychiatric harm. *See Wilkinson v. Downton* actions
international law, and child abuse, 3–4

*JD v. East Berkshire Community NHS Trust*
  comment, 151–154
  defensive practice reasoning, 150, 152, 153–154
  false accusations of abuse, 146–154
  foreseeability and proximity, 148–149
  justice, fairness and reasonableness, 149–151
  reasoning by analogy, 147–148, 196
  respect for family life, 159

judicial review
  adequacy of remedy, 74
  false accusations of abuse, 184
juries, and hypnosis, 205
just satisfaction, ECHR, 74–75

Kempe, R. S. & H., 2, 27

Lamm, J., 274, 279
language, and tort litigation, 47–49
legal representation, 158
libel, 185
'lifestyle' damage, 233
limitation periods
  arbitrariness, 245
  battery, 56, 58
  choice of actions, 24, 101, 255–258
    breach of fiduciary duty, 255–258
    *Wilkinson v. Downton* actions, 63–64, 258
  declaratory remedies, 281–282
  delayed discovery doctrine
    Canadian approach, 260, 268, 273–275
    and claimants' character, 270–273
    experts' role, 268–270
    generally, 260–276
    issues, 261
    judicial scepticism, 262, 284
    law reform, 283–284
    and nature of disorder, 274–276
    New Zealand approach, 266–267, 273, 284
    objectivity of test, 270–273
    recognition of causation, 266–268
    significant injuries, 262–265
    US approach, 275–276
  effect, 246, 281
  extension, 35
    avoidance behaviour, 279–280
    battery claims, 252–254
    delayed discovery, 260–276
    disability, 252–253, 260, 279–280, 283
    equity, 257, 276
    fraudulent concealment, 253–254, 260
    judicial discretion, 276–280

limitation periods (cont.)
  negligence, 260
  therapeutic delay, 280
 human rights challenges, 59–60
 issues, 286–287
 law reform, 61, 244, 282–284
 legal framework, 244–248
 Limitation Act 1939, 280–281
 Limitation Act 1954, 280
 Limitation Act 1980, 247–248
 negligence actions, 77, 259–280
 Northern Ireland, 255
 and post-traumatic stress disorder, 221–222, 265, 270
 potency of limitation defence, 48, 244–245
 preliminary issues, 246–247, 277
 procedures, 246–247, 250
 and public awareness, 28, 267, 284
 rationales, 38, 245–246
 and recovered memories, 24, 202
 Scotland, 255, 264
 *Stubbings v. Webb*, 248–251
   circumventing, 255–258
 third-party defendants, 258–280
 torts, 247–248, 280–281
   exception, 248
 two-tier system, 247–248
 vicarious liability, 258–259
 *Wilkinson v. Downton* actions, 63–64, 258
Linden, A. M., 43
List 99, 80, 82
litigation. *See* civil litigation; litigation by accused; tort litigation
litigation by accused
 against local authorities, 145–164
   Human Rights challenges, 157–161
   misfeasance in public office, 162
   negligence, 145–155
   witness immunity, 163–164
 against medical profession, 164–180
   negligence, 168–178
 comparative law, 180–184
 damage, 144
 defamation, 185–192
 forms of actions, 144–145

litigation by accused (cont.)
 intentional infliction of psychiatric harm, 194–195
 judicial review, 184
 malicious prosecution actions, 192–194
 types of claims, 144
local authorities
 duty of care, 89–90
 false accusations of abuse, 145–164
 foster home abuse, 90, 101–104
 iatrogenic neglect, 84–90
 *X v. Bedfordshire County Council*, 85–90, 145–146
London bombings, 131
loss of earnings, 239

malice, 162, 178, 188, 189, 190–192, 211
malicious prosecution actions
 burden of proof, 145
 and disciplinary proceedings, 193
 false accusation of abuse, 192–194
 and recovered memories, 178
margins of appreciation, 159
Meadow, Roy, 8, 44, 93, 163–164
media
 and abuse inquiries, 27–31
 moral panics, 28–29
medical profession
 confidentiality obligations, 164–166
  v duty to report abuse, 166–168
 doctor-patient relationship, 67–68, 91, 256–257
 false accusations of abuse, 164–180
  accused as non-patients, 168–170
  disciplinary proceedings, 178–180
  human rights challenges, 178
  implanting false memories, 172–174, 177, 204–206
  negligence, 168–178
  policy considerations, 170
  proximity, 181
  standards of care, 171–172
 patient autonomy, 174
 third-party liability, 168–170, 174–178
  Australia, 180–182
  negligence actions, 91–92
 training in child abuse, 172

## INDEX

memory hardening, 205
mental disability. *See* disability
Mertz, E., 177
mesothelioma, 227, 229, 235
misfeasance in public office
  actions against non-perpetrators, 107–108
  false accusations of abuse, 162
  forms, 107–108, 162
  malice, 162
  meaning of public office, 162
moral panics, 28–29
motor insurance, 41
Mullender, R., 39–40
Mullis, A., 59
multidisciplinary approaches, 2–3, 171
multiple personality disorders, 224
Munchausen syndrome by proxy, 5, 8

Neeb, J. W. W., 55, 255
neglect
  corrective justice, 38
  criminal injury compensation, 132
  educational neglect, 15
  iatrogenic neglect. *See* iatrogenic neglect
  nature of abuse, 14–15
  statistics, 4
negligence
  actions against non-perpetrators, 76–104
  actions by accused, 145
  benchmarks by regulatory bodies, 33
  breach of confidence, 165
  burden of proof, 201
  duty of care, 77
  employers
    liability, 77–79
    vetting standards, 79–84
  false accusation of abuse
    defensive practice reasoning, 150, 152, 153–154, 196–197
    foreseeability, 148–149
    implanting false memories, 172–174
    *JD v. East Berkshire NHS Trust*, 146–154
    justice, fairness and reasonableness, 149–151, 170, 181
    by local authorities, 145–155
    by medical profession, 168–178
    proximity, 148–149, 168–170, 181, 184
    standards of care, 154–155, 171–172
  hospital/NHS trusts, 93–94
  iatrogenic abuse/neglect, 84–99
  limitation periods, 77, 251, 259–280
  local authorities, 84–90
  medical profession, 91–92, 168–178
  non-intervening parents, 101–104, 282
  police and correctional services, 99–101
  primary and secondary victims, 76, 214–215
  pure psychiatric harm, compensation, 214–215
  requirement for actions, 76–77
  schools and teachers, 94–99
  social workers, 91–92
  transferred negligence, 173–174
  witness immunity, 92
nervous shock, 219
New Zealand
  Accident Compensation Scheme, 50
  declaratory orders, 281–282
  definition of homicide, 195
  disability, meaning, 253
  false accusations of abuse, 151, 162, 183–184, 194–195
  fiduciary obligations, 69
  legal responses to abuse, 286–287
  limitation periods, extension, 266–267, 273, 281–282, 284, 287
  punitive damages, 241–242
  tort litigation, 49–50
  trespass or negligence, 58
  vicarious liability, 110–111
  *Wilkinson v. Downton* actions, 194–195
NHS trusts
  iatrogenic neglect, 93–94
  non-delegable duties, 106
non-intervening parents, 47, 101–104, 282
North Wales Child Abuse Inquiry. *See* Waterhouse Report

Northern Ireland, limitation periods, 255
*novus actus interveniens*, 229–231
NSPCC, 24
nursery education, regulation, 33

Oedipus theory, 17
OFSTED functions, 32–33
ombudsmen, adequacy of remedy, 74, 156, 159
Orkney scandal, 29–31, 58
outrage, 214

paedophilia, 12, 112
parents, non-intervening parents, 47, 101–104, 282
partnerships, vicarious liability, 110
perpetrators
  breach of fiduciary duty, 54, 66–69
  insured, 128–129
  trespass to the person, 54–61
physical abuse
  bullying, 10–12
  corporal punishment, 5–8, 19
  fabrication/induction of illness, 8–10, 20
  forms, 5
  nature, 5–12
  psychiatric injuries, 19–20
  statistics, 4, 8
Pitcairn Islanders, 1
POCA list, 80, 82
police, iatrogenic neglect, 99–101
post-traumatic stress disorder
  'bodily injury', 127
  v borderline personality disorder, 223
  diagnostic criteria, 219–220
  effect of child abuse, 219
  generally, 219–222
  invention of psychiatry, 219
  legal convenience, 220–221
  and limitation periods, 221–222, 265, 270
  non-divisible injury, 221, 237
  physical characteristics, 209
  pitfalls for litigants, 221–222
  and sexual abuse, 17, 18

post-traumatic stress disorder (cont.)
  thin skull rules, 233
  with other disorders, 238
pregnancy, duty of care, 152
prevention of incidents, and litigation, 40–42
prostitution, 12, 233
proximity, and false accusations of abuse, 148–149, 168–170, 181, 184
psychiatric injuries
  *See also* specific disorders
  avoidance behaviours, 24, 279–280
  barriers to litigation, 20–24
  classification, 218–224
  compensation
    intentional psychiatric wrongs, 211–212
    negligence claims, 214–215
    pure psychiatric harm, 210–215
    recognised disorder requirement, 212–214, 215–217
    role of expert evidence, 218
    *Wilkinson v. Downton* actions, 212–214
  corporal punishment, 19
  credibility of claimants, 43–44, 225
  criminal injury compensation, 134–135
  damages in tort, 210–215
  distorted perceptions, 23
  emotional abuse, 20
  fabricated or induced illness (FII), 20
  and insurance policies, 126–127
  myths, 224
  non-sexual abuse, 19–20
  physical abuse, 19–20
  physical/mental overlap, 209–210
  proof issues, 35
  psychiatric damage, 209–210
  repressed memory. *See* recovered memories
  sexual abuse, 16–19
PTSD. *See* post-traumatic stress disorder
public authorities, human rights obligations, 72–73

public awareness
  and approaches to litigation, 27–28
  and foreseeability of abuse, 27–28
  and limitation periods, 28, 267, 284
  and tort litigation, 43–45
public inquiries
  See also specific inquiries and reports
  focus, 2
  media reporting, 27–31
public policy
  and consent defence, 55
  and escalation of claims, 53
  and false accusations of abuse, 170
  and insurance, 128
  vicarious liability, 125–126
  witness immunity, 163
punitive damages, 48, 241

quantum of damages
  aggravating factors, 240–241
  apportionment, 235–238
  contributions, 236
  and criminal fines, 242
  exemplary damages, 48, 241
  general and special damages, 239–240
  generally, 235–242
  loss of earnings, 239
  punitive damages, 48
  and seriousness of wrongs, 41–42
  supervening traumatic events, 238–239
  tort v criminal injury compensation, 37

recovered memories
  admissibility of evidence, 24, 201–206
  Brandon Report, 23, 202–206
  dissociative amnesia, 21–23, 283
  effect of litigation, 46
  implanting false memories, 172–174, 177, 204–206
  judicial scepticism, 177
  lack of consensus, 22–23
  legal barriers, 21–23
  limitation of actions, 24
  memory hardening, 205

recovered memories (cont.)
  reliability, 24, 177, 203–204
  sexual abuse, 12, 13
  techniques, 202, 205–206
  United States, 172–174, 175, 177, 206–208, 275
  corroboration, 208, 275
reflex anal dilatation test, 44
regulatory bodies
  benchmarks, 33
  reform onslaught, 31–33
rehabilitation of offenders, 81, 82
relatives
  claims against perpetrators, 69–71
  non-intervening parents, 47, 101–104, 282
  secondary victims, 70–71
religion
  and paedophilia, 112
  right to belief, 5, 6
remedies, right to
  adequacy of ombudsman remedy, 74, 156, 159
  declaratory remedies, 281–282
  ECHR, 73–74
  false accusations of abuse, 159
remoteness of damage, 231–233
repressed memories. See recovered memories
respect for family life
  false accusations of abuse, 157–160, 196
  margins of appreciation, 159
  remedies, 213
right of belief, ECHR, 5, 6
Rind, B., 17–18
risk allocation, 39
risk management, 40
Royal College of Paediatricians, 166
Royal College of Psychiatrists, 202

sadism, 12
Safeguarding Vulnerable Groups Bill, 82–83
Salem witch trials, 30
Salmond, J., 112, 117
satanic abuse, 204
schizophrenia, 222, 224

schools
  iatrogenic neglect, 94–99
  non-delegable duties, 106
  standard of care, 96–99
Scots law
  limitation and prescription, 245, 255, 264
  medical profession, third party liability, 170
  vicarious liability, 123
secondary victims, 70–71, 76, 135–138, 147, 214–215
seduction theory, 16–17, 30
self-blame, victims, 23, 268, 284
sexual abuse
  criminalisation of home abuse, 25
  discourse, 12–13
  dominance, 4, 16
  judicial responses to, 285–288
  nature, 12–13
  Pitcairn Islanders, 1
  psychiatric injuries, 16–19
  recovered memory, 12, 13
  social construction, 12–13, 34
  statistics, 4
  unique crime, 12–13, 20, 285
sexual offences
  criminal injury compensation, 133, 139–141
  redefinition, 34
  sex offenders' register, 81–82, 101
shell shock, 219
slander, 185
social construction
  evolution of child abuse concept, 1–3
  sexual abuse, 12–13, 34
social workers
  *See also* local authorities
  diffuse accountability, 3
  false accusations of abuse, 145–164
  malpractice cases, 29
  negligence actions against, 91–92
  standards of care, 154–155
  stress, 197
Soham murders, 82
solicitors, third party liability, 152, 153–154, 169

Southall, Professor, 36, 45, 153
speech impediments, 11
standards of care, and false accusation of abuse, 154–155, 171–172
Stocker, Petrina, 9
*Stubbings v. Webb*
  circumventing, 255–258, 286
  critique, 249–251
  effect, 30, 58, 101, 142–143, 282, 285–286
  experts' role, 269
  human rights challenges, 59–60
  judicial scepticism, 262, 284
  and law reform, 59
  limitation periods, 248–251
  and Scots law, 255
  sexual abuse as breach of duty, 57, 249
substance abuse, 223, 231, 233
sudden infant death syndrome, 44
suicides
  borderline personality disorder, 222
  bullying, 10
  emotional abuse, 20
  sexual abuse, 18
Sweden, ban on smacking, 8

teachers
  iatrogenic neglect, 94–99
  standard of care, 96–99
therapy
  and declaratory orders, 281
  hypnosis, 205
  recovered memories, 204
  tort litigation as therapy, 45–47, 54, 198
thin skull rules, 233
third-party defendants
  actions by victims, 71–126
  breach of fiduciary duty, 104–105
  breach of non-delegable duties, 105–107, 108
  breach of statutory duty, 75–76
  Human Rights Act actions, 72–75
  iatrogenic neglect, 84–99
  insurance policies, 129–131
  limitation periods, 258–280
  misfeasance actions, 107–108

third-party defendants (cont.)
  negligence actions, 76–104
  reasons for actions, 71–72
  types of non-perpetrators, 72
  vicarious liability, 108–126
tort litigation
  *See also* specific torts
  accountability function, 43–45
  adversarial process, 47
  and child abuse, 34–50
  choice of defendants, 54
  comparisons, 49–50
  compensation function, 36–40, 198
  costs, 46
  and defensive practice, 86–87, 150, 152, 153–154, 196–197
  forms of actions. *See* forms of actions
  functions, 36–47, 141–142
  and Human Rights Act 1998, 49
  judicial responses to abuse claims, 285–288
  language issues, 47–49
  lengthy procedures, 46
  limitation periods, 247–248, 280–281
  medico-legal joining of forces, 34
  and motor insurance, 41
  perpetrators as defendants, 54–71
  preventive function, 40–42
  proliferation of abuse claims, 35–36, 53–54
  psychiatric harm issues, 20–24
  public forum function, 43–45
  risk allocation, 39
  standard setting function, 40–42
  therapeutic function, 45–47, 54, 198
  time lag, 41
  *Wilkinson v. Downton* actions, 61–65, 194–195
trespass to the person
  actions against perpetrators, 54–61
  consent defence, 55
  limitation periods, 56, 58
  pure psychiatric harm, 211
  whether breach of duty, 56–58, 60–61, 249

Trindade, F. A., 62
Tucker Committee, 249, 250

undue influence, 67
United States
  battered child syndrome, 27
  employers' liability in negligence, 78–79
  extent of child abuse, 24
  false accusations of abuse, 145, 151, 172–174
  limitation periods, extension, 254, 275–276
  medical profession, third party liability, 174–177
  outrage, tort, 214
  preferential treatment of abuse, 199
  recovered memories, 172–174, 202, 206–208, 275
  sexual abuse discourse, 13, 18

vetting standards, 79–84
vicarious liability
  abuse in non-residential settings, 123–124
  actions by victims, 108–126
  adult victims, 124–125
  bullying, 11–12
  comparative law, 116–123, 125
  connection test, 113–120, 123
  course of employment, 112–123
  distributive justice, 39
  dual liability, 110
  employment relationship, 109–110
  entrepreneur test, 109
  fairness and reasonableness, 114–115
  insurance, 130–131
  limitation periods, 258–259
  *Lister v. Hesley Hall*, 114–116, 126, 142–143, 265, 288
  non-delegable duties, 115–116, 123
  non-employment relationships, 110–111
  non-profit organisations, 125–126
  and parents, 193
  public policy, 125–126
  spectrum of risk, 120–123

victims
- adult victims, 124–125
- bystander family members, 69–71, 135–138
- distorted perceptions, 23, 268, 284
- forms of actions, 54–131
- portrayal in court, 47–49
- primary/secondary victim dichotomy, 76, 214–215
- secondary victims, 70–71, 135–138, 147
- self-blame, 23, 268, 284

Vietnam War, 17

Waterhouse Report, 26–27, 31, 33, 42, 247

*Wilkinson v. Downton* actions
- actions by victims, 61–65
- conduct calculated to cause harm, 62
- damages, recognised disorder requirement, 212–214
- false accusations of abuse, 194–195
- generally, 61–65
- limitation periods, 63–64, 258
- recklessness, 62
- type of harm, 64–65

Williams, L., 22

wills, and duty of care, 152, 153–154

witnesses
- credibility of mentally ill claimants, 43–44, 225
- hypnosis, 205, 206
- immunity, 92, 163–164

*Working Together to Safeguard Children*, 4, 5, 12, 14

World War I, 219

World War II, 25

Wyatt, Geoff, 28